Praise for *Mengele*

"[David] Marwell comprehensively recounts this case of justice denied, and how—helped by his wealthy family, loyal friends and Nazi sympathizers—Mengele succeeded in evading his would-be captors."
—Steven Aschheim, *The New York Times Book Review*

"Has all the pleasures of a suspenseful crime novel, and all the inside detail of a police procedural.... This absorbing, exhaustively researched work is surely destined to become the standard reference on its subject."
—Bob Goldfarb, *Jewish Book Council*

"Compelling. . . . [A]t once a compact biography of the notorious war criminal, a detailed account of Mengele's flight to South America, and an absorbing narrative of the quest to bring him to justice."
—Patricia Heberer Rice, *Science*

"Authoritative. . . . [A]n adventure in pathology and criminology."
—Robert Siegel, *Moment*

"As this exceptional work clarifies, Josef Mengele was an ordinary person capable of extraordinary cruelty—and zealously mindful of his duty to a vicious regime."
—John Martin, *World War II* magazine

"Chilling and masterful." —Jonathan Mark, *New York Jewish Week*

"Gripping and disturbing." —Molly Odintz, *LitHub*, "Crime Reads"

"The most thorough-going account of Mengele's life available to date."
—Christopher Priest, *The Spectator*

"Masterfully chronicles Mengele's life and career."
—Janet Levy, *The Jerusalem Post*

"In *Mengele,* David Marwell has written the final and fascinating history of the 'Angel of Death.' His prodigious research results in many new insights into one of the most notorious Nazis. Marwell is convincing in unlocking the long-standing mystery of what motivated Mengele to undertake his gruesome medical experiments on twin children. He also manages to fill in important gaps in Mengele's postwar life on the run and conclusively settles any lingering questions about whether the bones unearthed in 1985 in another man's grave in Brazil were those of the fugitive war criminal. Marwell, who played a personal role in some of the events he recounts, displays not only the refined eye of a historian but emerges as a talented storyteller. The often infuriating tale he sets forth moves along effortlessly. At long last, in this important book, Mengele has been captured."

—Gerald Posner, author of *Mengele: The Complete Story*

"This is a book that only David Marwell could write after half a lifetime of studying and pursuing Josef Mengele. Marwell does more than portray the man—he details his multiple escapes, identities, and careers, the thirty-four-year search for his capture, the political intrigues and rivalries between countries, Nazi hunters, and intelligence agencies that led to Mengele's grave. A fascinating story of great importance."

—Michael Berenbaum, former director of the United States Holocaust Memorial Museum's Holocaust Research Institute

"Marwell's lucid and legend-busting account of Josef Mengele's life and deeds—and of the intricate and elaborate detective work required to find and conclusively identify him—is both absorbing and authoritative."

—Peter Hayes, author of *Why? Explaining the Holocaust*

"A fresh perspective on the notorious Auschwitz doctor, from his infamous experiments to the decades-long postwar search for him. Never losing sight of Mengele's monstrous activities, Marwell tackles common myths (Why was Mengele really interested in twins? And why his fascination with eye color?) and, chillingly, traces the underlying links between his 'research' and respected scientific institutions. Further: as an Office of Special Investigations historian committed to tracking down this elusive mass murderer, Marwell brings special insight and a wealth of detail to his riveting discovery tale."

—Debórah Dwork, author of
Flight from the Reich: Refugee Jews, 1933–1946

"Sharply written. Part-biography, part-memoir, *Mengele* is an outstanding achievement that conveys a sense of the man behind the myths and the difficulties of bringing closure for his victims."

—Richard Breitman, author of *The Berlin Mission* and
distinguished professor emeritus, American University

"David Marwell's *Mengele* is a fascinating historical work. How did Dr. Mengele come to epitomize the many medical atrocities committed by trained doctors at Auschwitz? How did he escape? How was he (almost) found? But it is far more than just exceptionally solid scholarship. It is also a thriller and a first-rate detective story written by someone who was part of the team that had to unravel this mystery."

—Deborah E. Lipstadt, author of *Antisemitism: Here and Now* and
Dorot Professor of Modern Jewish History and
Holocaust Studies, Emory University

"David Marwell is a credible and authoritative voice on Josef Mengele and his role in the Holocaust. Marwell's biography of Mengele offers a compelling depiction of Mengele as a man, as a monster, and as a symbol of the Nazi experiment of remaking the world. Anyone wanting to understand the perverse mentality of hate that lay at the center of Nazism needs to read this book."

—Abraham F. Foxman, director of the Center for the Study of Anti-Semitism
at the Museum of Jewish Heritage–A Living Memorial to the Holocaust
and national director emeritus of the Anti-Defamation League

"Part biography, part thriller, part detective story. But it is all history, thoroughly investigated and meticulously documented.... We need the scholarship of David Marwell and others now more than ever. They do more than add to the historical record, as important as that is; they also keep the Nazi offence squarely in our collective consciousness, direct us to differentiate between reality and fantasy and continue to remind us of the central irony of our humanity—that we live in a world not of sorcerers and dragons but of men and women who love their children, are loyal to their friends, and are capable of unimaginable evil."

—Kevin Stevens, *Dublin Review of Books*

MENGELE

MENGELE

UNMASKING THE "ANGEL OF DEATH"

DAVID G. MARWELL

W. W. NORTON & COMPANY
Independent Publishers Since 1923

Frontispiece: Mengele at Verschuer's institute in Frankfurt, 1935–36. *Archiv der Max-Planck-Gesellschaft, Berlin-Dahlem*

For information about permission to reproduce selections from this book, write to Permissions, W. W. Norton & Company, Inc., 500 Fifth Avenue, New York, NY 10110

For information about special discounts for bulk purchases, please contact W. W. Norton Special Sales at specialsales@wwnorton.com or 800-233-4830

Manufacturing by LSC Communications, Harrisonburg
Book design by Chris Welch
Production manager: Beth Steidle

Library of Congress Cataloging-in-Publication Data

Names: Marwell, David George, author.
Title: Mengele : unmasking the "Angel of Death" / David G. Marwell.
Other titles: Unmasking the "Angel of Death"
Description: First edition. | New York, NY : W. W. Norton & Company, [2020] |
Includes bibliographical references and index.
Identifiers: LCCN 2019033220 |
ISBN 9780393609530 (hardcover) | ISBN 9780393609547 (epub)
Subjects: LCSH: Mengele, Josef, 1911–1979. | Waffen-SS. SS-Panzer-Division
"Wiking," 5. | War criminals—Germany—Biography. | Auschwitz (Concentration camp) |
World War, 1939–1945—Atrocities—Poland. | Physicians—Germany—Biography.
Classification: LCC DD247.M46 M37 2020 | DDC 940.53/18092 [B] —dc23
LC record available at https://lccn.loc.gov/2019033220

ISBN 978-0-393-86750-3 pbk.

W. W. Norton & Company, Inc., 500 Fifth Avenue, New York, N.Y. 10110
www.wwnorton.com

W. W. Norton & Company Ltd., 15 Carlisle Street, London W1D 3BS

1 2 3 4 5 6 7 8 9 0

CONTENTS

PART IV: PURSUIT

A NOTE ON SOURCES

While this book is based on both primary sources from archives throughout the world and the careful research of a host of brilliant scholars, it also relies on the writings of Mengele himself. I read his correspondence and diaries from his later life and was exposed to the intimate details of his health complaints, frustrations, and private reflections, and to the style and rhythm of his thoughts. In addition, I had access to Mengele's own attempt at the very enterprise in which I was engaged. Late in his life, he undertook to write his life story but chose to do so in the form of an autobiographical novel, which was to be about a man "shaped in a very special way by his time." In a letter to his son, he accounted for this choice of genre by describing its advantages, which included:

> The possibility of a more liberal treatment of difficult themes; the interchangeability of one's own experience and that of other people; the typifying of events and people of that time; the easier clarification of inner connections, causes, and processes; and finally, the displacement of an individual fate onto entire groups.

He believed that through this type of "autofiction," which freed him from the bounds of literal truth, he could fashion from the raw material of his life a higher, perhaps more universal, message. For reasons related to security and protection, Mengele decided to fictionalize the names of individual characters and geographical locations. My challenge was to decipher his attempt at obfuscation and determine the real names of individuals and places that played key roles in his story. In doing so, my effort would complement Mengele's own—decoding what he had encoded. My success helped to clarify what he had sought to camouflage, making his "autobiography" an irreplaceable and invaluable source.

PREFACE

Josef Mengele was born on March 16, 1911, and died on February 7, 1979. At almost the exact midpoint of his life, in the summer of 1944, he spent long days and nights performing his duty on the ramp at the Auschwitz II concentration camp (Birkenau), sorting new arrivals and determining their fates. The Nazis' massive effort to murder the Jews of Hungary, the last remaining Jewish community they targeted, was well under way, and a seemingly endless procession of railcars along the newly constructed spur was routed through the main gate and into the heart of the camp, before coming to a stop a short distance from the gas chambers. Completed a few months earlier, this new entrance replaced an inefficient receiving ramp that had been located between the main Auschwitz camp and Birkenau and considerably simplified the unloading and processing of the doomed, disoriented passengers packed into the airless freight cars they had entered days before in Hungary. The camp had reached its zenith, operating at full capacity; between the end of April and late July, nearly 430,000 Hungarian Jews were deported there, the overwhelming majority murdered upon arrival. It could be said that Mengele himself had reached a similar high point in his life.

Were it possible to look into his mind, I imagine it would reveal enormous satisfaction in the path his life had taken. At a young age—

only thirty-three—he stood on the cusp of great success. His own study and preparation and hard work had brought him to an unprecedented place in the pursuit of the science that was his consuming passion. As he no doubt saw it, no one in history had had access to the raw material that stood before him or had been so liberated from the restraints that tamed ambition and limited scientific progress.

If the first half of Josef Mengele's life had seen a steady accretion of successes that led to that moment, the second half would see the dismantling of all he had achieved. The Third Reich would be driven, by that summer, from the farthest extent of its advancing empire back toward where it had begun. In the next months it would contract further, like a black hole folding in on itself. At the same time, Josef Mengele, once near the center of a brave new world, was moved increasingly to the margins. He saw the prospects for a promising future diminish, as everything that mattered to him moved beyond his reach.

As this process of dismantling was taking place, a complementary process began that would see his reputation grow to nearly mythical heights: to the world, he would become both the personification of the movement that so animated him and the most notorious author of its crimes. Referred to by some as the "Angel of Death," Mengele became a well-known character in popular culture and stalked the nightmares and haunted the daydreams of legions. At some point, he emerged as the embodiment not only of the Holocaust itself but also of the failure of justice in the wake of the war—a persona that helped to obscure any chance of our understanding who this man really was and what motivated him.

In February 1985, while working in the Office of Special Investigations (OSI) at the U.S. Department of Justice, I was assigned to the international investigation to locate Mengele and bring him before a court of law. Established in 1979 through legislation sponsored by Elizabeth Holtzman, a pugnacious and passionate congresswoman from New York, OSI had replaced an anemic effort to investigate Nazi war criminals living in the United States that had previously been housed in the Immigration and Naturalization Service. The new legislation not only created OSI but placed it in the criminal division of the Justice Department, provided it with a healthy budget, and supplied a legal framework under which Nazi criminals could be prosecuted for immigration fraud tied to their having misrepresented their backgrounds and their participation in Nazi persecution.

Initially, the office was organized like other federal prosecution efforts: under the direction of prosecutors, trained criminal investigators conducted the investigations, locating documentary evidence and witnesses. It soon became evident, however, that these cases were of a different sort. The crimes being investigated had been committed an ocean away, the evidence was in different languages, and the historical context into which the evidence needed to be placed was nearly lost to all but those who had lived it and the historians who studied it.

To investigate these crimes with the necessary sophistication, the prosecution team needed new members. I joined a small cadre of history graduate students and new Ph.D.'s, who, although initially hired to translate documents, soon effectively replaced the criminal investigators in the office. We developed, over time, a new discipline that might be called "forensic history"; for the first time, professional historians were hired as full-time members of a legal team, using their knowledge and skills to assist in legal proceedings. Our importance to OSI's mission was reflected in changes to the organizational chart; I started at OSI in March 1980 as the third historian, joining a staff that included ten or eleven investigators who had been detailed from various federal law enforcement agencies. By the time I left, nine years later, there were ten historians and only one investigator.

We worked as historians work, mining archives for evidence, interviewing individuals for elusive details, and consulting experts for context and continuity. But we were also advocates. And we labored under some constraints: the federal rules of evidence imposed new limitations on what we could offer as proof, and we memorized, like first-year law students, the exceptions to the hearsay rule.

Our standard fare at OSI were cases against low-level, non-German auxiliaries who, in the service of their "masters," had been involved in the persecution of innocent victims. The Germans had relied heavily on locals to assist them—as translators, policemen, and camp guards— in their occupation of conquered lands, and the indigenous population had had a powerful motive to link their stars to the German conquerors. As the tide of the war shifted against the Germans, forcing them to retreat, their helpmates followed, knowing that a return home would mean Soviet justice. They melted into the vast sea of displaced persons who flooded into German territory with no other place to go. Side by side with their victims, these victimizers benefited from Allied aid and found passage to a brighter future in America on the same ships that carried those they had helped to harm. Once in America, they left their pasts behind and established new lives. It took four decades and the effective pressure of a dedicated few to draw attention to the grotesque irony that the United States had become a haven not only for victims of Nazi persecution but also for those who had helped persecute them.

In March 1983 William French Smith, President Ronald Reagan's first attorney general, broadened OSI's purview by assigning us to investigate charges that American intelligence had recruited former Gestapo officer Klaus Barbie after the war. The allegation was particularly alarming since Barbie, who had been stationed in France, had been involved in the arrest and deportation of Jews and had been tried and sentenced to death in absentia by the French. Allan A. Ryan Jr. OSI's director at the time, issued a comprehensive report that chronicled how the United States had recruited Barbie as an intelligence asset, knowingly shielded him from French prosecution, and spirited him out of Europe to South America employing the so-called Ratline, an overland escape route to Italian seaports. Ryan made headlines when he recommended to the attorney general that the U.S. government offer the French an apology for having delayed justice.

After the Barbie investigation, a far more notorious figure emerged to capture the interest of the public: Josef Mengele. Mengele's twin personae—embodiment of both the Holocaust and the failure of justice—played a role in the political and moral calculus of the three nations that set out to find him in 1985. For the most outspoken of the Americans who pushed for the investigation, it was pure politics, a strategy for gaining the spotlight and scoring points. For the Germans, it was a compensatory effort to make up for past inaction. And for the Israelis, it was a curious mix of politics and emotion that saw them refuse to close the case for as long as they could. For me, although I know of no family member whom Mengele harmed, it was intensely personal. In the course of the investigation, I visited his hometown and his hideout; I interviewed his family, friends, colleagues, and victims; I inspected the scenes of his crimes and read his private correspondence and intimate musings; and finally, in the end, I held his bones in my hands.

Even after the Mengele case was officially closed, Mengele remained with me. I spoke about the investigation in scores of public presentations in the United States and abroad. The public I encountered remained fascinated by the figure of Mengele and what he represented. With his death and the availability of new sources about his life, Mengele remained the subject of serious scholarly and journalistic inquiry, and he continues to be a recognized and haunting figure in popular culture. Indeed, even now, a Google alert for "Mengele" yields nearly daily mentions of him across a broad range of topics from history to science, often as the benchmark for evil. In 2017 the prestigious French Renaudot Prize for literature was awarded to a novel about Mengele's postwar life, *La disparition de Josef Mengele,* by Olivier Guez, and the year before, a novel about Mengele at Auschwitz, *Mischling,* by Affinity Konar, was published in the United States to critical acclaim.

I continued to read and think about Mengele over the years, and at the beginning of 2016, I sat down to write a book about the investigation and my involvement in it. Bountiful new evidence about this unique international effort had been released and was available in archives in Germany, Israel, and the United States. The CIA file, declassified in 2000, detailed a part of the investigation previously unknown, and in September 2017 the Mossad, Israel's intelligence service, released a lengthy report in Hebrew, filled with new revelations, based on its classified Mengele file. All this material, along with my own recollections, provided a rich basis for understanding how and why Germany, Israel, and the United States decided to join forces to find Mengele in 1985.

My original plan to write solely about the investigation gave way under the weight of the intriguing body of recent literature and new scholarship I encountered in my research. I read deeply about Mengele's scientific education, experience, and work, and I learned surprising context and details. This material, much of it written in German, examines aspects of Mengele's life and career that had been unknown to me. Informed and intrigued, I decided to extend my subject beyond the investigation to an examination of the man—his life, career, and how he is both remembered and imagined by others. While a certain caricature of Mengele, given life by his role in films, books, and as an often-invoked symbol of evil, is well known, much less is understood about the man himself.

PART I

BECOMING MENGELE

CHAPTER 1

"BRILLIANT LUMINOSITY"

(March 1911–September 1938)

By all accounts, Mengele's childhood home was an unlikely incubator for the man who was to become the "Angel of Death." It is difficult to find evidence of the extreme politics, antisemitism, and capacity for murder that would define him. Studies about the social backgrounds and childhood experiences of men who would later commit crimes under the Nazis often describe the effect of World War I on their psychological and emotional makeup.[1] Many of those who were later judged responsible for carrying out horrendous crimes were of the generation for which the First World War played such an important role. One theory holds that the slaughter left many young Germans fatherless, and the sudden German surrender made shameful figures of the fathers who did return.[2] The psychological toll, it is argued, combined with postwar privations and political upheavals, molded a group of men who found in Hitler's message a powerful call to action, paving the way for his eventual success, and readying some to engage in an ideological struggle that would allow them to commit crimes and atrocities on an unprecedented scale.

Although Mengele's father, Karl, had served in the German Army at the beginning of the war, he was recalled after two years to resume his leadership of the firm that bore his name. It had shifted its production from farm machinery to equipment that would serve the German war effort. Manufacturing such items as metal plummets used in the deployment of naval mines, and two-wheeled, horse-drawn wagons to transport munitions, the Mengele firm increased the number of employees from fifteen in 1915 to ninety-one by the end of the war. Although not the largest employer in Günzburg, the firm was on its way to becoming a major economic force in the small town, which raised Karl Mengele's status and increased his wealth.

Mengele's mother, Walburga, three years her husband's senior, came from a well-respected Günzburg family. Whereas Mengele later described his father as "good-natured and soft-hearted," his mother was "extremely determined and forceful." An appearance by Mengele's mother at the factory was far more feared than when the father showed up, according to a family friend.[3] She was a devout Catholic whose religious devotion apparently affected Mengele.[4] Although not religious, he remained in the church and opted for a church wedding—both uncommon actions among SS members.[5]

In his autobiography, Mengele dedicated more than one hundred pages to his early life and painted a picture of a secure childhood surrounded by parents, grandparents, and household help. The family saw his birth as a significant event, coming in his mother's thirty-first year, especially after she had lost her firstborn just days after giving birth. The excitement that greeted Josef Mengele's arrival was a measure of how long he had been anticipated, and he took his place at the center of an attentive family. Joined by two younger brothers, Karl and Alois, within the next three years, Mengele had a relatively untroubled and uneventful childhood.

The atmosphere at home was, according to one childhood friend, "conservative, Catholic, conventional."[6] Mengele's father was, at least at some point, a member of the German National People's Party (Deutschnational Volkspartei, DNVP). He was not then a supporter of the Nazi Party, as suggested by some who cite his having made one of his factory buildings available to Hitler for a campaign event in October 1932. In fact, Karl first joined the Nazi Party in May 1933, only after it gained power, in connection with his own bid for a seat on the city council, which had eluded his prior attempts in 1924 and 1929. According to historian Zdenek Zofka, Karl Mengele's political aspirations were less ideological than grounded in his desire to influence the local business climate, and the local Günzburg Nazi Party officials accused him of purchasing his seat through a generous contribution.[7] Although Karl joined the SS in 1935, his membership was nominal, and he performed no service and attained no rank. The postwar denazification court found that his position as district economic adviser, which he held from 1936 to 1945, was technical in nature, and that he had had no political responsibilities and was not a "convinced or reliable National Socialist." The court found further that Karl Mengele had acted in a fair and generous manner toward individuals who had been targeted by the Nazi regime, including political opponents and Jews.[8]

Consistent with his father's conservative politics, Josef Mengele joined the Greater German Youth League (Grossdeutschen Jugendbund, GDJ) in 1924, and from 1927 until he left the organization in 1930, he was the leader (*Ältestenführer*) of the Günzburg chapter, which numbered sixty boys and thirty girls. Mengele recalled a summer solstice celebration that he organized with his group:

> We were proud of our big solstice fire, which blazed into the heavens on the ridge opposite the hometown, announcing that a small group of boys and girls today celebrated the solstice with fervent thoughts and desires in their hearts, to awaken and arouse the people of their homeland to the holy struggle of liberation from the shackles of the nefarious Versailles Treaty. The flames should liberate us and . . . illuminate our way, they should warm us with the love of our great people and of its high culture and they should incinerate all discord among us Germans.[9]

The GDJ did not accept Jews, as Mengele explained in his diary, in order that the "characteristic qualities of the German people" could finally be revealed and freed from alien "encrustation."[10] Some have interpreted Mengele's retrospective reflection on his time in the GDJ, with its clear nationalistic and antisemitic flavor, to suggest that his membership in the youth group defined a clear path to his later Nazi Party membership and wholehearted engagement with its ideology and worldview, but historian Sven Keller argues that such an interpretation goes "too far." To the extent that Mengele encountered antisemitic attitudes in his childhood home, it was more likely "the latent cultural anti-Judaism that was completely typical of the Catholic milieu of the time."[11] Antisemitism, Keller argues, was undoubtedly present in the GDJ, as it was in broad sections of the youth movement and in other right-wing conservative organizations in the Weimar Republic, but it was neither pushed into the foreground as an explicit objective nor comparable to the virulent racial antisemitism of the National Socialists.[12]

> Josef Mengele's membership in the GDJ cannot be regarded as a direct precursor, or as an indication of an already existing enthusiasm for the ideas and principles, of National Socialism. . . . They were oriented toward the ideas of Ernst Jünger or Moeller van den Bruck, not those of Adolf Hitler or Alfred Rosenberg.[13]

Mengele attended the *humanistische Gymnasium* in Günzburg, a secondary school that included instruction in Latin and Greek as the basis for European culture. His performance there was, at best, average, earning him a "satisfactory" in religion, English language, physics, and history, and a "deficient" in German language, Greek, Latin, and mathematics. While his behavior was judged acceptable, his effort and his interest in school were found wanting. Mengele's school records indicate that he suffered a series of infections, which began during the school year of 1927–28, including osteomyelitis, nephritis, and sepsis, and that these illnesses forced him to miss school for an extended period of time and also led to a chronic kidney ailment. This ailment prevented him from taking over the family company, which, as the oldest son, he might have claimed as a birthright.

Although the Great Depression had darkened the firm's prospects, it was still a going concern, and it would have seemed natural for Mengele to join his father in the business, especially since he had always been fascinated with things technical and displayed a keen interest in what took place in his father's workshops and factory. Mengele's mother, however, believed that her son's medical condition, with its need for a special diet and rest, argued against a job in the firm, which demanded a robust constitution. Mengele's youngest brother, Alois, who was attending a business preparatory school, was groomed to enter his father's business instead, leaving Josef, along with his other brother, Karl, free to choose his profession.[14] Mengele achieved his *Abitur* and earned his "certificate of maturity" in 1930, unsure what course of study he would eventually follow and unmotivated by any particular passion.

Munich

When Josef Mengele left his home in Günzburg, in April 1930, to begin his studies at the Ludwig-Maximilian University in Munich, he embarked on a journey of discovery and achievement. He threw himself into the study of medicine and its related disciplines of human genetics and anthropology. His choice of subjects was particularly timely since, with the rise of National Socialism, they would grow in importance and enjoy, as one historian has put it, "a symbiotic relationship" with the Nazi state,[15] one that would ultimately play a decisive role in the fate of millions.

His biology teacher at the *Gymnasium* in Günzburg had first inspired his interest in science, and he found anthropology "most exciting." After completing his *Abitur,* however, he fixed on dentistry as a subject of study, believing that he would earn a great deal of money, noting that "there was not even one dentist" in his hometown.[16] After arriving at the university, he had a conversation with Julius Diesbach, who, a year older than Mengele, also had attended his *Gymnasium* in Günzburg and was then enrolled at the university. Diesbach argued that dentistry was "too narrow a field and too specialized" and advocated convincingly for medicine. For Mengele, a particular attraction of medicine was its wide scope: "Since anthropology and human genetics belonged to the broader field of medicine, I finally opted for this discipline."[17] Despite the circumstances—a casual conversation—Mengele's choice was not superficial; indeed, he claims it awakened a "passion" in him:

> I had no idea then of the many-sided nature of medicine, but the kindled flame of enthusiasm would retain its warmth, if not its brilliant luminosity forever. How was it possible in so short a time to transform someone who was—one could almost say— "resigned," into someone who was "enchanted"?[18]

Mengele answered his own question by suggesting that his friend had unlocked a potential that was already present within him. Diesbach was a "magician," filled with the "beauty, grandeur, and high values of his science and art," who did not speak of the practical possibilities of medicine or the possibility for employment. Rather, he "knew only—probably quite unconsciously—how to incite my scientific curiosity and to translate it into enthusiasm for such a versatile subject. He needed only to tell me which subjects I would need to take in the first semester, and my decision was unshakeable, as if I had never even thought of another subject to study."[19] Mengele elevated the intervention of his friend, "at just the right moment," to mythic proportions, comparing the encounter to that of Athena visiting Odysseus disguised as a shepherd. The eerie fact that he never saw his friend again caused him to muse that perhaps it had really been Athena in disguise.[20]

Adolf Hitler understood the importance of medicine and had distinct ideas for how it should be practiced in the new Germany. In an early speech before the National Socialist German Physician's League (NSDÄB), he argued that, while he could do without lawyers, engineers, and builders, he needed National Socialist doctors: "I cannot do without you for a single day, not a single hour. If not for you, if you fail me, then all is lost. For what good are our struggles if the health of our people is in danger?"[21] When Hitler spoke of the "health of our people," he was not referring solely, or even primarily, to the well-being of individuals. Central to his concept of German medicine was the notion that the physician's first responsibility was not to the individual but rather to the nation, or Volk.*[22] This critical change in focus allowed German physicians to treat patients in ways that were previously unthinkable without, in their minds, violating their Hippocratic responsibilities, which were now cast in an entirely new light. The NSDÄB issued a demand for new medical ethics:

> From the first day, we have made it clear that the major turnabout in the world view of our days, an essential portion of which is vanquishing the individual through experiencing the "people" [Volk] must be the guiding principle of the morality and ethics of the medical profession.[23]

Hans Reiter, president of the Reich Health Office (Reichsgesundheitsamt), stressed the responsibility that fell to doctors under National Socialism, writing in 1939, "The physician fights as a biological soldier for the health of the Volk. If the doctor fails in this struggle, then no form of government will be able to secure the future of this Volk,"[24] and "The destiny of the German Volk rests entirely in the hands of the German physician."[25]

---

* Often translated as "people" or "nation," the German word Volk, as used by the Nazis, has no satisfactory one-word English translation. It refers to "a metaphysical entity that has both a life and a value of its own." Bruns, "Turning Away," p. 215.

Substituting the nation for the individual as the responsibility of the German physician made possible a new standard of care for the individual patient. The French medical historians Yves Ternon and Socrate Helman wrote:

> [The physician] must abandon his old humanitarian conceptions. He has one patient: the German People [*Volk*]. The individual is no more than a single cell of the whole people. The People are transcendent: they are the only Body. It is this Popular Body which must be preserved and treated. To maintain it intact, no sacrifice is too great. Just as a doctor will not hesitate to amputate a finger to save a limb, or a limb to save a life, so the Nazi physician is prepared to undertake all aggression against the individual who menaces the People, against individual Germans, and with even greater reason against strangers.[26]

In cases where the very existence of an individual challenged the well-being of the nation, the physician's responsibility was clear. On April 5, 1933, Hitler asked that the German medical profession move "with all its energy" to the forefront in the race question.[27]

Hitler's call for racial hygiene to become the primary responsibility of the physician in the new Germany was soon reflected in medical school curricula and in the infrastructure of the profession. Interest in these new subjects had already increased before the Nazi seizure of power with course offerings in genetics, anthropology, racial hygiene, and eugenics growing in the late 1920s and early '30s.[28] The establishment of the Kaiser Wilhelm Institute for Anthropology, Human Genetics, and Eugenics in 1927, with Eugen Fischer as its director, was "one of the most important events in the institutionalization of racial hygiene in Weimar Germany."[29]

MENGELE'S CHOICE OF study was dramatically confirmed when, on his first day of instruction, he attended a lecture by the Austrian ethologist Karl von Frisch. Frisch, who would be awarded the Nobel Prize for medicine in 1973,[30] was then the head of the Institute of Zoology at the University of Munich and had become famous for his study of honeybees in the 1920s (later published in English under the title *The Dancing Bees*). Known by the students as "Bees-Frisch," he delivered an introductory lecture for all students studying natural sciences and medicine. Having just returned from a lecture tour in the United States,[31] he stood before a large group of students and, as Mengele recalled many years later, seemed to speak directly to him:

> He began with a cursory reference to the system of Taxonomy starting with the Protozoa, and his words, which could be described as dry, had the ability, with the aid of simple but striking sketches on the board, to convey such a vivid picture of the material. It was something which I had never experienced before in my life. . . . If it were not difficult, in and of itself, to ignite the "zoological flame" in me, Frisch was able to do so not only for the moment . . . but in such a lasting way that I have kept this fire my entire life and have all too often been warmed by it.[32]

In other Frisch lectures,

> he described the insect's ability to see, smell, and taste, or the fish's sense of touch and hearing, or the balance organs of the crab. Everything sounded so easy, almost playful, and yet they were the results of fundamentally important and groundbreaking research activity.[33]

Where Frisch was riveting and inspiring to the young Mengele, his chemistry professor, Heinrich Otto Wieland, was the opposite: "he regarded this lecture more as an unpleasant interruption of his scientific research than as a creative option for a pedagogical requirement."[34] But whatever deficiencies Wieland displayed in the classroom, he made up for in the laboratory, where his work on bile acids had won him the Nobel Prize for chemistry in 1927.[35] He is said to have shielded Jewish students who studied with him by placing them under his personal protection.

Even after thirty years, Mengele recalled "with joy" the lectures of his physics professor, Walter Gerlach,[36] and "with reverence" those of the director of the university's anatomical institute, Siegfried Mollier. For a young medical student to have such a teacher, Mengele wrote, with his "beautiful sonorous voice" and "brilliant appearance," was a "blessing": "In a few words, this divinely gifted professor of anatomy had touched me—and probably all the others—to the depths of my soul and created in me an enthusiastic readiness for my studies."[37]

Mollier counseled his students that a good physician must "conceive of body and soul as a unity." He spoke of the "majesty of death" that they would encounter in their work. Later, when Mollier instructed them in the anatomy lab, Mengele wrote that the "great teacher" wanted them to have a deep, even intuitive, understanding of anatomy and not just memorize terms. He deftly demonstrated what was visible through dissection, "the functional relationship and the structural efficiency" of the components of the human body. Mengele was particularly moved by Mollier's introduction to the dissection labs: "My entire life—even in the most difficult situations—I can hear his solemn words from that time, when he spoke of the rights of the dead, that we should always approach the dead with dignity and gravity." Mollier trained not only a generation of physicians but a generation of artists who, attending his lectures at the Munich Academy of Visual Arts, also owed their understanding and appreciation of anatomy to him.[38]

In the short intervals between classes on the university's sprawling campus, Mengele needed to cover great distances, but his health issues made that difficult. So his parents gave him a car, a small Opel, that set him apart from most of his classmates and contributed to his active social life. Nevertheless, despite the intellectual stimulation and his clear engagement with his studies, Mengele seems to have been challenged by his separation from home and his first experience of independence. We know about his thinking at that time only through his sober and introspective autobiographical musings much later in life, and they may be more revealing of his later experience than an accurate account of a young man's coming of age. He wrote of loneliness and isolation: "It is precisely this feeling of being alone, the lack of an intimate connection to family, the lack of a true friendship that I felt so bitterly in the first few semesters." These feelings, he wrote, found expression in his "unrest, dissatisfaction, displeasure, superficial pleasure-seeking, and shallow existence." He took responsibility for the isolation, admitting that it was "more inner than outer" and that he did not tend to his family relationships or "seek an honest friendship." The reason, he suggested, was "deeper in his personality" and was "nothing more than inhibition." He claimed that in failing to "overcome" his isolation, he "disguised this inner inability in an—easily misinterpreted—preservation of the remoteness, cool impersonality, and unsocial arrogance," which may have had the effect of "discouraging all who otherwise came to me in friendship and affection." Mengele summed up his reflection by suggesting that it had taken him "more than half" his life to overcome his isolating inhibition and the "camouflage" he employed to protect himself, yet "their relics" were scattered "throughout" his life.[39]

Bonn

After two semesters at the university in Munich, Mengele transferred to Bonn. It was common for German students to study at a number of different universities, and Mengele would experience five before he was finished. He may have decided to transfer because the smaller school on the Rhine offered a more intimate experience, with less than two-thirds the number of medical students in Munich.[40] Perhaps in an attempt to connect himself more with those around him, he grew active politically in Bonn. In his autobiography, Mengele indi-

cated that he and his fellows were at first "not connected in any way
to a political party," although he had been "raised with a national consciousness," which had been reinforced in school. He claimed to feel
the "misfortune" that had been inflicted on Germany by the Versailles
"Diktat." When it came to party affiliation, however, he aligned more
with his parents' traditional "German National" stance than with the
National Socialist Party, which was attracting a surprising number of
followers, including the "older of his fellow students" who were able
to vote in the "memorable" September 1930 election, which catapulted
the Nazis to the second-largest party in the Reichstag, increasing their
representation from 12 to 107 of the 577 seats. Mengele admitted he
"felt a strong attraction" for the National Socialists' program and for
their entire organization, but in May 1931 (the same month he matric-
ulated in Bonn) he joined not the Nazis but the *Stahlhelm,* the Steel
Helmets, the national conservative group, founded in 1918, with ties
to the German National People's Party, to which his father and several
of his teachers at the *Gymnasium* belonged.[41]

The trigger for his emerging political engagement came shortly
after he arrived in Bonn. While standing with a schoolmate on Alter
Zoll, once part of the city defenses with a commanding view of the
Rhine, he observed a demonstration in Beuel, a working-class neighborhood on the other side of the river. A line of demonstrators were
crossing the bridge in the direction of the city center, carrying a
"bloodred flag" with a five-pointed star. They were marching in the
"well-known formation" of the Red Army, dressed in "Russian coats
and peaked caps." Mengele and his friend were deeply shaken by the
threatening scene of Communist activism, and when they parted,
Mengele said, "Well, we know what we have to do," implying that it
was not enough to believe in the nation; one needed to do something
to combat the looming danger from the Bolsheviks.[42]

Although Mengele had taken a step toward more political engagement, his was not yet the path of a committed Nazi; he could have
joined the party or any of its allied organizations but decided not to,

remaining connected to the conservative nationalism of his father. This is not to say that when Mengele eventually joined the Nazi Party and its vanguard SS, he did so out of the opportunism or the career building that motivated so many. Mengele's commitment to Nazi ideas and wholehearted support of the movement arose through the science that was to occupy him so intensely in the next years of his life.

Mengele remained in Bonn for three semesters and completed his fifth semester of the study of medicine, which allowed him to sit for the preliminary medical examination.[43] He passed this milestone, which tested him in six subjects (anatomy, physiology, physics, chemistry, zoology, and botany),[44] on August 12, 1932, with a grade of "satisfactory" (genüngend).[45] Mengele returned to Munich in September 1932 for his sixth semester at university, a semester that bridged the Weimar Republic and Nazi rule. The Nazi Party lost seats in the November 6 elections, and although many felt that its decline would continue, Hitler was appointed chancellor on January 30, 1933. Within a month, just a week before the end of the semester, the Reichstag burned, providing a pretext for the beginning of the end of parliamentary rule and the start of the Nazi dictatorship.

MENGELE SPENT THE SUMMER semester of 1933, his seventh of university study, in Vienna. He rented a room from a pharmacist, in a handsome apartment building on Bennoplatz, located near the city center and not far from the university clinic. But he had a bad experience, having found bugs in his room.[46] Although he may have objected to the condition of his apartment, he had no basis for complaints about the quality of instruction he received from the medical faculty. His teachers included Dr. Nikolaus von Jagic, head of the Vienna University Medical Clinic, and Dr. Wolfgang Denk, head of the university's surgical clinic. Denk enjoyed an international reputation as a surgeon and teacher,[47] although he was later involved in testing a blood coagulant developed at Dachau by Sigmund Rascher and Robert Feix.[48] Mengele studied, too, with Dr. Leopold Arzt, head of the university's clinic for dermatology and venereal diseases—who would be removed from his position in 1939 because of his previous support for the anti-Nazi Dollfuss and Schuschnigg regimes.

Finally, he studied with the head of the university's pediatric clinic, Dr. Franz Hamburger, a "stalwart representative of the right-wing *völkisch* camp" and a proponent of National Socialism. From 1934, Hamburger was active in the Nazi Party, when it had been outlawed in Austria.[49] In the 1940 edition of a textbook he coauthored, Hamburger and his colleague wrote:

> At all times should you be aware of the duties of the National Socialist physician, who keeps in mind not only the individual person, but the entire *Volkskörper* [people's body], in which the single person like the cell in the human organism is just a building block, just a cell of the people as a whole.[50]

Not only did Hamburger's clinic advocate euthanasia for babies with physical or mental disabilities, it routinely sent children to the infamous Spiegelgrund hospital, where hundreds were murdered under the Nazi euthanasia program.[51]

Dr. Berta Aichinger, a physician from Linz, lived with her twin daughters, Ilse and Helga, in an apartment on Gumpendorferstrasse, a twenty-five-minute walk from Mengele's residence. After the war, Ilse, by then a noted author, wrote vividly about a strange visit that had occurred many decades earlier. Her mother announced that a "friendly gentleman," whom she knew from the hospital, was coming to visit Ilse and Helga.

> "What do you want to know about them," [our mother] asked as he stood in the doorway. "I only have a few questions," said the man. "They are rather shy," our mother said, "I will stay with them." Then he asked [us] what it was like to have somebody constantly next to you who looked the same as you did. And a few

less spectacular questions. In between, he looked at my sister and
me with a great curiosity. . . . "A pity," we said when he was outside, "what does the man do all day?" "He is a twin researcher."
"Alas," again, we said disappointed. "And what is the name of the
man?" "He is called Dr. Mengele."[52]

When I asked Helga's own daughter, the artist Ruth Rix, if Helga had
ever talked to her about the encounter, she assured me that the visit
had taken place and that her mother "definitely" remembered it.[53]
Although Mengele was not a twin researcher or a doctor when he was
in Vienna, he was studying medicine and may already have had an
interest in twin research.[54]

Around this time, Mengele experienced a "turning point" in his
health. In his autobiography, he describes how, ignoring the limitations imposed on his physical activity by his kidney ailment, he ran a
ten-thousand-meter race and afterward experienced significant blood
in his urine. He claims not to have sought medical help and "a week
later" was able to satisfy the requirements for the German Sports and
Gymnastics Badge. Over the course of the next year, his condition
abated such that when he was thoroughly examined in 1937, in connection with an application for life insurance, he learned that he had
fully recovered from the disease.[55]

In the fall of 1933, Mengele returned to Munich where, in addition to medicine, he began to study anthropology under the prominent anthropologist Theodor Mollison, who became his *Doktorvater*
(supervisor; literally, "Doctor Father"). "One of the most prolific methodological and technical innovators in the field of measurement and
photography,"[56] Mollison had been born in 1876 to a father of Scottish
origin and a German mother and studied at Freiburg University. He
developed or perfected a series of measuring and recording devices
that helped to standardize and increase the precision of the essential measurements that were the basis of physical anthropology. His
standards and guidelines for the use of photography in anthropol-

ogical studies were designed to ensure "unambiguous and comparable" results,[57] and he created a new technique for displaying and
analyzing data that would have a profound effect on his field. Beyond
his methodological contributions, he was engaged in the study of
blood serum as a means of distinguishing races.

Mollison helped to redirect anthropology from an "epistemologi-
cal, methodological and conceptual blind alley,"[58] as historian Amir
Teicher put it, that "threatened to undermine the discipline's most
fundamental building block... the understanding of race itself."[59]
According to Teicher, to address this challenge anthropologists had
"to update their disciplinary toolbox... find practical uses for their
profession and... align themselves in the political aspirations of the
German state." As a result, "physical anthropology gradually turned
into 'Racial Science,' endorsing popular race classifications and adding cultural and mental components to earlier, purely descriptive
anatomical characterizations."[60] Mengele's new mentor Theodor Mollison would write in 1934:

> The new ideological attitude of our people has resulted in the use
> of the findings of scientific research that an earlier government
> greeted either with indifference or annoyance. The false claim of
> the equality of all people, which has been passed on to us for cen-
> turies and which nobody really believed, provided the pretext to
> support the inferior and to drag down the superior.[61]

The science that Mengele began to study would become an important resource for the new politics. Otto Aichel, deputy director of the
Society for Physical Anthropology, wrote in 1934:

> For the first time in world history, the Führer Adolf Hitler has
> translated what we have learned about the biological foundations
> of the development of a people—race, inheritance, selection—
> into action. It is no coincidence that this has happened in Ger-

many: German science has placed this tool in the hands of the politician.[62]

Hans Weinert, a professor of anthropology in Kiel, wrote in 1934 that "today biology is recognized and established as 'a core piece of the National Socialist worldview,'" adding, "among all sciences, anthropology...with its practical exploitation of race science and racial hygiene, is at the center of all biology."[63] Leading German scientist Fritz Lenz had written in 1931, even before the Nazis had taken power, that National Socialism could be considered "applied science.... above all as applied biology, applied racial science."[64] This symbiosis of science and politics transported Mengele's academic pursuits into a different dimension, equipping him to serve on the front lines of the racial struggle at the heart of the Nazi worldview.

For the next four semesters at the university, the name Mollison figured prominently on Mengele's list of courses. In addition to his clinical and theoretical studies in the full range of medical subjects (including childbirth, orthopedics, and surgery), Mengele studied anthropology intensively, and courses with Mollison represented a full two-thirds of his instructional hours.[65] Soon after the Nazis assumed power, Mollison proposed that the anthropological collection that belonged to the institute he headed be organized into an exhibition on racial science.[66] A previous exhibition at the institute had been closed down in 1917 by his predecessor, but Mollison argued that the time was right to mount a new exhibition that could serve not only the students at the university but also the public: "The anthropological exhibit wants to support in the most effective way the endeavor of the government to awaken an understanding of the racial question in the entire people."[67]

Mollison stressed that the principles of racial science, which he referred to as the "indispensable foundation of our worldview," would serve as an organizing principle for the exhibition and would make clear that individual races had "different values."[68] Historian Andrew Evans, in his book on German anthropology during World War I, concludes that the proposal for the Munich exhibition was clear evidence that anthropology had not only "been fully mobilized for the state and the nation but also had fully embraced a racist and *völkisch* perspective."[69] The several years it took for the exhibition to be approved and mounted—it opened on April 2, 1938—coincided precisely with the period of Mengele's work with Mollison. Given Mollison's preoccupation with the exhibition and Mengele's devotion to the subject as well as to his mentor, it seems more than likely that Mengele played a role in helping to plan and execute it.

For the subject of his dissertation, Mengele selected a topic that was entirely consistent with how anthropology was seen and practiced in Nazi Germany. In "Rassenmorphologische Untersuchung des vorderen Unterkiefersabschnittes bei vier rassischen Gruppen" (Racial-Morphological Examination of the Anterior Section of the Lower Jaw Among Four Racial Groups), Mengele wanted to "give a complete picture" of the racial differences that found expression in the front section of the lower jaw,[70] an effort that must be seen in the larger context of attempts to link differences in physical characteristics to race and ultimately to the development of a "racial diagnosis." He took issue with earlier attempts by anthropologists to discern race-based differences in the shape of the lower jaw, criticizing them for methodological failings.[71]

Mengele's research involved the careful examination of 122 lower jaws, originating from six different racial groups, which were part of the university's anthropological collection. Looking only at the very front part of the lower jaw—an area whose horizontal boundaries were the *foramina mentale* on each side and whose vertical limits were the edge of the tooth socket and the base of the jaw—Mengele determined thirty-two linear and five angular measurements relating to important landmarks within this region and derived nine ratios and other relative functions. Using these analytics, he examined their value as a racial indicator by creating a *Wertigkeitsindex,* or significance index, which was calculated by comparing variations of a characteristic within and between the various racial groupings. The higher the "significance index," the more important that characteristic was for racial discernment. He subjected the data to further analyses relating to statistical issues concerning the accuracy and reliability of his measurements.

Mengele's next challenge—to present his data in the most appropriate manner—was undoubtedly influenced by Mollison. In 1907 Mollison had devised a technique for displaying the results of anthropometric research into racial differentiation that changed the discipline and gave dramatic visual expression to the hard measurements that were the nuts and bolts of physical anthropology. Traditionally, data were summarized in tabular form, with columns for minimum, maximum, and computed mean values for particular measurements; such a presentation provided little useful analysis, especially when comparing data of several different populations, which was, of course, the goal of those studying racial differentiation. Mollison's method allowed for the comparison of mountains of measurements in such a way that simple observation could determine connections and influences that no amount of scrutinizing the raw data could reveal.

Mollison called his technique *Abweichungskurve,* or deviation curve, because it displayed the degree to which the characteristics of one tested sample deviated from the values of the baseline group. It succeeded in "transforming numerical values into points on a plane, and by connecting those points to create a curve, anthropologists turned numbers into visual entities. Statistical data now had a form that could be—perhaps even should be—visually assessed."[72] Mengele acknowledged the power of this method: "With a graphic presentation, it is readily possible to provide a clear picture of the characteristics among individual racial groups."[73]

Mengele's conclusions were unambiguous: "The jaws of the examined racial groups indicate in their front sections such distinct differences that they permit one to distinguish between the races."[74] But his methods, perhaps, were not. In one of the only critical analyses of

Mengele's Munich dissertation, Udo Benzenhöfer and his colleagues found in 2008 that Mengele's approach was essentially flawed, citing his failure to employ certain statistical techniques that were available to him at the time and criticizing certain of his analytic choices. They concluded, applying eagle-eyed hindsight, that Mengele could not establish a sustainable concept of race "since none existed (or exists)," citing population geneticist Luigi Luca Cavalli-Sforza's *Genes, People, and Languages* (2000).[75] Historian Michael Kater offered a similar critique when he wrote:

> From a formal point of view, Mengele's work moved on the exact scientific tracks on which his teacher Mollison had been trained. Nevertheless, there were alarming signs of inadmissible subjectivism already at the beginning of Mengele's scientific activity, which stigmatized the hopeful academic at an early stage. One was the postulated certainty that "races" differed from each other . . . and that therefore, as a consequence, qualitative value judgments should be made.[76]

Mollison apparently shared some misgivings about the quality of Mengele's work, focusing not on statistical methodology but on presentation: "The work, although it suffers from a somewhat clumsy manner of presentation and expression, may be described as fulfilling the requirements."[77]

Despite this lukewarm evaluation, Mengele redeemed himself during his oral examinations two weeks later. On November 11, 1935, he was examined in one of his minor fields, zoology, by Karl von Fritsch, and passed with the grade of II or *magna cum laude*. On November 13, he was examined in anthropology, his major field, by Theodor Mollison and received a grade I-II, which fell between *magna* and *summa cum laude*. For his second minor, he was questioned in the field of physiology[78] by Philip Broemser and received a I, or *summa cum laude*.[79] With his successful completion of all the requirements, Mengele was awarded a doctor of philosophy degree, *summa cum laude*, on November 13, 1935.

Mengele continued his medical studies and successfully passed the state examination in medicine in Munich in the summer of 1936. His next requirement was to perform a one-year practicum, equivalent to an internship in the United States, which he did, from September through December 1936, at the University Medical Clinic in Leipzig,[80] and then, beginning on January 1, 1937, in Frankfurt at the University Institute for Hereditary Biology and Racial Hygiene.

Frankfurt

The University of Frankfurt was the home of a man who would play an extraordinarily important role in Mengele's intellectual and professional life: Baron Otmar von Verschuer, a prominent German physician and eugenicist. An infantry officer during World War I, Verschuer had studied medicine in Marburg, Hamburg, Freiburg, and Munich, receiving his medical degree in 1923 with a thesis on protein content in blood serum—a subject related to that which he would take up with Mengele's assistance in 1943–44.[81] He received a position as a physician in Tübingen thanks to Fritz Lenz, one of the co-authors of the standard text, which came to be known as "Baur-Fischer-Lenz," that Hitler is said to have read while in Landsberg prison following the Beer Hall Putsch. In 1927 Verschuer published a study on genetics for his *Habilitation* based on twin research, a methodology that became his specialty. That same year Eugen Fischer, a luminary in the German scientific world, became the founding director of the Kaiser Wilhelm Institute for Anthropology, Human Genetics, and Eugenics (KWI-A) and appointed Verschuer to head the human genetics division, where he pursued his research on twins, which was supported in part by the Rockefeller Foundation.[82]

In 1935 Verschuer left the Kaiser Wilhelm Institute to head the newly established Institute for Hereditary Biology and Racial Hygiene at the University of Frankfurt. It would be hard to overstate Verschuer's impact and influence on German racial science during this period. Between 1923 and 1945, he published at least 109 articles and books and was the author of the medical textbook *Hereditary Pathology: A Textbook for Physicians and Medical Students*, which had three editions, the last published at the very end of the war in 1945. Verschuer also founded and edited the journal *Der Erbarzt* (The Genetic Physician), which was an influential venue for publication and discussion of ideas relating to racial science and state policy, and he published a number of Mengele's own book reviews and other writings.

The Frankfurt Institute had been founded in the spring of 1935 and inaugurated on June 19 of that year. Established within the faculty of medicine at the University of Frankfurt, the institute was the first of its kind to combine scientific research, academic instruction, and genetic practice.[83] Its raison d'être was the recognition that genetics and racial hygiene were necessary elements in the training of physicians as well as an independent field in medical studies. The work of the institute centered on three main areas: research, genetic practice, and instruction. Located in a huge building on the southern bank of the Main River, it occupied fifty-eight rooms on the second floor, with offices for the staff, laboratories, examination rooms, and the other elements of an academic institution that engaged in a public health service. Otmar von Verschuer described the public function:

> Just as the pathologist performs autopsies, the hygiene expert performs bacteriological examinations, and the clinician, alongside his research and teaching responsibilities, is also the head physician of a hospital, so the University representative for hereditary biology and racial hygiene is the consultant for hereditary medicine to health authorities and senior expert for the hereditary health courts and higher courts.[84]

In carrying out this function, the institute prepared expert opinions on the racial character of individuals.

Verschuer wanted his institute to be bound closely to the Nazi state through its science and the research it conducted:

> The history of our science is closely linked to our history of the recent past. The leader of the German Reich is the first statesman who has made the findings of genetic biology and racial hygiene a guiding principle in his governance. The scope of our science has thereby extended far beyond the boundaries of a specialized science.[85]

He envisioned an ambitious research agenda that would benefit and be supported by the state, based on the conviction that "practical goals" can raise important questions that "only tireless research" can answer. Claiming that "living science promotes ever new research," Verschuer pointed to the "rich results of genetic research" that were already "the basis for the racial policy of the National Socialist State and hereditary health care." He foresaw an expansion of such laws and a corresponding need for scientific support, making no secret of his attitude:

> We can only welcome the measures that have hitherto been taken for the hereditary recovery of our people, in the firm conviction that they are the right path that will lead to reconstruction. Our research is and will be responsible for the fact that hereditary and racial care, in which Germany is leading the world, is so firmly consolidated in its foundations that it can cope with any external attack.[86]

His plans included a large-scale project to identify and register all twins in the Frankfurt area, a clear indication that twin research was one of the most important approaches in the field of hereditary biology. Additional research projects involving family history sought to determine the hereditary pathology of a series of diseases by examining as large a sample of family members of an afflicted person as possible. Using this method, a series of illnesses and conditions were examined, including muscular dystrophy, diabetes, and certain physical malformations, like arachnodactyly ("spider fingers"), polycythemia (overabundance of red blood cells), and cleft palate. Moreover, an ambitious project was undertaken to study the entire population of an area in Hesse, comprising eight villages, from a hereditary biological perspective.

Mengele, having finished the first half of his internship in Leipzig, completed the second half at the Frankfurt Institute; when it ended on September 1, 1937, Mengele had fulfilled all the requirements for his medical degree and received his appointment as a physician. He worked at the institute as a volunteer for one month and continued there as a fellow funded by the Kerckhoff Foundation[87] beginning October 1. Mengele then started on his second doctorate, this one in medicine, with Otmar von Verschuer as his *Doktorvater*. Already a licensed physician, Mengele did not need this degree in order to practice, but it was necessary for an academic career—to teach or manage a university laboratory or institute—and required further study as well as the completion of a dissertation. Not surprisingly, the topic of Mengele's second dissertation was entirely consistent with the research program of the institute.

He chose to investigate the related birth defects of cleft lip, palate, and jaw—malformations that had emerged as particularly interesting in the context of racial hygiene, since new surgical interventions could correct them cosmetically, camouflaging a trait that would normally have identified a racially compromised individual. In approaching his topic, Mengele employed the research methodology of family history, which sought to identify and examine the relatives of an individual possessing a certain trait, to determine whether, and to what extent, they possessed the same trait. Previous research had failed to provide unambiguous answers to the question of whether cleft palate was a genetic defect,[88] and family history, based on broad research across generations, was seen as a promising approach, which Mengele hoped would provide clear and reliable results. The process was straightforward. After selecting a "specific characteristic or anomaly" to study, the researcher needed to identify and locate as many people as possible with the characteristic, along with as many of their family members. The family members were then carefully examined for any sign of the characteristic in question, and the results of the examination were entered into a family tree and statistically analyzed to determine whether the investigated characteristic was "inherited according to Mendelian transmission."[89]

For his dissertation, Mengele was able to identify 110 children who had been treated for an oral cleft by the surgical department of the university clinic in Frankfurt between 1925 and 1935. From these cases, he narrowed the number to seventeen, selecting those living in the Frankfurt area who had both a cleft lip and a cleft palate. Through discussions with the parents of these children, Mengele was able to reconstruct genealogical tables for the seventeen families, which contained entries for a total of 1,222 living individuals. Mengele himself examined 583 of them, and when he could not personally see an individual, he reviewed all their relevant medical records from local health offices. Within the seventeen families that were the subject of his research, Mengele determined that there were eight cases of "cleft formation," roughly half of the total sample, and believed that this was a clear indication of inheritance.

He then went one step further by identifying what he termed "micro-manifestations" in all seventeen families. A micro-manifestation was a "microform" of the oral cleft that could express itself in different ways, such as a submucous cleft, divided uvula, fold in the upper lip, or misplaced or missing teeth. Since he knew that such characteristics were not unusual in the general population, he made what appears to have been an arbitrary decision to consider the presence of two such microforms as significant for his study.[90] Using this standard, he determined that thirteen of the seventeen families exhibited either a fully developed oral cleft or at least two micro-manifestations of the condition, from which he concluded that there was a "singly dominant heredity" of the oral cleft. His examination of the seventeen families also led him to conclude that the "manifestation depended on other developmental disorders," noting a high correlation between the presence of an oral cleft (and its microforms) and other disabilities such as polydactyly, syndactyly, spina bifida, meningomyelocele, "feeble-mindedness and mental disorders,"[91] as well as more benign conditions such as hernias.

Mengele himself had at least two of the conditions that he had identified as micro-manifestations of an oral cleft: diastema and hypodontia, or missing teeth. He had also suffered from a hernia, a condition that had a relevant correlation to the presence of an oral cleft. One noted historian, Michael Kater, has suggested that this fact may have played a role in Mengele's choice of subject for his dissertation and certainly raises questions about his objectivity.[92] Indeed, one must wonder why the young scientist, who had spent so much time examining jawbones for his first dissertation, would focus again on that area of the body for his second. That he carefully described the existence of certain characteristics that he himself possessed as directly related to a physical defect, which, in turn pointed toward other serious developmental disabilities must have had its impact.

Mengele submitted and defended his dissertation in the summer of 1938. In his official evaluation, Verschuer wrote, "The dissertation of Dr. Mengele is an original, independently executed scholarly work, whose execution required not only great industry and tenacity in overcoming all the significant obstacles but also keen skills of observation and care in carrying out the examinations."[93] Verschuer echoed this enthusiastic endorsement of Mengele's achievement and talent in a more public way when he lauded his student's work in *Der Erbarzt*. In an article reviewing the accomplishments of the institute during its first four years, Verschuer chose to single out Mengele's dissertation as having gone beyond the work of others, who might have shown a hereditary basis for oral clefts but had failed to examine the subtle indications of the condition in a broad review of extended families or to establish a link to other developmental disabilities.[94]

Mengele's dissertation was published a year later in a respected journal, *Zeitschrift für Menschliche Vererbungs- und Konstitutions-lehre* (Journal for Human Heredity and Constitution Theory),[95] and it received due attention in the internationally respected *Handbuch der Erbbiologie des Menschen* (Handbook of Human Genetic Biology), which described it as a "careful work" that represented "an advance in the study of the genetic pathology of the cleft lip and palate because it points out the importance and the role of micro-manifestations."[96] Another respected journal published a long review article on the subject of cleft palates and referred to Mengele's work as "extensive and thorough."[97] Even as late as 1970, Mengele's work was referenced in a Japanese publication on oral clefts[98] and in a 1972 article in a British dental journal.[99] One historian, K. H. Roth, has argued that Mengele's dissertation made a significant impact on Verschuer, providing "the last building block for the final establishment of the new human-genetic paradigm.... Together with the first proof of the so-called Crossing-Over Mechanism in humans, in which Verschuer's Institute also played a leading role, a new human-biological basic science emerged, which was now about to give theories of selection a scientific basis."[100]

In the conclusion to his second dissertation, Mengele did not comment on the eugenic implications of his work, as another scientist, whom he cited, had done in his 1931 work on the same topic. It was unnecessary, thanks to the promulgation, on July 14, 1933, of the Law for the Prevention of Hereditarily Diseased Offspring, known as the sterilization law, which came into effect in January 1934. This statute allowed for the compulsory sterilization of any citizen who, in the opinion of a "genetic health court," manifested any one of a list of identified genetic disorders: "any person suffering from a hereditary disease may be rendered incapable of producing children by means of a surgical operation [sterilization], provided it is established . . . as very highly probable that any children he might produce would inherit some serious physical or mental defect." Concerning oral clefts, the "quasi-official" commentary on the law said, "A person with a harelip can be sterilized, if his offspring or other blood relatives display more severe forms of cleft-formation in the facial region . . . or other severe hereditary abnormalities."[101]

Mengele's work, with its "proof" of a high degree of heritability of oral clefts and their connection to other developmental disabilities, served to underpin the legislation, the enforcement of which resulted in the forced sterilization of 375,000 individuals between its enactment in 1934 and the beginning of World War II, on September 1, 1939. The Marital Health Law, promulgated in September 1935, prohibited the marriage of a healthy person to anyone who had a hereditary condition, including those with oral clefts. A 1936 modification of this law also prohibited marriage between healthy individuals and those who had been sterilized under other legislation.[102]

Mengele Joins the Nazi Party

Once the Nazis came to power in January 1933, consolidated that power after the elections in March, and passed the enabling legislation that ushered in dictatorial rule, many rushed to join the party, seeing advantage in aligning with the party in power. The new opportunistic allegiances to the Nazi Party were seen as a threat to its ideological purity, and an affront and challenge to those who had joined out of commitment and foresight. To combat this phenomenon, and to protect against Johnny-come-latelies, the party decided, in April 1933, to impose a ban on further party membership for an undetermined period of time, beginning on May 1, except for Hitler Youth members who had come of age after 1933, and a very small number of others. The party enforced the ban with such discipline that when it relaxed it in 1937, to permit applications from all who had been active in any party-related organizations since 1933, there was a rush of applicants, and party ranks swelled.

One of these 1937 applicants was Josef Mengele. Following the Nazi assumption of power, the *Stahlhelm,* which Mengele had joined in 1931, had been absorbed into the SA, a paramilitary group known as the Brown Shirts, and even though Mengele left that Nazi organization in 1934 because of his kidney problem, his membership made him eligible to apply to the party. His acceptance came a year later, in May 1938. Around the same time, Mengele also joined the SS.

The years of Mengele's university study changed him just as profoundly as they had changed both his country and the status of the science that had become his consuming passion. He had entered university at a time of political uncertainty; the impact of the Great Depression had not yet been fully felt in Germany. He emerged eight years later at the vanguard of a new science and committed to a new political vision, both of which promised to change Germany and the world. The combination of his studies in medicine and anthropology provided Mengele with a perfect scientific complement to Nazi politics. Indeed, Rudolph Hess, Hitler's deputy, said that Nazism was "applied biology." Through medicine, with its focus on the human body and its emphasis on genetic pathology, and through anthropology, with its focus on the racial body and its emphasis on the qualitative differences between races, Mengele had equipped himself to be a frontline soldier in the struggle that was at the heart of Nazi ideology and that defined its politics.

In September 1937, as an indication of his growing status as a young scientist with a promising future, Mengele attended the ninth meeting of the German Society for Physical Anthropology in Tübingen. During this meeting the organization elected to change its name to the German Society for Racial Research, a clear statement of the future direction of the discipline. Mengele published a note on the meeting in *Der Erbarzt,* in which he summarized the presentations.[103] A photograph

of the scientists assembled there reveals a young Mengele on the edge
of the large group, posing on the steps of a university building, with
the giants of the new science and Mengele's mentors—Eugen Fischer,
Otmar von Verschuer, Alfred Ploetz, and Theodor Mollison—in the
middle, occupying pride of place.[104]

CHAPTER 2

SCIENTIST AND SOLDIER

(June 1938–January 1943)

In June 1938, Otmar von Verschuer sought authorization to fill a vacancy at the Frankfurt Institute by hiring Mengele as a permanent assistant. In his letter of recommendation, Verschuer wrote that his prize student had "distinguished himself through extraordinary achievements." He praised his reliability and highlighted his "special anthropological training" as making him especially well-suited to work at the institute.

> He performs particularly valuable services in the genetic and racial assessments in connection with ancestry examinations, with his anthropological training serving him well here. At the institute's lecture series and on occasion of smaller lectures, he has proven that he possesses the ability to present even difficult intellectual subjects. Dr. Mengele has almost completed a major scientific work—family research on cases of cleft lip and palate. Another work on the issue of heredity in congenital heart disease is underway.[1]

The university approved the appointment, and Mengele took an important step toward what he hoped would be an academic career.

He continued to engage in scholarly activity, conducting research and publishing at least six book reviews and three articles, in addition to his dissertation. When Mengele's colleague Otwill Reichert died in 1939, Verschuer assigned Mengele the task of preparing Reichert's research for publication, which led to at least two articles on the heritability of *Thromboangiitis obliterans* (Buerger disease) and *Polyarteritis nodosa* (Kussmaul-Maier disease). In the 1940 issue of *Der Erbarzt*, Mengele published a paper on the inheritance of *Fistula auris congenita*, a sinus opening in the external ear.[2] The research for this paper emerged from a paternity case that had been assigned to Mengele, who found a correlation between the anomaly of the ear and a cleft chin. Mengele spent the summer semester of 1939 at the clinic for internal medicine at the University of Bonn, exchanging positions with Dr. Franz Grosse-Brockhoff.[3] He certainly enjoyed his mentor's confidence, standing in for him for two weeks in February 1940, teaching his course, "Human Genetics as the Basis for Racial Hygiene," and in March 1940 Verschuer recommended extending Mengele's period of employment. Verschuer underlined the last sentence of his letter of recommendation: "Following my experience of the past two years, I have become convinced that Dr. Mengele is suited for an academic career."[4]

Expert Opinions

Beginning with the civil service law of April 1933, new German legislation required that individuals prove their racial bona fides. Not everyone could provide the necessary documentation because of particular family circumstances (including adoption and birth out of wedlock), and in the case of so-called *Mischlinge* or mixed-race individuals, a clear racial designation was also missing. The Reich Genealogical Office (RGO), established in 1935 within the Ministry of the Interior, was responsible for resolving such questions. Historian Eric Ehrenreich notes that "during the twelve years of the Third Reich, State and Party authorities together issued two thousand statutes, ordinances, and regulations establishing legal rights on the basis of 'racial' status."[5] Much was at stake in terms of one's rights, status, occupation, and increasingly—with the passing of the Nuremberg Laws in 1935 and the violence of *Kristallnacht* in 1938—one's freedom and safety. Verschuer's institute was one of the first to be accredited by the RGO to produce racial certificates, and according to an article by Verschuer, between 1935 and the beginning of 1941 it prepared at least 448 of them.[6]

While at the Frankfurt Institute, Mengele placed his scientific knowledge at the disposal of the state by preparing so-called *Gutachten*, or expert opinions, for the RGO and the health courts, which had been created to enforce the various racial and eugenic laws designed to implement the Nazi worldview and to protect and "improve" the German race.[7] Mengele worked with Verschuer in conducting examinations and rendering professional judgments about an individual's paternity and "racial acceptability." Historian Sheila Faith Weiss examined 120 opinions rendered during Verschuer's tenure for which the examiner might be identifed; she found that Mengele prepared far more than the three other assistants at the institute—and that his judgment was more often than not beneficial to the person being examined, finding that the individual was not a "full Jew" more than two-thirds of the time. The prevalence of such a rating indicated not that Mengele was "soft" on Jews but rather that he viewed himself as an "objective scientist" whose findings were based on as "thorough" an analysis as possible.[8]

One of the cases Weiss describes in some detail is that of Heinz Alexander, who was accused of *Rassenschande,* or race defilement, a criminal act involving sexual relations between an "Aryan" and a Jew.[9] Alexander was, according to genealogical records, a "full Jew," even though both his parents had converted to Christianity and raised him in their adopted religion. He had admitted to having had an affair with an Aryan woman over several years, but defended himself against the charge of *Rassenschande* by claiming that he had been born out of wedlock and that his biological father was a "German-blooded" man, an assertion that was apparently supported by "a very large amount of written evidence," as well as by his blond hair and blue eyes. The prosecuting attorney requested that Alexander be examined by the Frankfurt Institute, and Mengele, assigned to the case in Verschuer's absence, completed his racial evaluation in July 1937, before he was employed as an assistant at the institute—demonstrating, according to Weiss, that Mengele enjoyed Verschuer's "great confidence" as an examiner.

Using a "similarity analysis," much like that used to distinguish fraternal and identical twins, Mengele compared Alexander with his mother and his "legal" Jewish father, and also with photographs of the alleged non-Jewish biological father, and concluded that Alexander "should be viewed as a full Jew." The court gave his opinion little weight, however, and acquitted Alexander of the charges in September 1937. It rejected Mengele's opinion as "illogical" since it had been contradicted by his own equivocal language, reiterated in his testimony in the courtroom, that there was only a "probability" that Alexander's biological father was his Jewish legal father.[10]

In reading Mengele's opinion,[11] one can find a firm basis for the court's finding that Mengele's seemingly ambivalent analysis clashed with his confident conclusion. Mengele's examination included, where possible, a comparison of twelve different areas, including blood type and factors, eyes and eyebrows, as well as finger- and footprints. He determined that there was nothing to rule out the paternity of Alexander's legal father, that some areas of similarity made the paternity "probable," and that there was no pronounced similarity between the photograph of the alleged biological father and the son. In this case, the prospect for high confidence was compromised by the lack of blood or fingerprint comparisons (since the alleged biological father was dead). Moreover, the use of photographs for comparison purposes weakened any conclusion, given their two-dimensional character and their lack of reliable color values for the evaluation of skin, eyes, and hair.

Verschuer, upset by the verdict, claimed that it "undermined" the

Nuremberg Laws, turning a "Jew into a half-Jew," and he appealed for a definitive way of determining racial ancestry that would be accepted by the courts and not be subject to the review of judges untrained in racial science. Dr. Walter Gross, of the Racial Policy Office of the Nazi Party, responded to Verschuer by criticizing Mengele for the "lack of clear and precise information" in his racial determination and for his "fickle" testimony at trial. He concluded, "I do not think that the court would have ignored a totally clear position of the assistant [Mengele]."[12] Mengele must have "learned from his mistake," Weiss noted, since she was unable to find any other instances where the court questioned a racial certificate that he issued.[13]

Marriage

While performing his practicum in Leipzig in 1936, Mengele had met Irene Schönbein, an attractive nineteen-year-old and the only child of Harry Schoenbein, a successful businessman from Freiburg, and his wife, Elise. Marriage for a member of the SS was not a private matter. Heinrich Himmler had issued the SS Engagement and Marriage Order on December 31, 1931, requiring all unmarried members of the SS to secure permission before marrying. As a racial elite, the SS had a significant interest in whom its members decided to marry, and it established an entire bureaucracy to evaluate and sanction prospective unions. A raft of paperwork was required, as was a medical examination proving the absence of congenital diseases and, above all, the capability to bear children; for the SS, marriage meant two people of racial quality procreating. The entire enterprise was, in many ways, a state-sponsored human breeding program.[14]

While Mengele was receiving military training in the Tyrol in the fall of 1938, Irene took the first steps necessary to become his bride. She requested the requisite forms to initiate the review of her family history and of her own physical and racial suitability. As a part of this process, she needed to obtain recommendations from two individuals who knew her well. The questionnaire contained a number of questions with binary choices, making clear the ideal qualities expected of an SS bride. Georg Schlick wrote in support of the marriage, claiming that Irene was "very reliable" (as opposed to "unreliable"), "very fond of children" (as opposed to "not fond of children"), "comradely" (not "domineering"), "thrifty" (not "wasteful"), "domestic" (not "flighty" or "vain"), and "efficient" (not "inefficient"). He went on to describe Irene as "well above the average" in intellect, and a "model for every German girl" in terms of her spirit and character. She was "particularly well suited" to become the bride of an SS member.[15] Similarly, Dr. Rudolf Schwarz described Irene and her parents as "reliable fighters for the National Socialist worldview" and judged Irene to be "a very well-educated and highly talented girl" who "is longing for a harmonious marriage, following the example set by her parents."[16]

The day after Christmas 1938, Irene had a physical examination in Frankfurt, performed by Dr. Schwarzweller, an SS physician. One section of the form called for an inventory of ten physical characteristics, with a list of associated values in descending order of desirability. For instance, for "Body Type," the physician could choose "muscular (athletic), plump, slim, or puny," with the first clearly being the most positive. For eye color, the following choices were available: "blue, gray, greenish, light brown, and dark brown." These physical attributes, thought to be expressions of the racial mixture that the person represented, were observed and noted. In Irene's case, Dr. Schwarzweller awarded her nine out of ten of the attributes with the highest value, and only one, "hair form," as the second highest: "sleek," which was one step down from "straight" but better than "wavy, curly, or crinkly." The combination of these features led Schwarzweller to conclude that Irene was primarily of the Nordic race with some Dinaric influences. She was found to be in excellent health and, perhaps of key significance, likely to be able to bear children, noting her "wide pelvis."[17]

Beyond her physical appearance, evident racial quality, and presumed reproductive potential, Irene needed to provide evidence that her family tree was free of taint. The form intended to examine this critical information provided an opportunity to catalogue the applicant's forebears going back to 1648, the date of the Peace of Westphalia, which had marked the end of the Thirty Years War. Along with providing the requested genealogical information to the extent possible, the applicant had to submit proof, in the form of certified copies of documents and similar verifications, which were subject to review by trained examiners, who had to certify each entry with a special stamp. Because Irene's paternal grandfather had been born out of wedlock, there was no way to identify his father's line with absolute certainty. One can find in Irene's file a court document from 1886 representing a settlement between Irene's paternal great-grandmother, Anna Schoenbein, and a man named Harry Lyons Dümler, according to which Dümler had undertaken to support Anna's child through his fourteenth birthday under the condition that Anna leave Dümler "completely alone." Furthermore, Dümler "expressly" rejected "that he [had] ever acknowledged that he [was] the father of the child."[18] Despite Dümler's seemingly dubious rejection of paternity, the SS official responsible for evaluating Irene's family tree wrote: "After consultation with SS Obersturmführer Osiander,[19] the fatherhood of Harry Lyons Dümler has not been proven. Ancestor number 4 [i.e., paternal grandfather] in the family tree of the future bride must therefore be considered as unknown."[20]

Although the office responsible for evaluating marriage applications introduced no objection to Mengele's marriage to Irene, Irene's compromised family history had a serious consequence. The SS Engagement and Marriage Order provided that once the SS authorized a marriage, the names of the family of the SS member would be entered in the *Sippenbuch* (clan registry), which was maintained by the Racial Office of the SS. Mengele was notified on March 9, 1939, that because Irene's grandfather was unknown, there would be no listing. With the formal evaluation out of the way and his choice of bride cleared, even if the result was not unalloyed, Mengele could, in the eyes of the SS, become officially engaged on April 21, 1939.[21]

Mengele and Irene were married on July 28, 1939, in Oberstdorf, first in a civil ceremony at the registry office (Standesamt) and then immediately following in a small chapel, where the Catholic service took place. Irene's father "wept in his handkerchief" during the ceremony.[22] In 1984 Irene would write to two researchers who were working on a book about Mengele, "I knew Josef Mengele as an absolutely honorable, decent, conscientious, very charming, elegant and amusing person. Otherwise I probably would not have married him. I grew up in a good, prosperous house, and I did not lack for marriage possibilities."[23]

Soldier

Five weeks after the wedding of Josef and Irene Mengele, Germany, responding to a manufactured provocation, invaded Poland and fired the first shots of what was to become World War II. From the Nazi point of view, the war, in addition to being a military campaign to conquer land and resources, was also a racial struggle, which was given a powerful pretext by the science Josef Mengele had studied and practiced in the nine years before its start. Because of the key role he played at Verschuer's institute, Mengele, in contrast to many of his colleagues there, was not immediately called on to trade his white coat for his country's uniform. He had been designated as important for "other service," preventing him, at least temporarily, from joining the fight on the battlefield.[24]

On June 15, 1940, his deferment behind him, Mengele joined the Sanitäts-Ersatz-Bataillon 9 (Medical Replace Battalion 9) stationed in Kassel, where he attended the "military physician training course" and passed the junior physician examination.[25] According to his friend Kurt Lambertz, Mengele's service in the unit was quite unpleasant thanks to the attitude and actions of a vicious noncommissioned officer, who wanted to "wear down his subordinates" by making them "crawl for hours around the base and clean clogged latrines."[26] Mengele's way out was to apply to the Waffen-SS, where he was assigned to the medical inspectorate on August 1, 1940. His first post was with the Central Immigration Office (Einwandererzentralstelle, EWZ) in Posen, where he was assigned to the health office as an expert in hereditary biology. The EWZ, a Nazi Party agency, had been established at the beginning of October 1939 to evaluate ethnic German immigrants to determine their suitability for resettlement.

For the Nazis, the war offered the possibility not only of removing threats to the German race but also of taking "positive" steps to preserve and cultivate the German racial community. Since race and nation were synonymous for the Nazis, they claimed the right and obligation to safeguard German blood wherever it was found. In a speech before the Reichstag on October 6, 1939, Hitler heralded the establishment of a "new order of ethnographic conditions, that is to say, a resettlement of nationalities," which, he suggested, would remove the source of further conflict in Europe. It was "utopian," he claimed, for "members of a highly developed people" to be "assimilated without trouble," and he called for a "farsighted ordering of the life of Europe." By this he meant, among other things, the resettlement of ethnic Germans to the new areas that had been added to Germany in the war. A secret annex to the Nazi-Soviet Nonaggression Pact, concluded on August 23, 1939, provided the means and opportunity for the kind of resettlement that Hitler conjured in his speech.

In addition to dividing up Poland and determining spheres of influence in the Baltic and Eastern Europe, the pact and its annexes allowed ethnic Germans in the Baltic states to migrate to Germany and so-called White Russians to pass from territory occupied by the Germans into the Soviet Union. The pact also allowed Germany to incorporate areas of western Poland, making them administratively and legally part of Germany. These areas, including Upper Silesia and the Warthegau, were to be emptied of their Jews and Poles, who were to be moved eastward into a rump Poland known as the General Government (Generalgouvernement); the annexed territories were to be repopulated with resettled ethnic Germans, who would occupy the empty homes and take over the appropriated farms and businesses. The resettlement of ethnic Germans from the Baltic, who would otherwise have come under Soviet control, was part of a huge effort to redraw the racial and ethnic map of Europe. In a similar effort, Hitler reached an agreement with Mussolini, in October 1939, that permitted ethnic Germans in the South Tyrol to opt for German citizenship and resettlement.

To accomplish this vast and complicated movement of people would require a correspondingly large and complex bureaucracy. The day after his Reichstag speech, Hitler appointed Heinrich Himmler as the Reich Commissioner for the Strengthening of Germandom (Reichskommissar für die Festigung deutschen Volkstums), a title whose English translation fails to convey its full meaning. Himmler saw his task as the creation of a new racial order that gave him a fiduciary responsibility to preserve, protect, nurture, and cultivate German blood. He was specifically charged with the repatriation of ethnic Germans, the "elimination of the harmful influence of alien [volksfremden] parts of the population, which represent a danger to the Reich and the German national community," and the establishment of "new German settlement areas."[27]

Two weeks later Himmler addressed a group of SS officers in Posen (Poznań), which had recently been annexed to Germany, and revealed his romantic vision of the impending resettlement:

> Germans have lived in the eastern provinces, where we stand today, for the past three thousand years. . . . These old German settlements have more or less maintained their racial identity in closed-off places . . . although, in part, the ability to speak German may have been lost. What was possible then must again be possible. . . . Since time immemorial German colonies have been a bulwark for the nation and have produced a flourishing peasantry. . . . The indigenous people were left to work as servants.[28]

The first phase included resettling ethnic Germans from Estonia and Latvia and was regulated by treaties Germany had negotiated with these two Baltic countries, which still maintained their sovereignty, although there was palpable fear that the Soviets would soon occupy them.[29] The treaties with Estonia, signed on October 15, 1939, and with Latvia, on October 30, regulated the disposition of property and the safe passage of any ethnic German who wished to go to Germany, which, from the Nazi perspective, was a "return home."

The resettlement of the Estonian ethnic Germans began just a few days after the treaty was signed and ended a month later with the movement of more than thirteen thousand people, 96 percent of whom were registered with the organization responsible for looking after their interests in Estonia.[30] In Latvia, the resettlement began on November 7, 1939, and ended on December 16. More than forty-seven thousand ethnic Germans, 88 percent of the total in Latvia, were transported to Germany,[31] where they were greeted by representatives of the EWZ. An SS physician conducted a physical examination, including a chest X-ray, paying particular attention to indications of potential genetic problems. A racial evaluation, much like the one carried out in connection with Irene's marriage application, was also required. An inventory of assets that had to be left behind, including real property and nontransportable goods, was created to assist in making compensation decisions. Perhaps most important was an interview that sought to determine how successfully an applicant had nurtured and supported their "Germanness": Did they, for instance, speak German, and how well? Did they belong to organizations that sought to foster and support a connection to German culture and heritage? Those applicants who scored well were resettled in the newly acquired territories, while those less connected to their German background were settled in the "old Reich," where they would receive support from the community in their efforts to become more fully German.

A single report among the surviving records of the EWZ revealed

Mengele's first wartime assignment. Drafted by Hermann Heidenreich, an SS officer and physician, it describes how he and two
colleagues—Mengele and a psychiatrist named Weber—worked for at
least two months, beginning in August 1940, to evaluate the EWZ's
work in resettling the Baltic ethnic Germans. Responding to concerns
about the quality of the health and racial evaluations, Mengele and his
colleagues carried out a systematic assessment of how major landown-
ers and farmers among the Baltic Germans were processed during the
first phase of the resettlement the previous year. Their report included
harsh judgments about sloppily executed evaluations, reserving
the sharpest criticism for the qualifications and performance of the
assigned personnel. They offered examples of carelessness and impre-
cision, including one, which surely came from Mengele, revealing
the failure of an examiner to discover a classic cleft palate that lay
behind a surgically repaired harelip. Their efforts were intended to
improve the EWZ's procedures. The stakes were high, they claimed.
The EWZ's judgments led to grants of land as compensation, and carelessness in its work could bring grave consequences: "the land is too
scarce and too valuable to be assigned to families which will produce,
within a generation or two, a stable full of idiots, imbeciles, epileptics,
or schizophrenics."[32]

It may be difficult for some to see the work of the EWZ, which often
led to a positive outcome for it subjects, in the same context as the
seemingly more sinister activity of others operating within the Nazi
system. Indeed, in postwar trials, SS racial experts freely admitted
their responsibility for the "positive policy" of resettling ethnic Germans during the war, and most escaped serious punishment.[33] Apart
from other crimes they may have committed, however, their work
in evaluating settlers on the basis of health and race was very much
an act of selection, with ominous consequences for those considered
unworthy. Mengele's work in Posen was in meaningful ways prologue
for what followed.[34]

Combat

We know less about Mengele's experience as a member of the Fifth Waffen-SS Viking Division, a frontline combat unit, than almost any other period in his life. Nearly all the works about Mengele have misconstrued even the most basic facts about where he was stationed, and for how long. And yet coming as it did almost directly before his assignment to Auschwitz, it marked an important transition from the young scientist to the SS officer who prowled the ramp at Auschwitz.[35] Although we cannot date with complete confidence when Mengele was assigned to the Engineers Battalion of the Viking Division as a *Truppenarzt* (troop physician or army doctor), it likely occurred sometime at the end of 1940,[36] and it is all but certain that he remained with this unit, without interruption, until the beginning of 1943, when he was transferred to Berlin.

The nucleus of the Viking Division comprised three motorized regiments: Nordland, created from Swedish, Danish, and Norwegian volunteers; Westland, composed of Dutch and Flemish volunteers; and Germania, consisting mainly of ethnic Germans. To this core was added an artillery regiment as well as the other components of an integrated fighting force. Christened "SS Viking Division" in January 1941, the unit was placed under the command of SS-Brigadeführer Felix Steiner, a veteran of World War I, who was awarded the *Ritterkreuz* for his performance leading the Waffen-SS regiment, SS-Deutschland, in the invasion of Poland in 1939 and in the defeat of France in 1940. Steiner, an early member of the SS, was selected by Himmler to lead the newly formed Viking Division, a unit that embodied the Nazi view that blood and nation were synonymous, and that Germany was engaged in a racial war.

Trained in both offensive and defensive activities, the engineers laid mines and cleared them, constructed fortifications and demolished them, built roads, and fashioned ways to defeat man-made obstructions, such as antitank ditches, as well as rivers and other natural impediments. In addition to carrying out these specialized tasks, the Fifth SS Engineers Battalion was a fighting force and was expected to take its place on the front line; in many ways, they were the pathfinders who led the way. While engineers are important for any army and for any military strategy, they took on immense importance for the Nazi Blitzkrieg, where speed and flexibility were paramount.

Mengele began with the unit as assistant medical officer, subordinate to Dr. Waldemar Ültzhöffer, and became the medical officer in mid-October 1941, when Ültzhöffer was struck by an asthma flare-up due to the mold caused by the moist conditions.[37] Although Mengele was supposed to treat acute combat-related injuries and wounds that were not handled by the medical units assigned to the division or by the relevant field hospitals, his major responsibility was to provide general care for the men in his unit, which included treating a wide range of maladies. For a physician with limited clinical experience, the responsibility was particularly demanding. Referring to this challenge later in a letter to Irene from the front, Mengele wrote, "I would be very grateful if you could get me a used copy of *Diagnostic and Therapeutic Vademecum*. One should master all disciplines here and that is a bit too much for a race hygienist. If one has such a small reference book, you can at least learn about specific diseases quickly."[38]

In April 1941 the men in the Viking Division, whose various components had been assembled in the area around Dresden in eastern Germany, experienced a change in intensity and activity. On April 4 all those on leave were ordered back. On April 8 Mengele's battalion boarded three transport trains and relocated westward to the area around Ulm for training exercises, which had the engineers building bridges across the Danube River. Mengele, with the battalion staff, was housed in the Sigmaringen city hall, just over an hour's drive from Günzburg and his own family. In early June 1941, the battalion received the order to decamp, and soon the men and equipment were loaded onto trains for a journey that took them eastward past Prague to Freudenthal (now Bruntal) in the Czech Republic, just ninety miles west of Auschwitz. From Freudenthal, the battalion moved northwestward past Breslau and arrived in Steinau on the Oder River late on June 7 and took up quarters in barracks once used by Reich Labor Service personnel. On June 18 they moved eastward, crossing the border into the General Government at Gross-Wartenburg and managing to traverse western Poland in three days. When they reached Parszów, they continued only at night and without illumination until they reached the staging area for the invasion, "disappearing" into the small villages and forests southeast of Lublin, just west of the German-Soviet demarcation line, where they waited quietly for the order to move.[39]

Late in the evening of June 21, 1941, the battalion commander, SS-Sturmbannführer Klein, called together his men, some of whom had to be woken up, and read the order from the High Command of the German Armed Forces that announced the imminent invasion of the Soviet Union. Operation Barbarossa would commence early the following morning on a broad front from the Baltic States in the north to Bessarabia in the south. Mengele and the Viking Division were part of Army Group South and were poised to enter Ukraine at the very south of the German front, with Romanian forces on their right flank. Only elements of the Viking Division's artillery and the Germania Regiment participated in the initial attack on June 22, with the main body of the division crossing into Ukraine only on June 30. Shortly thereafter it experienced its first engagement with the enemy and committed its first atrocities, which would mark the violence of this war beyond the scale and kind of any that preceded it.

The troops of the Waffen-SS were distinguished not only by their military bearing and discipline but also by their ideological commitment. Historian Kai Struve writes:

> The Viking Division was composed for the most part of recruits
> who had been socialized in the schools, Hitler Youth, and other
> organizations of the Nazi State, which had instilled in them to

a great degree the radical nationalistic, racist worldview of the National Socialist regime. They applied to the SS because they wanted to belong to the elite of the State.... The elevated ideological motivation, which was the basic reason for joining, was further intensified by the "ideological training" in this unit.... The necessity of a brutal, ruthless struggle against Bolshevism along with antisemitic themes was part of the central content of this training.[40]

Struve quotes a speech that Heinrich Himmler delivered to his generals in November 1938:

The war of the future will not be a skirmish but rather an existential struggle between peoples.... We would be ... merciless in such a struggle. It matters not if a thousand people in a city must be hunted down. I would do it, and I would expect the same of you.[41]

This training and indoctrination, as well as the expectations placed upon it by its leaders, created of the Waffen-SS a vanguard that viewed the war as both a military and a racial struggle.

Early in the morning of July 2, SS-Standartenführer Wäckerle, the beloved commander of the division's Westland Regiment, was shot and killed by a sniper near the village of Slowita. In the days that followed Wäckerle's death, members of the Viking Division carried out acts of extreme violence, claiming an estimated several thousand Jews as victims. Struve presents evidence from the records of various German Army units in the area, quoting, for example, the diary of a Lieutenant Kaesburg with the 295th Engineers Battalion: "Firing everywhere. It crackles. The SS bumps off anyone they get their hands on. It is horrific."[42] The chief of staff of the Fourth Army Corps observed that individual members of the Viking Division were seen "hunting for Jews." The war diary of a unit in the area noted that the SS was "indiscriminately" shooting Russian soldiers and civilians in large numbers. A member of the supply unit of the division, Hans Günther Otto, in a sworn affidavit after the war, claimed that his unit had been informed that Wäckerle had been killed by a Jew, and that their participation in the revenge actions marked the "beginning of the unit's participation in the extermination of the Jews."[43] Otto described an order that was read to his unit after Wäckerle's death: "The order said that we were no longer held accountable for the killing of any Jews we could get hold of and that we could indeed shoot any Jew we saw."[44]

The first large massacre by the Viking Division took place in Zoločiv, the next town after Slowita in the path of the advancing division. A prison in Zoločiv had been the site of a massacre carried out by the retreating Soviets. After the Germans marched into the town, two mass graves were discovered there, containing nearly 650 bodies, which led, two days later, to the murder of a thousand or more Jews in a pogrom sanctioned by the Germans, in which members of the Viking Division participated. A film taken during the pogrom shows that victims were beaten before their deaths. Shlomo Wolkowicz, who had fled from Lvov to relatives in Zoločiv, where he was in school, described the scene:

> It was a hot day, and many would pass out from the sharp odor of corpses, which did not bother our guards. The SS people stood around the pit, and from time to time, they ordered someone— especially men with beards and sidelocks—to come out and kneel in front of them. With sadistic pleasure, they hit their victim until he lay unconscious on the ground and they kicked them back into the pit. Sometimes family members tried to help the poor people, but then they often made their fate even worse. Some were taken out of the grave and beaten to death with unimaginable brutality. The killers allowed the injured to succumb to their wounds slowly in pain and agony. That went on all day. I was deeply shaken by atrocities, the likes of which I never saw again.[45]

The division moved out from Zoločiv and "liquidated" six hundred Jews in Zboriv, in what Kai Struve described as a further "escalation" of violence. In contrast to the pogrom in Zoločiv, where the SS along with local Ukrainians murdered a fraction of the Jewish population, Zboriv saw the killing of the majority of the Jewish men. Members of the Viking Division carried out the actual killing by themselves, receiving assistance from the Ukrainian militia only in rounding up the Jews and conveying them to the murder site, which was a bomb crater that served later as their grave. The sound of machine gun fire could be heard the entire day of July 4, 1941.[46]

After killing as many as two hundred more Jews in Jezierna (Ozerna), the unit moved on to Tarnopol, the third-largest city in eastern Galicia with forty thousand residents, 40 percent of whom were Jews. In a postwar memoir, August von Kageneck, who served with the Ninth Panzer Division, recalled how he learned of the massacre in Tarnopol. Someone in his unit had told him to go and see a comrade named Reiff, who had just returned from Tarnopol and was telling incredible stories:

> "Well," said Reiff, "they [the Viking Division] stayed two days and took the opportunity to murder all the Jews in the city."
>
> All Jews?
>
> Yes, all Jews.
>
> How did you know they were Jews?
>
> But it shows, huh? Their noses, their beards, their funny clothes. . . .
>
> How many dead were there?
>
> I do not know, but there were corpses everywhere, piles of corpses, against the walls of a square, along a bridge. . . . There were civilians, Polish or Ukrainian, who participated in the hunt.
>
> It lasted a whole day, and the next day they started again. An officer told them to save their ammunition and use spades and picks.[47]

As many as four thousand Jews were murdered in Tarnopol, and witnesses reported multiple incidents of rape by the German troops. Struve calculated that members of the Viking Division were involved in the murder of between 4,280 and 6,950 Jews in the week or so following their first engagement in the war against the Soviet Union.

Although there is no evidence that Mengele himself participated in these crimes, he surely knew of them, and they formed part of the context of extreme violence that characterized his service as a combat physician in the Waffen-SS. From the moment the division crossed the Soviet border at the end of June, it was engaged in nearly constant combat until the end of the year. In contrast to the two army groups, North and Center, which operated to their north, Army Group South met determined resistance from the start, and its progress was slow as it battled across the western Ukraine in July and August. The Viking Division moved from Tarnopol northeast to Zhitomir and then southeast to the Dnieper River. It continued south until it reached Dnepropetrovsk, which it took on August 25. On July 14 Mengele received the Iron Cross, Second Class (EKII), along with fourteen other division members; it was the first group since the invasion of the Soviet Union to be awarded the decoration for bravery in combat.[48] We do not know why he was decorated, but he was clearly pleased and reported the news to Irene, who passed it on to a friend in a letter dated August 15:

> Now [my husband] finally has his longed-for deployment! He is in the Ukraine, I must assume in all that heat. In the very first days he already received the EKII. The hardships must be incredible, yet their enthusiasm finally to be in battle and especially against this "hereditary enemy" can find no end![49]

Shortly after being awarded the Iron Cross, Mengele, along with his colleague, the battalion dentist Wilhelm Müller, put himself at significant risk to tend to wounded comrades, as Müller wrote in his diary:

In Ostroff, an enemy grenade launcher suddenly began shooting
very close to us.... There was a direct hit on the school which
housed the 2nd Company. Dr. Mengele and I go there immediately to provide aid. In the meantime, there was also shooting
from the cross street. There were three wounded and one dead
in the school.[50]

The battle in Ostroff cost the battalion seventeen dead and sixty
wounded.

Eberhard Heder, who would become the last commander of the
Fifth Engineers Battalion, described the experience of the first two
months of the division's activity:

On the march and in the attack, often interrupted by sometimes
heavy battles, as at Taraschtscha, the Viking Division and its
Engineers had their first extended stop when they reached the
large industrial city of Dnepropetrovsk.

By then, 700 kilometers had been overcome on mostly miserable roads, meager, softened sand paths, endless clouds of dust, or
deep mud, after many—sometimes harsh—offensive and defensive battles costing sacrifice and time.

That meant exertion in heat, dust and mud, no sleep and sometimes unnerving waiting.[51]

They were involved, at times, in bitter defensive actions in Dnepropetrovsk for another month, before moving south toward the Sea of
Azov at the end of September. In mid-November units of the division
participated in the seizure of Rostov-on-Don, a key port city and rail
junction, before it was retaken by the Red Army ten days later. The
division retreated to Uspenskaya on the Mius River, where it was to
remain until the following spring.

The division suffered significant casualties, having lost more than
20 percent of its strength in the first five months of combat.[52] One

of the casualties was SS-Hauptsturmführer Kurt Albert, the battalion commander, victim of a direct hit on his vehicle from a grenade that killed him instantly and also claimed a company commander, SS-Obersturmführer Maas.[53] The weather posed a significant obstacle as well. With heavy rains turning roads to mud, the Germans had to rely on horse-drawn wagons to make any progress, and even these conveyances were occasionally stymied in the muck. The engineers played a key role in the operations of the division, clearing obstructions and building bridges.

The division wintered over in Uspenskaya, commandeering local homes. Mengele wrote to Irene on January 4, 1942:

> We have turned our new Russian home into a comfortable abode. The local sick quarters have been furnished appropriately, and since yesterday I have a station with five beds. . . . It's hard for the infantry in this windy cold weather (–34.6 Fahrenheit). However, they seem to be doing better than the Russians, at least that's what the Russian prisoners of war are telling us.[54]

He wrote again on January 17, having learned that one of the battalion's noncommissioned officers was going back to Germany for a training course and would be able to mail a letter for him. This short note was, in fact, a wish list for things he wanted: sugar ("send on a regular basis"), jam, a comb ("very necessary"), a nail scissors, and shoe polish ("not for the high gloss, but for the stitching. It breaks without care"). He also thanked Irene for sending a small Russian/German dictionary, which he found more useful than the one issued by the army, which concentrated on military terms and did not provide much help for everyday life.[55]

Mengele wrote to Irene again a month later, still from the same winter encampment, sharing no news but revealing, between the lines, his homesickness and longing. In one reverie, he wonders when they will be able to be together again, in "1943?, 1944? 1945? Who knows when?"

and muses about what he would like to do, "well if we could be together now . . . we would be very happy without skiing. Yes? Yes. What would we do then? Well: Long 'sleep,' walk, good lunch, sleep again, drink coffee . . . walk, good dinner, . . . and 'sleep.' Yes? Do you agree? Just imagine it would be so."[56] He thanked her for sending a warm fur coat, which protected him from the "raging" cold. He had spent the night before reading Adalbert Stifter's *Waldsteig* in one sitting, by the "light of a car battery." "What a different world. So delicate, lovely, graceful, beautiful, good and pure, but also soft and unmanly," and he mused, "Well, after the war one can, perhaps—and rightly so—abandon oneself more to this world of only-beauty. However, our time leaves little room for such things."

With its failure to gain the swift victory in 1941 that it had planned, Germany, now also at war with the United States as of December 11, faced new and significant challenges. German war planners, led by Hitler himself, devised a strategy for 1942 that would place Mengele's division at the tip of the spear that they intended to drive deep into the oil- and mineral-rich Caucasus. Their manner of war-making, which depended on mechanized units and air support, combined with the vast territories they needed to conquer, created for Germany a nearly unquenchable thirst for oil. With its own reserves dwindling and its supply from Romania threatened by the Allies, Germany was in such desperate need of petroleum that Hitler is said to have said, "If I do not get the oil of Maikop and Grozny, then I must end this war."[57]

The Germans devised Case Blue, a summer offensive that would focus most of their forces' energy on the southern sector, with the twin aims of capturing the oil fields of Baku and the city of Stalingrad, of strategic and symbolic importance. The Soviets had believed the Germans would concentrate on Moscow, reinvigorating their attack on the capital that had stalled the previous winter. Misdirecting their defensive forces as a result, they suffered early and dramatic setbacks when the Germans unleashed their offensive on June 28. Within a week, the Germans in the north had reached the Don River and began to attack Voronezh. In the south, they retook Rostov on July 23. In a revision of the original plan, Army Group South was split into Army Groups A and B, with Army Group A's mission to capture the oil fields in the south and Army Group B's mission to capture the city of Stalingrad. Mengele's division, which was part of Army Group A and subordinated to the First Panzer Army, made early and significant progress. Salsk was captured on July 31, and the oil fields of Maikop, which had been badly damaged by the retreating Soviets, were taken on August 9. Mengele's unit had traveled more than three hundred miles in less than two weeks.[58]

Mengele wrote to Irene on September 2, when he and his unit were in Neftyanaya in the Krasnodar Krai, a little more than fifty miles from Sochi. The tone of the letter is decidedly less upbeat than his earlier missives:

> The forested area claims victims every day because it is a paradise for partisans. The day before yesterday, we had another five badly wounded, today, one. One is powerless against this type of warfare, I mean, although we do everything, it is almost impossible to avoid such attacks.
>
> I am fine. I have a lot of work at the moment. There are many infections with high fever, boils, and such things. . . . Yesterday I held long dialogues with the photos, during which I thought of you intensely.[59]

A month later Mengele's commander, Max Schäfer, recommended him for promotion to SS-Hauptsturmführer, providing a brief evaluation of his performance:

> Mature, upright, and absolutely reliable person who has the full confidence of his superiors and subordinates. Popular among his comrades. As a troop physician, he has always worked successfully, even in the most difficult situations, with great circumspec-

tion and absolute readiness to serve, so that the medical care of
the battalion was always fully guaranteed.[60]

The chief physician of the division endorsed the recommendation
enthusiastically: "Especially competent troop doctor. Promotion most
warmly recommended!" Mengele would receive the promotion the
following April.

By early October, Mengele's unit had reached the mountain city of
Malgobek, and by mid-November, Alagir, which marked the farthest
extent of their reach. They had traveled another three hundred–plus
miles, this time over two months, with frequent engagements with the
enemy on the ground and from the air. They suffered fuel shortages as
well as bad weather. At the end of November, Mengele came very close
to being killed in an air attack. Walter Hägele described the event in
the telegraphic syntax of the unit log: "Vigorous air activity again. . . .
Dr. Mengele buried. Bomb explodes next to foxhole and buried him."[61]
The summer offensive had failed to reach the Grozny oil fields. Hitler,
realizing they would not achieve that goal before the winter, ordered
the Luftwaffe to inflict as much damage on the oil installations as possible to prevent the Soviets from enjoying their output.

Meanwhile the German Sixth Army had advanced on Stalingrad and
reached its outskirts by the end of August. By mid-November, the Germans had captured nearly the entire city, and success seemed assured.
The Soviets, however, counterattacked on November 19 in a two-
pronged offensive against the Sixth Army's flanks, which were protected by Axis troops, primarily Romanians, who were understrength
and exhausted. The Soviets overwhelmed the Romanians and were
able to encircle the German Sixth Army, which Hitler had ordered not
to break out. Thus began a siege that would end with the destruction of
the Sixth Army and mark a significant turning point in the war.

At Christmas, the Viking Division was ordered to withdraw from
Alagir and move toward Stalingrad. After covering its withdrawal by
destroying bridges, it departed the area by train on New Year's Eve,

and on January 2 it arrived in Salsk, a key city with important rail and road connections as well as an airfield.[62] By the time the division arrived, the situation had worsened, and rather than move toward Stalingrad, it was deployed to cover the withdrawal of Army Group A from the Caucasus. Around this time, Mengele received the Iron Cross First Class (EK I), which was awarded for valor in combat and could be conferred only on those who had already received the Iron Cross Second Class.[63] At some point between his arrival in Salsk on January 2 and January 20, when the Germans destroyed the airfield prior to their withdrawal from the area, Mengele was evacuated by air. It is often claimed that he was evacuated because he had been wounded, but there is no evidence of a wound during this period.

What are we to make of Mengele's service with the SS Viking Division? Other biographical treatments of Mengele, with the notable exception of Sven Keller's, present a confusing and often contradictory picture of his military service, failing to describe what was essentially unbroken service that involved bloody and sustained combat as well as proximity to, and possibly involvement in, extreme brutality. There is no doubt that such sustained exposure to violence can have a profound effect on a person. According to Robert Jay Lifton, there were rumors at Auschwitz that Mengele was "shell-shocked."[64] If Mengele indeed suffered from some sort of post-traumatic stress disorder, his experience with the Viking Division might have been the reason.

Back in Berlin

In mid-January Mengele was transferred from the front, flying out of Salsk and making his way to Berlin. He wasted little time in contacting his mentor, Otmar von Verschuer, who had recently taken the helm of the Kaiser Wilhelm Institute for Anthropology in Berlin. Verschuer wrote to his predecessor, Eugen Fischer, and reported the news of Mengele's arrival, along with Mengele's account of the military fiasco at Stalingrad:

A few days ago, my assistant Mengele arrived in Germany after a two-day flight from Salsk. He had been involved in all the battles of the SS Viking Division and was awarded the EKI. He has been transferred to an office here in Berlin so that he will also be able to do some work at the Institute. He reported, very interestingly, that all the misfortunes to the right and left of Stalingrad had occurred as a result of the collapse of the Rumanian army. The officers had run away and abandoned their soldiers, resulting in a chaotic retreat. Some German armored divisions were introduced into this confusion but had to retreat in the face of overwhelming Russian superiority.[65]

In describing Mengele's departure from the front, Verschuer made no mention of a wound. In Berlin, Mengele was assigned to the SS-Infanterie Ersatz Battalion "Ost," a replacement unit.

Though Mengele was still formally associated with the Frankfurt Institute, he established a close connection to the KWI-A in Berlin and enjoyed the status of a "guest scholar," whose name even appeared on an "internal list" of birthdays of institute personnel. It appears, too, that Mengele gave expert opinions at Verschuer's request.[66] Despite his status as an assistant in Frankfurt, on combat leave, it is clear that he saw his future in Berlin, and equally clear that Verschuer had plans for his protégé. Fischer apparently also recognized Mengele's value for Verschuer, responding to the latter's letter on February 2, "I am happy for you that you have Mr. Mengele, at least part time."[67]

Verschuer's move to Berlin to succeed Fischer as director of the KWI-A had been part of a larger strategic plan conceived by Fischer, and agreed to by Verschuer, to chart a new course for the future of that institute. Fischer believed, according to Peter Weingart, that "the study of human heredity had advanced so far that it could describe the essential characteristics of normal and pathological hereditary traits, relate phenomenal appearance to these traits, and offer an approximate idea about the impact of environmental effects on them." What it could not do, however, was explain how a genetic disposition became a physical trait.[68] According to Hans-Walter Schmuhl:

> The idea, generally accepted up to that time, that every attribute was simply transmitted as dominant or recessive, monofactorial genetic information, did not hold up to the results of mutation research, population genetics and developmental physiology. Thus Mendelian genetics was giving way, in the words of the day, to "higher Mendelism, which presumed much more complicated mechanisms of heredity."[69]

This interaction between an individual's *genome* (their genetic make-up) and their *phenome* (the aggregate of their physical traits) involved what came to be known as *phenogenetics*. Fischer described the challenge in a report on the activities of the KWI-A: "The path from a given hereditary disposition [*Erbanlage*] to the readily configured hereditary trait [*Erbmerkmal*] in the individual is still unknown." The task of phenogenetics, according to Schmuhl, was to "disentangle the network of effects exerted by genes and environment." Fischer advocated a new emphasis on phenogenetics with a complementary reduction in focus on racial hygiene, which he believed should be the province of university institutes. He sought to reorient the KWI-A toward pure scientific research.

Bound up in this reconception of the KWI-A was Fischer's selection of Verschuer as his successor over the race hygienist Fritz Lenz. Fischer had been in communication with Verschuer for several years about his thinking regarding the future direction of the KWI-A, and he was confident that Verschuer would help realize his vision. Verschuer assumed the directorship in November 1942 and was able to secure necessary funding and procure appropriate staff to reinvigorate the institute's research, which had come to a standstill, largely due to the military drafting of its personnel.[70] He also "energetically pushed the concept of phenogenetics developed by Fischer."[71] In pursuit of this "new paradigm," argues Weiss, "a combination of experimental research on animals *and humans*" was necessary. She writes that "Dahlem Institute scientists could provide the necessary human clinical supplement to the ongoing experimental work in the developmental genetics of normal and pathological traits in animals."[72]

Mengele's four-month association with the institute in the winter and spring of 1943 laid the foundation for a crucial link between the scientists at the institute and a colleague who could be instrumental in supplying all manner of human specimens and data to advance their work.

PART II

AUSCHWITZ

CHAPTER 3

THE CAPITAL OF
THE HOLOCAUST

(May 1943–January 1944)

As a symbol of the Holocaust, Auschwitz seems particularly apt, even though well more than a million Jews had already been murdered by the Nazis before its gas chambers were operational. Almost unimaginable in its size and complexity, Auschwitz can be seen, in the words of historian Peter Hayes, as the "Capital of the Holocaust."[1] Both a concentration camp, with punishment and exploitation as its goal, and an extermination camp, whose raison d'être was wholesale murder, Auschwitz comprised the broad taxonomy of Nazi terror. It was made up of three main camps: Auschwitz I, Auschwitz II–Birkenau, and Auschwitz III–Monowitz, which housed the IG Farben factory. There were nearly fifty subcamps, ranging from agricultural estates to coal mines, in which people were forced to work, often to death.

Auschwitz was where the ultimate expression of Nazi racial policy was inflicted upon a broad mass of Jews and other victims from the far corners of Europe. At Auschwitz, one could hear a cacophonous babble of languages, including Yiddish, Polish, Romani, Slovak, Norwegian, Dutch, Ladino, Greek, Hungarian, French, Czech, Italian, Croatian, Russian, Danish, German, and even English. Economic exploitation extended not only to the fruits of a person's toil but also to the clothes on one's back and to one's physical body: teeth for gold, and hair as raw material for fabric. Here medicine and science were perverted and exercised on unwilling subjects, often to lethal effect. Industry was a co-conspirator, stealing labor and lives for profit. Auschwitz was the site of incomparable tragedy, unceasing fear, and unending sorrow, where countless families were torn apart and destroyed. And it was here that genocide found its most efficient expression.

Unlike Treblinka, Bełżec, and Sobibór, death camps located in Nazi-occupied Poland, where the Nazis tried to hide the evidence, the mechanism of murder at Auschwitz was easy to discover. From other death camps, only a handful of survivors emerged to recount what had happened; from Auschwitz, many thousands lived on to describe the horror they had witnessed and experienced. It is for this reason that we know so much about Auschwitz.

If Auschwitz, as place, stands as a symbol of the Holocaust, then Mengele, as perpetrator, has come to serve a similar role for the death camp itself. Perhaps for this reason, much of what is known about Mengele's time at Auschwitz is more trope than truth. Countless imagined encounters, misattributed deeds, and clichés about Mengele's activities have obscured the larger nature of his enterprise. This is not a question of guilt—for Mengele was indisputably guilty of innumerable crimes—but it speaks to the nature of his activity, its motivation, and its context.

Given the sheer number of people affected, the major charge leveled against Mengele by German judicial authorities seeking his arrest and prosecution involved his official activity at the camp as *Lagerarzt*: his participation in selections of arriving prisoners as well as those of inmates already admitted into the camp. Mengele himself admitted this activity to a number of people, including his son, and there is absolutely no question about his culpability. It is possible to detail, as prosecutors have done, many of the selections with the date and specific number and origins of the people involved. It was, however, Mengele's research at Auschwitz that has captured the most attention, fed our imagination with nightmarish images, and flooded our common vocabulary with superlatives of evil and depravity. Mengele's outsize reputation as a medical monster is in inverse proportion to what is known and understood about what he actually did.

There is some dispute about how Mengele came to be assigned to Auschwitz in May 1943. Did he apply for the posting? Was it arranged by his mentor, Verschuer? Or was he simply assigned in the regular course of business? We know that Benno Adolph, the physician whom Mengele succeeded as *Lagerarzt* in the Gypsy camp, had contracted scarlet fever at the end of April 1943 and needed to be replaced. At the same time Mengele, with the requisite rank and experience, was in a replacement unit available for assignment. Mengele's son Rolf told an interviewer in 1985 that his mother said Verschuer had "motivated" his father to go to Auschwitz and had actually applied for him to do so.[2] Hans Sedlmeier, an executive with the Mengele company in Günzburg and a confidant of the family, told German prosecutors in 1984 that Mengele said Verschuer had helped to arrange the transfer; a nephew of Verschuer's had been prepared to take the position but backed out at the last minute.[3] Although we will likely never know the precise circumstances that led to the assignment, it seems certain that Mengele did not go there against his will—as Verschuer maintained, after the war, in part to defend himself.[4] Given how quickly and passionately Mengele took advantage of the opportunities Auschwitz offered, it is easy to believe that he had requested the transfer. And it is true that Verschuer had clear motives for placing his prize student in Auschwitz, since his own research, and that of others at the KWI-A, received clear benefits from having Mengele there.

Whatever the proximate cause of his assignment, Mengele thrived at Auschwitz. Robert Jay Lifton believed that "Mengele's harmony with Auschwitz rendered him unique unto himself, *sui generis*,"[5] and that more "than any other SS doctor, Mengele realized himself in Auschwitz. There he came into his own—found expression for his talents, so that what had been potential became actual."[6]

A Doctor's Duties

Although Auschwitz was unique among concentration camps in its size and scope, its medical services (Department V) had an identical structure to those of the other camps. Mengele's direct supervisor was SS-Sturmbannführer Dr. Eduard Wirths, the *Standortarzt*, or garrison physician, who was the chief medical authority in the camp. Wirths reported not to the camp commandant, whom he advised on medical issues, but to SS-Standartenführer Dr. Enno Lolling, the chief physician of all concentration camps; Lolling headed the Department of Medical and Hygiene Affairs (Amt DIII) of the Administration and Economic Authority of the SS (SS-WVHA), which oversaw the concentration camp system. Wirths also had a reporting channel to the chief physician of the SS, SS-Obergruppenführer Dr. Ernst-Robert Grawitz.[7]

As chief medical officer, Wirths was responsible for the medical care of all SS members assigned to the SS garrison at Auschwitz and supervised a well-equipped field hospital with its complement of dentists, pharmacists, German Red Cross nurses, and medical orderlies. A "disinfection commando," which was recruited from the orderlies, was responsible for the disinfection facilities, which served legitimate public health needs, as well as the handling of the Zyklon-B gas, the active agent in the camp's gas chambers. In addition, Wirths oversaw medical care for the camp's inmate population, which was carried out by *Lagerärzte*, or camp physicians. The care of individual inmates was of little interest to the SS until, as the war progressed and prisoner labor became increasingly valuable, concern for their ability to work increased. Overall inmate health—as it affected the SS and civilian operators of the camp—was, however, of significant importance from a public health standpoint. Given the poor nutrition and sanitary conditions, disease and even epidemics were a constant concern, and SS camp physicians were on the front lines in combating them.

Mengele made a name for himself as an effective disease fighter when, in late 1943, he devised a technique that proved as efficient as it was radical. A non-Jewish Austrian inmate physician named Ella Lingens, who was imprisoned for having helped Jews in Vienna, described, in her 1948 memoir, Mengele's brutal approach to eradicating typhus:

> In fact, typhus was only stamped out when *Hauptsturmführer* Dr. Mengele, the ruthless cynic, became camp doctor. He collected the 1,500 worst cases among the Jewish patients in a hospital hut and sent them to the gas chamber. Thus he obtained an empty hut, which was disinfected and supplied with new paillasses [straw mattresses] and clean blankets. Then the patients of the nearest hut were de-loused, examined and taken naked into the vermin-free hut, which was put out of bounds. The same with the next hut, and so on, until everything was clean. Given the circumstances, this was the correct way of fighting and overcoming the epidemic. But that the camp authorities did not think it necessary to build a new hut for the purpose, that the cleaning-up began with the murder of 1,500 Jewish women—that was part of the horror of a situation in which everything was perverted from its meaning, in which evil was good and good evil.[8]

Mengele employed the same technique in other sectors of Auschwitz "to combat a scarlet fever epidemic among Hungarian Jews in camp BIIc and measles epidemics in the Jewish children's block (BIIa) and the Gypsy family camp."[9] The SS Hygiene Institute, which was located in nearby Rajsko, although not directly under the authority of Wirths, was an important institution for the entire range of medical services, including the identification and combating of disease. Essentially a medical laboratory, the institute carried out the full range of medical tests and pathological examinations on blood and other bodily fluids, and on other samples collected from members of the SS and inmates from the camp.

According to Polish historian Aleksander Lasik, the responsibilities of the camp physicians involved "more-or-less pro forma medical care for the prisoners," which included admitting and discharging prisoners from the camps' infirmaries, "performing diagnoses and recommending treatment," certifying the quality of the meals from the camp kitchens, and maintaining supervision of the infirmaries.[10] They were also required to "check the medical condition of newly arrived and released prisoners," and toward the end of the war, they examined German prisoners for their fitness for military service. In cases of the "accidental or violent deaths of prisoners," the camp physician was required to perform or supervise an autopsy to determine the cause of death. Beyond these tasks, which were more or less in line with a physician's traditional responsibilities, the camp physicians played an intimate role in mass murder. They carried out "selections" on the "ramp" of prisoners arriving at Auschwitz, determining who would be killed immediately in the gas chambers and who could first be exploited for their labor. They also carried out selections of already-admitted prisoners in the camp infirmaries to ascertain who was still capable of work and who should be killed. They certified the deaths of victims in the gas chambers, were present at the administration of corporal punishment, and attended executions.

In addition to their assigned, official duties, Auschwitz camp physicians engaged in experiments involving inmate subjects. Research in Auschwitz, like that conducted in other camps, included projects to serve "practical" goals, such as the research at Dachau into methods of rewarming bodies suffering from hypothermia, of importance to the Luftwaffe in its treatment of rescued pilots, or drug trials on inmates to evaluate efficacy and side effects. There was also research, like that of Mengele's, which was conducted for less practical purposes—to advance knowledge and careers. Although the medical research at Auschwitz was not carried out under Wirths's supervision, he was certainly aware of it, and he himself worked with his younger brother, also a gynecologist, on experiments involving cervical cancer.

The most extensive series of experiments at Auschwitz involved perfecting a method for reliable and efficient mass sterilization, which the Nazis planned to use on Slavs, so-called *Mischlinge*, and others. The experiments were ordered by Himmler and carried out by Professor Carl Clauberg, an expert on infertility, who was able to devise a nonsurgical method, using X-rays, which he estimated could sterilize up to a thousand women a day, given the right staffing and equipment.[11] Another parallel series of experiments on sterilization was carried out by Dr. Horst Schumann, who irradiated the testicles and ovaries of Jewish male and female prisoners, seeking the appropriate effective dose. SS-Obersturmführer Dr. Johann Paul Kremer carried out experiments on the effects of starvation and was particularly interested in "brown liver atrophy." Kremer was a professor of anatomy at the University of Münster, and like Mengele, he had both an M.D. and Ph.D. Polish historian Irena Strzelecka described Kremer's process:

> Every morning, at the outpatient clinic in block No. 28 in the main camp, he reviewed the prisoners applying for admission to the hospital. Among them were many extremely starved and exhausted prisoners ("*Muselmänner*"), the majority of whom were put to death by lethal injection of phenol. Just before putting them to death, as they lay on the autopsy table, he asked them for information he regarded as important, such as their weight before arrest, or the last medicine they had taken. . . . Samples of the liver, spleen, and pancreas were removed while the corpse was still warm.[12]

A number of camp physicians, including Friedrich Entress, Helmuth Vetter, Eduard Wirths, and to a lesser extent, Fritz Klein, Werner Rohde, Hans Wilhelm König, pharmacist Viktor Capesius, and head of the Hygiene Institute, Bruno Weber, used Auschwitz prisoners "to test the tolerance and effectiveness of certain drugs" on behalf of IG Farben.[13] Experiments were undertaken by Entress and Vetter to determine the precise incubation period of typhus in order to discover when patients with the disease were most contagious and when they ceased to be contagious. The experiment required intentionally infecting prisoners with typhus.[14]

Strzelecka described a particularly odd and little-known series of experiments carried out on unwilling subjects in an attempt to address a mounting problem within the German armed forces. In the late summer of 1944, a Dr. Emil Kaschub was sent to Auschwitz on behalf of the Wehrmacht in order to "unmask the various methods of malingering that were becoming widespread among German soldiers, especially on the eastern front . . . including self-inflicted wounds, abscesses, fever, and infectious hepatitis."[15] Using Jewish prisoners, Kaschub attempted to "provoke" the same symptoms displayed by the malingering soldiers.

Prisoners from Auschwitz were also supplied to physicians at other camps for research. For instance, twenty Jewish children were selected by Mengele in Auschwitz and sent to the Neuengamme concentration camp to serve as subjects for experiments on tuberculosis conducted by Dr. Kurt Heissmeyer, in the course of which they were infected with the disease.[16] According to Strzelecka, the children were hanged "from the heating pipes in a school on Bullenhuserdamm in Hamburg" in April 1945 to eliminate evidence of Heissmeyer's experiments.[17]

Historian Christian Dirks, in his book about Mengele's Auschwitz colleague Dr. Horst Fischer, describes a program of experimentation that Fischer conducted in Auschwitz III in 1943–44, using electroconvulsive therapy (ECT). ECT was at that time "considered to be the most advanced method for the treatment of the most seriously ill patients, often suicidal, suffering from schizophrenia and depression."[18] A Polish inmate physician, Dr. Zenon Drohocki, who had studied medicine in Krakow, conducted research on ECT in Bern, Brussels, and Paris and had "acquired practical experience in electroencephalography in Grenoble."[19] Drohocki recommended to Fischer that they construct an

ECT device to treat prisoners. Fischer, trained as a surgeon, had no knowledge of ECT but, intrigued, was able to secure approval from Wirths and allowed Drohocki to proceed. With the help of another prisoner, Drohocki was able to "organize" the necessary parts from supplies at IG Farben and build the machine. Small groups of supposedly mentally ill inmates were brought to Auschwitz III from other parts of the Auschwitz complex to undergo the treatment. The effort attracted a great deal of attention, and Mengele is said to have attended one of the experiments. The goal of the treatments was to treat incapacitated prisoners so that they were again capable of work. Some of the subjects of the experiments were then transported to Birkenau and gassed, and some witnesses reported that most of the experiments led to the death of the subjects.

In contrast to those experiments conducted ostensibly for practical reasons, Mengele's research, which was carried out on his own time in addition to his other official duties, was undertaken almost exclusively in his pursuit of the science that had occupied him since he had begun his university studies. He was almost certainly planning to use his Auschwitz research as the basis for his *Habilitationschrift*, a postdoctoral thesis, which was a prerequisite for an academic career.[20] In this pursuit of academic advancement, Mengele was not alone. Dr. Heinz Baumkötter, chief physician at the Sachsenhausen concentration camp, completed his dissertation only in 1942, while serving there,[21] and Mengele's colleague at Auschwitz, Dr. Hans Delmotte, had access to a Jewish inmate physician, who had been a professor and "widely acclaimed scientist," to help him with his dissertation.[22]

Selections

Perhaps the most chilling and familiar image we have of Auschwitz is the confrontation on the "ramp," where incoming prisoners, disoriented and frightened, exhausted and starving, were forced from the train car. These innocents were the objects of a well-choreographed and efficient process that came to be known as "selection." It stripped them of their remaining property, wrenched them from their loved ones, and sorted them into two categories: those who would be kept alive to work—at least for a while—and those who would be murdered within hours. As a camp physician, Mengele's duties included carrying out selections upon the arrival of new transports and also, routinely, culling inmates after they had been admitted to the camp. Although selections had not always been performed by medical personnel, in the spring of 1943, Eduard Wirths was able to reserve this responsibility for his medical staff, who would, he argued, be more professional and avoid past mistakes, such as condemning able-bodied prisoners to death.[23] The use of physicians also reinforced the view that the killing of Jews was a matter of public health, an effort to protect and preserve the racial community. Physicians were, in other words, carrying out a medical task for the benefit of the *Volk*.[24]

In 1982 Rudolph Vrba, who escaped Auschwitz in April 1944, described to me how the arrival of a train and its unloading proceeded. Until the spring of 1944, the ramp was a rail siding located outside the Birkenau camp at the site of the Auschwitz freight station. When a transport was announced, a unit from the guard battalion was deployed. The locomotive would be detached from the railcars, and the SS guard unit would surround the ramp completely to prevent escape and secure valuables thrown from the train. The doors of the train cars would be opened, and all the prisoners would be ordered out. A careful count was conducted, and the prisoners would be divided into two lines, men in one, women and children in the other. These groups would be made to file past the camp physician on duty, who would carry out the "selection," dividing the oncoming line to the left and right—life and death. The weak, the sick, the elderly, the young, and the pregnant were selected for death; mothers with young children were condemned to die with their offspring.

Three groups would have been formed after the selection: women who were to be admitted to the camp; men who were to be admitted to the camp; and those men, women, and children who were to be gassed immediately. Those who were to be admitted were marched the short distance to Birkenau, and those doomed to die were taken by truck to one of the two gas chamber and crematorium complexes nearby. A group of prisoners gathered the luggage and other belongings and transported the loot to the warehouses, nicknamed "Canada," where it would be inventoried and made available for local use or transported back to Germany for distribution. A crew entered the trains and cleaned them, and clerks completed and checked all paperwork. Depending on the size of the transport, the entire operation could be over in an hour or two. Every attempt was made to reduce anxiety among the prisoners by offering a catalogue of lies and reassurances about their fates. Josef Erber, an SS noncommissioned officer, told an interviewer in 1979 that the motto was "Keep everything as calm as possible on the ramp so that everything runs smoothly."[25]

On August 3, 1964, in the course of the Frankfurt Auschwitz trial, Richard Böck, a member of the motor pool at Auschwitz, which was responsible for conveying doomed prisoners to the gas chamber complexes, gave detailed testimony about a selection. Böck, who came from Günzburg and knew Mengele and his family, described to the court how he had witnessed Mengele on the ramp:

> There were the tracks, and the train stood there, and over there I saw Mengele. And there were a couple of officers; I didn't know all of them.... And I saw Mengele there and the rest of them.... Then they talked a bit at first, and I leaned against my truck, leaned against the fender and looked on.

Mengele then called for anyone with a medical background to step forward:

> Mengele ... said, "Doctors and pharmacists forward!" ... And then the men came slowly, real gentlemen came forward. Their

suits are wrinkled, but they were better dressed, some wore glasses.... They were elegant people, it seemed. And then Mengele made a gesture like that.

Böck gestured with his own thumb, "then they went by him, over to the left," and then he described a heartbreaking encounter as Mengele began to separate the people on the ramp:

A blond woman was the very first to come. I looked at her so closely, I would recognize her even today. I immediately thought that was the film actress. Lilian Harvey. And then Mengele said to her, "How old?" And she said, "Twenty-nine." Then Mengele asked, "Are you pregnant?" Then she said, "Yes." Then Mengele said, "In what month?" Then she said, "In the ninth." And then Mengele did so.

Böck gestured again with his own thumb.

And she walked over there, over the tracks, over and to the right.... Then came a young man, twenty-four years old. "Healthy, strong?" Mengele asked. Then he said, "Yes." Then Mengele did so, with the thumb—always with the thumb he did so and so—over and over. Then he went over to where the doctors were standing.

Böck continued, "Then came an old man who had a beard. [Mengele] asked nothing, he just went so." Again, Böck gestured with his thumb to the right. And finally, he described Mengele as being bored, or impatient, or simply tired, concluding the entire selection procedure, with a verbalized shrug of his shoulders.

And then after ... half of the train had walked by him, Mengele suddenly said, "Ach was. ..." Everybody went over there ...

women came with children, then the women came pushing carriages, and everyone is over there.[26]

They congregated to the right on the other side of the tracks from the doctors and the healthy and strong young men. Böck would later testify to the fate of those from the train who were sent to the right side—he had witnessed an actual gassing and described it in harrowing detail.[27]

In preparation for the huge anticipated influx of Jews that would come with the deportations from Hungary, a rail spur was built in the spring of 1944 that led through the main gate at Birkenau and terminated in the heart of the camp, very close to Crematoria Complex II/III. With this improvement, the unloading of trains could take place inside Birkenau, removing the need for the deployment of a guard company and the motor pool, thereby increasing the efficiency of the process immensely.

Dr. Mauritius Berner, a physician from Hungary, also testified at the Frankfurt Auschwitz trial about his experience arriving at the ramp in Birkenau on May 29, 1944:

> And the flow of people went forward, and I said to my wife—I was with my wife and three children, three little daughters: "Don't do anything. The main thing is that we five stay together." And: "We'll see how it goes."
>
> I had hardly said this when another soldier came between us and said, "Men to the right and women to the left," and separated us. I didn't even have the time to embrace my wife. She yelled after me, "Come, kiss us!" Perhaps out of some kind of woman's intuition, she sensed the danger that threatened us.
>
> I ran back through the cordon to them, kissed my wife and my three children. And then I was shoved back to the other side, and we went on in parallel but separated. Between the two tracks,

between the two trains, parallel but apart. Then I got pushed by
the crowd and I lost sight of them, my family.[28]

He then heard someone call out, "Physicians and pharmacists, assemble here!" Berner joined a large group, which numbered, he recalled,
around seventy. From his city alone, there were thirty-eight physicians and several pharmacists. They were approached by two German officers, one of whom Berner knew; it was Viktor Capesius, who
used to visit his practice as a pharmaceutical sales representative for
IG Farben. Capesius translated into Hungarian the words of the other
German, who Berner later learned was Josef Mengele.

Berner told Mengele that he had his diploma in his suitcase, which
had been collected with all the others on the ramp, and asked if he
could retrieve it. After finding his suitcase and grabbing his diploma
and several photographs of his family, Berner returned to the group of
physicians and pharmacists. By that time, Mengele had moved on and
stood some twenty or thirty meters away. Berner observed him standing in front of the crowd, which was moving toward him and which he
was separating with a movement of his hand. Some went to the right,
and others, including women and children, to the left. Berner testified:

> All of a sudden, I saw my wife and three children walking further
> away from Mengele. It occurred to me: I would ask Dr. Capesius
> one favor. I went up to him and said: Herr Captain . . . , I have
> two twins, who require more care. I will work as you wish, only
> please allow me to remain together with my family. I did not
> know why we were there, where we were supposed to go. He
> asked me, "Twins?" "Yes." "Where are they?" I pointed, "There
> they are." "Call them back," he told me.
>   Whereupon I called out the names of my wife and children.
> And they turned around, and I indicated they should come back.
>   They came back, and Dr. Capesius himself took them by the
> hand, the two children, and led us to Dr. Mengele. And at his

back, he said to me, "So tell him." And I said, "Herr Captain," I did not know his rank, "Herr Captain, I have two twin children," and wanted to continue to speak, but he said to me, "Later, I have no time." And with a dismissive gesture, sent me away.[29]

Capesius indicated that Berner's wife and children should rejoin their group and that Berner should rejoin his. Dr. Berner never saw his family again.[30]

The vast majority of people who encountered Mengele on the ramp shortly after arriving in Auschwitz did not survive. Those who did recall the brief meeting did so with anguish, as it marked the moment of separation from their loved ones. There are some who recall a confrontation with Mengele but are mistaken, having confused him with another SS doctor or simply having assumed it must have been Mengele who carried out the monstrous deed that left them alive while taking so many they loved. Historian Zdenek Zofka notes that many survivors recall Mengele speaking to them in Hungarian, a language he did not speak but which was spoken by his colleagues, the pharmacist Viktor Capesius and the physician Dr. Fritz Klein. "Often Mengele would be described as tall and blond, when he was only 5ft 8½ inches tall and dark-haired."[31] "Almost all inmates" at Auschwitz, according to Zofka, maintain that they had been selected by Mengele.

Hermann Langbein, a former Auschwitz inmate and author of the authoritative *People in Auschwitz,* wrote of this phenomenon, which he deemed the "Mengele Effect," a particular form of "memory displacement":

If a member of the SS is repeatedly named in public in connection with especially monstrous deeds, it is possible that survivors will project their experiences on to him. . . . More than once I heard survivors say that Mengele did this or that to them, even though Mengele had not yet arrived in Auschwitz at the time. Olga Lengyel has described him as a blonde angel, even though

Mengele was a markedly dark-haired type. In short, crimes of an anonymous SS physician were imputed to Mengele, about whom people had read so many bad things. . . .

Some well-known SS men have been positively idealized after the fact. Thus Fania Fénelon has called Mengele a "handsome Siegfried," and Therese Chassaing writes, "Mengele is immaculate in his belted uniform, tall, with shiny black boots that bespeak cleanliness, prosperity, and human dignity." Elie Wiesel mentions as one of Mengele's characteristic attributes "white gloves, a monocle, and the rest."[32]

Langbein saw Mengele "almost every day in the office of the SS infirmary where he was doing routine bureaucratic work," and he claims that Mengele never struck him as either attractive or elegant. He never saw him with a monocle. Doris Bergen, describing the work of Israeli historian Na'ama Shik, wrote about the "so-called Mengele Effect," noting that survivors' accounts decades after the fact could be shaped by what "they have read and heard in the meantime."[33]

Geoffrey Hartmann, who wrote extensively on survivor testimony, observed that "every Auschwitz survivor seems to have gone through a selection by Mengele, as if he manned his post 24 hours a day."[34] In fact, Mengele took his turn at "ramp duty" like the rest of the medical staff in the camp. There is no evidence that he served there more frequently or for longer hours than his colleagues. It does seem, however, as Zofka suggests, that "the name Mengele had become detached from the man" and had become "a synonym" for every doctor at the Auschwitz camp.[35] Similarly, historian Christopher Browning, in describing witness testimony about a selection by Mengele that was proved never to have occurred, called such an encounter with the Angel of Death on the ramp in Auschwitz "one of the most broadly recognized archetypical episodes of the Holocaust, widely disseminated in both books and films."[36]

Mengele took advantage of his service on the ramp to "recruit" a cadre of exceptional physicians, anthropologists, technicians, and other medical professionals who could assist in his research. In addition to calling out for physicians and other medical personnel during the selections, as described by Böck and Berner, he also consulted the registration records of admitted inmates. Helen "Zippi" Spitzer, a prisoner who worked in the camp administration and maintained a "card file," which included information about prisoner professions, described how Mengele would show up in the camp office and inquire about prisoners with a particular medical specialty.[37]

Camp physicians regularly conducted selections inside the camp and in camp infirmaries, to make room for arriving inmates and to "cull" the camp population, ridding it of "unproductive" people who were too ill or weak to work, or who posed a public health threat because of sickness or disease. Wolfgang Sofsky wrote:

> Camp selections marked the entire history of the concentration camp system throughout the war. They were instrumental for creating a balance between labor and death, productivity and annihilation. Prisoners who appeared weak or who were regarded as superfluous were regularly weeded out and killed. The camps functioned as a kind of revolving turntable of death. To make room for new arrivals, the SS liquidated exhausted inmates, exchanging them for fresh prisoners. And in order to close the gaps created by the pressure to annihilate, new groups were incarcerated, and then they too were replaced. In the bureaucratic logic of the system, the selections were a murderous means for system maintenance and guided organizational growth.[38]

Dr. Horst Fischer, who was tried and executed by the East Germans for his crimes at Auschwitz, provided some insight into the criteria for these selections, in his testimony at trial:

> There were a number of conferences of all SS physicians in Auschwitz for the purpose of working out firm criteria for the

selections. These discussions produced essentially the following characteristics as prerequisites for selections: starvation edemas; the complete lack of fatty tissue in the buttocks (to diagnose this, the physicians had the naked inmates turn around); the suspicion of TB (because of the deficient medical equipment actual TB was difficult to diagnose, and it evidently seemed too bothersome to perform X-rays in the main camp); accidents that cause broken bones; and severe suppuration. Roughly speaking, these were the cases in which selections appeared to be indicated.[39]

Many survivors recounted with horror the impact that Mengele's arrival would have whenever he appeared unannounced at an infirmary for an inspection. According to Robert Jay Lifton,

> Specific prisoner responses to Mengele's selections were dominated by a special quality of fear and helplessness. Dr. Gisella Perl wrote, "We feared these visits more than anything else, because . . . we never knew whether we would be permitted to live. . . . He was free to do whatever he pleased with us."[40]

In one often-recounted story, Mengele carried out a selection by submitting a group of children to a height test—a board suspended at a specific height, under which the children were forced to walk—sending those too short to hit the mark to their deaths.[41]

Although there is no evidence that Mengele performed selections more often than his colleagues, he appears to have served as an example for those who found the assignment difficult. Hermann Langbein, relying on an account by Hans Münch, an SS physician at Auschwitz assigned to the Hygiene Institute, described how a newly arrived SS doctor, Hans Delmotte, having been so affected by his first session on the ramp, refused any further such duty and requested to be transferred to the front. Delmotte was assigned for an "extended period" to accompany Mengele, who, Münch told Langbein, had presented an argument to Delmotte aimed at convincing him of the "necessity of eliminating the Jews." He said that "in exceptional situations" a doctor must "take the responsibility for selections," pointing out that "every medic in the Army has to make selections at the front because after battle he cannot possibly treat all urgent cases simultaneously." In making the triage selection, Mengele maintained, the combat physician was, in effect, selecting who would receive treatment to the detriment of someone else. Mengele added that the physician on the ramp was simply deciding "who should first be admitted to the camp," an act that was not so "momentous," since "a firm decision had already been made to eradicate the Jews."[42] The Jews, in other words, were already dead upon arrival. Delmotte reportedly was able to conquer his revulsion and proceeded to conduct selections like the other physicians. He committed suicide at the end of the war rather than be captured and have to answer for his crimes.

Christian Dirks described how another SS physician, Horst Fischer, was wracked by doubt after his first selection, in which he participated "merely passively." It was of a transport from Galicia, which comprised "only extremely poor and starving people." According to Dirks, Fischer "asked himself repeatedly in the next weeks and months why precisely these starving figures, 'the poorest of the poor, who could not possibly have an influence on the economy or politics, had to be killed.'" When he posed the question to Mengele, the latter explained that he was seeing the question incorrectly:

> It was precisely from this reservoir of people that the Jews drew new power and refreshed their blood. Without the poor but supposedly harmless Eastern Jews, the civilized West European Jews would not be capable of survival. Therefore, it is necessary to destroy all Jews.[43]

Fischer described Mengele as not "seeing a human problem," only one of race; as a "fanatic proponent," especially of the "racial issue";

and as being "the most convinced among us of the necessity of the destruction of the Jewish people." Fischer, who had known Mengele as a "very reserved and modest" colleague in the Viking Division, where they both served as unit physicians, encountered in Auschwitz a "changed" man.[44]

CHAPTER 4

"SERENDIPITOUS TRANSFER"

(May 1943–January 1945)

In a sense, Mengele created his own research institute at Auschwitz. "Staffing" it with inmates, he collected specialists in a wide variety of medical and scientific fields, as well as a cadre of technical assistants, nurses, illustrators, and clerical help. At the beginning of his time there, he dedicated a barrack in the Gypsy camp as his laboratory and supplied it with medical instruments and equipment. The scientific program of this "institute" included the treatment of *Noma facies,* a form of oral cancer; twin research; the collection of eyes from individuals with heterochromia (eyes of different colors); experiments relating to eye color; the collection of blood samples for a project on specific proteins; the collection of growth anomalies (like dwarfism and giantism) and physical anomalies (club foot, hunchback); the preservation of Jewish skeletons, human embryos, and deceased newborns;[1] and the anthropological study of Gypsies. The "institute" conducted research not only in the service of Mengele's own professional interests and professional advancement but also in collaboration with colleagues at the Kaiser Wilhelm Institute for Anthropology (KWI-A), and it supplied specimens to the SS Medical Academy in Graz for the training of the next generation of SS physicians.[2]

Auschwitz provided access to unprecedented resources for all the research areas of interest to Mengele. The sheer number of people who came through the camp ensured that a robust sample of human beings, with the full range of human traits, was available. Although twin births vary by population, they occur in approximately 1.1 percent of live births. Given the number of people deported to Auschwitz—approximately 750,000 during Mengele's time there—it follows that a large number of twins were available to him. Current rates of dwarfism are about one in forty thousand, suggesting that Mengele would have encountered a number of dwarfs among the deportees. The same holds true for the wide variety of rare conditions that affect human beings. For the anthropologist and the geneticist, access to the sheer number of these unusual cases, in a context that permitted unbridled research, was unprecedented.

Mengele had a special interest in Gypsies and took advantage of not only the twins who could be found among them but also the anthropological insights they offered. Inmate artist Dina Gottlieb, whom Mengele enlisted to paint portraits of his Gypsy research subjects, described Mengele's intense focus on them and suggested a possible explanation:

> He showed me the differences between types of Gypsies: how in the Aryan type the hairline matched the line of the eyes, how the blue of the Gypsies' eyes was different from the Aryans' blue, and which color was deepest. He was using these experiments to gather material for a book on the physical similarities and characteristics of Gypsies from different countries. He talked about it constantly.
>
> He used books and charts when working on his test subjects. He had templates to work out their eye and skin color, which he'd hold up to make a reading. One of his descriptions for the shape of someone's lips was the letter, M.[3]

Gottlieb was convinced that Mengele was going to use her paintings as illustrations for his book. Auschwitz offered a unique opportunity for the study of Gypsies; Mengele could conduct fieldwork within a population of thousands from a variety of geographical areas without needing to travel beyond the confines of the Gypsy camp. By contrast, Georg Wagner, an assistant at Verschuer's institute, while conducting research for his dissertation on Gypsies in the period before they were deported to Auschwitz, had had to travel more than fourteen thousand kilometers through Germany, Austria, and Czechoslovakia—and, even then, had access more limited than that available to Mengele.[4]

Noma Research

In the early 1980s, while I was working at OSI but before I got involved in the Mengele investigation, I traveled to the International Tracing Service in Arolsen (now Bad Arolsen), Germany, to conduct research for one of our Auschwitz cases. I was working in its historical collection, which contained copies of records from other institutions, and I came across a form signed by "Dr. Mengele" requesting that histological sections be made from an accompanying medical specimen, which had been sent to the SS medical laboratory on June 29, 1944. The form was one of many in the collection, the vast majority dealing with the transmission of blood, urine, or stool samples for analysis. This particular document, however, upset me greatly at the time, and I recall the feeling to this day. It indicated that the "specimen" being sent to the laboratory was the head of a twelve-year-old boy. At that time, I was unaware of any conceivable reason why such a specimen would be of interest to Josef Mengele, and this document only reinforced my notion of him as a wildly sadistic, grotesque monster.

Learning the reason for Mengele's interest provides important context for what might appear to be a symptom of unfathomable perversity. At the same time, the circumstances that led Mengele to request histological slides from the severed head of a child are no less chilling, even if seen in a scientific or medical context.

That context was a rare disease rampant in the Gypsy camp when

Mengele arrived in the summer of 1943. Known since ancient times, the disease was given its modern name, *noma,* by a Danish physician in 1680, who derived it from the Greek word *nemo,* which means "to graze" or "devour," underscoring its astonishingly rapid development. Noma can still be found today in developing countries where malnutrition, poverty, poor sanitation, and limited access to quality health care are present, and also among patients suffering from HIV and other immunodeficient conditions. Although once common in Europe and North America, the disease had virtually disappeared in developed countries by the twentieth century—except for its recurrence at Auschwitz and Bergen-Belsen.[5] Referring to cases of noma in present-day Nigeria, Dr. Cyril Enwonwu, former director of the Nigerian National Institute for Medical Research, described the course of the disease:

> Noma generally starts as a gingival ulceration that can be treated easily at the early stage with local disinfection, antibiotics, and nutritional rehabilitation. If the ulcer is left untreated, it progresses rapidly to involve the cheek or lip; swelling is often the earliest externally visible sign of disease. The swelling increases, and within days, a blackish furrow appears where intraoral tissue is being lost. The lesion finally establishes itself with a well-demarcated perimeter surrounding a blackened necrotic center. Sequestration of exposed bone and teeth occurs rapidly after the separation of the soft-tissue slough. A hole remains after the scab is removed.[6]

A Czech inmate-physician, Dr. Jan Cespiva, who worked in the Gypsy camp hospital, testified after the war about the effects of noma: "Whole chunks of flesh would come off [the affected areas]; lower jaw was also affected. I never saw such severe cases of gangrene of the cheek. Specimens of heads of diseased children were prepared for the SS Academy at Graz. . . . The heads were preserved in formaldehyde."[7]

Dr. Lucie Adelsberger, a Jewish physician born in Berlin, was sent to Auschwitz in May 1943, around the time Mengele arrived at the camp, and was assigned to work in the Gypsy camp hospital. Writing in the British medical journal *The Lancet,* in March 1946, as a displaced person in Amsterdam, she recalled:

> In 1943 there was a widespread outbreak of Noma, confined almost entirely to children. They showed deep and extensive ulceration of the mucous membranes of the mouth and cheek, with slimy necrotic holes inside the mouth, upper lips missing, and holes in the cheeks: this did not deter them from eating anything on which they could lay their hands.[8]

The outbreak of noma and its many victims offered Mengele a rare opportunity to conduct medical research, and he decided to study the disease, its causes, and its possible treatment. To lead the study, he "recruited" a world-famous pediatrician, Dr. Berthold Epstein, who was then assigned to Auschwitz III, and placed him in charge of this project.

Born in Pilsen, Bohemia, in what was then Austria-Hungary, in 1890, Epstein had been the director of a pediatric hospital in Prague and before the war was president and co-founder of the German Pediatric Society of Czechoslovakia. After unsuccessfully attempting to emigrate to England, Epstein was able to get to Norway in 1940, where he was granted a license to practice medicine. The German occupation of Norway began in June 1940, and at the end of November 1942, Norwegian police arrested him. A few days later he was deported along with his wife to Auschwitz.[9] Initially placed in the Buna satellite camp, Epstein was transferred to Birkenau and the Gypsy camp in August 1943, specifically to undertake the noma research. Assisting in the project was Dr. Rudolf Vitek (known as Weisskopf in the camp), a Czech Jewish dermatologist. Mengele had the noma-infected children moved to barrack 22, which he placed under Epstein's supervision.[10] Epstein researched possible treatments of the disease, including sulfonamides and vitamins. Other medications and dietary regimens were tested, and some claim that Mengele experimented with injections from noma sufferers to the healthy.[11] Inmate-physician Lucie Adelsberger described some of Epstein's therapies:

> At that time the disease was inevitably fatal: later, Prof. B. Epstein, working in the camp, clarified the problem of the condition's pathology; and by introducing treatment with a combination of sulphonamides and nicotinic acid provided an effective cure. At the same time, permission was received to give these children special high calorie diets, with meat and added vitamins. It was then possible, with nicotinic acid and injections of "Globucid" (suphanilamido-ethyl thiodiazole), to arrest a severe gangrene's stomatitis, even when oedema of the cheek indicated an impending perforation: in a few days a line of demarcation could be seen between the necrotic area and the adjacent healthy tissues, and the necrotic slough then separated.[12]

Mengele showed great interest in the noma research, recruiting an inmate-photographer, Wilhelm Brasse, to photograph a number of children afflicted with the disease as well as corpses of children who had died from it.[13] He had the Czech Jewish artist Gottlieb make drawings of the noma lesions, disliking, according to Gottlieb, color photography and preferring her ability to capture skin tone and color.[14] Kazimierz Czelny, the son of an inmate-physician from Poland, who was assigned as a corpse carrier in the Gypsy camp, recalled that he had to remove the heads from the bodies and place them in glass vessels filled with chemicals.[15] These heads, accompanied by a document like the one I saw in Arolsen, were then sent to the SS Hygiene Institute in Rajsko for histopathological study. The institute, in turn, sent selected specimens on to the SS Medical Academy in Graz for study and the education of SS physicians and scientists.[16] Without access to a medical library in the camp, Mengele asked a friend to borrow at least one book about noma from the university library in Breslau on his behalf.[17]

According to Miklós Nyiszli, an inmate pathologist forced to work with Mengele, research into noma, because of its prevalence, "had been greatly facilitated and considerable progress had been made towards finding an effective method of treating it." A new treatment for noma was developed, "consisting of a combination of malaria injections and doses of a drug whose trade name was 'Novarsenobenzol'" with "most promising results."[18] Yet despite Epstein's efforts to develop a successful treatment for the children afflicted with this disfiguring and usually fatal disease, it must be kept in mind that the disease was a product of the camp itself. Simple measures of sanitation and a modest standard of nutrition were all that would have been necessary to prevent an outbreak. Epstein might have solved the riddle of treatment, but no child he cured of this disease survived the camp.

Twin Research

Why was Mengele interested in twins? A surprising number of scholars, journalists, and others posit that he was searching for the secret of multiple births. His goal, it is said, was to discover an efficient way to increase the German birthrate and hasten the propagation of an Aryan future. The first to offer this explanation was probably Dr. Miklós Nyiszli, the Hungarian pathologist who worked closely with Mengele; he wrote an account of some of Mengele's scientific activity at Auschwitz in March 1946, and claimed that Mengele was "in search for a solution to the mystery of reproduction of the race. The great goal of this research was to increase the birth rate of 'super humans' who were destined to become the 'master race.' More specifically, this would in the future mean every German mother giving birth to twins."[19] Nyiszli's hypothesis was, however, wrong. It ignored the long tradition of twin research that had been a defining pursuit of Mengele's mentor, Verschuer, and the two important institutes that he led. It also failed to consider that, if there were a secret to twin births, the evidence would likely be found in the parents of twins and not in the twins themselves—evidence that Mengele seems to have made no effort to pursue or preserve.[20] To understand Mengele's interest in twins, it is necessary to understand the theory, practice, and history of twin research.

On the eve of World War II, in June 1939, Otmar von Verschuer delivered a lecture to the Royal Society of London, entitled "Twin Research from the Time of Galton to the Present-Day."[21] He told the gathering that a single picture hung in the library of the University Institute for Hereditary Biology and Racial Hygiene in Frankfurt, the institution that he founded and led: that of Francis Galton, whom he described as the "founder of our science." He went on to quote from a paper Galton had written in 1875:[22] "Twins have a special claim upon our attention; it is, that their history affords means of distinguishing between the effects of tendencies received at birth and those that were imposed by the special circumstances of their after-lives." Verschuer conferred upon Galton the distinction "founder of twin research," a field that he credited with being "alongside research into family history, the most important method of research into human heredity."

The methodological foundation of German twin research, which had been established in 1924 by Hermann Werner Siemens in *Twin Pathology*, involved comparisons between and among identical and fraternal twins. It was guided by a simple approach:

> Identical twins, which proceeded from the cells of a single fertilized egg, were held to be genetically identical—accordingly, any differences between identical twins were conceived of as exclusively environmental. Fraternal twins, on the other hand, which proceeded from different egg cells fertilized at the same time or in short succession, shared just over half of their genomes—like other siblings, so that differences between fraternal twins were understood to be the result of the coaction of a genetic *and* environmental factor. . . . . The twin method represented a "nearly

universally utilizable instrument for the practical investigation
of the problem of heredity vs. environment," as every characteristic that could be measured or counted could be tested "for rates
of concordance/discordance."[23]

In 1933 Verschuer called the method the "superior means of genetic
research in humans," and in 1936 Eugen Fischer referred to it as the
most important "instrument of human genetic research."[24]

A prerequisite for twin research was the successful determination of whether a pair of twins was fraternal or identical. This distinction, which may now appear straightforward, was nothing of
the sort to scientists in the first half of the twentieth century.[25] It
was initially believed that a careful examination of the placenta and
fetal membranes could yield confident conclusions about the nature
of the twin birth, but this notion was disproved. Siemens introduced
a breakthrough method for determining whether twins were mono-
zygotic or dizygotic, and Verschuer further developed it. Known as
the "Polysymptomatic Similarity Diagnosis," it relied on the careful
examination and comparison of a number of physical and physiologi-
cal characteristics of each member of a twin pair. The characteristics
chosen for comparison had to be those that were relatively stable and
not susceptible to environmental influence, "for only in such traits can
one expect that they would appear similar in one-egg twins but more
frequently different in two-egg twins." The compared traits should
also be hereditarily complex: "if a trait is based on a larger number
of genetic factors, then the probability that two people happened to
have all the conditions necessary to produce the same trait is low."[26]
In the 1930s, fifteen such characteristics were commonly used, beginning with blood groups and factors and including handprints, eye
color (defined with sixteen shades), the shape of the ear (described
with nineteen different variations), hair color and form, the shape of
the nose and lips, the placement and shape of the teeth, freckles, and
fingerprints, as well as a series of anthropological measurements.[27] A

careful application of this technique could, it was believed, reliably identify whether a twin pair was identical or fraternal.

The twin method was used throughout the Third Reich to prove the heritability of "everything from epilepsy, criminality, memory, and hernias to tuberculosis, cancer, schizophrenia, and divorce."[28] More than two hundred dissertations dealing in some way with twin research were published,[29] and funding for twin studies was "lavish," offering, as it purported to do, proof that there was a hereditary basis for human talents and imperfections.[30] The KWI-A also received support from abroad, with the Rockefeller Foundation underwriting twin studies there until the mid-1930s. When Rockefeller stopped its support, philanthropist James Loeb gave $1 million for continuing the research.[31] In his work at the KWI-A, Verschuer employed the twin method to study a range of conditions. He and a colleague, Karl Diehl, published a book about tuberculosis in 1933 in which they claimed to have determined the precise "relative influence of heredity and environment for various diseases" in identical and fraternal twins. There was, for example, a high degree of concordance for schizophrenia in identical twins, and none in fraternal twins.[32] Twin research was also pursued at the institute in areas beyond hereditary pathology: genetic immunology, race research, serology and blood group research, hereditary psychology, and criminal biology.

Although twin research was well funded and promising in its potential to produce meaningful results, its pursuit presented a number of obstacles. It was an extremely involved undertaking, requiring personnel to carry out the various measurements and record-keeping. A supply of appropriate twin pairs had to be identified, located, and induced to participate. The entire process required a huge investment of time and money. In the case of Verschuer's own research at the KWI-A, it took more than seven months to distribute twelve hundred questionnaires to schools in search of twin subjects. That effort produced one thousand possible twin pairs but resulted in only forty who were actually examined.[33]

Once a suitable twin pair was identified, their permission, or that of their parents, had to be secured, something that could not be relied upon. Participation in a twin study required a not insignificant sacrifice on the part of the twins' parents, beginning with at least a half-day visit to the institute, where a comprehensive medical history was compiled along with a complete medical examination. The Polysymptomatic Similarity Diagnosis took many hours to complete, and the observation form used by the KWI-A, which had to be completed for each twin, consisted of seventy-two fields. Photographs and fingerprints had to be taken. The proposed experiment might be unpleasant, painful, or have side effects. Beyond the disincentives presented by the inconveniences and unknowns of the process, there were also legal hurdles. It was forbidden in Germany, even under the Nazis, to intentionally infect a German citizen with a disease, a prohibition that led many scientists to conduct experiments on themselves. Given all these obstacles, Verschuer and his colleagues typically had to offer inducements to prospective twins and their families, which included a good meal or a vacation in one of the summer camps created especially for twins.[34] Verschuer was tireless in his pursuit of twins, creating by 1935 a database of more than four thousand in the Berlin area, a task that required close cooperation with hospitals, midwives, schools, and social services.

Twin research became even more difficult with the onset of the war. The supply of subjects dwindled as children were moved out of cities to the countryside as the war progressed. The number of scientific personnel was also reduced as the war effort consumed available professionals. As a result, research projects based on twin studies were dramatically slowed or had to be put off until after the war. In his annual report for the Institute of Racial Hygiene for the year 1943–44, Fritz Lenz reported:

The work of research has been quite impeded by the circumstances of the war, especially since summer 1943. It is very dif-

ficult and frequently impossible to acquire sufficient observation
material for certain essential scientific and practical problems.
As a consequence of the evacuation of women and children, family research and twin studies are practically impossible. Not even
surveys can be conducted anymore.[35]

Given this context, it is easy to see why Auschwitz, with its promising potential to supply twin subjects without cumbersome limitations,
offered such an attractive venue for a scientist in the field of genetics
who was willing to exploit the situation, and also able to surmount the
barriers that traditional medical ethics and basic humanity placed in
his way.

Mengele was able to do both. Hans Münch (Dr. Ernest "B") recalled
"Mengele saying that not to utilize the possibilities Auschwitz offered
would be 'a sin, a crime' and 'totally irresponsible' towards science."[36]
According to Dr. Horst Fischer, another physician at Auschwitz,
Mengele often spoke "enthusiastically" of his scientific work and
about the "material" that was available to him, describing "a unique
opportunity that would never again be offered."[37] Engaging in twin
research at Auschwitz was for Mengele a reflection of his commitment
to science and an opportunity to advance it beyond what he could have
only dreamed of a few years before. He was at the cutting edge, made
sharper by the unique potential that Auschwitz opened up for him.

To assist him in conducting measurements of the twins, he had
recruited a Polish anthropologist, Dr. Martyna Puzyna, who was Polish royalty thanks to her marriage to Stefan, a Polish count and the
son of a famous mathematician and rector of Lvov University; she settled in London after the war, where she was eventually interviewed
by German investigators. She had been arrested in March 1943 as a
member of the Polish Underground, held in prison in Lvov, and then in
August 1943 was sent to Auschwitz, where she was interned in Birkenau. After getting injured on a work detail, she was admitted with an
infected foot to the camp hospital, where she contracted typhus and

remained for a number of weeks. An inmate physician befriended her and learned of her training as an anthropologist, a background that she mentioned to Mengele, who then summoned Puzyna to meet with him. He asked if she had indeed been trained by Jan Czekanowski and was impressed when she confirmed that she had studied with the world-renowned anthropologist. Czekanowski's professional stature was on par with that of Theodor Mollison, Mengele's mentor in anthropology, with whom Czekanowski had professional contact. Czekanowski was famous for his work on the taxonomy of races and his eponymous "diagram," which permitted the effective identification of clusters of similar elements—a method of data visualization—and was useful in a variety of applications. He also deserves credit for having saved the Karaim national minority in Lithuania, who, despite their observance of Jewish ritual, were spared by the Nazis as a result of his having argued persuasively that they were of Turkish and not Jewish origin.[38] Mengele would have been conversant with Czekanowski's work and reputation, and he would have savored his good fortune in having as his assistant one whose pedigree within the field was royal indeed.

Mengele shared with Puzyna his "considerable interest in the field of anthropology" and that he was "particularly interested in doing comparative research on twins."

Mengele made it clear that he was ultimately interested in all types of twins. It was obvious that the special circumstances of a concentration camp the size of Birkenau offered unrivaled opportunities for the availability of a large number of twins. In other words, work should be done on a large scale in order to obtain results of recognized validity by statistical methods. Mengele described to me the procedures to be followed. Especially skull measurements should be taken, i.e., the length and width of the skull, and, of course, stature. There was also a multi-point screening scheme which, for example, included the shape of the ears, of the nose, color of the eyes and similar features. These values always had to be collected by means of a questionnaire. Mengele also provided me with measuring instruments, in particular, calipers.

I was given a special room for my work, and an inmate girl was provided to me to record the results of the measurements. While working, I had to wear a white lab coat like a doctor's. There was also a former anthropology student available, who had already taken measurements with the gypsies before I began my work. So we worked together for the measurements. We measured practically every day.[39]

Puzyna told Robert Jay Lifton that she considered Mengele's method "more or less standard for the time, the norm for anthropological work," and that she "recognized it as the same approach she had been trained in at her Polish university."[40] Another inmate anthropologist whom Mengele recruited, Erzsebet Fleischmann, described how they had to fill out a form with ninety-six points for each twin examined.[41] Puzyna thought Mengele's approach was "terribly detailed," more than necessary. Although Mengele never shared his research aims with her, she considered the work "scientifically legitimate."[42] To German investigators in 1972, she said:

It must be made clear again and again that Mengele was certainly a Nazi, but, in my opinion, he had, at certain times, an apparent genuine and serious interest in scientific work. As I myself was a scientific assistant, I felt that Mengele was capable of doing serious and objective scientific work.[43]

Equipped with the "latest Swiss precision measuring instruments," Puzyna followed a particular protocol in determining anthropometric values, particular ratios, morphology, and the color, tone, and texture of certain anatomical features.

There is ample evidence and testimony of particular procedures carried out on twins by Mengele and his assistants, but we do not know their ultimate objective. Much of what twin survivors remembered were the successive measurements and examinations undertaken in the course of the Polysymptomatic Similarity Diagnosis to determine whether they were identical or fraternal. Zvi Spiegel, an adult twin whom Mengele had assigned to look after the twin boys housed in barrack 14 of Camp BIIf, took on the title and metaphorical role of *Zwillingsvater,* or twins' father:

> The moment a pair of twins arrived in the Barrack, they were asked to complete a detailed questionnaire from the Kaiser Wilhelm Institute in Berlin. One of my duties as twins' father was to help them fill it out, especially the little ones, who couldn't read or write.
>
> These forms contained dozens of detailed questions related to a child's background, health, and physical characteristics, . . . the age, weight, and height of the children, their eye color and the color of their hair. They were promptly mailed to Berlin when they were completed.
>
> After the form was filled out, I would take the twins to Mengele, who asked them additional questions. Because many of the children spoke only Hungarian—and Mengele spoke only German—I would serve as the translator. . . .
>
> Much of the information Mengele was seeking had to do with demographics—where the family was from, what the parents had done for a living.[44]

It appears as though Mengele, in conducting his work, was following the same protocol as at the KWI-A—which would, of course, have been important in order to receive the imprimatur of that institution.

Yoav Heller, who wrote a dissertation about Zvi Spiegel in 2012, pieced together through interviews and witness testimony a description of how the twins were treated. Usually the day before a set of twins was needed, Spiegel "would receive a note with the relevant names. Obviously, they needed to be disinfected and had to take a shower, and then we would wait for the SS man to come and pick us up." Another twin recalled that they were also fed a meal before the experiment in order to arrive in "good shape."[45] One of the twins, György Lusztig, who had been eighteen years old at Auschwitz, described the examination room to an interviewer in 2000:

> It was like an old, primitive surgery.... There was a white bed with wax-cloth...as there were probably people who were examined lying down.... There was a table, and a typist. And there was a little cabinet with some equipment inside.[46]

In talking about the "typist," Lusztig was likely recalling the Polish inmate who acted as a clerk for Mengele, Janina Prazmowska.

Another twin, Kalman Baron, who had been fourteen years old at Auschwitz, told Yoav Heller in 2011 about the examination, which many twins recalled as "exhausting" and "frightening": "I was afraid. There was a stone bed. I was constantly given orders: take off your clothes, lie on your stomach, now turn on your back. I never knew what was coming—a needle, a cold stethoscope or something else."[47] The examinations could last several hours or more, and the twins were forced to stand naked in unheated rooms, which was particularly exhausting for small children.[48]

One twin, Thomas Simon, who had been eleven years old at Auschwitz, told an interviewer in 1995 about what was, for him, the most uncomfortable part of the examination:

> [Mengele] would measure everything.... He did all sorts of measurements...everything from the head and the eyes. I know one of the most unpleasant things I can recall...was when he took impressions of our teeth, because I recall he used plas-

ter of Paris . . . and, of course, they filled our mouths and it was extremely unpleasant. I mean I was gagging for several hours until that thing dried and was taken out.[49]

The twins were also fingerprinted, which required that their hands be washed with ether to remove dirt and oils.[50] One aspect of their examination, recalled by many surviving twins, was having blood drawn, often in perceived great quantities and on multiple occasions. Witness estimates of how much blood was drawn from each twin range from twenty cubic centimeters to fifteen times that volume.[51]

Beyond giving Mengele access to an extraordinary number of twins within a very short time frame, with no need for consent or for protective safeguards, Auschwitz provided him with an opportunity available to virtually no other scientist working with twins: he could determine when they died.

Certain research, as Benoît Massin observed, required the simultaneous death and dissection of twins:

Certain questions could only be answered by comparative histological or anatomical-pathological examinations of the internal organs. These required serious physical interventions, if not the deaths of the subjects. What's more, the scientists needed twins who had died at the same time in order to be able to do simultaneous autopsies.[52]

Although the procurement of corpses for scientific study had always been a problem for medical schools and research institutes, this shortage was alleviated in Germany after 1933 with a steady supply of bodies. Thanks to the Gestapo and SS, the bodies of victims of Nazi persecution were brought to various institutions for study. The supply of bodies of sets of twins, however, remained a problem. Robert Roessle of the Institute of Pathology at the University of Berlin had, it was thought, the largest collection of "material from twin autopsies in Germany," which he collected between 1929 and 1940 and which comprised material from more than one hundred twins, including one highly unusual instance of an adult twin pair, each of whom had hanged themselves on the same day. Since such cases were so rare, Roessle and others were forced to collect the bodies of stillborn and newborn twins from clinics and maternity hospitals and used these for comparative postmortem examination.[53] The reorganization of the KWI-A, with its new emphasis on phenogenetics, made the requirement for twin corpses even more urgent.[54] And the creation of a "Central Collection for Hereditary Biology" called for the procurement and preservation of a range of biological specimens, including "organs from adult identical and fraternal twins."[55]

In ruling over his absolutely unique experimental environment, Mengele did not have to wait for material to come to him. He could use his power to cause the simultaneous death of both members of a twin pair, allowing a corresponding autopsy of two individuals with identical genetic makeup and identical ages.

Eye Studies

Multiple witnesses described Mengele introducing chemicals into an experimental subject's eyes, either with an eyedropper or by injection. His goal in these experiments is almost always explained as an attempt to change the subject's eye color to an Aryan blue,[56] but the "Aryanization" explanation for the eye color experiments, to which Robert Jay Lifton also subscribed, always troubled me. I questioned whether Mengele would spend any time or effort attempting to effect what would, in essence, be a cosmetic change and have no genetic meaning. The real explanation for Mengele's experimentation is no less disturbing, but it is more consistent with the science he sought to practice. Although he did put chemical drops in prisoners' eyes, he was not trying to Aryanize them, and his eye-related work at Auschwitz did include the "harvesting" of eyes from children with a particular condition and shipping them to the KWI-A in Berlin.

Both of these activities were carried out in collaboration with Dr. Karen Magnussen, an assistant at the KWI-A. Magnussen distinguished herself not only as one of very few female scientists but also as an early and fervent member of the Nazi Party (joining in 1931), a race hygienist, and an antisemite.[57] Writing in 1943, she "designated the solution of the 'Jewish Question' as the 'core racial problem in Europe'":

> From the European standpoint the Jewish question is not solved by the circumstance that Jews emigrate from the racially thinking states to the other states. We see that these immigrants merely breed unrest and incite the Völker ("nations") against each other. . . . The race policy goal of the struggle of nations thus must be: the spatial separation of the European races and nations from all aliens (Jews, Gypsies, Negroes).[58]

In September 1941 Magnussen received a fellowship at the KWI-A in the department of experimental genetic pathology. She had a long-standing interest in the phenogenetics of normal attributes, especially in eye pigmentation, and a particular fascination with heterochromia. Verschuer offered her a position as an assistant in 1943, seeing the value of her research project, "On the Investigation of the Heritability of the Development of Eye Color as the Basis for Examinations of Race and Descent." This practical study, funded by the Reich Research Council (Reichsforschungsrat), would have served Mengele in his earlier capacity as an expert on racial identification and paternity issues, and in fact, Magnussen emphasized the importance of her research for the "praxis of National Socialist race policy." At the same time, her research was primarily conceived of as theoretical and an "important building block" in understanding phenogenetics.[59]

According to historian Hans-Walter Schmuhl, Magnussen's study involved six areas of examination. In the first—and basic to all the other areas—she dealt with "methodological questions on the determination of the structure, color and pigment distribution of the human iris."[60] In the second, "for the purpose of determining the influence of certain genetic hereditary dispositions on eye pigmentation," she bred strains of rabbits with certain eye colors.[61] The third area involved experiments to "physiologically influence pigment development" in rabbits, during the course of which she studied "the action of several hormones and pharmacologically effective substances on the development of pigment in the eyes."[62] It is believed that adrenaline was one of the hormones Magnussen used in these experiments. The fourth area involved studies about the development of pigment in childhood and was carried out in schools and was combined with genealogical studies. The progress of the war made this inquiry increasingly difficult, as air raids forced the evacuation of children out of urban areas. Nevertheless, Magnussen reported in September 1943 that she had examined more than thirteen hundred schoolchildren in Holstein and recorded observations concerning iris structure and eye pigmentation.[63] The fifth area involved the histological examination of dissected eyes from rabbits and humans. And finally, the sixth area involved "anomalies of the eye, such as corneal conjunctivalization and heterochromia."[64] In October 1944 she announced that she was finishing work on a paper about the "histology of total heterochromia in humans," a study that benefited significantly from Mengele's presence in Auschwitz.[65]

After Mengele's return to Berlin in January 1943 from active duty on the Russian front, he was able to familiarize himself with the current research and personalities at the institute. During a visit there, he met Magnussen and learned of the project she had undertaken. As part of her research, she was examining a cluster of heterochromia in a single Sinti family. The family of Otto Mechlau had been brought to her attention by a colleague at the KWI-A, Georg Wagner, who worked in criminal biology and had written his dissertation on "Race-Biological Observations on Gypsies and Gypsy Twins."[66] The family was of particular interest not only because of its high incidence of heterochromia but also because it included several pairs of twins. The family offered a significant research opportunity for Magnussen as well, since the family members were interned nearby in the *Zigeunerlager* (Gypsy camp) in Marzahn, where she had access to them, could examine family members, and obtain a comprehensive family history.[67]

Although Magnussen was able to photograph the eyes of one set of twins, her research was dealt a blow in March 1943, when the entire Mechlau clan was deported to Auschwitz, as part of the massive deportation of Gypsies from the Greater Reich carried out by the Nazis beginning in December 1942. The internment of the family in Auschwitz, she claimed, severely complicated her work, indeed made it "nearly impossible," and only the "serendipitous transfer" of Mengele to Auschwitz as physician saved the situation. In her May 1949 denazification interrogation, she explained that her research was only "possible through the assistance of Dr. Mengele," who "enabled me to clarify inheritance" by "determining the eye color and establishing the relationships among the members of the family."[68] She wrote to Viktor Schwartz (who had been an associate of her *Doktorvater*, Alfred Kühn) that Mengele had "compiled the genealogy of the family and recorded the physical attributes precisely."[69] Mengele also prepared a genealogical chart of the Mechlau family for Magnussen.[70] Mengele's work on Magnussen's behalf—the careful research and recording of family history—was similar to his work in his own dissertation, in which he had identified and described a physical anomaly and its frequency and occurrence in relevant family histories and genealogy.

Magnussen claims that she learned from Mengele that members of the family had contracted pulmonary tuberculosis, and she asked him to send her the autopsy reports and the "eye material" should anyone in the family die.[71] Only the dissection and laboratory analysis of the eye itself would yield the histological data necessary for her research. In her postwar statements, she suggested that her request for the eyes was predicated on the natural deaths of the subjects. Writing to

Schwartz in 1949, she asked, "In cases of death should I thus dispense with the histological analysis of the unique, abnormal material just because the people happened to die in the camp?"[72] In her decidedly disingenuous May 1949 denazification interrogation, she said:

> From the impression I gained from medical histories and from Mengele's very responsible and humanely decent attitude toward his interned patients and colleagues (he told me that he hoped to have one of the Polish female physicians, who was interned at Auschwitz, join the institute as a colleague after the war), the idea never occurred to me that anything could occur in Auschwitz that violated state, medical, or human laws.[73]

Magnussen did receive eyes from Auschwitz, but, with Mengele's help, they were not removed only from the bodies of people who died from disease or other natural causes.

Nyiszli, the inmate pathologist, recalled that he performed autopsies on four sets of twins, whom he discovered had all been killed by a direct injection of chloroform into the heart. He had been instructed to remove the eyes from these twins—six of whom had heterochromia—prepare the harvested eyes in formalin, and send the specimens to the KWI-A.[74] Another pathologist, Dr. Iancu Vexler, recalled Mengele pointing out a Gypsy family named Mechlau, which included seven or eight children with heterochromia, and informing him that when they died, their eyes should be removed, placed in special laboratory bottles, and sent to Berlin "for examination of the iris pigmentation." Mengele added, "You understand. Question of genetics . . . very interesting."[75] Puzyna recalled being asked by Mengele to deliver a wooden box, which seemed to be of great value to him, to the camp post office. When she was alone, she stole a look inside the box and discovered, to her horror, that it contained preserved human eyes in glass vials.[76] The former KWI-A scientist Hans Nachtsheim wrote to a colleague in 1961, "It was the greatest shock that I had experienced during the entire Nazi period when one day Mengele sent the eyes of a Gypsy family that had been interned in Auschwitz. The family had hetero-chromia of the iris, and a female colleague at the institute, who worked on heterochromia, had earlier shown interest in these eyes."[77]

Mengele's cooperation with Magnussen extended beyond supply-ing her with the eyes of dead children. He was also actively involved through his experiments on living children. He was not, however, attempting to turn brown eyes blue by injecting methylene blue dye into the iris, as has been repeated not only by witnesses, who made assumptions about the nature and motives of the experiment, but also by countless journalists and scholars. Mengele was helping Magnussen in the third area of her research project, which involved attempting to determine the influence of "several hormones and pharmacologically effective substances" on pigmentation.

Benoît Massin described the problem[78]: "The heredity of human eye color was problematic for researchers from the beginning of Mendelian genetics and was still unclear in 1940." It gained importance during the Nazi period since eye color was considered an important indica-tion of race. "Family and twin research had proven that eye color was dependent on genetic factors and not influenced by the environment." Although the fundamental law of inheritance of eye color—the "dom-inance of brown over blue, pigment-rich over pigment-poor"—had already been understood for some time, the issue was greatly compli-cated by the fact that eyes were not only blue and brown but a "nearly unlimited range of other colors." Geneticists had concluded that eye color was not determined by a single gene. And to complicate matters even more, "eye color was not only the result of the amount of pigment but also of the structure of the iris." It was theorized that eye color was dependent on "various pigment-forming, pigment-distributing, and pigment-concentrating genetic factors." Moreover, eye color was not constant throughout a person's life; it changed as one aged. Mas-sin notes that Magnussen, in a paper she published in 1943, pointed to the fact that newborns of "brown-eyed European races" were born with dark blue eyes, which changed to brown only later. It was difficult to understand "how a gene that was responsible for eye color could express itself first in the blue eyes of an infant, and then, after two years, in the brown eyes of the same child." According to Massin, "This was one of the problems that Eugen Fischer, the former director of the Kaiser Wilhelm Institute for Anthropology, and other geneticists before him, subsumed under the concept of 'phenogenetics' or 'developmental genetics,' and wanted to solve."

In her denazification interrogation, Magnussen described the nature of the experiment that Mengele carried out on her behalf, though within the context of her testimony—defending herself against criminal sanctions—she changed its fundamental nature. After receiving the eyes of the heterochromic twin children, she was able to dissect and examine their histology in detail. She claimed that she and Mengele were in search of a treatment for heterochromia, which would change the color of one eye so that both eyes were the same. Suggesting that heterochromia was some sort of affliction, she cast their efforts to "cure" it in an innocent light:

> As a result of the histological examination, it was possible to determine a presumable cause for the disturbing abnormality. We decided immediately to use the results in the interest of the same family and to attempt to cure the abnormality in one of the children. Since animal experiments of this type had been successfully carried out by other researchers, and since we had in advance confirmed through the university pediatric clinic that no unpleasant side effects were to be expected from the planned treatment (introduction of drops of a naturally occurring substance for the restoration of a disturbed function), the treatment was started.[79]

Benoît Massin has suggested that Magnussen provided Mengele with the substance that he was to introduce into the children's eyes.

In her report to the German Research Foundation in October 1944, she described the series of experiments examining the "physiology of pigment development in rabbits," in which she tested the efficacy of unspecified "hormones and pharmacologically active substances on the development of pigment in the eyes" of rabbits.[80] The evidence suggests that Mengele used the same substances on the children at Auschwitz. One witness, a Polish inmate-physician named Rudolf Diem, stated that Mengele "ordered the inmate-physicians, including myself, to put drops into the eyes of [people with different color irises]. I know that these drops contained adrenaline, something he [Mengele] spoke of himself. He reckoned that the use of these drops would cause a change in eye color."[81] After the war, Magnussen herself experimented with the use of adrenaline (as well as physiostigmine, atropine, and doryl) in animal eye color experiments.[82]

If adrenaline was, in fact, the substance that Mengele introduced into children's eyes, it is instructive to understand its side effects: rise in blood pressure, disturbance in heart rhythm, feeling of weakness, faintness, perspiration, shaking, and pallor.[83] These symptoms would have been frightening, and not only for a small child, and it is understandable why twin survivors recall these experiments with such horror and dread. And it is also understandable why the motivation behind them has been so misunderstood.

The experiments were not conducted in an effort to Aryanize their subjects, a goal that lacked any scientific basis and hence would not have interested Mengele, Magnussen, or the institute, under whose auspices they were operating. Their ultimate goal was purely scientific—a contribution to an understanding of phenogenetics. They also had a more practical objective, which involved improving, in Massin's words, "the method of classification of the color and structure of the iris for 'the applied genetics,' as Magnussen called it, of 'paternity and ancestry determinations.'"[84] Magnussen's research, with Mengele's active assistance in Auschwitz, was intended to improve the method by which eye color, including all that contributed to it, could be used to make better judgments about a person's race and family connections. "The structure of the iris and its pigmentation should in the future serve as a kind of body signature, which, on one hand, would be unique to every person, almost like a fingerprint, and, on the other hand, display enough similarity to relatives to reveal a family connection."[85] Magnussen wanted to improve the very activity that Mengele had been engaged in when he was in Posen, working for the EWZ and making judgments about a person's racial identity. While the experiments Mengele conducted on Magnussen's behalf were not designed to change the race of a single individual, they had a "higher" goal of serving the Nazi regime's effort to strengthen and defend the Aryan race, by helping to identify its members and, of course, its enemies.

Specific Proteins

In September 1943 Verschuer filed a preliminary report to the German Research Foundation for a project, approved and funded by that body, with the formal title "Experimental Research to Determine the Heredity of Specific Proteins as a Basis for Hereditary and Racial Research." Given the short title, "Specific Proteins," the project was based on a method named for its developer, the Swiss-born biochemist Emil Abderhalden, in the first decade of the twentieth century. Biochemist and historian Achim Trunk described Abderhalden's discovery and the basis for his theory:

> [Abderhalden] had injected a test animal subcutaneously with foreign protein, then taken a blood sample from which he obtained the serum and observed that the serum now was capable of disintegrating the foreign protein.... He concluded that the organism of the test animal must have produced enzymes ... [which] evidently catalyzed a protective reaction against the

intruded foreign protein without, however, disintegrating the autologous proteins. Abderhalden introduced the term "defense enzyme" for his discovery. Moreover, Abderhalden discovered that this reaction proceeded in a rather specific way: only the foreign protein that had been added was disintegrated whereas other proteins remained intact. . . . Hence he concluded that the intrusion of foreign proteins triggered the creation of highly specific enzymes.[86]

By isolating and identifying the "defense enzyme," Abderhalden posited that one could identify the foreign protein and what gave rise to it. He developed what he claimed was a wide range of applications for his "defense enzyme" theory, including a test for pregnancy and diagnostic tools for the discovery of diseases like cancer, tuberculosis, and even mental illness.[87] He won international fame when the theory was first developed, but interest in it waned as it encountered scientific opposition—only to enjoy a renaissance during the Nazi era, as a possible means to determine a person's race. "According to Abderhalden, every individual, every family, every race, and every species possesses a unique biochemical signature that arises out of the protein structure."[88] Abderhalden maintained that on the basis of the "defense enzyme," he had developed a uniquely precise method to ascertain specific differences between, but also similarities among, the proteins of different organisms.[89] In 1939 Abderhalden published the results of animal studies that proved, he claimed, that his "test" could identify the race of individual sheep and pigs, and he sought to extend his research to human beings—specifically, twins.

Abderhalden had written to Verschuer in 1940 to inquire about the possibility of testing the Abderhalden reaction on the blood of identical twins. Verschuer responded that, given the war's significant impact on the availability of suitable twins for study, not to mention medical assistants, who had been called to military service, Abderhalden's proposed research would have to wait until after the war.[90] But Verschuer was clearly intrigued by the prospect of working with Abderhalden and applying his technique to address the important challenge facing racial biology, namely the development of a reliable "race test." Mengele's assignment to Auschwitz appears to have given Verschuer the opportunity to take on the project despite his earlier demurral,[91] as it effectively removed the barriers to Abderhalden's proposed research.

In May, around the time of Mengele's transfer, Verschuer sent one of his medical technicians, Irmgard Haase, to Halle for three months to learn the Abderhalden technique from Abderhalden himself.[92] Historian Bernd Gausemeier suggests that the project had three related aims. First, it sought to discover a biochemical basis for racial identification, the methods employed up to that point having relied on physical characteristics and anthropometric comparisons involving, among other things, the shape of the skull and the color of hair, eyes, and skin. Second, the method promised to provide an unambiguous means of distinguishing between fraternal and identical twins, a fundamental challenge for twin research. Finally, Verschuer hoped to discover a new basis for determining paternity and related ancestral questions, which occupied a great deal of his time and that of other experts at his institute.[93]

Verschuer's second progress report to the German Research Foundation, covering the period October 1943 through March 1944, described Mengele's role in the project:

> New difficulties occurred in testing this method, which have been resolved in consultation with Abderhalden. Rabbit series are being screened to trace animals suited for the test devoid of spontaneously produced enzymes. My assistant Dr. med. and Dr. phil. Mengele has entered this branch of research as a staff member. He is on post as *Hauptsturmführer* [SS captain]

and Physician in Auschwitz concentration camp. Authorized by the *Reichsführer-SS*, anthropological tests are being carried out in the diverse racial groups of this concentration camp and the blood samples are delivered to my laboratory.[94]

Verschuer's third and final report, from October 1944, detailed the extent of Mengele's work:

This research has been further advanced. Blood samples of more than 200 people of most diverse racial provenience have been processed and blood plasma substrates produced. Further research will be continued with Dr. Hellman, staff member of the Kaiser Wilhelm Institute for Biochemistry. Dr. Hellman is a biochemical expert on protein research. With his aid the original Abderhalden method has been perfected, so that the actual rabbit test can henceforth begin.[95]

Although not specified, it is clear that Mengele collected these two hundred samples from inmates in Auschwitz. An extremely important aspect of his effort in collecting the samples would have been the careful description of the "provenance" of each sample—details relating to the individual from whom the blood was taken—using anthropological terminology.

Since the only documentation that has survived concerning the research project are the progress reports submitted to the funding organization and a few letters from Verschuer, one can only attempt to reconstruct the exact nature and course of the project. Achim Trunk has deduced how the experiment would have been conducted. A blood sample from Auschwitz would have been converted into a protein substrate—or substance upon which an enzyme acts—and injected under the skin of a laboratory rabbit. Abderhalden's theory held that the rabbit would then produce a "defense enzyme," to be found in its urine, in response. A solution of the produced defense enzyme would then be "laced with the injected protein and another with substrates" produced by other Auschwitz blood samples.[96] The theory held that the enzyme solution would degrade the injected protein effectively, while it would degrade the other substrates only to the extent that they were similar to the first one. Trunk summarized, "The corresponding formula was this: the stronger the substrate degradation, the bigger the chemical similarity of the proteins and thus the genetic affinity of the individuals from whom the blood was taken." Trunk theorized that the entire project would have required the injection of two hundred rabbits, each with a substrate produced from one of the blood samples, producing two hundred defense enzymes. Each of these enzymes would then be tested against each of the two hundred protein substrates. Trunk concluded:

> The alleged strength of the project consisted in this large sample, supposed to capture human "racial" heterogeneity. By improving the identification of the products of the Abderhalden reaction, one expected to come close to an exact determination of a relationship. In this context samples of twins (monozygotic as well as dizygotic) and "clans" were of particular importance.[97]

According to Irmgard Haase, in an interview with Benno Müller-Hill, the course of the war prevented the research project from developing beyond the stage of injecting the "the first rabbits" with the dried substrate.[98]

Collecting Specimens

On July 13, 2014, the student magazine for the Free University of Berlin ran the headline "Human Bones on Campus." Construction workers had come across human remains during renovation work on the grounds of the university library. The discovery was particularly newsworthy since it occurred "in the immediate vicinity" of the former KWI-A, whose original building still stands today and houses the university's Otto Suhr Institute for Political Science. There was immediate speculation that they had been among the specimens Mengele had sent to the institute from Auschwitz. "Ten round plastic markers with handwritten figures" were discovered with the bones, which appeared to be "labels for biological/medical specimens."[99] Before the origins of the bones could be determined with certainty, however, they were cremated and buried in a Munich cemetery, where there is a memorial to victims of euthanasia.

Regardless of whether Mengele had had anything to do with the discovered specimens, he certainly was responsible for supplying colleagues at the institute with medical and biological samples. Although the most infamous and best-documented example involved the eyes harvested from camp inmates, he undoubtedly collected and shared a range of other specimens. Inmate pathologist Miklós Nyiszli described saving certain specimens from the autopsies he performed that might be of scientific interest and showing them to Mengele, who would instruct him to pack them and send them to Berlin, marked "Urgent, contents important for the war effort":

> During my work at the camp I sent innumerable parcels to the institute in Berlin-Dahlem, in reply to which we would receive exhaustive scientific comments or further instructions. I had to set up separate files for this correspondence, which also included letters from the institute thanking Dr. Mengele for sending particularly fascinating items.[100]

Nyiszli also described Mengele spotting a hunchback on the ramp, who had just arrived on a transport. The fifty-year-old man was accompanied by his teenage son, who had a deformed foot. Mengele sorted them out of the ranks and sent father and son to Nyiszli, who understood that he was to examine them in detail while alive and then conduct an autopsy after they were killed:

> He listens interestedly to my report concerning both the *in vivo* and *postmortem* observations made on the two victims. "These bodies must not be incinerated," he says, "they must be prepared and their skeletons sent to the Anthropological Museum in Berlin."[101]

There is no way to estimate the number and range of samples provided by Mengele, but his access to the huge reserves of human variation and his control of a well-staffed pathology laboratory provided him with every opportunity.

Mengele's interest in growth anomalies also fueled his curiosity about dwarfs, the most famous example of which was his mid-May 1944 selection of the entire Orvitz family, whose members were subjected to rigorous examination and anthropometric evaluations. A recent book about the experience of this family, published, unfortunately, without notes, suggests that Mengele featured them in his scientific presentation on the occasion of the SS hospital dedication at Auschwitz, in September 1944, which was illustrated by a detailed family tree and ancestral chart prepared for him by the inmate-artist Dina Gottlieb. We know that Mengele's colleague at the Berlin institute, Hans Grebe, researched dwarfism and would have appreciated any dwarf-related specimens that Mengele might have supplied.

We also know that the KWI-A planned to create a department of embryology and established its "central collection," which was to include a wide range of human samples and specimens, including those from twins, along with human embryos, fetuses, and stillborn and deceased newborns, all available in large numbers in Auschwitz. Indeed, inmate physician Dr. Giesla Perl described preserving for

Mengele an intact human embryo, which, he told her, would be "sent to Berlin."[102] Benoît Massin indicates as well that Dr. Wolfgang Abel, a KWI-A colleague, appeared to be in the process of creating an anthropological skeleton collection. As Massin writes, Mengele's colleagues at the institute "could count on deliveries from Auschwitz."[103]

GIVEN MENGELE'S AMBITION, his pursuit of his *Habilitation*, and his patronage from Verschuer, it is clear that he pursued his science not as some renegade propelled solely by evil and bizarre impulses but rather in a manner that his mentors and his peers could judge as meeting the highest standards. Historian Massin writes, "Mengele is sometimes portrayed as the embodiment of the pseudoscientific SS physician, who, in complete isolation, carries out his abstruse experiments. In fact, Mengele was very tightly connected to the scientific community."[104] For this reason, he sought to "recruit" the very best practitioners from the inmate population and kept, reportedly, comprehensive records of his scientific work. For the same reason, it is difficult to accept testimony about some of his experiments and their rationale, such as claims that Mengele attempted to create a Siamese twin by "sewing together" two twins,[105] or that he sought to "make boys into girls and girls into boys" through "cross transfusions," or even "connected the urinary tract of a 7-year-old girl to her own colon."[106]

The notion of Mengele as unhinged, driven by demons, and indulging grotesque and sadistic impulses should be replaced by something perhaps even more unsettling. Mengele was, in fact, in the scientific vanguard, enjoying the confidence and mentorship of the leaders in his field. The science he pursued in Auschwitz, to the extent that we can reconstruct it, was not anomalous but rather consistent with research carried out by others in what was considered to be the scientific establishment. That research was criminal—and monstrous—because of the absence of all barriers that ordinarily serve to contain and regulate the temptations and ambitions that can push scientific research across ethical boundaries. Relegating Mengele and his research to the ranks of the anomalous and bizarre is perhaps more palatable than understanding that he was the product—and promise— of a much larger system of thought and practice. It is easier to dismiss an individual monster than to recognize the monstrous that can emerge from otherwise respected and enshrined institutions.

CHAPTER 5

"I'LL NEED TO BUY
A CRIB FOR ROLF . . ."

(May 1943–May 1945)

An album of photographs donated to the U.S. Holocaust Memorial
Museum in 2007 by an anonymous former GI, who had found it in a
Frankfurt apartment after the war, contains remarkable photographs
that depict Auschwitz not as a center of persecution and genocide but
as a place where people lived and worked. Research at the museum
revealed that the album had belonged to Karl Höcker, an adjutant to
Richard Baer, commandant of Auschwitz from 1944 to 1945. Among
the 116 black-and-white photographs taken between June and December 1944 are a number that depict SS officers relaxing at Sołahütte, a
small subcamp of Auschwitz about thirty kilometers from the main
camp, which served as a rustic getaway for Auschwitz personnel.
Mengele, smiling and relaxed, is captured in eight of the photographs,
the only ones that we can be sure show him at the camp.

For members of the SS, a posting to Auschwitz had significant
advantages over a combat assignment. Beyond enjoying relative safety,
they had the opportunity to live with or receive visits from their
spouse and family members. Indeed, the camp administration encouraged families to live together or make visits, believing that this kind of
contact provided psychological support for the SS members performing such "difficult service." We know that Mengele's wife visited him
twice—once for an extended stay—and that his father visited at least

once. Many of Mengele's physician colleagues lived with their wives and children near the camp. For instance, three colleagues and their families shared a home on what is now Garbarska Street in Oświęcim: Dr. Wilhelm Frank, a dentist in the camp; Dr. Wilhelm Rohde; and Dr. Horst Fischer, who later moved with his family to his own home and was replaced by another physician colleague, Dr. Bruno Kitt and his wife. Each family employed a young Polish girl from the area to help with the children and to carry out other household tasks. Jehovah's Witnesses, interned in Auschwitz, were assigned to do cleaning.

There was a commissary, Haus 7, where SS families could shop for food, and the men serving in the camp had access to fresh vegetables and fruit from local gardens and orchards. Clothing and shoes were available, presumably from the camp's stores of expropriated property, and tailors and shoemakers at the camp would alter and repair items for SS members and their families. Dirty laundry and linens were taken to the camp laundry. Prisoners were available to remodel and repair SS homes, stock coal cellars, work in the gardens, and distribute fresh water for washing and cooking, since the well water was rusty. Fischer, who was Wirths's deputy, did a lot of entertaining in his home, according to Aleksandra Slawarczyk, the Polish girl employed by him, and Wirths and Mengele were frequently in attendance.[1]

A gynecological clinic served female SS personnel as well as the wives of SS men and was overseen by Wirths, a gynecologist. An inmate named Artur Radvansky, who arrived in Auschwitz in October 1942, managed an assignment there in April 1943 thanks to his false claim that he had completed two semesters as a medical student at Charles University in Prague. In addition to cleaning the clinic and Wirths's office, Radvansky was responsible for running the baths, which were reserved for SS personnel. According to Radvansky, Wirths used to convene a meeting, every week or two, for all the physicians in Auschwitz (including pharmacists and dentists in this group), and many who were assigned to Birkenau took advantage of this time to have a bath.

The SS officers had few opportunities for bathing. In Birkenau there was no bath so they bathed when they came for consultations. . . . I had to prepare a bath for Mengele, clean his suit, and give him a massage. At least once a week, I had contact with Mengele, sometimes several times a week. Mengele was a very polite, good-looking man. He never screamed, never beat the prisoners he needed. I also never saw him beat anyone in the camp. He always said [the formal] "Sie" to me: "Arthur, please make me a bath, Arthur please do you . . ." He behaved the same way to others: "Please, Mary, do this and that." On the other hand, Mengele sent thousands of people to the gas chambers during the selections and also performed the worst experiments on children, including adults. That was the devilish thing about him, that you could never believe his pleasant face.[2]

Irene

Irene wasted very little time in taking advantage of the option to visit her husband and did so quite early in his Auschwitz service. In an interview in 1985, Irene could not remember the date, but she placed this first visit in August or September 1943.[3] This likely provided her with an occasion to announce to Mengele that she was pregnant. Perhaps it was her pregnancy that prevented her from visiting Mengele later during the Christmas holidays. He had fallen ill and was diagnosed with typhus on Christmas Eve[4] and was clearly not in a position to travel to visit his family; nor was it advisable for his pregnant wife to visit him. It appears, however, that he was not alone for the holidays, since Wirths's wife remembered Mengele's father visiting him over Christmas 1943; he stayed in the Wirthses' home.[5] Mengele had follow-up tests over the next several weeks and appears to have recovered from the illness, although the residual effects seem to have lingered.

Mengele wrote to Irene on April 26, 1944, to report the news that he had been awarded the War Service Cross Second Class with Swords, a decoration acknowledging wartime service unconnected with combat against the enemy. It was conferred upon soldiers in rear areas who had distinguished themselves, and on civilians who had advanced the war effort. As Mengele made clear to his wife, it was by no means a difficult medal to get; in fact, more than two million were awarded during the course of the war. In Mengele's case, the medal was for his actions combating the typhus epidemic; he indicated the decoration was known in the camp as "The Typhus Medal," and he included a sketch of it on the first page of his letter. In spite of making light of the award, he seemed pleased to have received it:

> Occasionally, a small beam of light falls into the desolation of everyday life and K-L [concentration camp] operations. This afternoon, at 4:00 pm, I was ordered to go to the commandant [Arthur Liebehenschel] and was given the "K.V.K. II. Kl. m. Schwerten" [War Service Cross Second Class with Swords]. Even though it is no longer unusual to receive such a medal, and even though I also have some that are even more valuable, I very much appreciated the recognition of my work and commitment, which sometimes, and repeatedly, means the endangering of health and life. (So, dear Butzele, you see, the medals gradually gather on my hero's breast!)[6]

Normally the medal would have been awarded on Hitler's birthday, April 20, but Mengele had not been in Auschwitz that day; he had been visiting Irene and meeting his newborn son, Rolf, for the first time. After spending time with Irene and little Rolf, he stopped in Berlin on his way back to Auschwitz, where he visited the KWI-A. He informed Irene that it was "very nice in Berlin," mentioning that Emmi Nierhaus, the chief nurse at the Frankfurt Institute, who had followed Verschuer to Berlin, was especially hospitable. Heinrich Schade, a former colleague in Frankfurt, who had also moved with Verschuer to Berlin, had dedicated all his free time to Mengele. And finally, Mengele noted cryptically that he was able to "discuss everything" with the "boss," meaning, of course, Verschuer.

He wrote to Irene that a package from Günzburg was awaiting him upon his return from leave containing three bottles of wine and a bottle of Sekt, intended to celebrate Rolf's birth. Mengele did just that in a "circle of nice people," which included colleagues Horst Fischer, the dentist Willi Frank, and Hans Muslow, the head of the climatology station at the SS Hygiene Institute in Rajsko, along with their wives. They toasted Rolf's health and his dear mother.[7] Dina Gottlieb recalled that Mengele returned from his leave "beaming with joy, he told me all about the child. And he gave me a little pastry he'd brought from home. It was so unexpected."[8]

Mengele let Irene know that he was fine, that the work continued as usual, but that he intended "on the whole to be more restrained" in the future. Likely he was referring to his health—he had not felt particularly well in Berlin, and following the train trip back to Auschwitz, he experienced significant swelling in his leg and intended to have everything thoroughly checked out at the hospital. Regardless of Mengele's stated intention to slow down, he was just about to enter the most intense period in the history of Auschwitz, one that would demand his singular engagement. Within four months, more than four hundred thousand Jews would arrive from Hungary, and Mengele would be called upon to play his part in overseeing the murder of the vast majority of them.

Irene saw her husband again during her second visit to Auschwitz, a trip well-documented in her diary. She departed Freiburg alone on August 8, 1944, leaving Rolf with her parents, and arrived in Auschwitz the next day. Her visit came exactly one week after the liquidation of the Gypsy family camp (Camp II-Be) of Birkenau. The Gypsy camp, which had been established in February 1943 to hold more than twenty-two thousand Roma and Sinti, and, later, the so-called family camp in Sector BIIb, holding Jews who had been deported from the Terezin ghetto beginning in September 1943, had offered Mengele something very important for his research—access to families. Unlike the rest of Auschwitz, where men were separated from women, families in these camps were permitted to remain more or less intact, thus providing the important family histories that were crucial for some of Mengele's research interests.

On the afternoon of August 2, 1944, more than fourteen hundred Gypsies who had been selected from the Gypsy camp as well as from the main Auschwitz camp—918 men, including fifteen boys under fourteen years of age, and 490 women—bade farewell to their friends and relatives and boarded a train at the ramp in Birkenau, which departed at seven p.m., bound for Buchenwald. At the evening roll call, Mengele ordered all Polish doctors and nurses to step forward, and they were taken to nearby Camp II-Bd. After the roll call, the camp was locked down, the barracks were surrounded by armed SS men, and trucks entered. The remaining 2,897 Gypsy men, women, and children were forced to board and were taken the short drive to the gas chambers, where they were murdered that night and burned in the open pit next to the crematorium, which was not operational at that time.[9]

Two weeks after Irene's arrival, her husband received his first formal performance appraisal for his service at Auschwitz, written by his supervisor, Dr. Eduard Wirths.

> Dr. M has a straight-forward, honest, and stable character. He is absolutely reliable, upright, and straight in his demeanor, he does not show any character weaknesses, tendencies, or manias.
>
> His mental and physical dispositions can be described as outstanding.
>
> During his employment as camp physician at the Auschwitz concentration camp, he has put his knowledge to practical and theoretical use while fighting serious epidemics. With prudence, perseverance, and energy, he has carried out all the tasks set him, often under very difficult conditions, to the complete satisfaction

of his superiors, and has shown himself to be able to cope with every situation. In addition to that, he, as an anthropologist, has most zealously used his little off-duty time to educate himself further and, utilizing the scientific material that was at his disposal due to his official position, he made a valuable contribution in his work to anthropological science. His performance can therefore be described as outstanding.

In his attitude toward his superiors, he displays the impeccable demeanor of an SS officer. The very best military deportment, tact, and reserve. His character makes him a favorite among his comrades. Toward his subordinates, he knows how to hold his own with absolute justice and the required strictness but is, at the same time, very popular and respected.[10]

Irene may not have been aware of the precise nature of her husband's work, claiming after the war that he had told her not to ask about it and maintaining that she had never entered the camp itself but stayed outside the barbed wire that surrounded it. She saw it as "bleak and desolate" and described it has having a "sweet" odor, but nonetheless, she found enjoyment bathing in the nearby Soła River and picking blackberries, which she made into marmalade. It was for personal reasons that she made the trip to Auschwitz to visit her husband. She loved him very much; he was her first great love—"always charming, funny, very social," vain, too, and apparently sad that he was, in his opinion, "too short." In Auschwitz she felt he was "subdued and depressed," although he never said anything about it.[11]

She made particular note in her diary, during this second visit, of the dedication of a new troop hospital in Auschwitz on September 1. The more than twenty photographs of the festivities were preserved in the Höcker Album, obtained by the U.S. Holocaust Memorial Museum. They feature Dr. Enno Lolling, the chief medical officer for all concentration camps, who used the hospital dedication as an opportunity to host a gathering of SS physicians from other camps including his deputy, Dr. Heinz Baumkötter, the chief physician at Sachsenhausen concentration camp. Irene referred in her diary to a scholarly conference held on that occasion at which her husband delivered a formal talk on his scientific work at the camp, entitled "Examples of Anthropological and Hereditary-Biological Work in the Auschwitz Concentration Camp."[12]

The hospital was no small project. Located east of the area that housed the SS Guard Battalion, the nearly one-million-square-foot compound comprised nine separate buildings and was designed to offer comprehensive health services to a large community, with a capacity of 250 beds. It included operating rooms, a dental clinic, facilities to provide care for women, babies, children, and those with infectious diseases, as well as lodging for doctors and nurses, a kitchen, laundry, and garages. Irene likely did not imagine, on the day of the dedication and her husband's scientific talk, that she would soon make use of this impressive new facility. She also had no way of knowing that within four months, on the day after Christmas, the hospital would be nearly completely destroyed in an air raid.[13]

Although Irene planned to return to Freiburg on September 11, she fell ill with diphtheria and later developed myocarditis, a complication of the disease. She may have already begun to feel sick by September 5, the day a transport arrived at Birkenau from Westerbork camp with 1,019 Jews from the Netherlands. We don't know whether Mengele had been assigned ramp duty that day, but if he had, he would have encountered a German family from Frankfurt who had moved to Amsterdam after the Nazis came to power in Germany. The entire family—mother, father, and two daughters—survived the selection, but only the father survived the war. His wife died in January 1945, and the two girls were transferred to Bergen-Belsen, where they both perished—the younger one, Anne Frank, on March 31, 1945.

Irene lay in a hospital bed beginning on September 11, suffering from high fever and receiving care from personnel in "striped prisoner clothing." She was prescribed "absolute rest," and her husband visited her three times a day, sitting by her bedside and reading Balzac's *Le Diamant* aloud.[14] On the morning of September 13, the IG Farben works in Dwory was bombed by a squadron of ninety-six American B-24 Liberator bombers. Although Auschwitz I and Birkenau were not the targets of the attack, both were hit by errant bombs. Irene was transferred to the newly dedicated SS hospital on September 18, where she remained for a month.

During Irene's stay there, on October 7, she wrote in her diary about another air raid, this time noting the response of antiaircraft fire and that she had to retreat "on shaky legs" to the shelter. On the same day, a remarkable act of resistance took place in Birkenau involving the *Sonderkommando*, a unit of inmates who were assigned to the horrific duty of attending the process of the gassing of prisoners, emptying the gas chambers, and conveying the dead bodies to the crematoria. Because of the nature of their work and their intimate knowledge of the Nazis' genocidal activities, members of the *Sonderkommando* were isolated from the rest of the camp population and were routinely murdered and replaced by new inmates. On the morning of October 7, members of the camp resistance movement informed members of the *Sonderkommando* that the SS intended to liquidate them as soon as possible. The squad in Crematorium IV decided to commence an uprising that had been planned for some time. They killed a German inmate who threatened to reveal their plans to the SS and, at 1:25 p.m., attacked an approaching SS guard unit with "hammers, axes, and stones." They set the crematorium on fire and detonated several grenades that had been made from gunpowder smuggled to them by female inmates assigned to a nearby munitions factory. The *Sonderkommando* in Crematorium V followed suit, attacking SS guards and then fleeing into the woods.

The SS response was swift and overwhelming, employing heavy machine gun and artillery. In the end, all the *Sonderkommando* members were captured, and by the end of the day, more than four hundred had been killed. The SS suffered fifteen casualties, including three dead.[15] While all this was unfolding, Irene lay in her sickbed a little more than a thousand meters away, surely within earshot of the prisoners' makeshift explosions and the responding fire of the SS.

While Mengele was preoccupied with his wife's illness, a colleague, Dr. Heinz Thilo, carried out a selection in the twins barracks, which housed the male twins in Camp BIIf. Witnesses maintained that Thilo "had some kind of rivalry" with Mengele and did not approve of him keeping twins alive in the camp.[16] Likely on October 2,[17] Thilo selected as many as half the twins, as well as two of the dwarfs, and marked them for death,[18] and through a risky act, Zvi Spiegel, the "twins' father," was able to alert Mengele of Thilo's apparent sabotage. Mengele countermanded Thilo's orders, and the twins were saved. Perhaps as a result of his actions, Thilo was transferred to Gross Rosen the next week.

Irene was discharged from the hospital on October 18 and moved with her husband into the physician residence building, which was part of the new hospital complex. She noted in her diary that her new home was being cleaned by "incarcerated female Jehovah's Witnesses."[19] The move had an impact on Irene, who, having married shortly before the start of the war and her husband's deployment, had never really shared a home with him. Now she felt "newly married."[20] The day after the move, four thousand Jews were murdered in the gas chambers of Crematoria II and III. On October 20 fifteen hundred Jews arrived in Birkenau from the ghetto in Theresienstadt. Of these, 169 women and 173 men were selected and registered in the camp, while the remaining 1,158 were murdered in the gas chamber of Crematorium III. On the same day, one thousand young people between the ages of twelve and eighteen were murdered, including 357 who had arrived from a subcamp of Gross Rosen in the village of Dyhernfurth (Brzeg Dolny), which supplied labor to a German chemical weapons factory. On October 22 Mengele conducted a "two-hour selection" among female Jews sent from Plaszów concentration camp.[21]

The End of Auschwitz

On the road to recovery and rededicated to her marriage, Irene left Auschwitz, accompanied by her husband, on October 30. They stopped overnight in Günzburg to visit with his family. In his postwar autobiographical writings, Mengele recalled his farewell from his mother, who he quoted as saying, "My dear boy, it will be long, this time."[22] On November 2, Mengele and Irene headed to Freiburg to be reunited with Rolf, from whom the new mother had been separated for three months, far longer than anticipated. Mengele had not seen his son since shortly after his birth the previous spring. In a postcard that he wrote to Irene on his way back to Auschwitz four days later, Mengele thanked her for the "wonderful days" and admitted that he would have been very sorry had he not made the trip. "The 'little man' has been very much 'with me' the entire day, he is such a delight and will certainly bring us only joy."[23] Years later Mengele would write of his short stay in Freiburg:

> I remember so well how several times a day, during a short leave in Freiburg, I would rush—probably unnecessarily—the six-month-old Ro[lf] to the basement because of air raid warnings. I can still feel deeply—even today—that sense of worry and responsibility for the child.[24]

Irene's extended visit in Auschwitz and Mengele's brief encounter with his son in Freiburg had a significant emotional impact on them both.

Three weeks after his return to Auschwitz, Mengele wrote to Irene and referred to a plan that he had obviously already broached with her. On November 23 she had moved with Rolf to Günzburg, presumably for security reasons, since the small Bavarian town was not as likely a target of Allied air raids as the city of Freiburg. Mengele revealed in this letter that he was attempting to get out of Auschwitz by transferring to a field unit. He had prevailed upon his friend Horst Fischer to ask Wirths, the chief doctor at Auschwitz, to intercede on Mengele's behalf with Enno Lolling concerning Mengele's transfer, but the intervention was not successful. Mengele wrote to his wife that he wouldn't be getting "out of here so quickly, as least not until the spring." He then raised the possibility that she move with Rolf to Auschwitz so they could at least live together "as a family" for the few months that he needed to remain there. He asked her to respond quickly and counseled her not to be discouraged by his family in Günzburg, who would naturally want her to remain there with Rolf: "This time, you are really free to make your own decision, and I won't cause you any trouble if you should decide against it." And then, invoking perhaps the changed character of their relationship, he wrote, "You are better able to make a judgment about this question than you were in the summer." He concluded, "You know that I love you very, very much, and that I look forward already to our still 'imaginary' being together."[25]

Two days later Mengele wrote again and informed his wife that the wives of his colleagues were keenly interested in knowing when she would be moving to Auschwitz; he had apparently made arrangements for an apartment, and word of a move had gotten out. He asked Irene to make her decision so he would know how to proceed. He wrote about his social life at the camp, which included an invitation from Viktor Capesius, the pharmacist, and a "Comradeship Evening of the SS." The remainder of the letter dealt with news of the war, with mention of fighting in Schlettstadt in Alsace, about forty kilometers from Freiburg, as a result of the Allies' advance, and his hope that the "new weapons" would soon have their effect: the V-1 and V-2 rockets, which were heralded by the Nazi leadership as changing the course of the war. Likely referring to an attack on the IG Farben complex conducted by the U.S. Air Force on November 29, Mengele described his sense of relative safety: "The attacks here are focused on the industrial area. So far, we have emerged from them unharmed.

Of course, the squadrons are flying over us, but they are hardly likely to select a concentration camp for attack."[26] He was assuring his wife that, ironically, Auschwitz was a relatively safe place for her and their son to be.

He wrote again three days later, having heard nothing from Irene, and displayed a growing irritation:

> I am still waiting to hear from you. I hope you have decided, because if you come, you have to let me know soon, due to the slow mail. Christmas is almost here, and travel is so difficult in the pre-Christmas period! I am working hard on furnishing the apartment. I need to know because I'll need to buy a crib for Rolf.[27]

When Mengele received three letters from Irene in the next week, he discovered that she had already agreed to move to Auschwitz with Rolf to be with him. The only point of disagreement was the timing: Irene preferred to go after Christmas, which Mengele thought inopportune given the difficulty of traveling between Christmas and New Year's, and which would mean that they would be apart for a second Christmas, since he could not go to her and would also not be able to pick her up. He suggested that he might be able to ask Wirths to send a nurse who could travel with Irene, but he did not wish to do so, proposing instead that his brother Karl might accompany her, or perhaps Irene's father. Irene had indicated certain preferences to Mengele about their apartment, which Mengele relayed to Martin Wilks, an SS noncommissioned officer in Wirths's office responsible for housing issues. Mengele was clearly very frustrated and wrote to his wife that she might already have been there with him, had she been able to decide more quickly.[28]

Irene would never make the trip. At the beginning of 1945, the Soviet advance threatened the camp, and the SS prepared for withdrawal. Those inmates who were deemed able were forced to evacuate Auschwitz, embarking on the so-called death marches to camps in the west, without adequate clothing in harsh winter weather. Thousands succumbed to the elements or were murdered outright by the accompanying German guards. After dynamiting the gas chamber/crematorium complexes and destroying camp documents, the SS vacated Auschwitz on January 17. Anthropologist Martyna Puzyna spotted Mengele feverishly packing before he left. "I remember well that in January 1945, a few days before the evacuation, Mengele appeared in the room [where his files were stored] and like a madman packed up all the notes and prepared them for being shipped. He did not speak a word and then disappeared. I never saw him again."[29]

After leaving Auschwitz, Horst Fischer made his way to Gross Rosen concentration camp, where he met his colleagues Mengele and König. In a postwar interrogation conducted by the East German authorities, Fischer would claim that Mengele reported to him that he had blown up Crematoria II and III "before the Red Army arrived." Apparently there had been some technical problem with the explosives, and Mengele, calling upon his experience with the Engineers Battalion of the Viking Division, had been able to "expertly" solve the problem and succeeded in demolishing the facility, leaving the ruins that are visible to visitors in Birkenau today.[30]

Mengele and König also reported to Fischer that Gross Rosen was "hopelessly overcrowded with prisoners and SS men." Serving no useful purpose there, the three rode in Fischer's vehicle toward Berlin to report to Enno Lolling in Oranienburg, just north of the city. On their way, they decided to pay a visit to Ernst-Robert Grawitz, the *Reichsarzt SS*, in Berlin, and decided among themselves that another assignment to a concentration camp would not be advisable. Fischer explained, "We all agreed that we would be brought to account for the crimes committed at Auschwitz and hoped either to die at the front or, if we were taken prisoner, to escape being identified as a physician at a concentration camp."[31] It was better to seek a hero's death.[32]

Their collective wish was not granted. They stayed on the grounds of an SS barracks in Oranienburg for a few days, joining a number of other SS personnel from Auschwitz, while their future assignments were being decided. The three physicians discussed their current situation and possible futures. Fischer claimed that while he expressed his belief that the war was lost, Mengele remained confident that Germany could still win with the deployment of Hitler's "miracle weapons." They also discussed what consequences they might suffer in connection with their crimes.[33] After a few days, Lolling ordered Mengele back to Gross Rosen with a promotion of sorts: he was to be the SS garrison physician (*Standortarzt*), with responsibility not only for camp prisoners but for all SS personnel assigned there.[34]

Mengele assumed his new responsibilities by February 5 but was immediately involved in the evacuation of the camp, which was liberated by the Soviets on February 13. It was not the first time that Mengele had been at Gross Rosen, a camp near the city of Breslau. It enjoyed a relationship with Auschwitz; Auschwitz had supplied labor to the various factories and work sites within the responsibility of Gross Rosen and had received in return shipments of prisoners no longer capable of work to be murdered in Auschwitz's gas chambers. We know that Mengele selected 996 women from Birkenau to be shipped to the Hochweiler subcamp of Gross Rosen on October 20, 1944,[35] and historian Bella Guterman claims that Mengele performed a selection of women in the Kratzau subcamp in February 1945, and that he was recognized by an inmate who had "strong memories of him from a similar event in Auschwitz."[36] Mengele also visited the Bernsdorf and Ober Altstadt subcamps in the Sudetenland, and in March 1945, he spent time at the Bad Warmbrunn subcamp, leading a committee of officers investigating an epidemic that had broken out there.[37] Although there is some question about Mengele's next steps,[38] in the days before the liberation of the main camp at Gross Rosen, he probably moved, with the camp leadership, to the Reichenau subcamp, which remained under German control until the very end of the war. Around this time, a witness saw Mengele in Ober Hohenelbe, another subcamp of Gross Rosen, about thirty kilometers from Reichenau.

Despite Mengele's hope that Hitler's new weapons would somehow rescue the Germans from defeat, the Allies continued their relentless advance from both east and west. Mengele's faith in Hitler's miracle weapons was misplaced, and his optimism could no longer be sustained. The collapse of the Third Reich was almost complete, and Mengele, who had pursued its goals faithfully to the very end, faced a profoundly uncertain future. His accomplishments were now liabilities, his ambitions had no prospects, and his loyalty had no beneficiary. He was untethered and alone.

PART III

FLIGHT

CHAPTER 6

CUSTODY AND CONCEALMENT

(May 1945–June 1949)

Interned

In the final days of the war, Mengele appeared at a German military field hospital in Saaz (Žatec), in the Sudetenland, a town famous for its herbal and spicy hops. Saaz lay to the west of Reichenau, and one could imagine Mengele ending up there in his attempt to make his way back to Germany. By coincidence, the head of internal medicine for this unit, Field Hospital (Kriegslazarettabteilung) 2/591, was Dr. Otto-Hans Kahler, a colleague of Mengele's from the institute in Frankfurt. At Mengele's request, Kahler asked the hospital commander for permission for Mengele to join up with them.[1] By joining this medical unit, Mengele was able to shed his incriminating SS uniform and dress himself as a German Army officer.[2]

Mengele could not have hoped for a better situation. Shortly thereafter the unit, with its newest member, moved west toward Karlsbad, the famous spa town, and then north, to settle near Oberschlema, in a forested area in the Erzgebirge (Ore Mountains). As Mengele wrote in his autobiographical novel, "At the end of the war, my unit was in Czechoslovakia, and on the night of the cease fire, we set out towards the west and reached Saxony."[3] They arrived in an area not yet occupied by the Americans or the Soviets. Described by Mengele as a no-man's-land, this stretch of unoccupied territory became, in the late spring of 1945, a sort of demilitarized zone, caught between the jaws of the Allied vise that had cleared Europe of German hegemony—from east to west and from west to east—before final postwar positions were established.

In this forest encampment, Mengele got to know his new comrades and developed a cogent cover story for himself that omitted his service in the SS and at Auschwitz and recast him as a Wehrmacht officer. Kahler, Mengele's former colleague, was worried about him—he appeared depressed and even spoke of suicide—and introduced him to Dr. Fritz Ulmann, a neurologist, who he thought might be of some help. Kahler recalled that Mengele spoke about Auschwitz, about selections and gas chambers, and commented that "old people did not have a chance there."

Mengele apparently got separated from Kahler when they moved into the forest encampment, and he grew close to Ulmann, who later claimed that at that time he did not know who Mengele was, although he suspected he was SS. Ulmann had a leadership position in the unit and was responsible for keeping track of the men in his charge. According to him, Mengele had used several different names by this time, including that of a famous Bavarian painter, Josef Memling. During their forced idleness in the forest encampment, Mengele and Ulmann discussed, among other things, their common childhood illness, osteomyelitis.

The medical unit bided its time, apparently making contact with the Americans located to the west but staying in place until their food situation grew critical. At some point, they decided to "break out," driving their vehicles in an orderly column toward the American lines. This likely occurred in mid-June, when steps were begun to clear the no-man's-land; Mengele and his colleagues wanted to ensure that they were taken into U.S., not Soviet, custody. As Mengele wrote in his autobiography:

With a few vehicles . . . we formed a column and managed to . . .
reach the Bavarian area. In the vicinity of the first big city, we
were . . . brought to an American prison camp. We had reached
our objective just as our supply of gasoline ran out. The Amis
[German slang for "Americans"] dragged us then from one camp
to another in which the rations got steadily smaller and our hopelessness greater. Finally, as the remnant of a camp that was being
closed, we were released into the American occupation zone, as
it had become known.[4]

Many in the unit came from Thuringia, northeast of their encampment, an area under Soviet occupation. The nurses in the unit were
not detained and were allowed to return home,[5] while the remaining
members of the field hospital were taken into custody and interned
in Schauenstein, in the vicinity of the German city of Hof, in Franco-
nia, near the Czech border. Established in late April or early May 1945,
the Schauenstein camp was located in the C.A. Waldenfels spinning
mill, which during the war had produced ball bearings and served as a
cloth warehouse for the German Navy. Mengele remained in Schauenstein for about six weeks, until late July, when he, along with Kahler
and Ulmann, were transferred to another POW camp in Helmbrechts,
to the south.

The camp at Helmbrechts had been established in early July on the
site of a former German labor camp by units of the 302nd Field Artillery Battalion, which had been in charge of a POW camp in Gera in the
Soviet zone until that area was ceded to the Soviets in late June. Discharging German POWs was "the order of the day at Helmbrechts";[6]
according to a battalion monthly report, more than two thousand
POWs were released during July alone.[7] In early August, Mengele,
Ulmann, and Kahler were released, each receiving an *Entlassungs-
schein*, or discharge certificate, a crucial document that proved they
had been screened by U.S. authorities and properly released, allowing

them to register with local authorities when they got home and permitting them to receive rations and other necessities. For some reason, Dr. Ulmann had a duplicate of his certificate and gave it to Mengele, who was able to alter it so that it appeared to be in the name of "Fritz Holmann"; he would use this name until he left Europe four years later.[8] The document was signed by Capt. Claudius J. Walker, who was transferred out of the Helmbrechts camp on August 8.[9] Discharged POWs were transported by U.S. Army truck to drop-off points within the U.S. zone.[10]

Several factors explain how Mengele could have been interned by American forces and then released, even under his own name.[11] The war in Europe ended on May 8, 1945, with the unconditional surrender of Germany, leaving a staggering number of German soldiers under the direct control of the Allies.[12] German prisoners overwhelmed the infrastructure that had been established to hold and process them. The United States had planned well for the occupation of Germany, training civil affairs officers and eventual administrators of POW facilities, but the rapid end of the war in Europe and the continuing conflict with Japan frustrated the careful preparations. Further, the army had instituted a system that credited U.S. soldiers with points based on the nature and length of their service. Many of the newly minted—and well-trained—soldiers destined for civil affairs positions had accumulated few points and were, therefore, tagged to participate in the planned invasion of Japan, leaving the high-pointers—combat-tempered, long-serving soldiers—to take up the civil affairs positions. This unforeseen reversal of roles saw infantry and artillery officers running POW facilities and trained guard personnel being shipped out to the Pacific.[13]

Even if the POW camps had been staffed by well-trained experts, however, the challenges would still have been daunting. There was a shortage of supplies, leading Gen. Omar N. Bradley to inform Gen. Dwight D. Eisenhower on May 6, 1945, that the supplies used by the Seventh Army to feed the disarmed enemy troops would run out that day, and that within four days, all the supplies that could be obtained from civilian sources in the area would be depleted; he concluded that "these disarmed forces will either have to be fed or released" and asked for immediate authority to discharge German POWs.[14] Whereas the Supreme Headquarters Allied Expeditionary Forces (SHAEF) could not authorize a blanket release, it did issue directives intended to expedite the discharge of prisoners.[15] A report by the personnel division of SHAEF dated June 14, 1945, revealed "anxiety" that the "present rate of discharge is not sufficiently rapid to enable disposal of prisoners of war and Disarmed German Forces to be completed before the water and before the food situation becomes acute." Perhaps in response to this fear and the dwindling food supplies, the following attitude toward discharge developed, as reported in early June: "discharge as many as possible as fast as possible without a great deal of attention to categories,"[16] and on June 29, SHAEF authorized what had already been going on for some time: a general discharge of German nationals held as prisoners of war, except those in automatic arrest categories, SS men, and war criminals.[17] With over three million German prisoners in custody, dwindling food supplies, and a significant and growing displaced person population with its own pressing needs and problems, this seemed like the only feasible strategy.

Given the provision that members of the SS and war criminals were not to be released, steps were to be taken to identify those who were to remain in custody or, if at large, be apprehended. The same conditions that led to the mass release of prisoners, however, applied to the safeguards against the release of those who should have remained in custody. Bureaucratic inefficiency, challenging numbers, and competing priorities conspired to frustrate sincere efforts to identify and secure war criminals. The printing and distribution of wanted lists was an imperfect enterprise: although Mengele's name had been included in the UN War Crimes Commission Wanted List no. 8, issued in May 1945, it was unlikely that that list had reached the units responsible for interning him. The Central Registry of War Criminals and Security Suspects (CROWCASS), established in Paris in 1944, published its first wanted list, incorporating the names, including Mengele's, from the UN War Crimes Commission wanted lists, in July 1945, but the distribution of this list had not been completed as of October 1945.[18] Despite energetic and well-meaning efforts, mundane ineptitude and logistical hurdles contributed to undermining this crucial endeavor.[19]

An additional—and key—circumstance stands out in explaining Mengele's successful escape from detection: he had no SS tattoo. It was standard practice for members of the Waffen-SS to have their blood type tattooed on the underside of their left arm, so that in the event a wounded soldier was unconscious, his blood type would be evident to those who treated him.[20] The presence of a tattoo was considered conclusive evidence of membership in the SS, and tattoos could be used as a litmus test in evaluating prisoners. Prisoners, without shirts and with raised arms, were forced to file past inspecting guards, who would immediately filter out those with tattoos for further examination and interrogation. Members of the SS became aware of the damning nature of the tattoo, and some attempted to have theirs removed. Tattooing, however, was not a universal practice.[21] As an SS medical officer, Mengele had been responsible for implementing the blood-type tattooing in his unit but was able to avoid it himself.

Ulmann recalled that after his discharge, Mengele was dropped off in or near Ingolstadt, a Bavarian city about one hundred kilometers from Mengele's hometown of Günzburg. He decided to visit an old school friend, Dr. Albert Miller, a veterinarian, who lived in Donau-wörth, about sixty kilometers to the west. Mengele arrived at the Millers' door "in the summer of 1945," wearing a uniform without insignia. He stayed for lunch and told his friend about his experience as a POW and about the two discharge certificates, one in his own name and one in the name of another physician. Mengele described how on his way to Donauwörth, he had encountered a farmer with two bicycles who, since he was going in the same direction as Mengele, let Mengele ride one. Concerned that he might be stopped by American troops, he decided to hide one of the certificates, which he accomplished by rolling it up and inserting it into the open end of one of the bicycle's handlebars. When they arrived in Donauwörth, the farmer continued onward, taking with him the bicycle Mengele had borrowed and, along with it, Mengele's concealed certificate—the one in his real name.[22]

Following their meal and conversation, Miller offered to arrange for Mengele to be driven to Günzburg, but Mengele declined. He would not be going home, Mengele told Miller and his wife, and asked them to let his family know that he was alive and that he would be traveling to visit a female friend who lived "near Gera or Jena," the second- and third-largest cities in Thuringia, located at that time in the Soviet zone of occupation.[23]

In his autobiography, Mengele wrote that he went to the Soviet zone to visit one of the nurses who had been with him at the field hospital in the "no-man's-land." What might have been Mengele's motive in visiting the nurse? We know that he had packed his research notes before leaving Auschwitz, and that he was taken prisoner without them. Could Mengele have arrived at Kahler's field hospital with his most important notes, perhaps culled in Gross Rosen so that they would be easier to transport? Could he have prevailed upon one of the nurses to take the notes with her when she returned home to Gera? Could Mengele have journeyed there to retrieve the fruits of his work in Auschwitz, which he had hoped would be the basis for one or more scholarly works that could propel his career? Although this theory is pure speculation, it accounts for the highly risky and assuredly imprudent trip to the Soviet zone, and answers the question of how Mengele would have been able to save what might have been most precious to him.

Whatever his motive for going to the Soviet zone, the evidence suggests that Mengele made the trip, although we do not know how long he remained there or where he ventured immediately afterward. In his autobiographical novel, he indicates that he ended up in Munich, where he stayed until mid-October. In Munich, he visited Fritz Ulmann, who

introduced him to his brother-in-law, Hans Weigel, a physician in Riedering, a small village south of Munich. Weigel offered to help Mengele
find work and a place to live, taking Mengele home to Riedering and
pointing him in the right direction to begin his search.[24]

The farm where Mengele found work—and where he was to live for
the next three years—was located in the small hamlet of Mangolding,
near Riedering, in the Rosenheim district. Situated in the foothills
of the Bavarian Alps, an area dotted with many beautiful moorland
lakes, Mangolding is perched on a small rise, from which one has good
views of the surrounding area, including the Kampenwand, a well-
known Bavarian peak to the south. There were four farms in Mangolding, including the one that became Mengele's temporary home.
Known as the Lechnerhof, it was less than twenty-three acres in size
and, at the time Mengele was there, had ten cows and a few horses
and grew potatoes, grain, and fodder. It was well off the beaten path—
an ideal place to lie low. The farm was owned and operated by Georg
Fischer and his wife, Maria. Georg's brother, Alois, worked there as
a farmhand and shared one of the upstairs bedrooms with Mengele,
who was now Fritz Holmann.[25]

The Farm Period

Beyond providing an opportunity for Mengele to keep a low profile and
escape the notice of American and German officials, his "farm period"
allowed him to take stock of his position and prospects: he clearly had
no future in Germany. With the exception of interviews conducted
with the farm family, our only source for Mengele's stay on the farm is
Mengele's own description of this period in his autobiographical novel.
These cover only the first year or so, and although lengthy—nearly
two hundred typed pages[26]—are short on plot and long on lengthy
discursions into a variety of subjects. Nonetheless, if we deconstruct
Mengele's autobiographical writings and distill from them the infor-

mation concerning the farm period, we can piece together the most important elements of his brief but pivotal time as Fritz Holmann.

We know that Mengele had the "misfortune" of "ending up with a very conservative and hardworking farmer, who demanded the maximum work from himself and his people." This no-nonsense boss required that Mengele work every day but Sunday, rise at four-thirty a.m., and spend "12 to 14 hours" in the fields or in the barn, tending to crops and animals. The work, which earned him ten marks per week, was difficult, and Mengele described in great detail the various tasks that fell to him and the variety of ailments that attended the draining physical effort.

The farmer's brother, Alois Fischer, appreciated his roommate's work ethic. Interviewed in 1985, he said:

> There was no work that was too dirty for him, he did everything the farmer asked him to do. He was physically very strong and got steadily stronger with the work. He learned very quickly. You only had to show him or tell him once, and he could do it. But he never spoke much. And he said nothing about himself, his past, or about the war. He did not want us to ask about those things. Everyone noticed that very clearly. He was neither friendly nor unfriendly, but rather always very controlled, disciplined.

Alois did describe one incident where Holmann's control and quiet bearing broke:

> Only once was there conflict: Although he was just a farmhand, he ordered me once to haul hay down from the barn. I told him to do it himself. He became angry, only briefly, but very intensely. He looked at me with rage; I thought he was going to attack me. But then he was in complete control again. That only happened once and never again.[27]

Fischer described Holmann as having an immense appetite, eating everything that was placed before him, without ever commenting on how it tasted, and drinking astonishing quantities of milk, "by the liter." Holmann was "very good-looking, like a cat," intelligent, and he spoke with a "slight Bavarian accent, always very quiet and concise." It was evident to Alois that Holmann came from a good home.

Alois's sister-in-law, Maria, the farmer's wife, described Holmann as being set distinctly apart from the locals by his speech and the way he expressed himself. He was very industrious, although he gave the impression that he had never done farmwork before. She thought he might have had an intellectual profession; he was always reading and writing. She also noticed that he frequently washed his hands. Holmann was reserved, kept to himself, rarely spoke about himself, and performed his farmwork to her husband's satisfaction. He would occasionally go to church on Sundays and from time to time would be absent for a day, but he rarely left the farm.[28]

From his brother, Karl, who managed to visit him, Mengele learned about the fate of his family in the wake of the war. Both his father and his youngest brother had been interned: Karl Sr. by the Americans, because of his Nazi Party affiliation, and Alois as a POW in Yugoslavia. Irene and Rolf, along with Irene's parents and Mengele's mother, had been evacuated to Autenried, a small village nearby, shortly before the Americans "conquered" Günzburg. Karl Jr. himself was banned from working at the family firm because of his Nazi Party affiliation and could not enter the offices or the factory. He had appointed longtime employee and confidant Hans Sedlmeier as trustee and thereby was able to maintain control of the business and circumvent the measures taken by the occupation authorities. The business came through the war without significant damage, escaping Allied bombs, which fell instead on their grandparents' home and destroyed it.

Yet even though she survived the war, Mengele's mother died in January 1946. She was living in the vicarage in Autenried when she was taken ill and sent to the hospital. Mengele suspected, based on Karl's account, that she was treated by "substitute physicians" who replaced "suspended colleagues," and that these "idiots" had "flushed" his "mother's edema far too quickly." Mengele devoted significant space in his autobiographical novel to mourning his mother and emphasizing her role in his life, holding the family together. He dwelled on the influence of her Catholic religion and her efforts to raise her sons within the faith. In one unusual section, he reflected, in an imaginary conversation with his mother, on how she would have reacted to news about him and the "smearings and hate propaganda" she might have heard on the radio: "Naturally, you did not believe all that. You know me."

Mengele also describes how he saw Irene during this period, once when she visited him near Mangolding, and once when he surprised her on vacation in Oberstdorf, the village in the Allgäu Alps where the two had been married.[29] Irene told Mengele that she had never expected to see him again and had imagined that he committed suicide. She brought him up to date on what had transpired since they saw each other last, including a visit from American soldiers when they were living in Autenried.[30] She described a "nice" American officer who was very taken with Rolf, and his Jewish interpreter, who alleged that Mengele had been responsible for the death of five million of his "tribal brothers." She claimed that the American officer had not believed the number and "negotiated the number down" to four million. Irene also described how Martha, Karl's wife, had entered the occupied home of Mengele's parents under some pretext and had been able to take a photograph of Mengele off the wall and hide it between the cushions of a club chair, out of view of the Americans.

Neither meeting with Irene was satisfactory from Mengele's point of view. Irene was distant and pessimistic about the prospects of their ever being able to enjoy a normal life together. She knew of the allegations against her husband, having recorded in her diary in early May 1945, before the war was over, that his name had been mentioned on the radio in connection with Auschwitz and later, in early October, that a newspaper article mentioned a Josef Mengele, "who had watched people die with animal pleasure."[31] Her pessimism, which Mengele described as "hopelessness," was likely fueled by the news of the verdicts in October 1945 of the International Military Tribunal (IMT) at Nuremberg, the subject of a long, discursive detour in Mengele's writing, in which he described Nuremberg as "an unquestionable farce" and "political theater." There was news as well of preparations for a new set of trials, conducted by the Americans at Nuremberg, focusing on different components of the Nazi state. The first one, which began immediately following the IMT, placed twenty-three physicians in the dock and became known as the Doctors Trial, which started in December 1946.[32]

Irene was also clearly aware of the denazification effort, begun by the Allies and taken over by the Germans, intended to rid Germany of the influence of National Socialism by identifying and removing from public life anyone who had contributed to the Nazi state in any meaningful way. As a first step in the denazification process, every German male above a certain age had to fill out a questionnaire (*Fragebogen*), detailing his activities and memberships during the Nazi period.[33] Given these early and energetic efforts by the Allies to rid Germany of Nazi taint and punish those responsible for war crimes, it was natural that Irene would counsel her husband to leave Europe as soon as possible.

Aware of the threat to her husband posed by the Allies' ongoing attempts to seek out and prosecute Nazi war criminals, Irene did what she could to protect him: she pretended that he was dead. A former resident of Günzburg, Julia Kane (née Hebel), recalled that Irene Mengele had acted after the war as if her husband were indeed dead; a priest in Günzburg, Father Kneer, had told Kane that Irene had revealed to him that her husband was missing "in Poland" and requested that the priest conduct a "memorial mass." Charlotte Terstegen (née von Schmidt auf Altenstadt), a former employee of the U.S.

Military Government Detachment in Günzburg after the war, also recalled Irene wearing black and following other conventions of a woman in mourning. The wife of an investigator for the U.S. Military Government Detachment recalled in March 1986 that she had heard that Irene had "taken steps to have her husband declared officially dead by the authorities."[34]

The ruse apparently worked. Responding to an inquiry about Mengele in January 1948, Gen. Telford Taylor, the American chief counsel for war crimes, reported, "Our records show Dr. Mengerle [sic] is dead as of October 1946."[35] Mengele's father's denazification file indicated that his son was "missing."[36] Finally, a radio broadcast of April 1946 may have reported that Mengele had killed himself.[37] His family's deliberate misrepresentation clearly contributed to this widespread misconception on the part of the public and the authorities.

Though Mengele was still alive, his marriage, he realized, was dead. Irene raised the question of divorce at one of their meetings, to which he responded, "Perhaps later, as camouflage." When Irene then asked, "What does later mean?" Mengele understood that his marriage was over.

Leaving Europe

We can date Mengele's decision to leave Europe to the fall of 1948. He had many personal reasons for doing so, not the least of which was his belief that his wartime activity made it impossible for him to resume a normal existence. He had no desire to continue to live underground, and he knew his safety could not be guaranteed. If he ever wanted some semblance of a satisfying life, it could not be in Germany, certainly not at the moment and not for some time. He wanted to leave behind manual labor and anonymity and may have hoped for the possibility to resume the scientific pursuits that had so animated him.

Mengele's decision took place in a larger context that would have a profound effect on the postwar history of Germany. In June 1948 the Allies instituted a major currency reform in Germany's western zones, which involved a contraction of the money supply, with tax cuts and the elimination of price controls—a comprehensive restructuring that in essence denazified the German economy. These changes, in addition to the significant investment of Marshall Plan money, fueled the powerful engine that would drive the German economy forward in the so-called *Wirtschaftswunder*, which would resurrect Germany as an economic power.

The currency reform had an immediate and substantial impact on Mengele's life. The farmer who had employed him for three years would tell a journalist in 1985 that because of the currency reform, he could no longer afford to employ his farmhand, Fritz Holmann.[38] Mengele left the farm on August 1, 1948, and his whereabouts for the next nine months are a matter of speculation. Rolf would tell journalists in 1985 that his father spent this time living in the forests near Günzburg and maintained contact with his family, which makes some sense; he needed their help—both logistical and financial—to leave Germany.[39]

In the years after the war, business at the Mengele firm had resumed and soon took off. The patriarch, Karl Sr., had been released from detention and was joined by his two sons, Karl Jr., who was subjected to denazification, and Alois, who was released from internment as a POW in Yugoslavia in 1949. The business was well suited to profit from the immense effort to repair and rebuild Germany. Their most popular product in the immediate postwar period had a single wheel: the firm's wheelbarrows hauled away rubble and conveyed building material throughout Germany.[40]

The financial success of the company made it possible for Mengele to leave his homeland and, at the same time, made it necessary for him to renounce any claim on the firm. As long as he had a financial interest in the company, he could put it at risk should he ever be captured and brought to trial. In January 1949 Mengele visited a notary and formally abandoned his interest in the family business.[41]

THE SOUTH TYROL, or Alto Adige, as it is known in Italian, is a region in the north of Italy that played a significant role in the escapes of many Nazis and war criminals. Referred to by one historian as "Nazi Bolt-Hole Number One," this alpine region, known for its apples and wine, has always been a gateway of sorts to Europe by way of navigable passages through the Alps. Bordered by Austria and Switzerland, and offering access to the rest of Italy, the South Tyrol's history in the first half of the twentieth century suited it well as a means of entry and a way station for Nazis seeking a European exit.

Along with its majority German-speaking population, the South Tyrol had been separated from the Austro-Hungarian Empire at the end of World War I and annexed to Italy in 1920. Under Mussolini, there had been an attempt to Italianize the province, limiting German-language education, changing German names, and encouraging southern Italians to relocate there. Hitler's assumption to power encouraged the German-speaking population of the South Tyrol, but the Führer was more interested in gaining Mussolini's support than he was in inducing Germans to break away from Italy. In October 1939, Hitler and Mussolini agreed to the so-called *Option für Deutschland*, a referendum to be completed by the end of the year that would allow the ethnic German population of the province to decide whether they wished to remain in place, renouncing their German identity and retaining their Italian citizenship but surrendering their minority rights, or "opt" to emigrate to Germany and take on German citizenship. They were to be settled in areas of Austria or newly conquered land in the east as part of the massive shift in population that occurred at the beginning of the war.

About 85 percent of the affected population, approximately 250,000 people, "opted" for Germany; the rest, the so-called *Dableiber* (Remain-ers), elected to stay. By 1943, when the Germans occupied and virtually annexed the area, only about seventy-five thousand people had actually emigrated. With the end of the war, the status of the South Tyrol was an open question: would it go to Austria, or remain Italian? And the status of the ethnic Germans was likewise ambiguous. They had renounced their Italian citizenship and were considered by the Italians to be foreigners; they had the status, in effect, of displaced persons. As a result of the Optants Decree in 1948, those who had formerly chosen to renounce their Italian citizenship could now regain it. The South Tyroleans enjoyed a unique status among German-speaking minorities in Europe in that they were spared expulsion after 1945—a fate that befell their brethren in many other places.[42] Italian prime minister Alcide De Gasperi said at the end of 1945, "The only area that offers the Germans protection and asylum is Alto Adige."[43]

The preferred exit route for someone wishing to leave Central Europe was through one of the Italian ports. For Mengele, this meant crossing into Italy by way of Austria and the Brenner Pass. Once in Italy, he could obtain the necessary identification documents and make his way to Genoa. He, of course, was not alone. In the postwar years, literally millions of refugees undertook the journey, with a range of motivations. Some were trying to return home; some sought a reunion with loved ones; those with no hope of reaching home or family sought a future elsewhere. Many were war criminals, but there were also ethnic German expellees from Eastern Europe and the Soviet Union and other displaced persons who had no place to go. Holocaust survivors made their way to Palestine from Italian ports, and anti-Communists and Nazi collaborators sought refuge from Soviet-occupied lands. As historian Gerald Steinacher, an expert on Nazi escape routes through the South Tyrol, summed it up:

> Italy turned into a nerve center for streams of refugees . . . whose goal was to reach the Italian sea ports. Obstacles were especially

present in Central Europe: the internal German borders with their controls and restrictions and the Alps, a barrier to Italy, that had to be overcome. But there, structures were available that had been established for the purpose of smuggling. The border between Austria and South Tyrol had been under strict surveillance since 1918, yet in spite of that, it had always been porous. The system had worked itself out: experienced mountain guides knew the right paths and people.[44]

Mengele's departure from Europe was a challenge, but one that many others faced and for which there were people willing and able to help.

Mengele began his autobiographical account of his departure from Europe with a literary device, *in medias res*—diving into the middle of the story and then, in a flashback, revealing its beginning. He started with a lengthy description of a train trip from the South Tyrolean border town of Brenner: "Fate always accompanies you on a train journey." Can it be that when he wrote these words, several decades after the event, he made no connection to the hundreds of trains he had greeted at their last stop on the ramp in Auschwitz, or the fate that he had determined for the hundreds of thousands of people whom he encountered, the vast majority in the final hours of their lives? He displays no awareness of this irony as he describes in some detail his own fears and revels in his intense self-absorption as his train arrived in Sterzing, also known as Vipiteno, the northernmost city in Italy, just on the other side of the Brenner Pass from Austria.

He accounts for his successful entry into Italy by way of a detailed description of his departure from Innsbruck on Good Friday, which fell on April 15 in 1949. He was driven along a scenic alpine road about thirty kilometers south to Steinach am Brenner, an Austrian outpost very close to the Italian border, by one of several men who would assist him at every stage of his escape. There he waited until nightfall, when he was taken by taxi to the Kirschbaum Inn, in Gries am Brenner, a tiny village very near the border. In Gries, Mengele met the man who was to lead him across the border. Despite awkward literary foreshadowing—"The pendulum clock on the wall ticked noisily, and the half-hour stroke sounded metallic and intrusive. It was time to depart"—the actual crossing of the border proved, for the most part, unexciting. On foot, Mengele navigated the challenging terrain and descended toward Italy. Successfully avoiding a roving patrol of Italian border guards, he arrived at his destination on the other side of the first of several hurdles that stood in the way of his departure from Europe. In the early morning hours, he boarded the train with which his account began and arrived in Sterzing.

The Golden Cross Inn in Sterzing became Mengele's home for several weeks and served as a staging ground for essential preparations for his journey. One of Mengele's helpers arranged for him to be photographed for an identity card "like the ones issued in the period of the German occupation," and a few weeks after the photographs were taken, the identification documents arrived. Mengele described them as "really perfect and incontestable, if they were inspected by a representative of the Italian state who was prepared to accept as valid and sufficient such a bi-lingual document." Mengele benefited from the historical and geographic context from which his new identification purported to derive. Many from the South Tyrol had such identification, dating from the second half of the war; the Italian authorities accepted their IDs, satisfied, in the end, that at least some form of identification was being offered.

Mengele's ID, purportedly issued in Tramin on April 11, 1948, was in the name of "Helmut Gregor," born August 6, 1911, in Tramin; profession, "mechanic." Historian Gerald Steinacher found that Tramin was also the place of issuance for the ID cards of other Nazi escapees, including Adolf Eichmann and Joseph Goebbels' aide Erich Müller. Tramin, located south of Bozen (Bolzano), "was well known as a stronghold of the Völkische Kampfring Südtirol, a Nazi-oriented group. The provisional mayor of the town had easily managed to set aside blank ID card forms during Nazi rule in South Tyrol between 1943 and 1945."[45] Since mayors who had served during the period of German control were permitted to remain in office until the summer of 1945, they had both the means and the opportunity to produce fake IDs to accompany their motives to protect former Nazis and to profit from doing so. Steinacher points out as well that all applications made for identity cards in Tramin for the year 1948 had disappeared, despite the general policy and practice of the municipality to preserve them.[46]

A week later, in mid-May, "Erwin," one of Mengele's helpers,[47] shared greetings from Mengele's father and friends, whom he had seen in Germany. He brought with him more money; although Mengele had not yet spent a great deal, he would need the funds for his long journey. Erwin also brought with him a "box of scientific specimens"—a curious and provocative reference that could very well relate to the material that Mengele had collected through his experiments at Auschwitz. With the delivery of the money and the "box," Erwin announced, his optimism "as buoyant and comforting as the May weather," that all the necessary preparations for the departure had been accomplished. A few days later the guide appeared and informed Mengele that the date had been set and that the final steps of the journey would take him through Bozen and Milan to Genoa and finally to Argentina.

Mengele traveled by train to Bozen, where he met up with "Hans," who filled him in on what was going to happen. "This evening, when it gets dark, we will visit an influential individual, from whom you will receive an Argentine 'permesso de libero desembargo' [landing permit]. Before that, this afternoon, we will meet in a cafe the man, with whom you will travel to Genoa, by way of Milan."

When they arrived in Genoa, Mengele met his newest—and last— escort, "Kurt," who immediately purchased passage on the *North Queen*,* scheduled to depart five days later, for 120,000 lire. Kurt

---

* Mengele uses the name *North Queen* to refer to the ship; the ship's real name was *North King*.

explained that such "emigration ships" did not sail every day and were often quickly sold out. He then described the next steps:

> What you need now is a passport, which will permit you to travel, and that we will obtain from the Swiss consulate. There, on the basis of your identity card, you will be issued an International Red Cross passport. We'll take care of this this morning. And tomorrow we will take care of the formalities at the Argentinian consulate.[48]

They then headed to the Swiss consulate, and on the way, Kurt coached his charge about exactly what he should say.

When Mengele informed the older man who greeted him at the Swiss consulate that he had come to apply for a Red Cross passport, the man seemed not at all surprised. And when Mengele told the "no longer so very young" woman behind the counter what he sought and the reasons why, she absorbed it all with a patient forbearance, looked him deep in the eyes, and repeated as if by rote her petitioner's wish: "Okay, you want a Red Cross passport for emigration to Argentina because, as a South Tyrolean, who, during the war, lived in Germany, you cannot receive a passport from either the Italians or the Germans due to uncertain nationality. Your identity card serves as a basis for your claim." After a pause, she added, "It can be done because, according to new regulations, the Red Cross will help all those in need without extensive research." The woman went to work, writing intently and then asking for two photographs, which were dutifully provided. After only a brief wait, unheard of for a passport office, the finished Red Cross passport was handed to him with a "knowing smile." As Mengele left the consulate, the man who had greeted him at the door asked in a "confidentially prying" way, "Where do you really come from?" Mengele responded, with self-assurance, "From the South Tyrol, naturally. Quite honestly," and left the old man behind with an "annoyed and disappointed" look on his face.

Mengele was able to encapsulate in this short scene in his

autobiography both the rationale and the routine for acquiring a Red Cross passport, an essential element in the escape of so many Nazis for departing Italy and gaining entry to South America. The International Red Cross had been issuing such travel documents since 1945; Red Cross passports had been recognized by the United Nations since 1946 as substitute documents and could be used by refugees to emigrate to Brazil, Bolivia, Paraguay, Argentina, and North America.[49] This indispensable document was issued "to all persons who had been compelled by the war to leave their country of residence and could not obtain any passport." South Tyroleans, who had opted for Germany but still resided in Italy, were eligible for such refugee identification by virtue of their "unresolved" nationality. A close examination of the language used in the passport indicates both its lack of probative value and its desirability: "The present document has been established at the request of the bearer and because he has stated that he possesses no regular or provisional passport and that he is unable to procure one."[50] Contributing to the flimsiness of the document was its very composition; its photograph was attached with paste and had no stamped embossment, which meant that it could be replaced or substituted without evident trace.[51] The ease with which it could be obtained represented a low threshold for the many who wished to exploit it for illicit purposes.

Mengele's next task was to obtain a certification that he had no tax obligations, and then a so-called begging certificate, which indicated that he had never begged in Italy or been the recipient of public welfare. On the following day, when Mengele visited the Argentine consulate to have the *permesso de libero desembargo* certified and to obtain a visa, the sharp-eyed official noted that the Red Cross passport, which Mengele had received only the day before, had already expired. The woman at the Swiss consulate had mistakenly entered the same date for issue and expiration. This careless oversight required a return to the Swiss consulate, where the error was corrected without apology. Mengele went back again to the Argentine consulate, where, without further reason to deny him, the necessary seals and stamps were applied, and certifications were issued. Upon return of his papers, Mengele was informed that a physical examination was required: "Only physically and mentally healthy people could immigrate to Argentina."

Mengele and Kurt headed to the port, where Argentine physicians examined those passengers who would be leaving on the *North Queen* in a few days. They were concerned about infectious diseases and the highly contagious eye affliction trachoma, or Egyptian ophthalmia, but carried out the exam using the same "glass rods"[52] and the "same unwashed fingers." This lack of hygiene caught Mengele's attention; the search for the disease could very well be the agent of its spread. Armed with his health certificate, Mengele and Kurt headed to the city center, where he would be issued a certification from the public health authority stating that there was no record of his ever having been treated for a nervous or mental condition.

The objective for the rest of the day was to obtain a vaccination certificate, which he was able to accomplish through another contact of Kurt's, a Croatian physician who had been stuck in Italy after the war. The certificate was supposed to confirm that the bearer had been vaccinated within two weeks, and that a follow-up inspection revealed that it had been successful, but instead of a vaccination, Mengele received a cup of coffee, the necessary document, and despite the precariousness of the Croat's financial situation, a "professional discount" from his "colleague." With this additional piece of fiction, Mengele's collection of fraudulent documents, attestations, and certifications was complete, with the exception of his exit visa from Italy, which he would obtain the next day.

This last formality did not turn out as he expected. On the way to the prefecture the next morning, Kurt made a telephone call and discovered that the official who was supposed to issue the visa was away. "I can't take care of this for you, you must try it yourself," he told Mengele, giving him the folder containing all the documents they had collected over the past two days and advising him to place a twenty-thousand-lire note on top. With this file in hand, Mengele entered the prefecture, mounted the stairs, and was met by an official, who took the folder from him, extracted the "bookmark," and returned it to Mengele without saying a word. Mengele thought that perhaps the proffered bribe was not large enough, but he soon learned that something else was amiss. He was asked for a document that he did not possess and was aggressively interrogated, a process that ended with his arrest and confinement in a cell in the basement of the prefecture.

After a tense night, Mengele was interrogated by the same official, who accused him of committing horrible crimes against Italian prisoners of war. In response, Mengele simply smiled, shook his head, and repeated that he came from the South Tyrol. The next day the "inquisitorial" questioning focused on Kurt and whether Mengele had paid him any money, which Mengele denied. He was forced to lead the police to the pension where he was staying, and his baggage was retrieved and brought to the prefecture. In the course of the questioning, Mengele learned that the *North Queen*, which should have been under way by now, had thankfully not yet left port.

At this point, Kurt's contact reappeared, and everything changed for Mengele. His once-aggressive interrogator now became his friend, accompanying him to the ship's agent to straighten out his passage, which, because of his failure to report on time, was in jeopardy. When Mengele learned that there were no more places in tourist class and that a second-class ticket would require an increase in fare, he was ready to pay it. His companion, the police official, however, would not hear of it and was able to arrange for a four-man cabin in second class for the reduced tourist-class price.

The next morning Mengele and his baggage, including *"Preparados histo-patologicos para un estudiante de medicina no valor comerical"* (Histopathological specimens for a medical student, no commercial value),[53] arrived at the port and began the process of embarking. He presented his dossier with its hard-won contents, and after careful review, he was ushered along and finally made his way on board. Here Mengele's autobiographical novel takes on a philosophical tone:

> As the ship pulls away from the harbor and begins its journey in the Ligurian Sea [Mengele] stands on the deck, looking down at the gray-green waves divided by the keel, which run along the ship's side. He sees only the waves roll by inexorably and unchanging under him. His thoughts are as fleeting as the waves. "Waves," he says half aloud to himself, "waves, everywhere waves." When they announced that the ship had crossed the three-mile limit, he startles. So it is, if you emigrate, he thinks, and goes to his cabin.[54]

The ship would take him to a new continent, which would be his home for the rest of his life.

CHAPTER 7

CALM AND STORM

(June 1949–July 1962)

Mengele arrived in Argentina on June 20, 1949, beginning a period of relative stability. Following his years of hard labor, isolation, and caution, he could now reclaim some measure of his lost status and eventually his own name. He could again enjoy cultural pursuits, with visits to theaters and concert halls, which Buenos Aires offered in surprising numbers. He could cultivate the life of the mind, with access to libraries and bookstores, attendance at lectures, and contact with informed and sophisticated people. He lived unthreatened and in relative safety in Argentina for nearly a decade—until he was forced again to abandon his name and seek refuge elsewhere.

Argentina

When Mengele, under the name "Helmut Gregor," arrived in Buenos Aires after four weeks at sea, he expected to be welcomed by a Dr. Rolf Nuckert, a physician whom he had met in 1939. Nuckert was to pick him up at the port, arrange lodging, and introduce him to representatives of the German community in Buenos Aires.[1] But Nuckert never showed up; instead, Mengele had to go it alone and negotiate the arrival formalities himself. The customs officials showed particular interest in one of his suitcases, the one that "Erwin" had delivered to him and that may have contained his medical notes. When informed of the suitcase's contents, the customs agent summoned a physician at the port—who, not speaking German, could not understand what he was looking at; Mengele was allowed through. With no one there to meet him, Mengele joined two shipboard companions and moved into the "third-class" pension Palermo, with a shared bedroom and a toilet down the hall. The next day he set out to meet a Dr. Schott in search of employment. Schott worked as a consulting engineer for a textile firm in the center of Buenos Aires, and as Mengele made his way there on foot, he passed by the Casa Rosado, Juan Perón's presidential palace, and saw the palace guard in their military finery. The image so impressed him that he commented in his diary about the stabilizing influence of military traditions, lamenting that "the New Germans" had "sacrificed them on the altar of their feelings of collective guilt and servility."[2]

When Schott offered him a menial position as a wool comber, Mengele declined and accepted a position elsewhere as a carpenter, which came with a room in the Vicente López district that he had to share with an engineer. The arrangement was not satisfactory to Mengele, who had already had to put up with such close quarters, without privacy, during his years on the farm. The intimate living arrangement also allowed his roommate to draw some conclusions; having seen some medical equipment among Mengele's belongings and noting his refined speech, he suspected that Mengele was not originally a carpenter by profession. When the engineer's daughter, who lived with the engineer's estranged wife, became ill and could not get a bed at the German hospital, the engineer beseeched Mengele, whom he thought to be a physician, to treat her. Though at first hesitant to admit his medical background, Mengele soon relented—overcome by the Hippocratic oath's prescription to provide treatment to those in need. After swearing the engineer to secrecy, he agreed to treat his daughter.[3] Mengele discovered that she suffered from scarlet fever. Turning a storeroom in the pension into an isolation ward, he tended to her with cold compresses, ordered light meals and chamomile tea, and gave her sulfonamide tablets.[4]

Despite the disappointing start to Mengele's new life in Argentina, things began to look up for him in September 1949, when he was able to move into the home of Gerard Malbranc, a known Nazi sympathizer. Malbranc provided not only comfortable living arrangements, with his spacious colonial-style residence in the posh suburb of Florida, but also entrée into the circles of prominent expat Germans and influential right-wing Argentines. It was through Malbranc that Mengele met Willem Sassen, a Dutch Nazi collaborator and journalist, who became famous as the host of a series of taped conversations with Adolf Eichmann in 1957.[5] Sassen, a ghostwriter for many expat Nazis, contributed regularly to the right-wing German-language publication *Der Weg*. He was also, at the time Mengele met him, the driver for German air hero Hans-Ulrich Rudel, a Luftwaffe colonel credited with 2,530 combat missions—Hitler's most decorated soldier. Mengele grew close to Rudel, who had a network of friends who would prove very useful. Rudel had teamed up with Constantin von Neurath, the son of Hitler's foreign minister who had been imprisoned at Nuremberg, to form the *Kameradenwerk*, a "fund for legal and emergency aid, to help those who had been brought low by the failure of the Reich's final victory."[6] Mengele also befriended the prominent architect Federico Haase, who had his own influential circle; his wife's father would later become Alfredo Stroessner's finance minister when he seized power in Paraguay in 1954.[7]

Mengele obtained his Argentine "alien identity card," issued in the name of "Helmut Gregor," on September 17, 1949, listing the Malbranc home as his address. During this early period in Argentina, Mengele received significant support from his family, and his father visited him at least once, probably in July 1952.[8] Mengele also took advantage of the family firm: it exported expensive woodworking equipment (saws, planing and milling machines) indirectly to him in Argentina, which he then sold at a profit to customers in the building and lumber industries. In addition, he established a small business with only a few employees in Buenos Aires that produced wooden toys.[9] In 1953 Mengele moved into his own apartment and began to travel to Paraguay, where, through Rudel,[10] he made the acquaintance of Werner Jung and army officer Alejandro von Eckstein. Both were Nazi sympathizers and became valuable contacts. Von Eckstein was an old army buddy of Alfredo Stroessner, and Jung was branch manager of Ferreteria Paraguay SA, which represented a number of machine and tool manufacturers, including Karl Mengele and Sons.[11] According to Jung, Mengele "really started to push the family business from 1954 on." He was especially keen on selling "a device to distribute manure and carts to haul dirt and equipment."[12]

Mengele was doing well financially. He moved to the predominantly German suburb of Olivos and acquired a Borgward Isabella automobile in 1954, possibly arranged for by his father. He applied for a driver's license; his former landlord and friend, Gerard Malbranc, as well as another acquaintance, certified to his "upstanding" character. One can imagine Mengele's satisfaction at regaining some of his former standard of living and status, even if he was far from home. Although still living under an assumed name, he had a stable material base and a growing circle of influential friends. During this early period in Argentina, Mengele was introduced to Adolf Eichmann by Willem Sassen, though by all accounts, the two were never close friends; Mengele was reportedly uncomfortable with the "downtrodden aura of fear surrounding Eichmann, whom he regarded as a broken man."[13] Sassen assessed them as "completely different kinds of people," noting that Mengele had financial means, something that Eichmann never did. In their respective escapes from Europe to South America, both men took a similar route, though while Mengele spent the weeks of waiting in a comfortable hotel, Eichmann had spent his time in a monastery.

Mengele also returned to his science during this period, publishing an article on genetics under the name "G. Helmuth" that appeared near the end of 1953 in *Der Weg*.[14] Beyond the subject and the pseudonym, evidence that the article was written by Mengele can be inferred from Mengele's association with others who wrote for the publication: both Rudel and Sassen were frequent contributors. The article, "Heredity as a Biological Process," is an introduction to genetics, covering the basics of hereditability, Mendelian laws, and genetic pathology.[15]

As Mengele settled into his new life in Argentina, a major part of his former life came to an end. Irene, who refused to follow him to South America, sued for divorce. While Mengele was hiding on the farm in Mangolding, Irene had met Alfons Hackenjos, recently released from a POW camp, having been captured while serving with Rommel's Afrikakorps. By early 1954, she was prepared to marry him. Irene informed the Mengele family that she did not expect any support from them. There were, however, legal formalities that had to be addressed. Irene appeared in court in Düsseldorf and gave the following statement, misrepresenting when she had last seen her husband and couched in the formal terms necessary to meet the legal requirements for divorce under German law:

I last saw the defendant in November 1944. Since that time, I have had no personal connection to him. We have corresponded with each other concerning maintenance support. I no longer believe that the conjugal partnership between the defendant and me can be resumed. Our marriage is broken, the defendant did not return to me and in fact emigrated to South America in 1948, and no longer takes care of me. Under no circumstances am I prepared to resume the marriage with my husband.[16]

Why Irene had told the court that Mengele emigrated in 1948 instead of the real date, 1949, is unclear.

For his part, Mengele executed a power of attorney in Buenos Aires on November 16, 1953, authorizing his lawyers to represent him in the proceedings in Düsseldorf, where Irene was living at the time, and instructed them to offer no opposition to his wife's petition for divorce.

Irene wasted little time and married Alfons Hackenjos on October 5, 1954, in Freiburg, where she moved in July of that year.

With his son now divorced, Karl Mengele Sr. saw an opportunity to solve two problems. His second son, Karl Jr., had died suddenly of a heart ailment in December 1949 at the age of thirty-seven, leaving Karl's wife, Martha, a widow. Martha had fallen in love with Karl while still married to Wilhelm Ensmann, whom she divorced on March 9, 1948, in order to marry Karl on February 3, 1949. The paternity of her son, Karl-Heinz, born in 1944, was the subject of a court battle after the divorce, with the court ultimately deciding that Karl-Heinz was the natural son of Karl Mengele Jr. The family was now concerned that Martha would dilute the family's financial interests in the firm should she remarry outside the family, and Mengele's father hit upon the idea that she marry Josef. It is unclear how well Josef knew Martha; it was important that the two should meet to test the viability of Karl Mengele's scheme.

It took time to arrange the meeting, and Mengele received a number of visits over the next two years. Hans Sedlmeier, the trusted family friend and executive in the firm, traveled to Buenos Aires, as did Mengele's younger brother, Alois, along with his wife, Ruth. It was decided that Mengele would travel to Europe, which meant that he had to obtain a passport. He applied to the Argentine Federal Police in April 1955[17] for an "alien passport" under the name "Helmut Gregor," requiring a certificate of good conduct, which was issued to him on September 1, 1955, and he received the passport, valid for only 120 days, in mid-November.[18] In March 1956 he flew to Switzerland with a brief stopover in New York City. He was met in Geneva[19] by Hans Sedlmeier, who then drove him to Engelberg, Switzerland, where he registered at the best hotel in town. Waiting there were Martha, her son and Mengele's nephew, Karl-Heinz, as well as Mengele's son, Rolf—who believed Mengele to be his uncle. Mengele spent a week in Switzerland getting to know Martha and Rolf, who was apparently fascinated by his "Uncle Fritz," who gave him pocket money and told stories about gauchos on horseback in South America. He also talked about the war; Rolf recalled in 1986 that "nobody spoke about the war, it was taboo," and as young boys, he and his cousin, Karl-Heinz, were "very interested to hear about . . . the fighting and the actions . . . and he told us about his anti-guerrilla actions in Russia."[20]

Mengele spent some time in Günzburg visiting with family, according to Hans Sedlmeier, during questioning by the Frankfurt Prosecutor's Office (Staatsanwaltschaft) in December 1984. Sedlmeier said nothing about the gathering in Switzerland; instead he described how Mengele stayed in Martha's home in Günzburg. He also revealed that Mengele accompanied him on a business trip to northern Germany, during which he visited with colleagues from his time at Verschuer's Frankfurt Institute. Sedlmeier dropped Mengele off at the Nassauer Hof Hotel in Wiesbaden and collected him there a few days later. Mengele told Sedlmeier that he was meeting an Argentine manufacturer of gas meters, who was visiting Germany[21]—but he likely visited his mentor Otmar von Verschuer at his home in Solz, an hour and a half drive from Wiesbaden.[22] Rolf told an interviewer that Mengele also went to Munich during this trip and visited the couple who had helped him at the end of the war before he made his way to Mangolding. While in Munich, Mengele had a minor traffic accident but was able to avoid a confrontation with the police by giving the other driver some money.[23]

Mengele left Germany and returned, via Switzerland, to Argentina. In addition to his reunion with family, former colleagues, and friends, he had been able to see his son again and share relaxed and playful moments. Perhaps most important, his visit had proven his compatibility with his brother's widow. Mengele now began to plan for his wedding to Martha and her move to Argentina, and he made the decision to jettison his assumed identity as Helmut Gregor and resume his life as Josef Mengele. This decision, whether motivated by his relative success in recent years and the lack of any evidence that he was in danger, or by the impact of his trip to Europe, required that he approach the German embassy in Buenos Aires and secure the necessary documents to obtain an Argentine identity card under his true name.

On September 11, 1956, Mengele received a document from the German embassy certifying his identity as Josef Mengele, born March 16, 1911, in Günzburg, and that he was divorced. Mengele would have had to produce his birth certificate, presumably obtained during his visit to Günzburg, and testify that he had been living under a false name, "Helmut Gregor," since his arrival in Argentina in 1949. One wonders why the German embassy or Foreign Office was not suspicious of a man who clearly had something to hide. With the certificate in hand, Mengele applied for an Argentine identity card, which was issued to him under the name "José Mengele" on November 26, 1956. In the same month, he was issued a new German passport (no. 3415574), completing the official resumption of his old identity. Martha and her son, Karl-Heinz, joined Mengele in Buenos Aires in October 1956, and they moved into a new house that Mengele had purchased in Olivos (Virrey Vertiz 970), which was registered in the name of Karl Mengele & Sons.

With his identity once again intact and believing his years of hiding were behind him, Mengele began to resume his life's passion for science. Mengele had known Dr. Ernesto Timmerman for several years and, according to Elsa Haverich, an assistant to Timmerman, used to visit him almost daily at Wander Laboratory, a pharmaceutical firm. When she met Mengele, whom she knew as Dr. Gregor, he was running his small woodworking shop, which she and Timmerman visited once. In October 1957 Timmerman and a man named Heinz Truppel invited Mengele to join them as a partner in a fledgling pharmaceutical company called Fadrofarm. Mengele brought not only scientific sophistication and experience but half of the venture capital—five hundred thousand pesos—needed for expansion. Most of the money came from his family in Günzburg, and the rest from the proceeds of Mengele's sale of the woodworking business. Ulrich Völklein maintains that Sedlmeier, on a visit to Buenos Aires in 1957, conducted due diligence on behalf of the family firm before the deal was approved.[24] In a financial disclosure statement, dated August 24, 1960, Fadrofarm described its business as the "production and distribution of drugs, medicines, and medicinal specialties." In the same disclosure, "Dr. Jose Mengele" is described as "Dr. of Chemistry, a native of Germany."[25]

Elsa Haverich recalled her first encounter with Mengele at Fadrofarm, some years after she had met him with Dr. Timmerman:

> He came into the office one afternoon. I called him "Dr. Gregor" at that moment because to me he was "Dr. Gregor." Then he corrected me and told me that, "No it is Dr. Mengele." Joking a little bit, I asked him why he changed his name. He answered that it was for political reasons; when he got out of the war, he had to do it with another name.[26]

She said that Fadrofarm manufactured a drug for the treatment of tuberculosis called Resorpas, which was considered very effective. Likely Resorpas was a brand name for para-aminosalicytic acid, known by the acronym PAS, which, used alone and in combination with other drugs, was considered state-of-the-art in 1957. Truppel reported that Mengele used to "do studies of new products for treatment of tuberculosis" and used to read many "medical and scientific books."[27] Haverich said that Mengele, who worked every day at Fadrofarm, was not involved in production or administration but "used to make studies about tuberculosis and he used to prepare reports after that." It appears as though he may have been responsible for compliance issues, since Haverich noted that his reports were presented to "public health" officials. Mengele would read "German scientific books, for example about medicine." She described him as always whistling classical music.[28]

Although Martha and Karl-Heinz had by now joined Mengele in Argentina, their being together accomplished only part of Mengele's father's plan. His son now had the companionship and stability of a fam-

ily, but it was important that he also be legally and unassailably married to Martha to protect the family's legacy. Mengele had renounced
his own interest in the family firm when he left Germany in 1949, and
only through a legal marriage, recognized in Germany, would he be
able to regain it—or rather, the interest of his deceased brother, which
had been passed to Martha. He began the process in the summer of
1957; it was decided that they would get married in Uruguay, presumably because his divorce from Irene was less a problem there, given
that Uruguay, unlike Argentina, recognized "absolute divorce," which
meant that one was permitted to remarry after divorce.[29]

Nevertheless, Mengele needed to assemble documentation from
Germany that would prove that both he and Martha were in a legal
position to wed. The necessary records proving the death of Martha's
husband and his divorce from Irene needed to be certified, by the relevant officials in Germany, and those certifications then had to be
authenticated, in turn, by the Uruguayan consul in Munich and the
Uruguayan Foreign Ministry. The red tape stretched from August 1957
to the spring of the following year, when Mengele was finally able to
submit the requisite paperwork to the civil authorities in the Uruguayan
town of Nueva Helvecia (New Switzerland), where the wedding was
to take place. Located a few miles from the coast in the Department
of Colonia, Nueva Helvecia was about a four-and-a-half-hour car ride
from Buenos Aires, including a ferry ride across the Río Plata. It had
been founded by Swiss immigrants in 1862 and became the home for
immigrants from Austria, Germany, and France who were welcomed
with open arms by Uruguay.

In organizing the marriage, Mengele was helped by the lawyers
Himoff and Germán, who prepared the relevant documents and used
their influence to expedite the proceedings. The judge who officiated
was a former priest named Pedro Izacelaya, and the witnesses were
the lawyer Juan Carlos Germán and his wife Lidia Florio de Germán,
both of whom testified, falsely, that Mengele and Martha were living in Nueva Helvecia. The wedding took place at five p.m. on July

27, 1958.[30] Uruguayan law required that a notice be posted publicly and published in the newspaper stating the intention of the couple to marry and inviting anyone who knew of a reason why the marriage should not take place to notify the civil authorities within eight days. The notice, which should have been published on July 17, eight days before the date of the wedding, did not appear in the newspaper until July 26, the day after the wedding. This delay was clearly intended to permit the bride and groom to leave town before their nuptials were made public.[31]

Schnabel and Schüle

While Mengele was putting the final touches on his wedding plans, a series of events were set in motion near his hometown in Germany that were to have a defining impact on the rest of his life. In March 1958 Ernst Schnabel, a prominent radio personality and author, who had been an officer in the German Navy during the war, published a book entitled *Anne Frank: Spur eines Kindes* (Anne Frank: Trail of a Child).

The slim volume was the idea of Anne Frank's father Otto, who had survived the war, and the head of a German publishing company, Dr. Gottfried Bermann Fischer. Although Anne Frank's diary was first published in German in 1950, it did not sell well, and Frank, believing it important that his daughter's work be distributed widely in Germany, organized an inexpensive paperback edition, which was published by Fischer Bücherei in 1955. It sold thirty thousand copies in the first month. The wide popularity of the book, which reached sales of 375,000 by the spring of 1957, led to a demand for more information about Anne Frank, including her fate following the events described in the diary.

At the same time, questions were raised about the authenticity of the diary, spurred in part by differences between the Dutch- and German-language editions. To address the thirst for more information and to dispel the doubts, Otto Frank and Dr. Fischer approached

Ernst Schnabel to write the rest of Anne's story based on interviews with individuals who had encountered her. Frank contacted the New York–based German-Jewish immigrants' magazine, *Der Aufbau*, seeking publicity for the project in the form of an article or advertisement that could help identify anyone whose path had crossed that of Anne or her mother or sister in Auschwitz or Bergen-Belsen. Schnabel contacted Anne's childhood friend Miep Gies in 1957, seeking "living, tangible people so that the reader can feel that Anne was living among real people and not among paper witnesses."[32]

Schnabel's book was a great success, appearing in many editions and in twenty-one languages. Following its publication in March 1958, it was serialized in a number of newspapers throughout Germany, including in the *Ulmer Nachrichten* that summer. One reader, a young girl, having read the excerpt of Schnabel's book published on July 1, 1958, felt moved by a single sentence to write to the author. The sentence maintained that "no one knew . . . where Dr. Mengele was, whether he died or whether he still lived somewhere." The "young reader" wrote on July 7, 1958:

> Apparently, some people do know. . . . Otherwise the older Herr Mengele in Günzburg would not have told his former housemaid . . . that his son, who was an SS doctor, practiced medicine in South America under a different name. And because he was so homesick, Mr. Mengele sent the widow of another son over there.[33]

Not knowing where Ernst Schnabel lived, the young girl addressed her letter to the newspaper in which the excerpt from Schnabel's book appeared, the *Ulmer Nachrichten*, which forwarded the letter on to Schnabel's publisher, which, in turn, delivered it to him.[34]

Receiving the letter, Schnabel wasted little time. On August 3 he wrote to the state prosecutor in Ulm, a city close to Günzburg, the town mentioned in the letter as the residence of Mengele's father: "I feel compelled to bring to your attention several issues that could—I am obviously not competent to judge—potentially lead to an inquiry by your office."[35] He went on to describe his book, the broad public exposure it had received, and the anonymous letter that he had recently received and was enclosing. "The letter concerns itself with the concentration camp physician Dr. Mengele, who is mentioned on page 138 of my book. Mengele appears to have been one of the most dreadful people in Auschwitz." Schnabel provided the prosecutor with a reference to Gerald Reitlinger's 1953 book *The Final Solution*, which contained information about Mengele, and concluded his letter:

> The anonymous tip about Dr. Mengele is a tenuous reason to get involved in the case. One would usually throw such a letter in the trash. . . . [However,] if her message helps to prevent a monster, like Dr. Mengele from Auschwitz, from continuing to work as a physician anywhere in the world, it would accomplish something very good for humanity, for us Germans, and for our deeply sullied German name.[36]

Without knowing it, Schnabel, in his desire to do something positive, both helped to initiate the case against Mengele, and significantly contributed to Josef Mengele's escape from justice.

Schnabel's letter landed on the desk of Erwin Schüle, a senior prosecutor in Stuttgart, who was, at that moment, immersed in a criminal case that would represent a watershed in West German justice. Over the past two years, Schüle had single-handedly revived a moribund investigation that would fundamentally alter the way Nazi war crimes were investigated and prosecuted in Germany. The changes he helped usher in were part of a larger process of *Vergangenheitsbewältigung*— coming to terms with the past—that for more than a decade had taken a backseat to the more pressing priorities that occupied the energy and focus of the German population, and to the emerging realities of the Cold War.

Schüle's case, which he had investigated and prepared with unprecedented determination and ingenuity, was, by the beginning of August, winding down after a three-month trial. He was seeking the conviction of ten men who had served together in a Nazi killing unit in the days following the invasion of the Soviet Union. These men, all members of Einsatzkommando Tilsit, were charged with participation in the murder of more than five thousand Jews in the German-Lithuanian border area in 1941. The lead defendant was Bernhard Fischer-Schweder, a member of the Nazi Party and a high-ranking SS officer, who had been the head of the police in Memel at the beginning of the war and had personally led the mass killing of Jews. Fischer-Schweder had only himself to blame for coming to the notice of German prosecutors; it was his own narcissism and self-promotion that had led to his prosecution, not the work of investigators and prosecutors.

Many of the Nazi war crimes cases in West Germany in the 1950s came about not through systematic investigation but through flukes and coincidence. But even after charging an individual, German prosecutors faced significant hurdles in proving their cases. Their biggest obstacle was, in some ways, the law itself. The West German criminal code was ill suited to prosecuting Nazi crimes, which had been committed within a state structure. These murders were not, for the most part, ordinary criminal acts but were committed with the knowledge, encouragement, and sponsorship of the state. As such, the question of individual motivation was muddied at best, and here German law proved itself particularly ineffective since, in the case of murder, the question of motivation under the German code was central and far more nuanced than it is under U.S. law.[37] Already wielding a dull instrument, German prosecutors also operated in an inauspicious environment, given the pressures of the Cold War and German reintegration, and compounded by the presence of so many with compromised pasts within the judiciary and police. All these factors conspired to make the 1950s a period of relative immunity for Nazi war criminals, a state of affairs that clearly benefited Mengele.

Before Erwin Schüle assumed control of the investigation into

Fischer-Schweder, it had lumbered on under its various burdens for more than a year, yielding a collection of contradictory allegations that would not, in all likelihood, have met the burden of proof for an indictment. With the case against Fischer-Schweder headed toward dismissal, Schüle took command, approaching it with considerable energy and creativity, charting a new course for investigating Nazi crimes. He sought the involvement of archives—he was the first prosecutor since Nuremberg to use the Berlin Document Center—and of historians and Jewish organizations, and he initiated judicial assistance requests to locate witnesses and evidence in other countries. His approach was to not focus exclusively on the criminal himself but to extend the inquiry to the crime and its all-important context. His indictment read in part like a history text: in addition to describing the specific crimes in question, he laid out the organizational structure of the police and the systematic nature of the criminal acts that had been committed. Anticipating the likely defense claims of superior orders, he carefully accounted for the role of personal initiative and individual conduct.

All ten defendants were convicted of being accessories to murder, arguably a lesser offense than they had committed. This discrepancy was another consequence of the German criminal code and how it was applied to Nazi crimes. German courts deemed the leaders of the terror structure of the Reich—Hitler, Himmler, and Heydrich—to have been the chief perpetrators, leaving those who served under them vulnerable only to charges of being abettors and accomplices. Still, ten men were found guilty of having participated in the mass murder of innocents, and the carefully prepared case served a didactic purpose of educating the public about crimes of which many were ignorant, and about the men who had carried them out.

In the aftermath of the Fischer-Schweder trial, justice officials of the West German *Länder* began to try to coordinate future activities in connection with investigations of Nazi crimes. They created a central authority, staffed by prosecutors and investigators, who would initiate investigations and assist in the prosecution of Nazi-era crimes that had taken place outside German borders. The Central Office of the Justice Administrations of the *Länder* for the Investigation of National Socialist Crimes (Zentrale Stelle der Landesjustizverwaltungen zur Aufklärung nationalsozialistischer Verbrechen) opened its doors on December 1, 1958, and Erwin Schüle was named its first director. Within a short time, it launched hundreds of investigations and set in motion a systematic approach to the investigation of Nazi crimes. Historian Jeffrey Herf summarizes the impact of the Fischer-Schweder trial: "Journalists, liberal politicians, lawyers, and intellectuals now called for a systematic examination and judicial prosecution of Nazi war crimes and crimes against humanity. The era of democratization based on silence and integration was coming to an end, and a more intensified period of West German judicial confrontation with Nazi crimes was beginning."[38]

When Schüle received the August 3 letter from Schnabel, he interpreted it as a *Strafanzeige,* or criminal complaint, and forwarded it, on August 12, to the state prosecutor in Memmingen, the office that had jurisdiction over Günzburg. That Schüle considered Schnabel's letter seriously and forwarded it to the relevant authority so quickly was surprising given that he was immersed in the Fischer-Schweder case, having delivered his closing argument only the day before. Perhaps Schüle's work had sensitized him to the particular weight and significance of Josef Mengele's crimes. Schüle's accompanying memorandum named an individual who, it was believed, could provide additional information about Mengele and his whereabouts. In addition, Schüle informed his colleague in Memmingen that he had received information that Josef Mengele's father had recently shipped an automobile to him in Argentina, and he suggested that the customs authorities in Günzburg might be able to supply a current address. He cautioned that such an approach should be made without alerting Mengele's family to the existence of the investigation.

The prosecutor's office in Memmingen acted upon Schüle's letter within a week and tasked the Bavarian criminal police to pursue all the leads that it contained. They, in turn, assigned the job to the police branch in Günzburg, which handled the assignment with thoroughness and dispatch, providing a response to Memmingen five days later, on August 25, 1958, a few days before the verdict in the Fischer-Schweder case.

The police, based on inquiries to their colleagues in Freiburg, Frankfurt, Düsseldorf, and Munich, and confidential information received through the mayor of Günzburg, were able to compile a detailed report on Josef Mengele.[39] It traced his whereabouts through his official residential registrations, from birth through 1944, his marriage to Irene Schönbein in 1939, the birth of their son in 1944, and his divorce in 1954, with the important information, contained in the court file on the divorce, that Josef Mengele's address in Argentina was, at that time, Sarmiento 1875 Olivos, in Buenos Aires. The police also reported that Mengele did not return to Günzburg following the war and was considered missing in action for a long time. Several years before, a rumor had begun to circulate that he lived in Argentina. His father was supposed to have visited him in Switzerland and, another time, traveled to Argentina to see him. There was also much speculation about Martha Mengele's move, along with her son, Karl-Heinz, to Argentina, in 1956, supposedly to marry a rich American there. A note in the files from the guardian court in Günzburg indicated that Martha and her son lived in Lalucila, Argentina. However, no records could be located to confirm the widely suspected marriage between Martha and Josef, which had occurred exactly one month before. The police were also able to learn that, in the summer of 1957, Hans Sedlmeier, a senior executive in the firm and an intimate friend of the family, spent four weeks in Argentina.

The three important results of their investigation were the proof that Josef Mengele had survived the war; that his last known address in Germany had been in Freiburg; and that he resided in Argentina. The first provided a crucial predicate for an investigation, the second determined its jurisdiction, and the third introduced an enormous obstacle before it even began.

Hermann Langbein, the general secretary of the International Auschwitz Committee, was also hard at work building a case against Mengele and was in contact with German judicial officials and with Simon Wiesenthal. Langbein, who had been a prisoner in Auschwitz and had worked in the office of *Standortarzt* Eduard Wirths, had had frequent contact with Mengele in Auschwitz. When Gerald Posner interviewed him in April 1985, Langbein recalled how he had found the records relating to Mengele's divorce from Irene in 1954, which indicated that he was living at that time in Argentina.[40] Langbein wrote a memorandum outlining nine criminal charges against Mengele and submitted it to the federal prosecutor in Bonn on September 19, 1958.[41] Without a last known address for Mengele, however, the appropriate jurisdiction for the case could not be identified, since jurisdiction was determined by the residence of the accused. On November 12, 1958, Langbein's associate, the lawyer Henry Ormond, wrote to Langbein and reported that he had been able to view Mengele's personnel file from Frankfurt University and determined that Mengele had been married to Irene, who bore him a son in Freiburg in 1944 and resided at "Sonnhalde 81." Ormond suggested that Langbein might be able to determine "through his friends" whether Mengele had been registered in Freiburg, indicating that, while he could make the inquiry himself, he did not want to "warn the man" unnecessarily.[42] Langbein turned to the prosecutor in Freiburg,[43] who took six months, with significant assistance from Langbein, to develop the case and seek a warrant for Mengele's arrest, which was issued by the Freiburg court on February 25, 1959.

With a warrant and evidence that Mengele was living in Argentina, the obvious next move was to petition the Argentine government to arrest Mengele and extradite him to Germany—though German justice officials had reason to doubt that an extradition request to Argentina would be successful, given that a number of previous attempts had been unsuccessful.[44] Responding to the Foreign Office, which had reported on its poor record with such requests, the Freiburg prosecutor wrote:

> To orient you, it should be noted that there is extremely incriminating witness testimony against Mengele, that he is repeatedly mentioned in the literature about persecution, and that, according to surviving Auschwitz prisoners, he was one of the most responsible for the atrocities that occurred there. There is likely to be, therefore, considerable political interest in getting hold of him.[45]

The argument worked. The prosecutor in Freiburg issued a second, revised arrest warrant on June 5, 1959, and, a month later, the German Foreign Office asked its embassy in Buenos Aires to begin the process of petitioning for Mengele's extradition.[46] Since there was no extradition treaty between Germany and Argentina, the case would have to be submitted first to the solicitor general for a recommendation, and then the Argentine Foreign Ministry would have to determine that the extradition was in the "best interest" of Argentina.[47] It took more than a year for the German extradition request to make its way through the warrens of the Argentine system, slowed by technicalities and a lethargic bureaucracy.[48]

The Argentines' handling of the matter led officials at the embassy to believe that there was little hope of extradition.[49] Nevertheless, on June 2, 1960, the Germans were finally able to perfect their submission, leading Attorney General Lascano, on June 24, to decide that the extradition could proceed.[50] Ten days later Judge Jorge Luque issued an order for Mengele's arrest.[51] Much, of course, had happened in the year since the decision had been taken to seek Mengele's extradition. By the time his arrest was ordered, Mengele had been gone from Argentina for months, had settled in Paraguay, and had obtained Paraguayan citizenship.

The prosecutor's office in Memmingen had made a crucial mistake in including the local police in its investigation. Günzburg was a company town, and the Mengele firm was the company. The business dominated its economic life, and the Mengele family played a significant and deeply rooted role in many aspects of the community. It would have been nearly impossible to conduct any kind of investigation there without encountering someone with a connection to the firm or the family, and news of the inquiry was sure to spread. The chain of events precipitated by Schnabel's letter to Schüle on August 3 led to the involvement of the Günzburg police in mid-August, and then, most certainly, to the Mengele family being informed, and, in turn, to Mengele learning of the ominous news.

Schnabel's letter defined an inflection point in Mengele's life; sent six days after his marriage to Martha—an act designed to secure his future—it heralded, instead, the end of any sense of security he might enjoy and marked the beginning of his new life on the run. By the end of September, Mengele, anticipating flight, executed a general power of attorney granting his wife authority to act for him in all matters and legal transactions.[52] At the same time, the Israelis, whose sights were on Adolf Eichmann, learned from Germany's failed attempt to extradite Mengele that, if they wanted to place Adolf Eichmann on trial, they would have to take matters into their own hands.

Paraguay

According to Gerald Posner, Mengele arrived in Paraguay on October 2, 1958, on a ninety-day visitor visa. Mengele had been traveling to Paraguay for years, but this time he knew that his life in Argentina would never be the same, and he likely began to explore the possibility of making Paraguay his new home. It had much to recommend it. The political environment in Paraguay was far more welcoming than in Argentina, now that Juan Perón, with his broad acceptance of Nazi émigrés, was gone. The current Argentine president, Arturo Frondizi, a former human rights leader, had less sympathy for the former Nazis who had taken refuge in his country. After Perón's departure, Paraguayan strongman Alfredo Stroessner, who had family roots in Bavaria, opened Paraguay to Nazi fugitives, and it even became a haven for the deposed Argentine dictator. There were well-established German communities in Paraguay, and Mengele had good friends and contacts there. Perhaps most important: Paraguay prohibited the extradition of its citizens.

Mengele returned to Argentina at the end of 1958, and a short time later the prosecutor in Freiburg issued the first arrest warrant for him. We must assume that Mengele learned about this ominous event through his family and their connections with local law enforcement. The news removed any chance that Mengele could remain in Argentina, whose new government could not be counted on to protect him. Mengele had to dissolve his relationship with Fadrofarm to free significant capital to fund a new life in Paraguay. Elsa Haverich recalled Mengele arriving at the office one day and simply saying he had to leave the country.

> I asked him "Why? What is going on?" I thought maybe it was his
> family, or an illness, or even an accident. Then he told me, very
> sadly, no, it was because of political reasons. I didn't ask too many
> questions, because he looked a bit worried. The following day, the
> day he had to go, he arrived later, at noon. He looked very quiet
> that day. He was very sad, very worried. It was about 5:30. He took
> some books to return to the library—he was always reading science
> and medical books—we got in the car. He gave me a lot of advice
> about the company and what we should do and I said, "I'll see you
> again?" Then he told me, "Elsa, we will never meet again."[53]

Mengele officially separated from the pharmaceutical firm on March 31, 1959, selling his share to Ernesto Niebuhr.[54]

Mengele made his move to Paraguay sometime before May 1959, when he registered with the Paraguayan police; the alien registration files carry the name "José Mengele." On October 24 he applied for Paraguayan citizenship and, six days later, was issued a "good conduct certificate" and a residency permit by the police.[55] Accompanied by his friends Alejandro von Eckstein and Werner Jung, who served as witnesses, he appeared in November before the supreme court in Asunción in connection with his naturalization. During the proceedings he had to swear, supported by the testimony of his witnesses, that he had lived permanently in Paraguay for five years and that he intended to renounce his German citizenship. In addition, he had to demonstrate through the submission of the good conduct certificate that he had no police record or legal encumbrance that could interfere with his naturalization, and he had to show proof that he had deposited five thousand guaranis in the Bank of Paraguay. Having satisfied the requirements, José Mengele became a citizen of Paraguay on November 27, 1959.[56]

Ten days before Mengele's naturalization, his father died in Günzburg. It has long been speculated that Mengele traveled to Germany in order to attend the funeral, but had he done so, he likely would have been apprehended. On November 21 Henry Ormond, an attorney who represented several Auschwitz survivors in restitution cases and as civil plaintiffs in the Frankfurt Auschwitz trial, notified the prosecutor in Freiburg that Mengele might try it; the relevant border and customs officials were warned, and the Günzburg police undertook to stake out the funeral.[57] If Mengele made plans to return home, his contacts in Günzburg likely warned him against doing so.

The protections he enjoyed as a newly minted Paraguayan citizen notwithstanding, the fact that Mengele was still the subject of an active arrest warrant, with German judicial and diplomatic agencies attempting to have him extradited—albeit from a country he had already exited—argued for him to keep a low profile in his newly adopted country. He did exactly that, living on a farm in Hohenau in the southeast of Paraguay as the guest of Alban Krug, a friend of Hans-Ulrich Rudel.

Mengele did venture out of his secure location at least once, in April 1960, when he met with Hans Sedlmeier and Martha in Asunción at the Grand Hotel.[58] There was much to discuss now that Mengele had moved, including a new, safe communication system and the details for his continued financial support. They then spent a few days in Encarnación in the Gasthaus Tirol, owned by Armand Reinaerts, a Belgian friend of Mengele's. Sedlmeier later told German prosecutors that he did not visit Mengele's home, but that Martha had confided that her husband lived in "extremely primitive" conditions. Martha would later claim that this visit was the last time she saw her husband.[59] She lived in Buenos Aires for a short while after Mengele's move, but in early 1961 she left for Switzerland, where Karl-Heinz was attending a boarding school, and later settled in Merano, Italy.

The abduction of Adolf Eichmann in Argentina in May 1960—and his removal to Israel to stand trial—changed everything for Mengele. Although he may have been safe from extradition, the proven ability and willingness of the State of Israel to reach beyond its borders and engage in extralegal actions to mete out justice made all previous calculations meaningless. Emerging from a pseudonymous existence and resuming family life would now be impossible. He had to disappear, in a place that was large enough and in which there was not yet a trace of him. Although he had contacts in Paraguay, his visits there over the years had left footprints that he feared Israelis could follow. He chose Brazil. Because he could not simply venture there without help, he turned to Hans-Ulrich Rudel.

Mengele left Paraguay for Brazil in mid-October 1960, carrying a Brazilian identity card under the name "Peter Hochbichler," supplied to him by Rudel, who also introduced him to Wolfgang Gerhard, the man who would become his guardian. Gerhard, an Austrian in his mid-thirties who lived in São Paulo and operated a textile printing business, made the practical arrangements for Mengele's life in his new home. He was only too happy to help, writing to Rudel that he considered the opportunity to be of service to "Dr. Dr. Mengele"* not only a significant "vote of confidence" from Rudel but also a "huge personal honor."[60] Before emigrating to Brazil in 1949, Gerhard, who had risen to a leadership position in the Hitler Youth, had lost none of his passionate connection to the Nazi cause, choosing to name his firstborn son "Adolf" in 1958.[61] In Brazil he distributed *Der Reichsruf,* the organ of the Socialist Reich Party (Sozialistische Reichspartei, SRP), an extreme right-wing political party backed by Rudel that had been banned by the German Constitutional Court in 1952.

"We've found him, the little shit!"

Mengele's decision to go to Brazil carried substantial risk. The Mossad report on Mengele, published in 2017, provides considerable detail on just how close it had come to capturing him and how quickly and thoroughly it had penetrated the security that was supposed to protect him. That he was not captured once the Israelis identified Wolfgang Gerhard in 1962 was a confounding failure, made all the more baffling given the exquisite instincts and ingenuity that brought them so close.

On January 8, 1960, Mossad chief Isser Harel, alerted to the possible presence of Mengele in Argentina by Simon Wiesenthal, asked his associate Efraim Ilani—the Mossad representative in South America—to look into the matter. Ilani was unable to provide concrete intelligence but informed Harel about the German extradition request and the less than helpful response offered by the Argentine government. In the late winter and early spring 1960, while the Mossad was planning its operation to capture Eichmann, it also attempted to find Mengele's address and looked into a number of possibilities without success. It did not know that Mengele had already left Argentina for Paraguay.

On May 15, 1960, five days after Eichmann's capture, and while he

* Mengele's two doctorates meant that he could be referred to as "Dr. Dr."

was still in an Israeli safe house in Buenos Aires, his Israeli captors questioned him about Mengele. Eichmann admitted that he had met Mengele three times. The first was in 1951, in a pension in Vicente López. In 1952 they had met in a garage while Eichmann was having his company car repaired. He claimed that Mengele shared space with the car repair shop, probably describing the business Mengele operated before he bought a share in Fadrofarm. Their third meeting took place in 1954 or 1955, in a plumbing business in the Buenos Aires suburb of Florida. At first Eichmann knew Mengele only as Dr. Helmut Gregor, though he assumed it was an alias; only later, after there had been a lot of publicity about Mengele and his crimes, did it occur to him that Gregor might have been Mengele. Willem Sassen confirmed his suspicion.[62]

Before leaving Argentina with Eichmann, Isser Harel made one last attempt to locate and capture Mengele. He sent an agent to the address of Mengele's workshop inquiring after "Gregor," who, the agent claimed, had once sold him machine parts, which he needed again. That operative having no luck, Harel sent another to check Mengele's other known addresses, but neither calls to the current occupants nor inquiries of the mailman turned up anything useful. Robbed of the satisfaction of adding a second prize to his ambitious mission, Harel and his team departed Argentina in the final act of a brilliant operation: Mossad operatives, posing as flight crew, helped a sedated Eichmann, dressed in the uniform of an El Al flight attendant and appearing drunk, aboard a waiting El Al plane, which was in Argentina to transport the Israeli delegation to the sesquicentennial of Argentine independence from Spain.*

The Mossad then turned its attention to another figure who was in a position to provide significant information. Within a day of being

---

* One member of the Israeli delegation was the future Israeli foreign minister Abba Eban, who was then unaware of the Eichmann abduction or the presence of the long-sought Nazi on his plane.

apprehended, Eichmann told his captors about the Dutch journalist Willem Sassen, who had recorded many hours of conversation about Eichmann's role in Nazi Germany and his activities related to the capture and deportation of Jews. Born in 1918, Sassen had volunteered for the Waffen-SS in June 1941 and had been wounded twice on the Russian front. He became a military correspondent and in 1944 was appointed editor of the journal *Telegraph*. Though taken prisoner by the Canadians, Sassen was able to escape at the end of December 1945 and made his way to Argentina, arriving in 1947. There he worked in theater and took up his former profession of journalism, writing for American and German newspapers. In Buenos Aires he met Eberhard Fritsch, the founder and publisher of *Der Weg*, and became an editor of that publication. After Eichmann's capture, unsigned articles based on the taped conversations with him appeared in *Life* magazine in the United States and *Der Stern* in Germany, which the Mossad concluded had been written by Sassen.

The Mossad reasoned that if Sassen had been successful in getting Eichmann to talk, he was likely to know a great deal about other Nazis in Argentina. Moreover, his publishing of the inculpatory Eichmann "memoirs" implied that he was willing to "betray" people whom he had befriended, and the modest $2,500 fee he received for the Eichmann articles suggested he needed money. This combination of factors led the Mossad to begin an active operation to recruit the Dutchman.[63]

The Mossad turned to a contact in Buenos Aires, a Jewish journalist who had been in touch with Sassen, and were able to convince him to meet with the Israelis. Harel assigned Zvi Aharoni, who had played a major role in the abduction of Eichmann, the task of recruiting Sassen, and Aharoni was finally able to meet him in October 1961. He showed Sassen the German extradition request sent to Argentine authorities, which detailed the crimes of which Mengele was accused. According to Aharoni, Sassen expressed shock at the alleged actions of the man he had known in Buenos Aires. "I believe it, but I do not want to," he said, though Aharoni was not certain that the reaction was authentic.

Aharoni assessed Sassen as motivated more by the pursuit of "sensation and money" than by "ideals, principles, and conscience." Aharoni learned as well that Sassen had another powerful motive for working with the Israelis. The Dutchman was afraid that the Israelis would promote the claim that he had assisted them in the capture of Eich-mann; a false rumor to this effect had been circulating in right-wing circles in Argentina, and the Israelis were more than willing to exploit it. Aharoni concluded that his new recruit possessed significant information about Mengele and was willing to share it.

At a meeting in Paris at the beginning of December 1961, Sassen told Aharoni that he knew a man who maintained regular contact with Mengele. "Mr. X," as Sassen referred to him, met with the fugitive every six months. Sassen admitted that he had had contact with Mengele's wife, Martha, and his business partner Ernesto Timmermann, as recently as December 1960, but that only "Mr. X" maintained contact with Mengele himself. Sassen reported that Timmermann had assisted Mengele with his flight to Paraguay in 1959, after the extradition request had been filed. He indicated that Martha Mengele had returned to Europe, settling in Switzerland, and that the Timmermann family had adopted the Mengele family dog. Sassen said he was convinced that Mengele would not be in communication with Martha, whom he described as a "big fool."[64]

The two met again five days later, in Munich, and Aharoni was able to persuade Sassen to reveal the identity of Mr. X: Hans-Ulrich Rudel. Based on his conversations with Rudel, Sassen had learned that Mengele was living about thirty miles outside São Paulo, in an isolated house, guarded by armed men; that he was depressed and had considered suicide; and that he was not in contact with his family in Europe. Rudel also informed Sassen that the German prosecutor suspected a man named Hans to be the link between Mengele and his family in Günzburg, though he claimed they suspected not him, Rudel, but Hans Sedlmeier, who worked for the family firm.

Aharoni and Sassen had another meeting that December, this time at the airport in Zurich, during which Sassen shared his fear that Rudel was suspicious of him. Rudel was aware that transcripts of Sassen's tape-recorded conversations with Eichmann had come into the hands of Israeli prosecutors and had been mentioned in Eichmann's trial; Sassen believed that Rudel suspected him of providing this damning evidence to the Israelis and was consequently reserved with him during their most recent meeting. Nevertheless, Sassen concluded that the former air ace was the only person in Europe to have contact with Mengele, and that with "90 percent certainty," Mengele was now living in Brazil. He provided Aharoni with the name and telephone number of a pharmacist in São Paulo, Robert Schwedes, a close friend of Rudel's with whom Rudel stayed when he was in São Paulo.[65]

In early April 1962, the Mossad sent an officer to São Paulo to try to locate Schwedes. In addition to surveilling the pharmacy and Schwedes's home, the Mossad, with the help of local agents, made inquiries with local government, utilities, and tax agencies. Later, Sassen informed Aharoni that Rudel was going to visit Brazil in mid-June 1962. Sassen offered to assist Israel in apprehending Mengele on the condition that Rudel receive immunity—a condition that Aharoni immediately accepted. After the meeting, Aharoni wrote to Harel:

> I am almost convinced that [Mengele] is not in [Paraguay] and has not been there since June 1960 when he left in the direction of [Argentina]. All the threads point to [Brazil], and the thread that seems to me the most reliable from all the threads (Artist-Singer [Sassen-Rudel]) points to [São Paulo].[66]

Aharoni was able to persuade Harel, who directed that the appropriate resources be committed.

The Mossad believed it had identified Rudel's forthcoming flight— a KLM plane from Amsterdam to Rio with a stop in Lisbon—and had even placed two spotters on the plane, but Rudel postponed his departure from Europe. All efforts to account for Rudel's whereabouts failed; he seemed to have simply "vanished." Finally, on June 29, 1962, Sassen telegraphed the Mossad in Brazil that Rudel had arrived in São Paulo, and the agency dispatched officers to commence their surveillance of individuals in São Paulo, including a man called Hens and the pharmacist Schwedes. On June 30 they observed Rudel and Hens leaving Hens's residence by taxi and riding to the city center. There they met an unknown person and rode in his white Chevy convertible to Schwedes's pharmacy, where they picked up his wife and drove to their home. That night Rudel and Hens were dropped off at Hens's residence by the unknown man; the Mossad surveillance team noted the license plate on the white convertible—which they learned was registered to one Wolfgang Gerhard.

The next day Rudel was observed taking a bus to the airport in São Paulo, where he boarded a Lufthansa flight that had originated in Berlin and, after the stopover in São Paulo, was to continue on to Asunción. Sassen met Rudel in the Paraguayan capital a few days later, and with Aharoni in Montevideo on July 5. Sassen reported that Rudel would return to São Paulo within two weeks, and that the two of them would then fly together to Europe for business purposes.

In Rudel's absence, Aharoni flew to São Paulo to supervise the surveillance and also gathered additional information about Wolfgang Gerhard, who lived in a rural area twenty kilometers south of the São Paulo city center. Aharoni learned that Gerhard had been born in Austria on September 3, 1925, and had arrived in Brazil on April 26, 1949, with his wife, Ruth. He often visited an isolated farm on a dirt road about two kilometers west of mile marker 58 on the main road that led south from São Paulo. Aharoni surveilled the farm: it was one of two on the road, consisting of a main building and several auxiliary structures, including a small outbuilding about one hundred meters away that appeared to house someone at night. The main building was under renovation, clearly marked by the presence of scaffolding. A small brook that flowed next to the farm powered a generator. The farm was run-down, but its isolated setting offered advantages for someone like Mengele, who would want to live undisturbed. Never-theless, Aharoni estimated the likelihood of Mengele residing there at no better than 20 percent.

But on July 23 the Mossad team, while approaching the farm, observed a group of men—one of whom looked exactly like Mengele. Agent Zvi Malkin reportedly exclaimed over his radio in Yiddish, "That's him! We've found him, the little shit!"[67] The cable sent to Mossad headquarters in Israel was less colorful: "Zvi saw a man at the Gerhard farm who matches Mengele in shape, height, age, and clothing."[68] The response came promptly from headquarters to delay any action in the area until additional information could be collected, and until explicit permission was granted.[69]

Aharoni met with Sassen in São Paulo three days later, and again two days after that, in Rio de Janiero; although Sassen did not supply definitive proof, he had gathered significant evidence, which Aharoni found persuasive, that it was indeed Mengele who had been spotted on July 23. Sassen reported that he had met Gerhard for the first time on July 24, in the presence of Rudel and Hens in the latter's house. Gerhard had been introduced as "Lange," a nickname based on Gerhard's height (lange means "tall" in German). Every time Mengele's name was mentioned, a discernible reaction among the assembled men suggested that the subject of Mengele was not to be discussed. Later, after leaving Hens's home, Sassen had invited Gerhard for a drink and, after more than one, guided the discussion around to Mengele. Gerhard downplayed Rudel's role in hiding Mengele; Rudel did not even know where Mengele was at the moment and had not visited him recently. Gerhard claimed that he was the person in daily contact with Mengele, and the one who had provided him with a place to hide and who had taken care of everything.[70]

Despite the promising lead and the obvious excitement of the men on the ground, the Mossad, strangely, elected not to follow up with anything close to the necessary level of engagement. Indeed, at the very time its efforts appeared to be bearing fruit, making the apprehension of the "Angel of Death" seem like a possibility, the operation was essentially halted. The Mossad made no further attempt to confirm the identification, and if the man spotted had indeed been Mengele, he was allowed to burrow further underground, below the radar of the Israelis.

Aharoni claimed in a 1997 book that he and his team had been called off the Mengele hunt to work on "one of Harel's surprise projects"—the search for Yossele Schumacher, a boy who had been smuggled out of Israel by his ultra-orthodox grandparents, who disapproved of their daughter raising him in a secular fashion.[71] But Schumacher was reunited with his parents in Israel on July 4, 1962, several weeks before Aharoni was supposedly assigned to look for him.[72]

The 2017 Mossad report offers a different explanation for the diversion of resources from the Mengele search in midsummer 1962. It was not the Schumacher case but rather the threat emerging from the contribution of German scientists to the Egyptian missile program that occupied Harel.[73] Thanks to Operation Damocles, which involved Mossad attacks on German scientists and intimidation of their families, as well as Israeli diplomatic initiatives aimed at improving relations with Germany, the collaboration of German scientists in the Egyptian rocket program ended. The operation also led to the removal of Harel as head of the Mossad and the appointment of Meir Amit, a change in leadership that significantly influenced the Mossad's approach to hunting Nazi criminals.

We now know that Wolfgang Gerhard played a key role in protecting Mengele in Brazil, and it is significant that the Mossad was able to identify him so early. There is, however, a question about whether Aharoni and his colleagues actually encountered Mengele on that July day in 1962.

After arriving in Brazil and living temporarily in São Paulo, working at Gerhard's textile printing company, Mengele was introduced to Geza and Gitta Stammer, acquaintances of Wolfgang Gerhard. The Stammers had purchased a farm in Nova Europa, not far from the city of Araraquara in the state of São Paulo, where they grew coffee. They took Mengele on as farm manager, and he moved there sometime in 1961. According to Gitta Stammer, she discovered Mengele's true identity after seeing a photograph of the Nazi doctor in a Brazilian newspaper, published in connection with a story occasioned by the seventeenth anniversary of the liberation of Auschwitz, on January 27, 1962. After confronting Mengele, who admitted his identity, the Stammers approached Gerhard and complained that they had assumed a significant risk in harboring Mengele, and that they needed a more suitable residence if they were to continue to do so. Gerhard contacted Hans Sedlmeier in Günzburg, and it was decided that the Stammers would acquire another farm with more appropriate security features, which Mengele would help finance.

The farm in Nova Europa was put on the market, and a new farm was procured in Serra Negra. While the actual purchase date is unknown, Mengele wrote in his diary on August 19, 1962, that he had moved to Serra Negra "almost four weeks" earlier, placing his moving date some time shortly after July 23—the very date when the Israelis encountered a man thought to be Mengele at the Gerhard farm. It is entirely possible that Mengele was staying there temporarily until the acquisition of the Serra Negra property had been completed or until accommodations were ready for him there.

That Mengele actually stayed on the farm received further support from an unlikely source, more than five years later. On January 23, 1968, a woman informed the Israeli consul in São Paulo that her brother-in-law, a man named Wolfgang Gerhard, had harbored Josef Mengele on a farm located at the sixty-two-kilometer marker on the São Paulo-Curitiba road, nearly the exact location of the farm that had been the object of Israeli interest in 1962. The woman, Thea Maria Kleyer, was the sister of Gerhard's wife, Ruth. She claimed that she quarreled with Gerhard and that he had threatened to kill her and her sister. Two Mossad officers met with Kleyer on February 3 and listened as she explained that she was seeking custody of her youngest son, aged eight, from her second marriage. She offered to assist the Israelis in finding Mengele if they agreed to help her get her son back, and the Israelis agreed to help.

Kleyer provided a number of details about Mengele that we now know were accurate. He spent Christmas 1962 at Gerhard's home and had moved in with a family whom she described as "very simple people"; the woman was Hungarian, and the man, Kleyer claimed, was German. (She was presumably speaking of the Stammers, although Geza Stammer was Hungarian and not German.) She also mentioned another figure, Wolfram Bossert, who had contact with Mengele.[74] She told the Israelis that she had seen Mengele since then; that his hair had gotten grayer and was thinning; that he looked as though he had gained weight; and that Gerhard, every six to eight weeks, retrieved money from the post office for Mengele and delivered it to him. Mengele, she claimed, had stated that he was not guilty of the crimes of which he was accused.

The leadership of the Mossad took this new lead in the Mengele hunt seriously and deployed an officer to São Paulo to supervise the operation. After a number of meetings with Thea Kleyer, the officer, Benjamin Rotem (code named *Mirambo*), determined that her information concerning Mengele's location was stale, dating back to 1962–63, but her statements concerning the importance of Gerhard were accurate; *Mirambo* recommended that the Mossad kidnap Gerhard and force him to reveal where Mengele was hiding. The plan was rejected, however, and *Mirambo* returned to Israel.

A Legal Victory

Although Mengele succeeded in avoiding those who sought him in the early 1960s, he was held accountable in one little-known incident, which saw him the subject of legal proceedings in Germany. In September 1960, while Mengele was still in Paraguay, Hermann Langbein, the secretary general of the International Auschwitz Committee, wrote to the University of Munich, informing it that the prosecutor in Freiburg had issued a criminal complaint against one of its graduates, Josef Mengele, and asking whether Mengele should be allowed to continue to have the right to the doctor title, in view of the heinous allegations against him.[75] The university eventually agreed that he should not, but before taking any further steps to announce or to enact its decision, it wanted to coordinate with the university in Frankfurt, which faced the same issue.

As in Munich, the University of Frankfurt referred the question of Mengele's degree to a committee, which was scheduled to issue a decision on July 6, 1961. Unlike their Munich colleagues, however, the Frankfurt officials decided first to provide an opportunity for Mengele to respond to the charges, as would be the procedure in any other case. Since they had no current address for the missing Mengele, they advertised his right to respond on the university's "blackboard" and in the media. Although it probably surprised no one that Mengele failed to appear, few likely expected an attorney to show up in his place. Martha, who had received Mengele's power of attorney in September 1958, engaged a law firm to fight the proposed removal of her husband's academic degrees. The firm, Dr. Laternser & Steinacker, was building a reputation in postwar Germany for its defense of accused Nazi war criminals, including defendants in the Frankfurt Auschwitz Trial.

Mengele's attorneys tried to force the university to wait until a court had established Mengele's guilt or innocence, but they failed. The university decided to rescind Mengele's medical degree. In a ten-page opinion, relying on the witness statements that formed the basis of the arrest warrant, it concluded that Mengele was "unworthy" of the academic title. It found that through his flight abroad, he had escaped his responsibility to the public and to the academic community to face the serious charges that had been leveled against him. As Stefanie Harrecker points out in her book about the postwar removal of academic degrees, *Degradierte Doktoren* (Demoted Doctors), the Frankfurt committee, in its decision, made no distinction between indictment and conviction; Mengele's refusal to face his accusers was sufficient evidence of his unworthiness.

Though Mengele's lawyers appealed, the University of Frankfurt stood by its decision. An action brought before the Frankfurt Administrative Court and a subsequent appeal to the Hessian Administrative Court to have the university's decision annulled also failed; the case was dismissed in the summer of 1964 without the possibility of further appeal. With all avenues of legal action now closed, the decision of the University of Frankfurt was final. Shortly thereafter, the University of Munich reconfirmed its own four-year-old decision, which it had never made public, and announced that it had rescinded Mengele's degree. These actions taken by two German universities and confirmed by the court had absolutely no practical impact, but the symbolism was enormous, and one can imagine that the effect on Mengele himself was profound. To lose the right to carry his academic titles removed an essential part of his identity and distanced him even further from his homeland and the life he had been forced to abandon.

PART IV

PURSUIT

CHAPTER 8

PRELUDE

(1961–1985)

It was "the most ambitious international effort since World War II to hunt down a former Nazi," according to Ralph Blumenthal of the *New York Times*.[1] Germany, Israel, and the United States had agreed to form a cooperative effort to locate Josef Mengele and bring him to justice. The agreement, which established "direct lines of communication at the prosecutorial and investigative levels," had been the result of two days of meetings in Frankfurt on May 9 and 10, 1985. Although all three countries had their own decades-long histories of searching for Mengele, or responding to allegations about his presence, a confluence of circumstances and public interest had brought fifteen investigators and prosecutors together days after the fortieth anniversary of the end of the Second World War in Europe. Political and emotional forces had produced a powerful motive for each nation finally to find the Angel of Death and, in so doing, redress past inaction, failure, and missed opportunities.

Israel

Although the Mossad had been on the right track in the early 1960s in Brazil, its search for Mengele is a history of repeated failures and false steps, despite creative and persistent efforts that began soon after the Eichmann capture. The public and self-appointed Nazi hunters reported sightings, and the Mossad reacted,[2] but it considered it much more productive to develop leads of its own. In the summer of 1961, for instance, it learned from one of its agents that Martha Mengele was going to meet "someone" while visiting her parents at their lakeside country home in Uffing in Bavaria. The Mossad mounted a full-scale surveillance of the home from a boat on Lake Staffelsee—but could identify no one except Martha, her parents, and her son, Karl-Heinz. Intercepts of Martha's mail revealed another tantalizing clue when, writing to her family from Merano, where she was vacationing in October 1961, she included the phrase, "We are having a good time." The Mossad knew that Karl-Heinz was then in Switzerland, and the question emerged: who accounted for the plural "we"? The Mossad dispatched a team to investigate, only to discover that it was Martha's mother, who was staying with her at the Hotel Eurotel.[3] Another time they learned from an Israeli woman that her son, who was studying in Germany, had learned that Rolf Mengele and his mother were in regular correspondence with his father. The Mossad took steps to recruit their informant's son in the hopes that he could befriend Rolf—but the operation was unsuccessful.

In August 1964, Meir Amit, the head of the Mossad, agreed that Martha Mengele's home should be entered surreptitiously in search of correspondence or other written material that might provide evidence of Mengele's whereabouts. It took more than two years before the Mossad was able to enter Martha's apartment in August 1966, and it was disappointed by the items the agents found, which included Martha's calendars and address books from the years 1956 to 1961, the certificate of her marriage to Mengele in Uruguay, and a condolence letter from Mengele on the occasion of the death of her husband (and his brother), Karl. Although the break-in yielded no current, tangible link to Mengele, the Mossad believed that he was still somehow connected to Martha and decided to enter the apartment once again, this time to install listening devices. This second operation, carried out on

November 29, 1966, also included active surveillance of Martha and monitoring of the audio feeds from December 1966 to January 1967. The team listening in on her daily activities identified regular visitors and even a possible "lover," a certain Siegfried Pereda, a dentist. On Christmas Day they came upon something that must have raised their heart rates. They reported, with 90 percent confidence, that Mengele himself was visiting Martha. Amit ordered Rafi Eitan and others to go immediately to Milan, where, within twenty-four hours, they were able to listen to the tapes themselves. But after listening, they reached the conclusion that the man identified as Mengele was actually Fritz Will, Martha's father.

In early May 1967, the Mossad again infiltrated Martha Mengele's home, photographing, among other things, her personal diary, her 1966 calendar, and her correspondence with friends in Argentina. They found references to her son and her parents but not a single reference to her husband, a fact that surprised them and led them to speculate that Mengele was dead, that he and Martha had broken completely, or that there were particular grounds for disciplined security. A conversation monitored at the end of August led the Mossad to understand that Mengele was still alive and that, moreover, Siegfried Pereda knew a great deal. This revelation caused the Israelis to consider an active provocation that might induce Martha to reveal what she knew about her husband and his whereabouts. They decided to contact Pereda and offer to pay for information about Josef Mengele, reasoning that his response to this request might yield valuable intelligence regardless of how he acted. He might know something and agree to sell that information, or he might tell Martha about being contacted, in which case she might reveal information herself or decide to get in touch with Mengele. Any potential response would, of course, be overheard by the ever-present Israeli "ears."

An Israeli agent, posing as a patient seeking treatment, visited Pereda in his office. When they were alone, the agent identified himself as a representative of the state of Israel, informed him that the

Mossad knew all about his relationship with Martha, and asked him for his help in discovering Mengele's whereabouts. Pereda responded immediately that he knew nothing about Mengele but was willing to help, adding that he believed it highly doubtful that Martha had any relevant information or, in light of their intimacy, that she would discuss the subject with him. The agent returned the next day and found the dentist nervous, with "trembling hands," but still willing to cooperate. Pereda, however, initiated no conversations with Martha about her husband. After yet another clandestine entry into Martha's apartment, and numerous further attempts to induce Pereda to act, with no results, the Mossad decided to end the expensive operation. On October 27, 1967, it removed its listening devices from her home and, a few days later, gave up its nearby apartment, which had served as its base of operations.

The new head of the Mossad, Zvi Zamir, with the approval of Prime Minister Levi Eshkol, decided that thereafter the Mossad would lower the priority of the pursuit of war criminals, choosing to dedicate its resources to combating more immediate threats. The order invoking this change in mission was signed by Eshkol on December 31, 1968, and was subsequently ratified by his successors, Golda Meir and Yitzhak Rabin. As a result, the Mossad essentially ceased any active measures to capture Mengele for nearly a decade, responding only occasionally to over-the-transom leads, including the stakeout of Alois Mengele's funeral in 1974, which failed to identify Josef Mengele among the mourners.

Things changed with the election of Menachem Begin in May 1977.[4] According to Ronen Bergman, Begin informed his Mossad chief, Yitzhak Hofi, during their first meeting after his election, that he wanted the Mossad to undertake a "large-scale targeted killing campaign" against Nazi war criminals. Hofi's response was that Israel had "other missions that concerned the security of Israel now and in the future," and that he gave "priority to today and tomorrow over yesterday." Hofi later said that Begin understood his point of view but did not like it. "In the end, we decided that we'd concentrate on one target, [Josef] Mengele."[5] With Begin's vigorous backing, on July 23, 1977, the cabinet's security committee resolved "to order the Mossad to resume the search for Nazi war criminals, in particular Josef Mengele."[6] A special unit was created on March 13, 1978, whose sole purpose was to locate and capture Nazi war criminals and put them on trial—or if that proved impossible, to kill them.[7]

Among the many plans hatched by the Mossad to locate and capture Mengele under this new directive, one involved a German journalist named Gerd Heidemann, code name *Zaluza*, whom the Mossad targeted for recruitment in 1979 since, despite his good salary, "he always has money difficulties." Heidemann told the Mossad that he was planning to travel to South America to write a series of articles about fugitive Nazi war criminals. (To provide credible entry, he took along the former SS general Karl Wolff, who had been released from prison after serving a sentence for war crimes.) Heidemann's journey was chronicled in some detail, but it yielded no useful information about Mengele.[8]

In 1981 the Mossad turned its focus again to Hans-Ulrich Rudel, the pursuit of whom had led them to Wolfgang Gerhard in 1962. The team came up with an extreme proposal that involved kidnapping Rudel's young son, twelve-year-old Christoph, and presenting the father with an ultimatum: divulge Mengele's whereabouts or the child would be killed. Their planning advanced to the point of drafting a proposed ransom demand, which was to come from a member of an organization of Auschwitz survivors:

> We are aware of the fact that you have fought for Germany. You have received the highest award for excellence, and we accept you as such. On the other hand, Mengele is a human monster and he has to give account for his actions. . . .

We believe that CHRISTOPH is dear to you and you do not
want his fate to be like the fate of our children. . . . Don't risk
his life.

Give us Mengele's address and save Christoph's life.[9]

The leadership of the Mossad rejected the plan, and Rudel died shortly
afterward, obviating any additional schemes to induce his cooperation.

In the spring of 1982, the Mossad began to plan for an elaborate and
expensive operation focused on Rolf Mengele, who was then working
as an attorney in Berlin. The operation, which took many twists and
turns, involved inspecting Rolf's mail and installing listening devices
in his apartment. Initially, the plan was centered on the date March
16, the birthday shared by Rolf and his father, given the possibility
that the two might be in telephone contact that day. Mossad operatives
installed listening devices on March 12, and for seven straight days,
they heard mostly "business-like" conversations. There were many
birthday calls since it was not only Rolf's and his father's birthday but
also that of his wife, Almuth, and the operatives learned details about
the family, including the dates of their planned vacation. There was,
however, no call from or to Josef Mengele.

Aware that Rolf and his family would be on vacation, the Mossad entered Rolf's apartment on April 4 and again a few days later
to install additional listening devices and photograph personal documents, including passports. They discovered a letter, dated March
21, 1983, indicating that Rolf had lost his job. This news would have
a significant impact on its operation, though that would not be evident for a few months. In the meantime, the Mossad continued with
its audio surveillance and considered a "stimulation plan," which
would have involved making a phone call to Rolf informing him that
his father was gravely ill; the operatives would have monitored Rolf's
subsequent movements, in hopes that he would make plans to be by
his father's side. To accomplish this ambitious program, they needed
a base of operations close to Rolf's apartment. After searching for an

appropriate rental unit without success, the Mossad, with the approval of Yitzhak Hofi, purchased a nearby apartment on June 10, 1983. In early July, however, it became evident that Rolf was away from his home, and the Mossad slipped into it on the night of July 15. The operatives' entry lasted only a "minute or less," long enough for them to discover that it was completely empty. Rolf had moved with his family to Freiburg on July 1; without his job in Berlin, he had returned to the city of his childhood.

The Mossad followed him there and rented an apartment at the end of November, resuming its audio surveillance. Rolf had started a legal practice in Freiburg, and after two weeks of listening to his conversations, the Mossad concluded that they were entirely related to his business activity. It did pick up one provocative detail, however. In one conversation, Rolf was heard to say the phrase "morning a few times in Brazil," without providing any details about when he had been there or whom he might have met. In reporting this remark by cable to Israel, Igo Sommer, a Mossad officer, included the handwritten comment, "In the early days, Willem Sassen told me that [Mengele] lived in Brazil. It turned out that the information was not accurate."[10] Sommer's comment makes clear that by the early 1980s knowledge of the Mossad's early work in tracking Mengele to Brazil was closely held, was no longer considered credible, or had simply been forgotten.

Over the next year, the Mossad initiated an operation against Rolf in which a Mossad officer, Rafi Meidan, posed as a real estate customer who approached Rolf indicating his interest in doing business. The two met a number of times and developed a pleasant relationship, but Rolf was not enthusiastic about the business proposition. Meidan engaged him in discussions about politics and history in the hopes that he could lead Rolf to admit who his father was and reveal whether he was still alive. Meidan was impressed by Rolf and his political opinions, describing him as "anti-Nazi."[11] But he made no mention of Josef Mengele. The Mossad then introduced Meidan's "secretary" into the operation and explored the possibility of a romantic connection between her and Rolf. After testing the waters, however, the Mossad operative who posed as the secretary made it clear that she believed nothing would come of the romance scheme, leaving only one possibility: "violence, abduction, and blackmail."[12] Mossad staff began to plan to kidnap of Rolf Mengele, but the leadership of the organization rejected the idea.

The Mossad considered a variety of other operations, including a plan to enlist the help of Oscar-winning screenwriter and producer Abby Mann, involving a movie about Mengele in South America. It also contemplated an operation in Haiti following news that Rolf Mengele was planning to vacation there. The scope, expense, and creativity of the Mossad's schemes and the kinds of activities it was willing to contemplate are clear indications of the depth of its commitment to finding Mengele. But it failed to capitalize on its early and brilliant success in discovering Mengele's network in Brazil.

ON THE FORTIETH ANNIVERSARY of the liberation of Auschwitz, in January 1985, a group of Mengele's twins made an emotional pilgrimage to the camp that had been the scene of such suffering. The group was led by Eva Kor, an Indiana homemaker and real estate agent, who in 1983 had founded the organization CANDLES, an effective acronym for the awkwardly named international society Children of Auschwitz Nazi Deadly Lab Experiments Survivors. CANDLES sought to identify and bring together all the surviving twins who had been subjected to Mengele's experiments in Auschwitz.[13] The 1985 group included Eva and her sister as well as six others, "all survivors of pairs of twins," who traveled to Poland not only to commemorate but also to bring attention to their history, and to underscore the fact that Mengele remained unpunished and at liberty. The seventeen camera crews that followed the group allowed the world to witness their journey to the site that represented such profound loss to them and hundreds of thousands of others.

Kor, who had arrived at Auschwitz in 1944 at age ten, explained of her decision to return, "This [was] the beginning of the end. My children asked me so often what happened. I do not have the answers. My biggest problem is that I never said goodbye to my mother."[14] Like so many others, she and her sister had spent the rest of their lives dealing with the trauma that they had experienced.

Among those gathered was Marc Berkowitz of Brooklyn who, as a small boy, had acted as a messenger and aide to Mengele; he was here now, he said, because he "hoped to find the child I was before this happened."[15] His twin sister remained at home in the United States, not wishing, Berkowitz claimed, to "say anything to a world she feels ignored us when we were orphaned and suffering."

By early 1985 the twins and their story had already received a great deal of publicity. In early 1984 *Parade* magazine commissioned Lucette Lagnado, a reporter for Jack Anderson, a widely read syndicated columnist, to write a story about the child survivors of Mengele's experiments in Auschwitz. In reporting her story, Lagnado was helped by Eva Kor, who placed ads in Israeli newspapers and gradually assembled a list of Auschwitz twins that she shared with Lagnado, who visited Israel in March 1984 to conduct interviews. With the help of Eva and her twin, Miriam, Lagnado was able to overcome the reluctance of many of the twins to tell their stories and gradually assembled a picture of Mengele and his activities in Auschwitz.

Lagnado's article began, "He was at the same time their savior and their demon," communicating an odd ambivalence that animated the widely varying recollections. For instance, one Tel Aviv housewife found Mengele "gentle" when he drew her blood and insisted that "even though he was a murderer and a killer," she believed he "loved children." Lagnado created a remarkable portrait of the twins, describing the profound impact that Mengele had on them not only as children in Auschwitz but throughout their lives. *Parade* was an influential publication with a massive circulation, and putting Lagnado's article on its cover gave the story of the twins tremendous exposure.[16] The article was reprinted in newspapers in several foreign countries and led to a significant response from readers.[17]

After their visit to Auschwitz, the twins traveled to Israel, where they were joined by another ninety or so twins, dwarfs, and others who had survived Mengele's experiments. There they participated in a "tribunal," with the slogan "I Accuse." The mock trial was part of "The World Convention of Twins and Others Who Underwent Experiments by Mengele," the first-ever symposium for surviving Holocaust twins, which sought to collect evidence of Mengele's crimes, along with information about the details of his experiments. Invoking the authority of past war crimes trials, the six-member board of inquiry was headed by Gideon Hausner, the former attorney general of Israel and prosecutor of Eichmann, and it included Telford Taylor, the American chief counsel for war crimes at Nuremberg; Zvi Terlo, a member of the Eichmann prosecution team; and the famed "Nazi hunter" Simon Wiesenthal, who commanded worldwide respect for his singular efforts to bring Nazi war criminals to justice. Simone Veil, an Auschwitz survivor, former minister in the French government, and president of the European Parliament, participated in the tribunal as a witness. Held in the auditorium at Yad Vashem, Israel's Holocaust memorial, the three-day event included dramatic testimony from thirty twins and dwarfs, much of which had never been heard before.

At the conclusion of the proceedings, the tribunal announced that there was sufficient evidence to try Mengele "for war crimes and crimes against humanity," including "acts of murder, the causing of grievous bodily harm and acts of brutality against the bodies and souls of men and women."[18] Of course, before Mengele could be tried, he had to be located. Wiesenthal, at the time considered by the public and the press to be the most reliable source of information about Nazi war criminals—a reputation that would suffer in the course of the Mengele case—stated during the proceedings that he believed Mengele was "in a closed military area in Paraguay."[19]

In November 1984, when they first learned of the planned tribunal, German prosecutors wrote to Menachem Russek, an Israeli police colonel who headed the unit charged with investigating Nazi war crimes, to request a record of the proceedings, including a list of witnesses with addresses.[20] The German embassy in Tel Aviv followed the hearings closely, reporting to Bonn that although the tribunal would produce little of value for the ongoing investigation of Mengele, it was important to avoid the potential allegation that the German government was indifferent to the proceedings or lost interest once they were over.[21]

Germany

One of the most persistent tropes surrounding Mengele's escape from justice is that the Germans did nothing to prevent it or to rectify it. In this regard, it is worth remembering that West Germany did not exist as a sovereign state during the period when Mengele still resided in its territory; he had left Europe on May 25, 1949, two days after the establishment of the Federal Republic, and had vacated occupied Germany six weeks before that. It was the Allies who had the responsibility and opportunity to capture Mengele before diplomacy, foreign police cooperation, and extradition laws would become essential and complicating factors. Understanding how the Allies had failed was a major goal of OSI's investigation. The Germans' thirty-year failure to locate and capture Mengele, on the other hand, is a far more complex question. The easy explanation—reluctant actors working on behalf of an unwilling state—tells only a part of the story.

There are indeed legitimate grounds to question the willingness of the Germans to mount a sustained and effective search for Mengele and to advocate for his arrest and extradition. Germany's record in pursuing Nazi war criminals, although often underestimated, fell far short of what was possible and of what the victims of Nazi crimes were entitled to expect. With the clarity of hindsight, one can easily see that an even modest effort might have discovered Mengele's ongoing connection to individuals in Germany, which would likely have revealed his whereabouts. However, a formidable task faced German investigators, even assuming they operated with pure and unambiguous motives. One well-placed mail intercept could have unraveled the entire system employed to protect Mengele in his various hideouts, and considering the number of people necessary to surveil, and the duration of the surveillance, the challenge is evident. In addition, German investigators had to operate under the constraints of a legal system that offered important protection to family members of an accused person, as well as significant safeguards for personal privacy. Designed to prevent the egregious violations of individual rights and privacy that had characterized the Nazi regime, these protections imposed meaningful hurdles for carrying out intercepts of telephone and postal communication.

Mengele became the subject of interest for German justice and police authorities beginning in the late summer of 1958, and the first arrest warrant was issued by the court in Freiburg in February 1959.[22] That April Fritz Bauer petitioned the German Supreme Court to move jurisdiction for the Mengele investigation to Frankfurt, where it could be included in the massive Auschwitz investigation already under way. Mengele was number sixty-one on the list of ninety-five subjects, which included twelve other physicians.[23] This investigation resulted in the Frankfurt Auschwitz Trial, which ran from December 1963 through August 1965 and put twenty-two defendants in the dock. In April 1968 the Mengele case was separated from the overall Auschwitz proceedings, and a preliminary investigation (*gerichtliche Voruntersuchung*) was initiated against him, to be conducted not by the prosecutor but rather by an examining magistrate (*Untersuchungsrichter*), Horst von Glasenapp, who collected more than three hundred witness interviews from around the world detailing Mengele's activities and crimes. However, this effort was closed in December 1974, and the investigation was temporarily suspended by the court in Frankfurt in January 1975 because of Mengele's unknown

Mengele's student record card from the University of Munich, 1930–36.
Universitätsarchiv München, Stud-Kart II, Mengele, Josef

The building housing the University Institute for Hereditary Biology and Racial Hygiene in Frankfurt on the bank of the Main River.
Archiv der Max-Planck-Gesellschaft, Berlin-Dahlem

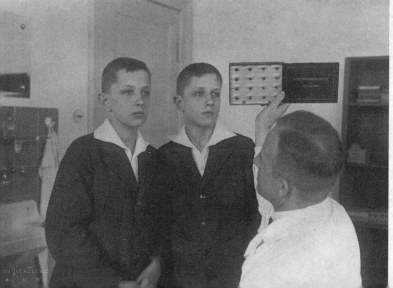

Otmar von Verschuer assessing the eye color of a pair of twins.
Archiv der Max-Planck-Gesellschaft, Berlin-Dahlem

Mengele at Verschuer's
institute in Frankfurt, 1935–36.
Archiv der Max-Planck-Gesellschaft, Berlin-Dahlem

Mengele (second from left) joking
with colleagues at Verschuer's
institute in Frankfurt, 1935–36.
Archiv der Max-Planck-Gesellschaft, Berlin-Dahlem

The ninth meeting of the German Society for
Physical Anthropology, held in Tübingen in
September 1937. Mengele can be seen in the second
row, on the far left. His mentors Theodor Mollison,
who supervised his dissertation in anthropology
at the University of Munich, and Otmar von
Verschuer are in the center of the same row (tenth
and fourteenth from the left).
Archiv der Max-Planck-Gesellschaft, Berlin-Dahlem

Mengele serving with the Fifth SS
Engineers Battalion of the Waffen-SS
Viking Division, in Ukraine, October 1942.
Collection Hermann Abmayr

Hungarian Jews undergo a selection on the ramp at Auschwitz-Birkenau, May 1944. Mengele not only determined who would be murdered immediately and who would be exploited for their labor first, but also sought out appropriate subjects for his medical experiments as well as well-trained physicians and other scientific specialists to assist him in his work.

United States Holocaust Memorial Museum, courtesy of Yad Vashem (public domain)

Laboratory form signed by Mengele requesting "histological sections" to be made from the head of a twelve-year-old child, July 29, 1944.

Photo by David G. Marwell

Three SS officers socialize on the grounds of the SS retreat of Sołahütte, outside Auschwitz, July 1944. From left to right: Richard Baer (commandant of Auschwitz), Mengele, and Rudolf Höss (the former Auschwitz commandant).

United States Holocaust Memorial Museum, courtesy of anonymous donor

An accordionist leads a sing-along for SS officers at their retreat at Sołahütte, July 1944. Mengele can be seen to the immediate left of the accordionist.
United States Holocaust Memorial Museum, courtesy of anonymous donor

Child survivors of Auschwitz, wearing adult-size prisoner jackets, stand behind a barbed wire fence after Soviet troops liberate the camp, 1945. Eva Kor and her sister, Miriam, are in the knitted caps.
United States Holocaust Memorial Museum, courtesy of anonymous donor

Application for Red Cross travel document in the name of "Helmut Gregor," the alias Mengele used to leave Europe in 1949.
International Committee of the Red Cross. (CICR, V-P-HIST-03349-21 ACICR C TV, N°100.501)

Mengele's Brazilian driver's license, issued under his alias "Wolfgang Gerhard," 1976.
Photo by Betina Anton

From left: Israeli police officer Menachem Russek with OSI attorney Rod Smith and OSI deputy director Neal Sher, in Israel, 1982.
Photo by Eli M. Rosenbaum

The exhumation of a body thought to be Mengele's in Embu, Brazil. José António de Mello, assistant director of the São Paulo morgue, standing in the container used to hold the bones, shows the skull to the gaggle of reporters and photographers who witnessed the spectacle, June 6, 1985.
AP/Shutterstock

Slide of Mengele's femur used to determine biological age of the skeleton exhumed in Embu, 1985.
Gift of Dr. Lowell J. Levine, Museum of Jewish Heritage, New York

Television monitor at the Institute for Forensic Medicine in São Paulo displaying the photo-skull superimposition technique developed by the German expert Dr. Richard Helmer, June 1985.
Courtesy of Jerry Whistler Snow

U.S. expert Leslie Lukash stands before Mengele's bones, arranged in anatomical order at the Institute for Forensic Medicine in São Paulo, June 1985.
Photo by Eric Stover

American forensic experts meet to draft a preliminary report on the identification of Josef Mengele's remains, São Paulo, June 20, 1985. Left to right: Ellis Kerley, Clyde Snow, Eric Stover, Leslie Lukash, John Fitzpatrick, Ali Hameli.
Courtesy of Jerry Whistler Snow

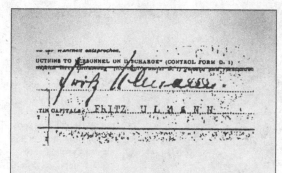

Signature of Dr. Fritz Ulmann from his discharge certificate. Mengele modified Ulmann's name and signature to become "Fritz Holmann," the name he used while hiding on a farm in Bavaria right after the war.
Office of Special Investigations, In the Matter of Josef Mengele.

Flyer announcing the CANDLES Inquest, November 1985. A chorus of doubt greeted the news that the skeleton exhumed in São Paulo was that of Josef Mengele. Survivor Eva Kor and her organization of twin survivors organized a public "inquest" to examine the evidence.
Courtesy of CANDLES Holocaust Museum and Education Center

Author in São Paulo during an investigative trip, April 1986.
Hessisches Hauptstaatsarchiv Wiesbaden

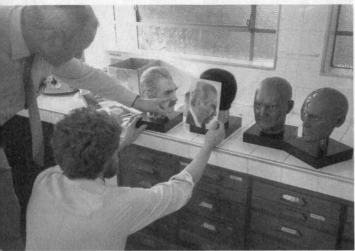

German police officers Horst Gemmer (left) and Dieter Sack examine a reconstruction of Mengele's face carried out by Brazilian experts by applying modeling clay to a replica of his skull. Campinas, Brazil, April 1986.
Photo by David G. Marwell

Dennis Gouldman (left), chairman of the Israeli interagency committee on Mengele, with Brazilian police official Dr. Aparecido Laertes Calandra, São Paulo, April 1986.
Courtesy of Dennis Gouldman (unknown photographer)

U.S. Department of Justice
Criminal Division

In the Matter of Josef Mengele

A Report to the
Attorney General
of the United States

October 1992

Prepared by:
Office of Special Investigations
Criminal Division

Neal M. Sher
Director

Eli M. Rosenbaum
Principal Deputy Director

OSI's report to the attorney general, William Barr, October 1992. OSI waited until after DNA tests confirmed the identification to issue its report.
Photo by David G. Marwell

whereabouts. In January 1981 the prosecutor in Frankfurt issued a new, much more comprehensive arrest warrant for Mengele, an expression of a renewed and more energetic effort to locate and bring him to justice.

Over the years, the Germans investigated a large number of allegations about Mengele's identity and whereabouts and followed up on numerous reported sightings. For instance, in February 1961 they examined a tip that Mengele was living under a false name in Ethiopia, but they ruled it out because of a significant difference in the height of the suspect. That same month they investigated a forester in Rendsburg, Germany, near Itzehoe, but concluded that he was not Mengele. When Martha Mengele returned from Argentina in 1961 and moved to Switzerland, German investigative officials traveled to Zurich to consult with Swiss officials but found no evidence that Mengele was there. Within an eight-month period in 1961, they investigated leads in Argentina, Egypt, Peru, Chile, Brazil, and Ecuador.[24]

The Germans also undertook active efforts to surveil family members within the severe constraints of German law. They were present as observers at Mengele family events, covering the funerals of Mengele's father in 1959 and his brother in 1974, and they initiated or stepped up surveillance of key people on important dates, like Mengele's birthday. At one stakeout involving a celebration of Martha Mengele's family in Munich in June 1984, the German surveillance team observed another group surreptitiously filming the crowd. It turned out that the British journalist Bill Bemister had had the same idea as the German investigators—except that he had better equipment and secured a better vantage point. The Germans suspended their operation fearing that they would be detected and approached Bemister, who agreed to share the fruits of his clandestine filming.[25]

Regardless of the earlier attempts to locate Mengele and to bring him to justice, by early 1985 the German government was clearly prepared to commit substantial resources to getting it done. On January 31, 1985, the Hessian minister of justice announced a twenty-fold increase in the reward for information leading to the arrest of Mengele, an unprecedented sum of one million Deutschmarks (approximately $800,000 today). Though this amount would soon be overshadowed by far larger sums offered by the Simon Wiesenthal Center and the Israeli government, the significant increase, along with the rushed negotiations that led up to it, highlights the political calculus at play within Germany as well as internationally, and the tensions that can exist between public prosecutors and politicians.

On January 25, 1985, two days before the group of Mengele twins visited Auschwitz, the director of the Hessian Criminal Police, Walter Löw, met with an undersecretary in the Hessian Ministry of the Interior, Wolf von Hoerschelmann, to discuss the Mengele case. Löw strongly recommended an increase in the reward,[26] reasoning that the level of the existing reward had resulted in no relevant leads and that, given Mengele's power as a symbol for the "atrocities of the Nazi regime," his arrest would be of "immense political and historical importance." A spectacular increase would, he argued, prove the strong interest of law enforcement and provide an incentive for people to come forward with information. It would have a worldwide ripple effect, earning special attention in South America, where Mengele allegedly lived, and might cause him to make a false move. He suggested that the planned "tribunal," organized by the CANDLES organization in Jerusalem, scheduled for early February, would offer a suitable forum for announcing the increase.

Considering Mengele's advanced age—he would be seventy-three—Löw argued that only a high-pressure investigation, which could be generated mainly by a broadly public investigation, could lead to quick success. To that end, the year 1985, with its many planned events commemorating the fortieth anniversary of the collapse of the Nazi regime, appeared particularly suitable for harnessing existing investigative approaches and attracting new ones. Löw recommended that the investigation be intensified, employing new measures like telephone and mail monitoring of Mengele's wife in Merano and initiating similar surveillance of Mengele's son in Berlin. He promised a new investigative plan in the coming weeks.

In a strongly worded letter to the Hessian minister of justice dated January 31, 1985, Von Hoerschelmann, on behalf of Hesse's minister of the interior, laid out his recommendation, which essentially echoed Löw's points.[27] The time was ripe, he stressed.

Christoph Kulenkampff, the Justice Ministry official responsible for handling the reward issue, was opposed to an increase at that time, seeing such a move as tantamount to an admission that Germany would act only under pressure of international public opinion. This view was shared by Gunther Mitscher, from the office of the Hessian state prosecutor, who also believed a dramatic increase would lead to that "false impression." What's more, he claimed that the state prosecutor had already in recent years taken every conceivable step to pursue every lead.[28] At the same time, the senior state prosecutor in Frankfurt, Heinz Haueisen, argued against the efficacy of the reward, suggesting that it would not stimulate useful new leads and might, indeed, have the opposite effect, by increasing the number of erroneous and intentionally false ones, which would only hinder the investigation. Echoing Mitscher, Haueisen warned against the impression that the Germans had done nothing, or not enough, and were moved to action only by the "Israel-Tribunal" and the fortieth-anniversary commemorations, suggesting, in the end, that "an increase . . . by a factor of twenty rates less as an investigative measure than as a purely political display."[29]

On January 31, after carefully weighing the competing arguments presented by the Ministry of the Interior and the state prosecutor's office, the Ministry of Justice decided to reverse its position, reasoning that the chance that increased publicity would lead to substantive information about the whereabouts of Mengele was too great an opportunity to ignore.[30] That same day the ministry issued a press release to announce the reward as unique in the history of German law enforcement, and it took steps to ensure that it would be publicized not only in Germany but, through the Foreign Office, around the world.[31]

The United States

It was a shot in the dark, but it paid off in ways that Rabbi Marvin Hier could not have imagined. His October 25, 1984, letter to the National Archives invoking the provisions of the Freedom of Information Act (FOIA) sought all documentation relating to Josef Mengele. The response two weeks later yielded a handful of documents, the most explosive of which was a memorandum from Special Agent Ben J. M. Gorby of the 970th Counter Intelligence Corps (CIC) Detachment, who wrote that his unit had "received information that one Dr. MENGELE, fnu, former *Oberarzt* (chief medical Doctor) in AUSCHWITZ Extermination camp has been arrested in Vienna."[32]

Hier, an Orthodox rabbi, had founded the Simon Wiesenthal Center (SWC) in 1977. Small of stature, he had an outsize personality and a genuine charm that proved irresistible to countless donors who had helped make the SWC into one of the most successful nonprofit organizations in the highly competitive Jewish philanthropic world. Keenly attuned to marketing and public opinion, the center made an arrangement with the famous Nazi hunter that permitted it to take on his name and immediately enjoy recognition and status that would have taken years longer to attain otherwise. The SWC has achieved remarkable success in the fields of education, advocacy, and human rights, and it played a significant role in the Mengele case.

Hier followed up on his initial FOIA request with another query on November 20, 1984. The response, again arriving two weeks later, included notification that four documents had been withheld because their release could reasonably be expected "to cause damage to national security" or because they originated with a foreign government. On December 10, Hier appealed to the secretary of the army, John Marsh, and on December 19, without waiting for Marsh's response, he wrote to President Reagan calling on him to "launch an official investigation in the case of Dr. Josef Mengele." Until the Gorby memorandum came to light, it had been assumed that Mengele's whereabouts following the war were unknown to the Allies. Now the news that Mengele might have been arrested by U.S. forces challenged this assumption. Only a "full-fledged investigation by the administration, and a thorough analysis of the documents" could "determine whether the United States had played a role" in Mengele's postwar activities.[33] On January 14 the general counsel of the Defense Department informed Hier that his appeal for the release of the four withheld documents had been denied, indicating that one document had been properly classified and that the other three were of foreign origin; the originating country had to be consulted before they could be released.

In the meantime, the SWC located Benjamin Gorby in Israel, and Hier spoke with him over the phone. Without adding significant new information, Gorby explained the context in which he had written the memorandum, emphasizing to Hier that there was "no doubt" that he had considered the source of information "as fully trustworthy"; otherwise he would not have acted upon it by writing the memorandum.[34] The Gorby memorandum and its implications concerning the activities of the U.S. Army in the postwar period were invaluable for the SWC as a means of drawing attention to Mengele as well as the entire subject of Nazi war criminals, and the organization decided to publicize the information. Hier and his colleagues did so with exquisite media savvy and were able to command the attention of an already primed public. The possibility that Mengele had been in U.S. custody was too tempting not to be fully explored—and exploited—by the news media and certain politicians.

The SWC held a press conference in New York City on Wednesday, January 23, 1985, with New York senator Alfonse D'Amato, among others, in attendance. The timing was not accidental; Hier was clearly capitalizing on the fortieth anniversary of the liberation of Auschwitz, which was to fall on the following Sunday, January 27, and which was

to be the occasion for the well-publicized visit of the twins to Auschwitz. At the press conference, Hier released the documents he had
received and called for a "full government investigation." He also
informed the press of the documents withheld by the government and
threatened a lawsuit if they were not released, an action that D'Amato indicated he might join.[35] True to his word, on January 29 Hier
instructed Martin Mendelsohn, SWC general counsel, to file a lawsuit
in federal district court on behalf of the SWC and D'Amato for the
release of the withheld documents.[36]

Hier's efforts bore fruit almost immediately. Elliott Abrams, assistant secretary of state for human rights and humanitarian affairs, said
that there was "agreement within the Reagan administration that the
case should be examined, at least initially, by the Justice Department's
Office of Special Investigations." A similar effort by the SWC to prod
the Canadian government was also effective, as Prime Minister Brian
Mulroney directed his justice minister to conduct "an urgent investigation" into the possibility that Mengele had found refuge in Canada.[37]

The publicity resulting from the release of the Gorby memorandum
and other documents led to further revelations. On January 31 a former GI named Walter Kempthorne wrote to the SWC that during the
first week of July 1945 while he was stationed in Germany, he had seen
a man identified to him as Josef Mengele. While serving as a "perim-
eter guard at an Army Counter-Intelligence post in Idar Oberstein,
fifty miles east of Trier in southwestern Germany," he had encountered a male prisoner, standing at attention and perspiring profusely,
apparently having recently engaged in strenuous physical exercise.[38]
When Kempthorne asked two guards nearby what was going on,
one responded, "We're getting him in shape to get hung. This here's
Mengele, the bastard that sterilized 3,000 women at Auschwitz."
Kempthorne claimed that he had thought about Mengele over the
years but never believed anyone would be interested in his story until
he'd read the news reports of the SWC's investigation. "I always visu-
alize the name of Mengele with the face of the man I saw in the camp

because I connect it with 3,000 sterilized women," Kempthorne told a reporter. "That's a mental image that is hard to forget, especially for a 19-year-old kid." Kempthorne presented himself as a believable witness. He was a retired engineer and a Stanford graduate, who provided a photograph of himself in the guard tower at the POW camp and supplied credible details about his service there.

Hier hosted a press conference at his Los Angeles center on February 14 to introduce Kempthorne and his story. Senators D'Amato and Arlen Specter were invited and took advantage of the opportunity to comment on the expanding case. D'Amato declared that the "noose was tightening," describing Kempthorne's revelations as the "most credible evidence we have had to date" that U.S. authorities had had contact with Mengele before he fled Europe, and adding, "I intend to communicate this to the president."[39] Raising the possibility that U.S. officials might have helped Mengele escape, Specter commented, "The United States Army has a lot to explain why Dr. Josef Mengele was not brought to justice."[40]

The chairman of the Juvenile Justice Subcommittee of the Senate Judiciary Committee, Specter had announced, at an earlier press conference at the center, that he intended to hold hearings on the Mengele case the following week in Washington. The hearing would "come at a time of heightened international interest in bringing the notorious 'angel of death' of Auschwitz to justice and will focus on the testimony of survivors of Mengele's gruesome experiments during World War II.... We will seek to uncover new leads and information as to the nature and extent of involvement of American, Canadian and other Western governments with the fugitive Nazi war criminal from 1945–85."[41]

ON THE MORNING OF February 19, 1985, the *Washington Post* carried a front-page story about the improving prospects for the Republican senators who were running for reelection in the middle of Reagan's second term. Among the twenty-two Republican seats up for grabs in 1986 were the twelve that had been won for the first time in Reagan's

landslide victory of 1980; two among that freshman Republican class
were Alfonse D'Amato and the former and future Democrat, Arlen
Specter. The senators found themselves together later that morning in
room 124 of the Dirksen Senate Office Building, Specter in his capacity as chairman of the Juvenile Justice Subcommittee of the Senate
Judiciary Committee, and D'Amato as the first witness to be called
in a hearing on "Searching for Dr. Josef Mengele." Specter, who had
earned a reputation for seeking headlines, ignored Judiciary Committee chairman Strom Thurmond's challenge that the "Judiciary
Committee didn't have any real jurisdiction to hold hearings on Josef
Mengele," according to the Wall Street Journal.[42] He proceeded with
the claim that his Juvenile Justice Subcommittee did have jurisdiction
by virtue of the fact that there "were a lot of children who were victims" of Mengele's experiments.[43]

D'Amato's role as leading advocate for the Mengele investigation
holds some irony when one considers that he had defeated Elizabeth
Holtzman, perhaps the most outspoken activist for action against
Nazi war criminals, for his Senate seat. Known as "Senator Pothole,"
for championing the special causes of his constituents that he thought
would work to his political advantage, he took up the Mengele case
with great engagement, knowing that it would be a highly emotional
and newsworthy one, no matter the outcome. On Thursday, January
24, the day after the New York Times ran an article describing the
Gorby memorandum, he had written to William Casey, the director
of the CIA, to ask him to form a "special team to conduct an inten-
sive search of intelligence records for any and all information directly
or indirectly concerning Dr. Josef Mengele."[44] CIA analysts worked
through the weekend in a "herculean effort" to locate relevant documents,[45] and CIA general counsel Stanley Sporkin and his assistant
briefed D'Amato in his office on the results on January 29. The most
newsworthy information relayed to D'Amato came from a December
1984 memorandum written by the American ambassador to Paraguay,
Arthur Davis, about a conversation he had had with a Paraguayan offi-

cial named Conrado Pappalardo on December 11, 1984. Pappalardo told the ambassador that from 1959 to 1965 Mengele had split his time between Costa Nu, near Encarnación, and Asunción, and that he had moved to Brazil in 1965 because "various 'Nazi hunters' were on his trail." Pappalardo indicated that Mengele had later moved to Portugal, and that friends in Paraguay used to receive Christmas cards from Mengele that were sent from Portugal. The cards stopped coming "around 1980," leading some to believe that he had died.[46] D'Amato asked whether the CIA could confirm Mengele's presence in Portugal and whether he was dead.[47] The CIA was unable to "substantiate" the "rumor" that Mengele had ever been in Portugal.[48]

In February, D'Amato sent a letter to his "fellow New Yorkers" vowing to dedicate his efforts in the Mengele case. "I have made finding Mengele a personal priority," he wrote, describing his individual efforts with the CIA and the Department of Defense and his joint efforts with Hier and the SWC.[49] The night before the hearing, he received the 1985 American-Israel Award at the annual B'nai Zion dinner in New York City. In his remarks, he intoned, "We cannot allow Mengele to avoid justice. We are now in a race against time, if we don't catch him soon, he may be free to die in bed of old age. This is a far more peaceful fate than this mass murderer and torturer deserves." He continued:

> Published information leads me to believe there was official involvement by US and other allied government agencies in the exodus of Nazis from Germany after World War II. I want to know if Mengele had any official assistance in his escape from justice. If he did, I want to know who helped him. Any person who was involved in helping war criminals escape punishment must be held to account for his action.[50]

The junior senator from New York State had clearly found an issue he could run with.

CHAPTER 9

THE INVESTIGATION

(February 1985–June 1985)

Even before the scheduled Senate hearings, the work of the Simon Wiesenthal Center and the senators from Pennsylvania and New York moved not only public opinion but also the levers of government. On February 6, 1985, Attorney General William French Smith announced that the Justice Department would open an investigation into the whereabouts of Josef Mengele and the allegation that he had been in U.S. custody after the war. Promising a thorough and speedy investigation, Smith said that the Justice Department's Office of Special Investigations (OSI) would "seek to compile all credible evidence on the current whereabouts of Mengele as well as information concerning his movements in occupied Germany and his suspected flight to South America." Five days later he ordered the U.S. Marshals Service (USMS) to join OSI in the investigation. Explaining the basis for the investigation, Smith said that there "have been enough allegations to warrant" it, noting the newly declassified documents that suggested Mengele "was in a United States–occupied area after the war and was known to U.S. authorities." Smith indicated that the Justice Department would receive support and assistance from the Pentagon and the CIA.[1] The announcement of the investigation came on the final day of the mock trial in Jerusalem.

The most significant outcome of the Senate hearing, from the point of view of OSI, came as a result of the appearance of Lt. Gen. William E. Odom, the army's assistant chief of staff for intelligence. Appearing with army general counsel Susan J. Crawford, Odom was prepared to discuss the documents that had been identified through the FOIA request made by the SWC and to describe the army's activities in relation to their discovery and release. He was not prepared for the kind of questions the senators had in store for him. The focus of their interrogation was the Gorby memorandum and the steps the army had taken to follow up on the information it contained. Had the army, for instance, identified the commander of the 430th CIC Detachment in Vienna to whom the memorandum was addressed? When Odom responded that they had not but would if instructed to, Specter gave him a tongue-lashing he clearly had not expected:

I don't consider it a sufficient response for a Lieutenant General, and the Assistant Chief of Staff for intelligence, to say to this subcommittee that you will pursue it if the Chief of Staff and if your Army superiors think you should. You're not a private, you are not a corporal, you are not a Lieutenant—you are a three-star general. It seems to me you have the responsibility to take that initiative and to pursue it, and that when you know about a letter that exists like this in 1947, that the first question you ought to ask and you ought to demand some answers for, is what effort has been made to find out who this commanding officer is, and not to come to a Senate subcommittee hearing and say you don't know.[2]

When I later learned about this confrontation, I remember questioning the wisdom of embarrassing a three-star general in such a public way. But I was wrong.

The Department of the Army created a Mengele Task Force to assist us in our investigation and to "facilitate access to the extensive documentary material in its possession."[3] Maj. Nick Ruiz was assigned as our liaison, and with his help, we were able to identify and locate former U.S. military personnel and obtain relevant records about their activities in postwar Germany. The army activated a reserve intelligence unit to work in the Intelligence Records Repository at Fort Meade, Maryland, to review and index more than 325 reels of microfilm containing copies of CIC and other investigative files. The U.S. Army had suddenly become the most active and committed resource that OSI could have imagined.

The Four Questions

As soon as the attorney general ordered us to investigate the questions raised by the public, we began to search for relevant documents and witnesses both in the United States and abroad. With the able assistance of the army task force, we identified and located all surviving American personnel who had served in units relevant to our research. In the course of the investigation, we interviewed more than one hundred individuals and reviewed a vast quantity of documents in archives, record centers, and private hands. Our Israeli researcher, Efraim Zuroff, conducted parallel research and interviews there. With the help of the State Department, we located and interviewed witnesses in France, Austria, and Germany, and we made document requests of archives in a range of countries, including East Germany and the Soviet Union.

The allegations we were charged to investigate fell into four broad questions, which provided an organizing structure for the investigation and the public report that we later published.

The first question, which we framed as the "Idar-Oberstein Question," dealt with the early allegations raised by Walter Kempthorne and publicized by the SWC, that Mengele had been in U.S. custody immediately after the war and had been knowingly released. Our approach to the allegation was to examine it more broadly and not restrict ourselves to the specific details that had been asserted. We investigated, rather, the subject of U.S. policy toward the custody and release of prisoners of war.

The "Günzburg Question" involved the widespread belief that Mengele had lived openly in his own hometown of Günzburg, which was located in the U.S. Zone of Occupation, for a period of time after the war with the tacit approval of the U.S. personnel and agencies operating there.

The "Gorby Question" involved the specific allegation that Mengele had been taken into custody as a war criminal by U.S. authorities, and it examined the U.S. effort to seek out, apprehend, and prosecute Mengele.

And finally, the "Barbie Analogy" examined the claim that Mengele might have been used by U.S. intelligence and aided in leaving Europe via the Ratline, in a manner similar to that which OSI had discovered in the 1983 Klaus Barbie investigation.

SENATOR SPECTER SPONSORED a second hearing of his Juvenile Justice Subcommittee on April 22 in Philadelphia, scheduled to coincide with the inaugural ceremony of the American Gathering of Jewish Holocaust Survivors, which attracted several thousand Holocaust survivors from around the country. Six survivors testified about Mengele at Auschwitz. Neal Sher, on behalf of OSI, told the committee, "We believe that this notorious criminal must be apprehended, and we are optimistic," an affirmation that drew "wild applause" from the audience.[4]

The survivors also passed a resolution condemning President Reagan's planned visit to Bitburg. German chancellor Helmut Kohl had invited the American president to join him on the fortieth anniversary of the end of World War II to lay a wreath on a German grave in the Kolmeshöhe military cemetery near the city of Bitburg. Following Reagan's acceptance of the invitation, it was learned that among the men buried in the cemetery were some members of the Waffen-SS.

Even after being informed of the presence of the SS graves, Reagan did not change his mind about Kohl's invitation. The survivors in Philadelphia expressed "anguish" and "outrage" at the president's decision to go through with the visit, claiming that he had "reopened many wounds" with his "lack of understanding and lack of sensitivity."

On the question of Mengele's current whereabouts, we had received one apparently solid lead in the spring of 1985—though it would turn out to be the product of a combination of wishful thinking and outright fraud. For a time, however, it captured the imagination of the press and the pursuers of Mengele. This lead originated with a journeyman German journalist who approached the *New York Post* with a story about a man living in Uruguay who claimed to be Josef Mengele. It had all the ingredients of a cheap thriller—a mysterious man of great wealth, a collection of luxury homes, and a beautiful mistress—and therefore the ring of truth for those who imagined a certain kind of existence for Mengele. Rupert Murdoch, the owner of the *Post,* was intrigued but careful as well, having recently been taken in by another German journalist who had peddled the forged "Hitler Diaries" to another of his papers. Despite his understandable wariness, Murdoch was looking for a splashy exclusive that might help restore his reputation after the embarrassment of the forgery.[5]

The *Post* invested considerable resources in trying to verify the story, sending reporters to Uruguay to stake out the mystery man's villa. After several attempts, high-quality surveillance photographs of the man were obtained and presented for evaluation to three noted forensic anthropologists, each of whom had been trained to compare two photographs of individuals to determine whether they were of the same person. Peggy Caldwell, a consulting anthropologist within the New York City medical examiner's office; Larry Angel, from the Smithsonian Institution; and Ellis Kerley, a professor of anthropology at the University of Maryland, were provided with a set of the surveillance photographs along with a copy of a photograph of Mengele (from his SS file) and one of an unrelated person as a control. After

careful study, the three experts delivered a unanimous finding that
the Uruguayan man was Mengele—and theirs was not a lukewarm
opinion. Kerley, when asked whether he would stake his life on his
opinion, reportedly responded, "Well, in a way, I'm betting my professional life on this,"[6] and Angel said he was "willing to go to court
if that is necessary," adding that it was "pretty much like seeing an
automobile coming down the street at about fifty feet away and saying,
'That is a Mercedes.' It is of that order. We ordinarily act on that kind
of thing."[7] While Kerley and Angel placed their level of certainty at 95
percent, Caldwell was quoted as having enough confidence to send a
man "to the electric chair," based on her conclusion.[8]

The story was eventually debunked after John Martin and ABC
News got ahold of it. They simply confronted the suspected Mengele,
who turned out to be a Uruguayan citizen by the name of Walter Branaa, who was able to provide ample proof of his bona fides.[9] The case
illustrated the healthy appetite for dramatic stories about Mengele as
well as the fallibility of forensic identifications.

The Marshals' Plan

At the end of March 1985, the State Department used the secret Roger
Channel to distribute a cable to its embassies in Chile, Argentina,
Uruguay, Brazil, and Paraguay,[10] announcing that the United States
had decided "to mount a major effort calling on all available intelligence resources, to locate Nazi war criminal Josef Mengele—if he
is still alive—and endeavor to have him brought to trial, most likely
in the Federal Republic of Germany."[11] The cable described what it
termed a "two track approach" on the part of the Department of Justice, "involving parallel initiatives carried out by the Office of Special
Investigations and the US Marshals Service." While OSI was to "compile a comprehensive archive" of what was known about Mengele
and was working with West Germany and Israel, the USMS had been
tasked to develop and implement a "comprehensive program to gather

by overt and clandestine means all intelligence necessary to identify and locate Mengele." All indications were that Mengele was in South America, and consequently, the marshals would focus a "good part of their initial effort" there.

In early April Howard Safir, associate director of the USMS, met with the CIA for initial discussions concerning the assistance he sought from the agency for his nascent operation. The CIA's Director-ate of Operations "pledged all possible support" and, as an immediate result of the meeting, assigned a cryptonym, or codeword, to identify the project to capture Mengele. Normally a cryptonym was composed of two parts: a two-letter combination or digraph, and a word, usu-ally drawn from a random list. The CIA assigned the cryptonym LW-CATCH to the operation—a choice that appeared to be anything but random given the clear aspirational and optimistic message it seemed to convey.

Two days after meeting with Safir, the CIA contacted its rele-vant posts in South America setting out its position on the Mengele investigation and offering guidance concerning the "get Mengele program" and particularly its "joint effort nature." Although CIA headquarters claimed that it was "readily apparent" that the mar-shals were "of necessity dealing with the vast amount of rumors, unsourced reports, and unsubstantiated information of probably dubious nature, nearly all of which has appeared in the press," it believed they could make a "worthwhile contribution" to the effort by cutting through "this chaff by concentrating on the clandestine collection of hard intelligence which may lead to Mengele's arrest (or prove his demise)." Headquarters instructed its posts to report on the existing assets available to be "tasked for information about Mengele" as well as the "potential for recruiting new sources."[12] Responses to this cable arrived at the CIA over the next several days, describing the steps that the various CIA stations planned to under-take in response to the task that had been set.

The accepted wisdom, shared by nearly all involved in the case, was that Mengele was in Paraguay, and there were many reasons why this small South American country, with a population less than half the size of New York City, should have invited such a suspicion. First, it was Mengele's last known place of residence, a country he had entered in early 1959 and where he had been naturalized as a citizen in November of that year. Nazi hunters Simon Wiesenthal and Beate Klarsfeld were convinced he was there, as were German prosecutors and police.

Paraguayan president Alfredo Stroessner had gained power through a coup in 1954 and would be ousted by another in 1989, taking refuge in Brazil. His father was from Hof, in Bavaria, and Stroessner was rumored to have offered haven to Nazis and to have enjoyed their company. Stroessner's German ancestry and reported fondness for Nazis notwithstanding, he was steadfast in his denial that Mengele remained in Paraguay following his brief residence there after his departure from Argentina.

Benno Weiser Varon, the first Israeli ambassador to Paraguay, had been sent there in 1968 to establish an embassy and to cultivate the Paraguayans who had begun a two-year term as members of the UN Security Council, where their vote was critical for the Israelis. Given that his mission was to make nice with the Paraguayans, he soon found the flood of Mengele sightings, as well as information of his whereabouts, an annoyance and a distraction. Not only was Israel making no effort to look for Mengele at that time, but Varon's acting on the proffered information might have alienated the Paraguayans, whom he was charged with cultivating.[13] Nevertheless, Varon did not have the "smallest doubt" that Mengele was in Paraguay as "everybody took it for granted."[14]

The American embassy in Asunción created a task force to focus attention and resources on the search for Mengele. Composed of the CIA station chief, the defense attaché, and senior diplomats, the task force met on May 21 with the U.S. marshals, who were visiting South American countries to lay the groundwork for their operation. The meeting represented a "quantum leap" in their efforts, which had been "devoted to generalities" until then.[15] Beginning with the assumption that "they could not expect cooperation from the Paraguayan government, and their effort . . . would have to be entirely covert,"[16] the marshals outlined a plan that would employ two kinds of activities. First, they would recruit covert agents who would gather information in Paraguay; indeed, the marshals claimed they already had "a stable of assets" that they intended to deploy.[17] Second, they would "ask the embassy to provide information, analysis and to run down leads in response to specific requests." Integral to the proposed plan would be stationing one or more marshals "in Paraguay or a neighboring country, preferably undercover, within an Embassy," in order to support these covert operations.[18]

The embassy task force members agreed that Asunción would be a poor choice for the marshals' base of operations "due to the difficulties of running clandestine operations on the scale envisaged in the fishbowl environment of Asunción, coupled with the fact that the small size of Embassy would make it difficult [to] accommodate USMS presence securely."[19] São Paulo or Montevideo were thought to be more suitable alternatives, from which the USMS could run "third country operations into Paraguay."[20] The embassy officials were clearly concerned about "the adverse effects on US-Paraguay bilateral relations" should Stroessner ever learn about the USMS operation, a prospect that was "almost inevitable, given the use of Paraguayan sources," even if run from a third country: "Paraguayans will talk and eventually Stroessner will hear of it."[21]

CIA headquarters provided guidance to their station in Asunción on May 24, agreeing with the judgment that Paraguay would not be "an appropriate operational base" for the USMS, even on a temporary basis.[22] The Marshals Service decided, instead, to locate its men in Buenos Aires. CIA headquarters agreed that the marshals would have access to Buenos Aires station communications and recommended that they be declared to local security services and receive nominal State Department cover.[23] Safir met with Ambassador Davis on May

28 and the American ambassador to Argentina, Frank V. Ortiz, on June 4 to iron out the details.[24]

Meeting in May

Our May meeting in Frankfurt came three months after the attorney general had ordered the investigation. Much had happened in that time: two Senate hearings in the United States, and the mobilization of intelligence and executive resources. The Germans, with their renewed focus on the Mengele case, had been open and accommodating, sharing the status of their investigation with us and even allowing us to copy much of their file during a late February visit to Frankfurt with representatives of the USMS. The Israelis, likewise, had ratcheted up their efforts, appointing an interagency committee to coordinate their Justice and Foreign ministries and the Mossad. It was time for the representatives of the three nations to come together.

The meeting was hosted by Hans-Eberhard Klein, a senior state prosecutor in Frankfurt in charge of the German investigation. I liked and respected Klein very much and knew him to be a kind and committed professional who did his best to make his way through the minefield that the case laid before him. Klein not only understood the particular legal and investigative challenges that faced him, but he had a keen sense of the case's political dimensions. He was joined at the table by his colleagues, Jürgen Hess, a journeyman prosecutor, and the laconic and no-nonsense Eberhard Galm, who had little patience for the nods to politics and diplomacy that Klein knew were needed. The German police were represented by Horst Gemmer, a particularly talented officer in the Hessian State Police and the brother of the police president of Frankfurt. The German Federal Police (Bundeskriminalamt, or BKA), equivalent to our FBI, were represented in the person of Johannes Horn, a senior official.

The Israeli delegation was led by Dennis Gouldman, an English-born lawyer who had spent some time in the United States. Gouldman, chair of the Israeli interagency committee, was a precise, careful, and dedicated professional who devoted himself fully to the case, representing his country faithfully and with tact and diplomacy. He was joined by Menachem Russek, who headed the unit responsible for investigating Nazi war crimes. Menachem's duties generally involved aiding other countries in their pursuit of Nazi war criminals. As a part of my responsibilities at OSI, I supervised a contractor, Efraim Zuroff, who represented our interests in Israel, and I visited Israel and met with Menachem and got to know this intense and experienced police officer. A survivor who carried with him an unmatched motivation and commitment, Menachem, a native of Łódź, Poland, had been interned by the Nazis from the beginning of the war, and among the places on his path of persecution had been Auschwitz, where he told me he had come face to face with Mengele.

The U.S. delegation was headed by Mark Richard, who enjoyed a well-deserved reputation for his sober and selfless commitment serving both Republican and Democratic administrations. Neal Sher, who had headed OSI since 1983, had the polish of an articulate, well-educated, and passionate advocate, as well as the resourcefulness and attitude of a street kid from Queens; it was a winning combination. Howard Safir of the USMS, intense and ambitious, had already had a long and successful career in federal law enforcement, which included service with the Drug Enforcement Agency and chief of the marshals' witness security division. He and his colleagues were bent on changing the reputation of the USMS, which had always been the poor cousin in federal law enforcement. Wresting from the FBI the responsibility for a certain type of fugitive investigation, the USMS sought to make a name for itself by planning and carrying out inspired and dramatic operations to sweep up large numbers of federal fugitives. The Fugitive Investigations Strike Team (FIST) lured unsuspecting fugitives with attractive bait, like Super Bowl tickets, and scored big headlines. The USMS also ventured into international waters in pursuit of high-profile criminals who had eluded the efforts of others. Mengele was high on its internal list of targets.[25] Don Ferrarone, the soft-spoken and talented chief of international operations for the USMS, accompanied Howard Safir, as did Al Matney, who had previously worked at OSI, and Arnold Stolz, a German-speaking marshal who acted as interpreter for his colleagues.

Despite the unexpected press and the unusual context of our meetings, they proceeded without drama. Each side described its activities to date and pledged cooperation and transparency in the future. The formal agreements included the formation of a working group on the police level, which would involve the exchange and coordination of investigative findings, consultation on activities, and additional joint meetings as needed. We also agreed that each nation should establish contact with its respective intelligence services and seek to reduce statements to the press, since they tended to invite a large number of low-quality leads that would only serve to complicate an investigation.[26] The most important development announced at the meeting was the Germans' plan to conduct a search of the home of Hans Sedlmeier, a close friend of the Mengele family and a former executive of the family firm. Sedlmeier had long been rumored to have acted as a link between Mengele and his family, and we all welcomed Klein's announcement of the impending search.

Sedlmeier Search

Sedlmeier had been the subject of German investigative interest since the very beginning of the case; he was a prime suspect when the question was raised about a link between the fugitive Mengele and the firm and family that had the means to support him. Sedlmeier was interrogated by German prosecutors on at least four separate occasions, beginning in March 1964, when his home and automobile were also searched.[27] In July 1964 Simon Wiesenthal claimed in a letter to Fritz Bauer that Sedlmeier was in regular contact with Mengele.

Bauer responded that he knew there had been contact in the past but was unaware that it was ongoing.[28] Beginning in December 1984, in the new phase of the Mengele investigation, Sedlmeier was questioned three times in three months. During an interrogation in March, Sedlmeier admitted that he had repeatedly visited Mengele in Argentina in late 1957.

In March 1985, perhaps spurred on by the reward and certainly by the renewed publicity surrounding the search for Mengele, a professor from Gießen, Jürgen Harte, reported to authorities that a few years earlier, he had overheard a tipsy Sedlmeier describe going to South America "for years" to bring money to Mengele. The professor's revelation provided the basis for the prosecutor's office in Frankfurt to seek a court order to search Sedlmeier's home:

> The witness Sedlmeier is to be regarded as the central figure in the relationship between Mengele and his family. For this reason, he has already been interrogated four times. Sedlmeier admits that he had kept contact with the accused until 1960. However, he has always denied having supplied him with money.... In contrast to this, he indicated, in 1982 or 1983, that (after consuming alcohol, which means according to the proverb, that he spoke the truth) he had gone to South America routinely over the years and delivered money to the accused.... It must be assumed that he knows more than he revealed in his interrogations.[29]

The initial petition for a warrant to search the "home, automobile, and person" of Sedlmeier for evidence concerning the whereabouts of Mengele was denied by the court on April 15, 1985.[30] Prosecutors were, however, successful in appeal, and the warrant was issued on May 2, 1985.

Not until the final day of May could the search, a combined effort of relevant federal, provincial, and local police, take place. The original plan to begin the operation at six a.m. was modified out of consideration for Sedlmeier's advanced age (he was seventy-five) and rescheduled for eight a.m.[31] It did not take long for the search to bear fruit. Within a few hours, Kriminalhauptkommissar Schöller from the BKA called his headquarters in Wiesbaden to announce the discovery of some correspondence concealed in a cupboard in Sedlmeier's wife's bedroom, along with a 1985 datebook belonging to Hans Sedlmeier.[32] One letter in particular raised a red flag: a three-page, single-spaced, typewritten letter, with the salutation "Lieber Messerle!" and beginning with the sentence, "I am very sad to have to tell you today of the death of our mutual friend."[33] Reading through the letter, one quickly grasped its conspiratorial nature: "We believe that we are all unanimous in wanting to continue to maintain the secrecy as before. Not only in order to avoid personal difficulties, but also to let the other side continue to waste time and money on something that is already obsolete."[34]

The police knew they had an important lead and believed that the letter might have come from Mengele himself. Although there was a good deal of material still to digest, they now had a solid indication that Mengele could be in Brazil. Comparing names that appeared in the letter with Sedlmeier's datebook, they determined that one of the people mentioned in the letter, Geza Stammer, lived in São Paulo. In addition, a telephone number with area code indicated that the letter writer also lived in São Paulo. Sedlmeier fueled their suspicions when he refused to testify about the address and behaved "strangely" when asked.[35] If the police were surprised by the discovery, they were certainly joined by Sedlmeier, who had not known his wife had preserved the correspondence. Commenting later to a *New York Times* reporter, he quipped, "My wife stupidly kept it. Stupid. I don't know why she did it, but that's what got us in the end. They came here and found it."[36]

By noon, the Germans were drafting a memorandum describing the new evidence for their diplomatic posts in Brazil and the Brazilian Federal Police. As police officials in BKA headquarters in Wiesbaden prepared to extend their investigation to Brazil, the search in Günzburg continued, and additional evidence mounted. In late afternoon, contact was established by telephone with the German embassy in Brasilia, and an official there agreed to request the necessary support from the leadership of the Brazilian Federal Police. The Wiesbaden officials believed it was crucial to act quickly, since word of the search and its outcome could likely not be contained, and it would only be a matter of time before the news would spread to Brazil and Mengele or his protectors would be warned. The BKA called the German consulate in São Paulo and appealed for immediate action.

The German consular official, Sepp Wölker, made an appointment with the responsible police authorities in São Paulo for two p.m.— six p.m. German time—that afternoon; he had already secured their agreement to assist. There followed a number of hurried telephone calls and exchanges of information that, compounded by less-than-ideal communications, led to considerable confusion. Wölker reported that the Brazilian police had dispatched teams to apprehend and question the individuals whose names or addresses had been sent by the Germans, only to indicate early the next morning that it had been a misunderstanding. The Germans, in turn, discovered that they had transmitted some incorrect information in their rushed early reports. The Brazilians identified residents at the addresses supplied by the Germans as being extremely unlikely to have had anything to do with Mengele. For instance, one was the head of the Nestlé operation in São Paulo—a third-generation Brazilian citizen.

The next day, Saturday, Wölker reported that the Brazilians had not yet confronted anyone and that their analysis had not yet identified a suspect. Furthermore, he informed the German police that they could not count on any investigative activities over the weekend. Dr. Aparecido Laertes Calandra, chief of the operations center of the Brazilian Federal Police in São Paulo State and a graduate of a BKA training course, had requested a telephone meeting with the BKA on Monday morning to discuss further tactical steps, imposing a much-needed breather on what had been a too hectic and undisciplined effort. The

Germans welcomed this enforced pause, realizing that the scope of the evidence seized at the Sedlmeier home did not "permit a comprehensive evaluation" on so tight a time frame.

With more time, Dieter Sack, a high-ranking BKA officer, analyzed the material from the Sedlmeier search, focusing on the undated letter from "MUS" to "Messerle," among others.[37] Based on the physical evidence, he concluded that the typewriter was from a country whose language did not use umlauts, since the umlauts in the letter were rendered by superimposing a quotation mark over relevant letters. He determined the identity of "MUS" by cross-referencing a telephone number in the letter to the name "Bossert," which appeared in Sedlmeier's datebook. Sack was able to fix the approximate date that "Uncle" died since the letter describing his death was referred to in another letter—this one dated April 20, 1979—as having been written "two months earlier." A reference to the marriage of "Messerle's son" provided clear evidence that "Messerle" and Sedlmeier were one and the same.[38]

Sack summarized the content of the letter, describing how Bossert reported the "detailed circumstances" of the death and burial of their mutual friend, "Uncle." During a vacation "at the sea," "Uncle" suffered a stroke while swimming. Bossert was able to pull him from the water, but "Uncle" died on the beach. "Uncle" was buried under the name "Lange," in a double grave alongside the real Lange's mother, an eventuality that "Lange" had prepared for by informing the cemetery administrator that an old and "ailing relative" might soon be buried there. The cemetery administrator almost "ruined everything," however, when he wanted to open the coffin to bid farewell—a Brazilian custom—to Lange, whom he had known. To prevent the opening of the coffin, which would have unraveled their plans, Bossert's wife launched an "attack of hysteria," which Bossert described as only "half pretense."[39]

The discovered correspondence revealed that "Uncle" had lived with a maid in a house whose official owner was Geza Stammer, located not too far from São Paulo, since "Uncle" often visited the Bosserts there. Following the death of "Uncle," Stammer wanted to be "rid of the connection as soon as possible." Sack concluded his analysis with the following: "In analyzing the letter in combination with the other secured correspondence, it is clear with high probability, that 'Uncle' is the wanted Josef Mengele, who died in Brazil in February 1979 and was buried by the Bossert family under the name 'Lange.'"[40] Instead of seeking to locate Josef Mengele alive, the Germans now had to reckon with the likelihood that their search had ended. They needed only to confirm the death of their long-sought quarry.

On the afternoon of Monday, June 3, 1985, Hans Klein met with officials from all German parties involved in the investigation, including the Hessian Ministry of Justice. He had much to report. He summarized the evidence located during the Sedlmeier search and revealed that the BKA had concluded, with high probability, that Mengele had died in 1979. There was a discussion about the possibility that the new evidence had been "planted" to fool the investigators into believing Mengele was dead; the assembled group judged the odds to be "50–50." The group questioned why the Mengele family had not reported Mengele's death, given how much they had been inconvenienced by the authorities and harassed by the press, and how their business had suffered. One explanation, they reasoned, might have been that the family had a strategic reason for keeping silent—wishing to wait out the five-year statute of limitations, which would protect nonfamily members, like Sedlmeier, from criminal exposure for obstruction of justice through their protection of Josef Mengele.

The group agreed that the new developments in Brazil had to be pursued and decided upon a number of concrete steps, including renewed interrogation of Sedlmeier and members of the Mengele family, as well as a judicial assistance request to Brazilian authorities to question Bossert, Stammer, and others. They also called for the exhumation of the body in Brazil and requested that the BKA reach out to the Brazilian police through the German consulate in São Paulo, and possibly send German police officials to São Paulo. Finally, they decided not to inform their Israeli and American partners until there was more clarity, and to keep the press in the dark.[41]

Later that day, direct contact between the BKA and Calandra of the Brazilian police was established, and it was decided that two BKA officials as well as Horst Gemmer from the Hessian Criminal Police (Landeskriminalamt) would travel to Brazil. A new and final chapter in the Mengele case was about to begin. No one knew how complex and drawn out it would prove to be.

CHAPTER 10

SÃO PAULO

(June 1985)

A Body Is Exhumed

Despite the agreement that all significant evidence would be shared among their partners in the tripartite investigation, the Germans feared that the news would leak, and that Mengele, if still alive, would go even further underground, or that important evidence would be destroyed by those who had sheltered him. News of the significant turn in the case and the Germans' hurried departure for Brazil reached U.S. officials only on the morning of Thursday, June 6. The director of the BKA called a contact in the CIA in Germany, reporting the likely death of Josef Mengele in a "swimming accident in 1979" and that his body had been buried in São Paulo. He indicated that this information resulted from a search of the premises of a "Mengele contact," that the Germans had sent a representative to São Paulo to "check out the story," that they "now believe the story is most likely true," and that the grave "reputed to be Mengele's" would be opened later that day. In what turned out to be a most accurate prediction, the Germans told their American contact that they expected a "great fuss" in the media as soon as news of the exhumation became known.[1]

The two marshals, John Pascucci and Rafael Fonseca, who had been scheduled to travel that evening to Buenos Aires to initiate their search for Mengele in South America,[2] were redirected to São Paulo instead to follow up on the recent development. While Pascucci and Fonseca headed to Brazil, the German police officers Gemmer, Sack, and Schöller had already spent a full day's work there. They had met with Brazilian Federal Police chief Romeu Tuma and his deputy, Aparecido Laertes Calandra, to show the Brazilians the material they had secured during the Sedlmeier search and to clarify the details of their cooperation. They were keenly aware of their status in Brazil and sensitive to the diplomacy required by their working outside their jurisdiction. Formally, they were operating under an investigative assistance agreement that had been executed between, on one side, the Frankfurt Prosecutor's Office, the BKA, and the Hessian Criminal Police, and, on the other, the German consulate general in São Paulo and the Brazilian Federal Police. In their first report home, they described assisting the Brazilian police by providing information and analysis and carrying out interviews of witnesses "at the request" of their hosts.

On the afternoon of June 5, immediately after they had arrived, Sack accompanied the Brazilian Federal Police as they searched the home of Wolfram and Liselotte Bossert, where they discovered three files of letters that corresponded with those found in the Sedlmeier search. Confronted with this evidence, the Bosserts admitted they had known Mengele and confirmed that he had died on the beach in Bertioga, about one hundred kilometers away, and had been buried under the name "Wolfgang Gerhard." The German police were permitted to question them informally, the first of six interviews that they would conduct with the Bosserts over the next two weeks. These sessions, and two with Gitta Stammer, whose husband was on a trip and would remain away throughout the Germans' stay in Brazil, provided a seamless and relatively detailed account of Mengele's residence in Brazil.

In the late 1960s the Bosserts had been introduced to a certain "Senhor Pedro" by Wolfgang Gerhard, a mutual acquaintance, who was from Austria. At that time "Senhor Pedro" was living on a farm in the vicinity of São Paulo with Gitta and Geza Stammer. A year or so after meeting "Senhor Pedro," the Bosserts became aware of his true identity. Around 1969 Mengele moved to a house in the Eldorado section of São Paulo, where he remained until his death. Wolfgang Gerhard returned to Austria around 1974, where he died in 1978; before leaving Brazil, he gave Mengele his ID card, along with other personal identification, which Mengele modified with a photograph of himself and used as his own. The Bosserts told the investigators that Rolf Mengele had visited his father in São Paulo in 1977 or 1978 and had returned to visit at the end of 1979, after his father's death. At that time he retrieved some of his father's personal possessions and photographed his grave.

The Bosserts' physical description of Mengele included mention of a wide gap between his two upper front teeth. They claimed he had had a procedure in Argentina to alter this distinguishing feature, which led to his having to wear a dental prosthesis in later years, and that Mengele had also undergone a failed plastic surgery attempt that had left scars. They could not, however, provide any information about wartime wounds, physical defects, or any other surgeries. The Bosserts also provided an assessment of Mengele's temperament, describing him as a difficult and demanding man with a strong personality—a man who sought to dominate. He had spoken often about his life in Germany but avoided any talk of his time at Auschwitz.

Wolfram Bossert explained how Mengele had used a "cutout" to manage his correspondence with Germany: letters would be sent in a double envelope to a certain Herr Schweigard in Augsburg, who would pass the sealed inner envelope on to Hans Sedlmeier or Karl-Heinz. He explained that they had kept the news of Mengele's death a secret, fearing retaliation from the Israelis, and stressed that they had been motivated by "humanitarian" and not "political" concerns; for Bossert, "a refugee's fate is worse than a death sentence."[3]

ON THE AFTERNOON OF June 6, the German police officers accompanied their Brazilian colleagues to witness the exhumation of the grave, identified by the Bosserts as Mengele's, in a cemetery in Embu, a suburb of São Paulo. In the spare syntax of their telexed message back to Germany, they reported on the unearthing of the body and the unorthodox circumstances that surrounded the event:

> On June 6, 1985, from 1:30 pm to 2:45 pm, the exhumation took place under the supervision of a Brazilian forensic pathologist in the presence of several hundred representatives of the international media. Essential findings:
> — Bosserts identified the remains of the coffin
> — Condition of the vegetation on the grave and the soil are consistent with a long period of being undisturbed;
> — Skeletonized body with an upper jaw prosthesis and the remains of a suit.
>
> Despite repeated attempts, neither German police officials nor the deputy consul general, who was present, could influence the preparation or execution of the exhumation or do anything about the presence of journalists in the immediate area of the grave.
>
> The skeleton was not secured intact along with the casket but was rather removed unsystematically as individual pieces. What remained of the casket remained in the grave.[4]

Even a casual viewer of American television in the last two decades, with its many programs dedicated to forensic science, both crime dramas and documentaries, would be able to identify the significant problems that attended the exhumation carried out by the Brazilians. The public nature of the spectacle and its hurried manner prevented the requisite painstaking and systematic approach. Before a shovel ever met the ground, the entire site should have been secured, mapped, and photographed. Great care should have been taken to excavate the burial container so it could be removed from the grave intact, ideally to a place where it could be opened and the body within examined and photographed in situ. Each of the skeleton's 206 bones, some of which are quite small, should have been retrieved. The clothing and any other objects in the container should also have been examined and photographed. Few, if any, of these steps were taken, and the gravedigger, under the supervision of the Brazilian police and the forensic pathologist, disturbed the evidence in irreparable ways. Perhaps most egregious was his breaking of the casket, which resulted in damaging the skull of the skeleton within. This unprofessional performance compromised the identification of the body before any real work had even begun.

The U.S. consulate general was closed on June 6 in observation of the Feast of Corpus Christi, and Consul General Steve Dachi was at home when his press attaché called to report that the exhumation of a grave thought to be that of Josef Mengele was being broadcast live on television. Dachi tuned in and witnessed a man standing in an excavated grave handing bones, one by one, up to a colleague. The dramatic high point echoed a scene out of *Hamlet*: a skull hoisted out of the grave, accompanied by the cacophonous, cricket-like clicks of scores of cameras recording the macabre event.

That evening Dachi met with a German BKA official for three hours and later provided the State Department with a clear and cogent summary of what had led to the exhumation. Dachi related the German claim that they had had "no time" to share news of their findings with the Americans or the Israelis, since they feared Mengele might still be living and had to act quickly. He reported on what had been gleaned from the interrogations of the Bosserts and Gitta Stammer about Mengele's residence, death, and burial in Brazil and conveyed the Germans' evident frustration with the conduct of their Brazilian colleagues:

According to the BKA agent, São Paulo Federal Police chief Romeu Tuma and Forensic Pathologist Jose Antonio Melo spent more time and effort showing off to the television cameras than they did looking after the evidence. At the Bossert residence, they failed to wear gloves while fingering through all the papers, even though the German experts practically thrust them into their hands. At the gravesite, they failed to record or photograph the remains including pieces or shreds of hair and clothing in their original relationship, instead dumping everything indiscriminately into a large container, after holding up various bones to the television cameras.[5]

Summarizing the Germans' attitude at the end of the first eventful day of the investigation in Brazil, Dachi wrote:

> Although the German officers on the scene are convinced of the strength of their recently seized evidence that Josef Mengele lived in São Paulo from 1967 and died there in 1979, they cannot be certain that the [exhumed] remains . . . will prove to be his. What worries them the most is that the Brazilian identification process will be a cursory or unscientific one, and that whatever conclusion they reach will not be acceptable or convincing to either the German or to the experts of other identified countries. . . . The BKA representative fears that the Brazilians have a strong, politically motivated interest in a quick, positive identification, and may not study or work through the evidence seriously enough to be convincing to outside experts. The latter prospect, given the years of effort which has gone into this case, has left the German team present in São Paulo, at least for the moment, profoundly depressed.[6]

Although nothing could undo what had already occurred, the Germans hoped, as did their American colleagues, that the Brazilians would allow other experts to join in the work that awaited them.

The key Brazilian official in charge of the Mengele investigation was Romeu Tuma, chief of the Brazilian Federal Police in the state of São Paulo, a handsome, well-dressed figure with jet-black hair and moustache who was keenly interested in making an impression on the press. The atmosphere at the police headquarters in downtown São Paulo, located on the upper floors of a nineteen-story building, seemed chaotic to a first-time visitor. As crowds of people waited for an audience, interview, or interrogation, a platoon of liveried waiters served coffee from large round trays they carried above the heads of the milling crowds. In a *New York Times* profile published during the investigation, Tuma emerges as an intriguing figure, a "different kind of policeman," who carried no gun, eschewed alcohol and tobacco, and was a practicing Roman Catholic.[7] He was armed with a sense of humor and a welcome frankness—two important qualities that would help him in June 1985. He knew something about survival, having managed to emerge intact from the period of military rule in Brazil ending in March 1985, during which he had served in the notorious Department of Political and Social Order (DOPS). Although DOPS had used torture as a tool against opponents, Tuma, trained as a lawyer, was never accused of human rights abuses. He is quoted as opposing torture as immoral, unethical, and inefficient. In 1978 Tuma had gotten involved with his first case involving a former Nazi when he arrested Gustav Wagner, the "hangman" of Sobibór, who was living in São Paulo.[8]

Tuma accounted for his ability to operate effectively in both regimes by explaining that he was a "professional." But the Mengele case called upon more than a police officer's professionalism; it thrust Tuma into the spotlight of intense interest from the huge contingent of international press that had descended upon São Paulo. He was faced with having to protect the dignity and reputation of his own police force while satisfying the acute pressure from the United States and Germany, whose representatives were unnerved by what they had seen during the exhumation and concerned about the reliability and expertise of the Brazilian authorities. Displaying some of the humor noted in the *New York Times*, Tuma commented to the press assembled at the gravesite following the exhumation that he could assure them of one thing—that the body buried there was "well and truly dead." He also claimed that he was "100 percent convinced" that the body was Mengele's but quickly added that he would "await the results of the medical examiners."[9]

On the morning of June 6, 1985, OSI director Neal Sher was in a Washington, D.C., Metro train on his way to the office from his suburban Virginia home. He did not normally take public transportation, but he had a speaking engagement in Boston that evening, and rather than leave his car at the airport or in a downtown garage overnight, he had opted for the train. OSI historian Peter Black coincidentally boarded the same car a few minutes later and, seeing Sher, greeted him by saying, "I guess you've heard the news?" "What news?" Sher remembers responding. When Black related what he'd heard of the exhumation from the morning news, Sher was surprised and skeptical. Surely, if this were a legitimate lead, the Germans would have told us, he thought, though when he got to the office and called Hans Klein, Klein confirmed the story. Sher's travel plans changed dramatically. Instead of Boston, he would be going to Brazil.[10]

Sher was not the only skeptic. Hans Klein's boss in the Frankfurt Prosecutor's Office, Heinz Haueisen, told the New York Times, "We have to be careful. We do not want to say that it was in fact Mengele until we have proof."[11] Senator Alphonse D'Amato warned that the body in the grave might be "a Mengele Smokescreen," explaining that "a man like Mengele" might have "faked" his own death. He called upon the Justice Department to send a team of forensic specialists to Brazil to "examine the exhumed body." Simon Wiesenthal, who had just arrived in New York for a previously scheduled visit, also expressed doubt, saying that Mengele's reported death was inconsistent with "many reported sightings." Rabbi Marvin Hier claimed to be "very skeptical," questioning why Mengele's family would not have announced his death earlier, putting a halt to all the negative publicity that the very public search for him had brought upon the family.

Serge Klarsfeld voiced a similar concern but said he would await the results of the forensic examination. The *Frankfurter Rundschau*'s article on the discovery of the grave and exhumation was titled "An Open Grave Should Bring Clarity." Nothing could have been further from the truth.

Tensions

The first challenge facing the Americans and the Germans was to secure a role in the forensic examination of the exhumed body. The Brazilians, who were sensitive to the optics of foreigners swooping in and taking over, had much at stake. Not only were issues of sovereignty at play, but the competence and dignity of Brazilian police and medical personnel could be seen as being challenged. At the same time, the governments that had joined together in the investigation had much at stake as well. The Brazilians had shaken all confidence in their ability to reach a decisive and unchallengeable conclusion, and confidence was key.

Sher arrived in São Paulo on June 7, in the middle of a highly sensitive public drama. According to the Germans, he almost immediately placed Tuma under "considerable pressure" to depart from the bilateral German-Brazilian approach that had been functioning up to that point, arguing that the case was "of international importance" and should be handled on an international basis. An international team of experts could assume leadership, Sher believed, or at least teams of experts in forensics, interrogation, and securing of evidence could have responsibility in their respective areas. Tuma turned Sher down flatly.[12] Concerned, Wölker took Sher aside to warn him that his approach to Tuma "threatened to destroy ongoing cooperation on the working level." He assumed that the Brazilians would not "accept a usurpation of their control of the case," and that a "formal" rejection of Sher's proposal, once given, might scuttle the opportunity for finding a reasonable solution.[13] Wölker advised that the only way to secure the cooperation that Sher had suggested was to appeal to the Brazilian government in the capital, Brasilia.

Dachi also witnessed Tuma's entrenched attitude when he met with him on the morning of June 7. Tuma insisted that his police force was "quite capable of carrying out a thorough investigation without outside assistance" and was bothered that both U.S. Marshal Rafael Fonseca and Sher had arrived in São Paulo uninvited.[14] Realizing the prospects were shaky for changing Tuma's view of the matter, Dachi evidently spoke with higher-ups at the State Department and the U.S. embassy in Brasilia, which resulted in the deputy chief of mission (DCM) at the embassy making an informal démarche to the Brazilian Foreign Ministry.

The DCM met with the acting foreign minister that evening and explained "that the Embassy had heard reports that police authorities in São Paulo might not be handling the analysis of the evidence in the Josef Mengele case in accordance with the highest standards." He suggested that this impression "could prompt doubts around the world about whether the exhumed remains were really Mengele's, as well as about Brazilian capabilities and intentions." After an energetic and tactful exchange, peppered with tough talk, the Brazilian diplomat told the DCM that his government was being "as cooperative as it could" with foreign officials and said he would call the minister of justice and urge him to instruct the police to do so as well.[15]

On Sunday, June 9, Dennis Gouldman, the chairman of the Israeli interagency Mengele team, reached Sher in his hotel room and was brought up to date on the progress of the case.[16] Sher told Gouldman of the current plan to proceed on two paths: an examination of the documents that had been discovered, and an examination of the body. The documents, if found to be authentic, would establish that Mengele had lived in Brazil, a necessary condition for his having died there. Sher revealed that the press had been used strategically to put pressure on the Brazilians to allow outside experts to participate in the investigation. He also informed Gouldman that the day before, Tuma had agreed to allow U.S. and German experts to review the documents, and that U.S. experts, along with Mengele's original BDC file containing examples of his handwriting for comparison, would arrive the next evening. The pathological examination of the remains would be conducted by the Brazilians. Sher advised Gouldman that if the Israelis wished to send experts, their ambassador should request that they be allowed to take part as observers.

After their initial intransigence, the Brazilian police were gracious hosts. While emphasizing that the case was "a Brazilian matter," Tuma ultimately conceded, in an elegant turn of phrase, that "science has no borders" and "welcomed" U.S. and German assistance in weighing the evidence.[17]

Rolf Speaks

Before the experts even began their work, Mengele's son, Rolf, issued a statement that removed all doubt about his position and that of his family concerning his father's death. When news of the discovery in Brazil broke, Rolf had been in Spain on vacation with his wife and child. Touring in a motor home without a set itinerary, he was cut off from the world, and there was no way anyone could reach him.[18] When he returned to Freiburg on Friday, June 7, the day after the exhumation, he switched on the television and learned that the secret he and his family had been harboring for more than six years was now out. In an interview with Gerald Posner, Rolf said:

> I thought to myself, "this is serious." I thought that [my cousin] Dieter must have leaked the story. We had all had an agreement that none of us would act without consulting the others, so I was a little surprised. The last time we met in March, Dieter had been very anxious to get the story out but without involving the Stammers or the Bosserts or the family at this end. So I thought not only had Dieter leaked it but that it had all gone wrong.[19]

He soon discovered, however, that his cousin Dieter had been trying to reach him for some time to explain what had really tipped the authorities off. As the story of the grave in Brazil and the very public exhumation spread, Rolf found his home under siege from the media and his phone ringing off the hook. He proposed to his cousins in Günzburg that the family issue a statement. "I didn't see how we could avoid it anymore," he told Posner. "The Stammers were talking, the Bosserts were talking. It would all come out sooner or later."[20] But Dieter and Karl-Heinz refused, still believing that they could continue to hide their involvement.

Everyone in Günzburg was "paralyzed," and so Rolf decided to act on his own. He was advised to go public by a journalist friend of his secretary and sister-in-law, Sabine Hackenjos. According to Posner, Rolf realized that he could not only quench the public's intense thirst for information about his father's fate, but also make a great deal of money. He tried unsuccessfully to contact *Stern* magazine on June 9, but he was able to meet with representatives of *Bunte* the next day, and they came to terms on a deal that would permit *Bunte* to have access to his father's correspondence and notebooks, which he had retrieved from São Paulo in 1979.

The next day Rolf issued this short statement, which was telexed to Klein in Frankfurt and read by Sabine Hackenjos to the press:

> I have no doubt that the corpse exhumed at the cemetery in Embu, Brazil, on June 6, 1985, is the remains of my father, Josef Mengele. I am certain that the forensic examination will confirm this fact soon. The family is prepared to provide material evidence [*Hinweise*] for the identification. I confirmed the details of his death myself in 1979 in Brazil. Out of respect for those who were in contact with him for 30 years, I have remained silent.[21]

The statement included a sentence that expressed Rolf's "deepest sympathy," and that of his family, for "all victims and their relatives."

Rolf's cousins were not happy; he told Posner that Dieter and Karl-Heinz were "totally opposed" to his issuing the statement. His cousins may have had a point, for if Rolf had thought he could somehow quiet the public's interest or settle any questions with his statement, he was to be disappointed.

German officials urged caution, warning that Rolf's statement "could be a camouflage tactic" and that they would wait for the results of the forensic inquiry. For his part, a confident but cautious Romeu Tuma "was not surprised by Rolf Mengele's statement. . . . I would have been surprised if it had contradicted our evidence. But we must await the results of the scientific tests."[22] On the other hand, Menachem Russek, the Israeli police official, saw no reason to wait; Rolf's statement did not change "his opinion." He reasoned that "if the family were convinced that he was dead, they would have been the first to come out and announce it, so that people would leave them alone." Miriam Zeiger, a representative of CANDLES speaking on behalf of Mengele twin survivors, agreed: "All of us twins are sure that it is simply a deception."[23]

Document Examination

OSI was very familiar with document and handwriting forensics; many of our cases relied on documents received from the Soviet Union, which were often challenged in court as forgeries. To establish the authenticity of these documents, we engaged forensic experts, often Tony Cantu from the Secret Service, to prove through chemical analysis that the documents' paper and ink were consistent with their date.[24] To establish the identity of handwriting or signatures, we used a handwriting expert, usually Gideon Epstein from the Immigration and Naturalization Service, who would compare the questioned handwriting with known samples. Epstein was already familiar with the Mengele case, having previously identified Mengele's hand behind the signature of "Helmut Gregor" in the Red Cross document Mengele obtained to travel to Argentina in 1949.[25]

Cantu and Epstein, along with David Crown, a former CIA document expert then in private practice, were selected to perform the examination of the purported Mengele documents found in São Paulo. The three experts departed for Brazil in the early evening of Monday, June 10, 1985. As a clear indication of the change of attitude on the part of the Brazilian authorities, the three, along with Michael Wolf, Sher's deputy, who replaced him as OSI representative in São Paulo, were given VIP treatment when they arrived at the airport on the morning of June 11, with Brazilian Federal Police taking care of all customs and immigration formalities. Dachi described the new Brazilian attitude as "not only one of tolerance, but of genuine appreciation," thanks to the "discreet handling of media and cultural sensitivity" displayed by U.S. representatives in São Paulo and Washington. He emphasized that it was "imperative that we continue to maintain a low profile and let the Brazilians prove it's their show."[26]

The actual work of examining the documents began in earnest on June 12. Cantu's role was to look for anachronistic characteristics or ingredients in the paper and ink used in the documents—a forgery's smoking gun. It was just such an analysis that had identified the notorious "Hitler Diaries" as forgeries just a few years before. Although the fake diaries had supposedly survived the careful scrutiny of historical and handwriting experts,[27] an analysis of the paper and the materials in the binding revealed them to have been manufactured after the period during which the diaries were supposedly created. The scandal that erupted in the wake of the fraud invited a healthy skepticism of the work of document examiners and handwriting experts.

When Cantu completed his work later that summer, he found that eight different inks had been used in the fourteen documents that he examined, and he compared them to those in the standard ink library of the Bureau of Alcohol, Tobacco and Firearms. One of the inks, a black ballpoint pen ink used in two of the documents dated 1979, had been manufactured by the Bic Pen Company in Milford, Connecticut, between November 1, 1974, and August 4, 1977, but was not distributed in Brazil. A "black fluid ink" used in another document had been manufactured by the Parker Pen Company of Janesville, Wisconsin, between 1958 and 1968 and was available in Brazil. The other inks had "characteristics found in standard inks available before 1965." There were no watermarks on any of the examined papers, which precluded a precise determination of the source or date of their manufacture, but they all had "characteristics of papers manufactured prior to 1979." Cantu concluded that there was no evidence that would "eliminate the possibility that the samples were prepared prior to 1979." The one ink not available in Brazil could have been brought there by some means other than commercial sales.[28]

Crown and Epstein agreed that they would independently examine the documents, which were divided into fourteen lots, and compare their findings when their work was complete. Their assessment included "microscopic work" for the "purpose of studying the line quality of the writing," "transmitted and oblique light analysis" to evaluate the surface of the paper, and ultraviolet light work to "identify the absence or presence of unusual fluorescence with the ink or paper." Without discovering any such evidence, they moved on to compare the handwriting in Josef Mengele's BDC file—the original of which had been brought to Brazil[29]—with the material discovered in the home of the Bosserts.

Epstein admitted great confidence in the results of his handwriting analysis, claiming that it "reconfirmed, more clearly than ever before," that handwriting habits,

> once firmly established through time and use, will change only slightly over the years, and that even the most blatant and insignificant characteristics remain with us through good times and bad. But most of all it has reconfirmed that there exists within a large collection of handwriting from one person changes in

rhythm, speed, legibility, and degree of abbreviation in the same way these changes occur in our speech.[30]

The prerequisites for a successful analysis were present in the generous quantities of both known and questioned samples. Mengele's BDC file contained two handwritten autobiographical statements with "much the same material repeated in both," which provided the examiners with what amounted to a handwriting exemplar written twice, allowing them access to the same words and, in some cases, identical sentences displaying the natural variations that characterize handwriting. When Mengele wrote these short autobiographical pieces, his handwriting was that of a twenty-seven-year-old, and he had already established "firmly unconscious handwriting habits." For comparison, there was also a rich trove of handwritten letters, essays, and notes written over a long period of time, which offered more than a sufficient opportunity to examine and compare characteristics and idiosyncrasies. Epstein identified several of these features in both the questioned and known samples. For instance, there was an obvious "baseline habit," with the writing "going downhill," being higher on the left than on the right, whether there was an actual line on the paper or not. Similarly, he discovered similarities in "letter construction, connecting strokes, height ratios, and spacing habits as well as the internal slant characteristics" present in both the questioned and the known samples. Epstein also made note of distinctive forms of the German diacritical umlaut and the diagraph double-S.

Epstein concluded, and Crown concurred,[31] that eight of the questioned documents were written by Josef Mengele and two were not. They also found that the typewritten parts of one of the documents were not prepared by either of the typewriters seized in the search of the Bossert home. Their findings, described as "definite," were announced at a press conference hosted by Tuma. Crown said, "[We] made a thorough examination and are definitely convinced beyond a shadow of doubt that [the documents] are written by Josef Mengele. . . .

If we'd had any doubt, we would have expressed it. . . . It's a definite identification. We're staking our reputations on it."[32]

The stage had been set for what might be the long-sought denouement of the Mengele drama. Witnesses had testified to his demise, and his son, breaking his long silence, offered confirmation. There was, however, still much work to do. Through diplomacy and the power of their presence, Germany and the United States had overcome the initial intransigence of the Brazilian authorities and secured a role for their experts in the case. Exacting analysis of the documents that Mengele had left behind proved that he had lived in Brazil. What remained was to determine if he had died there.

CHAPTER 11

"A BIOGRAPHY OF BONES"

(June 1985)

While events were unfolding in Brazil, efforts were under way in the United States to assemble a team of forensic medical and anthropological experts to examine the Embu remains. What was known about the case at the time suggested that the choice of experts would be important. There was unlikely to be a single test or comparison that could render an unambiguous judgment; the skill, experience, and reputation of the experts would make all the difference. Reflecting the immense public interest in the case, two teams were ultimately sent—one by the U.S. Department of Justice and the other by the Simon Wiesenthal Center with the help of Senator Alfonse D'Amato.

The Experts

D'Amato heard the news of the impending exhumation in Brazil from his aide, Morgan Hardiman, on June 6. Hardiman told the senator that he had just spoken by phone with Sher, who "doesn't know any more than we do" and was on his way to Brazil.[1] D'Amato's immediate reaction was to call Dr. Leslie Lukash, the chief medical examiner of Nassau County, whom he had known since the 1960s. Lukash was among the most experienced and respected forensic pathologists in the country, and D'Amato asked him to go to Brazil to "keep an eye on things."[2] Lukash was willing to go, but not alone, and counseled that a team would be necessary. To do it right, he explained, he would need an anthropologist, an odontologist to evaluate forensic dental evidence, and a radiologist. With D'Amato's encouragement, Lukash began to contact colleagues as an initial step in forming a team.

His first call was to Clyde Snow, a legendary, hard-drinking anthropologist from Oklahoma, just back from a trip to Argentina, where he had helped to identify the bodies of those murdered by the government during the military regime. Snow was game. Lukash's next call was to John Fitzpatrick in Chicago, a forensic radiologist with a sterling reputation. Fitzpatrick was willing to go. The last call was to Lowell Levine, an odontologist who had worked with the Nassau County medical examiner's office for some years. Lukash couldn't locate Levine, who, it turns out, was on active duty with the navy reserve in New Orleans.

That evening Lukash watched the exhumation on the evening news. Eric Stover, a human rights worker with the American Association for the Advancement of Science, who was to join Lukash's team as an observer and a chronicler, quoted Lukash muttering to himself, "Christ, they're making a goddamn carnival show out of this," and, later, "They exhumed that skeleton like a bunch of Keystone cops. The only thing they didn't do was serve drinks and hamburgers."[3] Snow, who had seen the same coverage in Oklahoma, appeared on *Nightline* the next night, telling Charlie Gibson, "Having a policeman dig up a skeleton is a little bit like having a chimpanzee do a heart transplant. . . . Skeletal remains are extremely fragile. . . . Small items, such as teeth, bullets, other personal effects, which could be helpful in identification, do tend to get lost. And what you need to use is the same sort of painstaking, methodical technique that archeologists have used for a hundred years in excavating prehistoric remains."[4]

The U.S. marshals, who had taken responsibility for assembling the Justice Department team, rejected Lukash, Snow, and Fitzpatrick but were able to locate Levine and secure his agreement on June 10 to go to

Brazil on their behalf. They also added University of Maryland anthropologist Ellis Kerley, who had misidentified Walter Branaa as Mengele two months earlier, and Ali Hameli, the chief medical examiner for the State of Delaware. Senator D'Amato could not have been happy when his man, Lukash, was passed over, leaving him distanced from the case. Morgan Hardiman told Eric Stover that D'Amato "wanted the best scientists, the very best team. Then he's snubbed. So we dug in our heels."[5] Hardiman called Rabbi Marvin Hier in Los Angeles and secured his agreement to send Lukash, Snow, and Fitzpatrick to Brazil as a separate team representing the Wiesenthal Center.[6]

The two teams represented the first rank of American forensic specialists, each experienced in a range of cases from large-scale tragedies, like airline disasters and mass atrocities, to individual murder cases. They were routinely called upon to determine the cause of death in a given situation and, with increasing frequency, the identity of the victim. From the mass suicides at Jonestown to the assassination of John F. Kennedy, these men had offered their professional opinions. There was a major distinction, however, between the two teams. Hameli, Kerley, and Levine were being paid and were working for the U.S. government, while Fitzpatrick, Lukash, and Snow had volunteered their services and were working on behalf of the Simon Wiesenthal Center and its dean, Rabbi Hier, who took care of their travel and per diem expenses. Although the scientists were serving different masters, the differences in compensation and chain of command had no effect on their easy interaction and cooperation. They were, after all, longtime colleagues who had worked together in different combinations many times before.

Meanwhile the Germans were lining up their own experts: Dr. Rolf Endris, an odontologist associated with the Institute for Forensic Medicine at the Johannes Gutenberg University in Mainz, and Dr. Richard Helmer, a forensic anthropologist from the Institute for Forensic Medicine at the University of Kiel. Helmer had developed a new technique that he would employ in the Mengele case and that would have a significant impact on anyone who witnessed it, providing stunning, if not-as-yet universally accepted, evidence.

In today's world, with DNA analysis a commonplace, it may be difficult to appreciate how determining whether the suspected skeleton was indeed that of Josef Mengele could have presented such a vexing scientific challenge to forensic experts. A definitive test did not exist, and only high-quality comparative evidence (such as X-rays or detailed dental records), which were not available as they started their investigation, could lead to confident conclusions. The challenge was to extrapolate from the skeleton the characteristics and eventually the identity of the person it once had been. Snow described the process as reading and interpreting the "osteobiography" written in the bones of the skeleton, or, as he put it, "the biography of bones—a brief and informative biography of an individual . . . if you know how to read it."[7] Snow was fond of saying, "Bones make good witnesses. Although they speak softly, they never lie and they never forget."[8] Eyal Weizman and Thomas Keenan, in their book *Mengele's Skull*, describe Snow's approach: "The bones, no longer the living human but not simply an object, bear the imprint of a lived life. . . . A sequence of illnesses, incidents, and accidents, along with conditions of nutrition, labor, and habit—that is fossilized into the morphology and texture of bones."[9] They go on to quote Snow:

> When we see bones on the table, they are dead. But in the living body, the bone is very dynamic tissue, and it is very responsive to stresses, occupational stress for example, sports, injury, other activities. We take that osteobiography, we compare it with our missing person. In that way, we can gradually come down to eliminate more and more deceased until we identify the person we wanted to find.[10]

With the teams in place, the bones waited in the laboratory, ready to tell their story.

Osteobiography

The recovered remains were incomplete and in poor condition, having rested in a wet environment for more than six years. There was no soft tissue remaining, only bones, some hair, and the vestiges of clothing. What is more, the cemetery worker who had broken through the lid of the coffin during the exhumation had damaged the skull, and the Brazilians had failed to recover every bone. These factors notwithstanding, it was possible to determine certain basic characteristics of the deceased person: stature, sex, age at death, and right- or left-handedness. Bones can also reveal aspects of an individual's medical history and significant injuries that may have been suffered during life, and they sometimes point to distinctive features that would have marked the individual's appearance. It was relatively straightforward to reject an identification if there were significant disparities in stature, age, or sex, but a positive identification relied on adding indices of consistency, moving toward a conclusion that, layer by consistent layer, increased the likelihood of the identification.

The Brazilian team, stung by the chorus of concern for the manner in which the exhumation had been carried out, ventured back to the cemetery in Embu early on Sunday morning, June 16. Their mission, unannounced and with no press in tow, was to recover any material that their first attempt, ten days earlier, had failed to find. They must have been surprised and surely chagrined when, partway through their secret mission, they saw the two German specialists, Helmer and Endris, accompanied by a TV crew, approaching the grave. The Germans, with a day off, had decided to visit the grave, and the TV crew had somehow gotten wind of the supplemental exhumation and decided to cover it.[11] Despite their embarrassment at being caught in the act, the Brazilians did retrieve "sacks of dirt" from the grave and brought them to the Institute for Forensic Medicine (Instituto Medico Legal, IML), where it was sifted and washed.[12] Their efforts resulted in the recovery of four teeth, several small bones, and a number of small bone fragments.[13] Having ameliorated the results of their first clumsy attempt, they were able to ensure that the skeleton waiting to be examined was nearly complete, with only some tiny phalanges and other bones from the feet and hands still missing.[14]

Ellis Kerley and Lowell Levine were the first American forensic specialists to arrive in São Paulo. They went to the IML to see the facility and meet with their Brazilian colleagues and encountered Dr. Wilmes Teixiera, a Brazilian pathologist known to them from scientific meetings. Teixiera, having international experience and a good knowledge of English, had been appointed as the liaison with the international experts. They agreed that all the assembled scientists would work together and present a "joint report," estimating that the examination would take at least through June 21.[15]

By Friday afternoon, June 14, a total of fifteen foreign representatives, more than half of whom were American, were either present or expected shortly in the Brazilian metropolis. With the departure of the document and fingerprint experts and the arrival of the Wiesenthal team, there would be a total of seven American forensic experts, including Eric Stover, two German forensic experts, and the complement of German police, U.S. marshals, and a lone OSI representative, Mike Wolf, since Neal Sher had departed. The Israelis had made the curious decision not to send a forensic specialist, opting instead to dispatch Menachem Russek, who arrived before the weekend. Russek's work as the chief of the Israeli police unit responsible for Nazi war crimes investigations focused almost exclusively on supporting investigations and prosecutions carried out by other nations, pursuant to judicial assistance requests. An experienced cop, Russek was no forensic specialist, and although he carried significant moral weight and clearly made an impression on Tuma, he could offer little assistance to the forensic inquiry.

But the Israelis also sent a second man to Brazil. The Mossad report later revealed that a certain "N," a department chief, accompanied Russek but worked behind the scenes. Russek was to liaise with the Brazilian police, and "N" was to have no contact with Brazilian officials. The guiding assumption under which both men were ordered to operate was that the exhumed body was not Mengele—an assumption that Russek did not require any pressure to adopt. Indeed, before setting foot in Brazil and without seeing the body or any of the assembled evidence, Russek maintained that "Josef Mengele lives and breathes. . . . The trick with the skeleton in Brazil is the invention of this twisted mind and of his relatives who are aiding him to escape. They have already managed to play every sophisticated trick in the book to conceal Mengele's identity; this is just another desperate scheme."[16]

The Israelis also failed to reveal what would have been a major factor in the investigation: they had been aware of Wolfgang Gerhard and his connection to Josef Mengele for quite some time, having learned of the association from Willem Sassen in 1962 and having it confirmed by Thea Maria Kleyer, Gerhard's sister-in-law, several years later. Furthermore, they had been alerted by Kleyer to the existence and identity of the Stammers and Wolfram Bossert. That information, while certainly not dispositive, would have contributed significantly to our ability to evaluate the evidence that we encountered in Brazil. The Mossad report raises a question about this oversight:

> One may conclude with certainty, that the [members of the Mossad], not to mention, the Mossad leadership, were not aware in 1985 of the information from 1968 about Wolfgang Gerhard, and of the fact that at least one of the Mossad members at the time had known Gerhard and tailed him in the context of his search for Mengele.

The report blames "obliviousness" and "compartmentalization" for this failure, which "probably made the task of coming to a conclusion about the skeleton bearing [Mengele's] name more difficult."[17]

Work began in earnest on Monday, June 19. While the Germans

functioned as a team, the other scientists organized themselves by discipline. The bones were laid out in rough anatomical order on a table, and the scientists noted for the first time the extent of the damage to the skull. It was a "mess," with some of its delicate bones "crushed to the size of pumpkin seeds."[18] This was not an auspicious beginning. For Helmer, the skull was especially significant, since it was an essential element of the technique that he was planning to showcase. When Lukash asked Helmer whether he could repair the skull, the German anthropologist responded, "Oh . . . certainly. Yes, I can do it," displaying impressive confidence for a task that Stover compared to assembling a "holographic jigsaw puzzle."[19] Helmer succeeded, indicating later that he had been aided by the freshness of the fractures, which left clear margins and allowed "a seamless and unforced" assembly, so that "the skull attained its original form again."[20]

With the skull reassembled, the experts began their examination. Crucial for their work was reliable antemortem data on Mengele's physical condition and medical history, to which they could compare the information that they would distill from the bones. Their most important source was the Berlin Document Center file, which included Mengele's marriage application, with the findings of his medical and anthropological examination neatly recorded.

The age, race, sex, stature, and handedness of the individual whose skeleton lay before them were determined based on both morphological observations—relating to form and structure—as well as detailed measurements. To determine sex, it was customary to examine the cranium and the pelvic bones. In a male, for instance, the cranium will have a well-developed glabella, the area between the eyes and just above the nose. A male will also have a strong brow ridge, a large mastoid process, which is the bony prominence behind the ear, and a well-developed external occipital protuberance, the bump at the base of the skull. The pelvis, which is composed of the hip bone (innominate bone), the sacrum, and the coccyx, can also be an indicator of sex when examined properly. For instance, a male will have a deep and narrow sciatic notch (the channel in the pelvis that accommodates the sciatic nerve), and the pubic opening will be narrower than that of a female. After completing their visual and manual examination of the bones in question, they began their measurements with rulers and calipers. Employing the Giles-Elliott formula, they took five cranial measurements and compared them to established standards and determined that the skull was that of a male, within an 85 percent reliability. They also measured the diameters of the heads of the humerus and femur, the long bones of the arm and leg, which were consistent with those of a male.

The experts next assessed the race of the skeleton, which was accomplished by taking eight measurements of the skull, many identical to those used in determining sex, and analyzing them by means of the "cranial discriminant function" developed by Eugene Giles. The irony of this examination will not be lost on anyone aware of Mengele's own studies in the same area, including his first dissertation, which involved racial determination through the careful measurements of the lower jaw. (None of the metrics employed by Mengele were used by the American experts in Brazil, and the German team did not include a finding on race in their report.) The scientists concluded that the skeleton was Caucasoid and noted, in addition to the result of the metric-based analysis, that the skeleton displayed many other morphological and metric traits consistent with the racial determination, and none that were inconsistent.[21]

The Americans employed two methods for estimating antemortem stature, though they cautioned that stature was a traditionally undependable feature for comparison because the comparative data were unreliable, easily influenced by the posture of the person being measured or the skill and attentiveness of the person doing the measuring. In Mengele's case, the comparative height measurement came from his BDC file: 174 centimeters (5 feet 8½ inches). First, they combined the measurements of the skeleton's femur and tibia and projected the antemortem stature to have been between 167.5 and 179.5 centimeters.

They next combined the lengths of all the bones in the skeleton that contribute to stature and added a factor that accounted for the missing soft tissue, which yielded a result of between 168.3 and 176.5 centimeters. Both methods arrived at a stature that could be added to the growing list of consistencies.

For the determination of age at death, or biological age, the American team took two approaches, one that examined age-related changes visible in the skeleton, and another that used a microscopic analysis of changes in bone structure. Nearly every bone in the human body changes with age, and anthropologists have analyzed these changes and arrived at standards for interpreting them and correlating their age-specific characteristics. The experts in Brazil looked first at the cranium, which consists of twenty-two bones joined by sixteen sutures. The sutures close progressively over time, and an analysis of how open or closed they are can correlate with age at death, allowing a skilled expert to arrive at an approximation of age.

The cranial suture method alone was not sufficient to arrive at a confident age determination, however, especially for skeletons that were older at death. The pubic symphysis, the joint that connects the lower part of the pelvis, reveals age-related wear; Snow and Kerley looked for patterns of wear in three areas of the pubic bone, assigning a value to each. The sum of the values was then compared to established standards. The sacrum, the triangular bone at the base of the spine, shows age by the degree of fusion of its component parts and the nature of its connection to the coccyx or tailbone. The ribs likewise reveal age by characteristic "cupping" where the rib attaches to the cartilage that connects it to the sternum, or breastbone. With age, the cartilage itself can display ossification as it hardens and turns to bone. The breastbone, shoulder blades, and vertebrae were also examined to disclose the degree of degeneration. The conclusion that the American team drew after their exhaustive review was that the skeleton's age at death was between fifty-five and seventy-five years—consistent, but not very precise. Had they been examining a younger skeleton, they would have been able to be far more exact, since many growth-related changes in the skeleton occur at younger ages.

In 1965 Kerley had developed a method of determining the biological age of skeletons with impressive accuracy based on the observation and quantification of microscopic changes in the cortex of the long bones. The Kerley method would be particularly important for the Mengele case, because it was well suited for older skeletons, promising accuracy for the entire age range from birth to ninety-five years. Described in lay terms by a former student of Kerley's:

> He would take a cross-section of a bone fragment and look for areas of altered bone. Bone gets weak as people age, and as new cells enter the original bone, they chew away older parts of the bone and then incompletely fill it in, in a process related to osteoporosis. . . . The new bone tissue forms concentric circles.[22]

The results of this process, which continues throughout life, can be quantified by identifying and counting these areas of new bone; Kerley described it to me using the metaphor of the rings of a tree that correlate to age.

Kerley took the skeleton's left femur to the University of São Paulo training hospital and carefully cut three cross sections from the bone, which he then sanded down with two grades of sandpaper until they were each one tenth of a millimeter thick; he placed these delicate wafers on separate glass slides and examined two under a microscope.[23] He counted the "tree rings" and plugged his results into a formula he had developed after rigorous work on a large sample of specimens. The first slide indicated a biological age of 70.5, plus or minus five years, and the second slide indicated an age of 68, plus or minus five years. Averaging the two, he came up with an estimate of 69.25 years at the time of death. Kerley took the third slide back home with him to Maryland, where he had a specially calibrated microscope, and came up with an estimate of 68 years. In the final report of the American team, an estimate of 64 to 74 years at death, with 69 being "the most probable," was agreed upon.[24]

To determine handedness, the anthropologists focused on bilateral asymmetries in the arm bones, with longer bones correlating with the dominant side. Although asymmetries can be the result of a complex interaction of environmental and nutritional factors, it was believed at the time that favoring one arm over another subjected its bones to increased mechanical stress, which caused a lengthening of that arm. Although today there is no clear agreement about this connection between asymmetry and handedness,[25] the experts in Brazil were following established practice when they declared that the skeleton belonged to a right-handed man, due to the clear difference in length of the bones in the arms.

They did encounter at least one apparent anthropometric discrepancy in their examination. While Mengele's BDC file listed the circumference of his head as 57 centimeters, the circumference of the skull in São Paulo was 51 centimeters. Helmer, the German anthropologist, later accounted for this discrepancy by suggesting that when the measurement was taken, it did not include Mengele's prominent brow ridge.[26] On the other hand, Snow did not question the measurement in the BDC file, arguing that there was a recognized standard method (Martin technique) for taking the measurement and that Mengele's own training in anthropology would have made him "quick to correct any error in technique" on the part of the physician making the measurement.[27] Snow asserted in a six-page paper with three pages of references that Mengele's 57-centimeter head circumference in life was entirely consistent with the smaller value derived from the skull. Through a multiple regression analysis, he projected what the antemortem head circumference would have been, based on the length and breadth of the cranium, adjusted to account for postmortem shrinkage of the skull, a studied phenomenon, and for the depth of soft tissue.

Probably the most promising area of inquiry in the identification of skeletonized remains at that time was dental evidence. The condition of the teeth in a skeleton can reveal a great deal, including the skeleton's approximate age as well as where dental treatment was received, since materials and practices vary widely. Appropriate antemortem dental records and X-rays make possible a definitive identification. In the case of Mengele, there existed only a modest dental chart in his BDC file, and the skeleton had only ten natural teeth along with removable partial dentures—not a great deal to go on, especially since Mengele's 1938 dental chart was unremarkable, showing the absence of two upper teeth and filled molars, top and bottom, on both sides. It might have been possible to rule out an identification if the absent teeth were present or if one of the molars had no filling, but that was not the case. The dental evidence marked another consistency linking the skeleton to Mengele, but it was a modest one by any standard.

In observing the skull, however, Lowell Levine noticed a very wide incisive canal in the center of the upper palate, where its two halves join, describing the condition as a near nonunion of the hard palate. Significantly, this anatomical feature would have meant the individual had a diastema, or gap, between his upper front teeth, a condition that, while not rare, is not widespread. A quick look at the photograph in Mengele's SS file shows clearly that he did indeed have a wide gap there.

Four decades before Levine discovered the anomaly in the Embu skull, Mengele himself had been pursuing his second medical dissertation under the direction of Otmar von Verschuer, passionately investigating the very anatomy occupying Levine's attention. I think it is more than likely that Mengele would have classified the condition of the skull's palate as one of the microform indicators upon which he relied to prove the genetic nature of the cleft lip and palate. Snow's metaphor that a postmortem examination is akin to reading a biography written in bones seems particularly apt.

The forensic pathologists' report included a catalogue of observations about the skeleton. Lukash and Hameli accounted for the condition of the bones, distinguishing between antemortem and post-mortem damage or changes, which would play a role in the identification. They noted, for example, the presence of "a roundish defect of the left anterior zygoma, about 8 mms in diameter ... with concentric rust color deposits on the margin"—a hole in the small diamond-shaped bone at the front of the skull that is often called the cheekbone. The assembled team was initially convinced that this was a postmortem artifact caused by years of water dripping off the end of one of the screws that secured the viewing window in the casket, wearing away the bone, but it would become the object of much speculation and disagreement. Another unusual feature, noted by the experts but not further identified, was described to me as a "bony spur about the size of the first joint of your pinky," projecting out from the hip near the hip socket, near evidence of an old fracture.[28] They were unable to supply any explanation for this anomaly, and it would take a visit from another expert to São Paulo some six months later to provide an explanation.

Perhaps the most important finding in the experts' report was not the presence of some anomaly but rather the absence of one: there was no evidence of an illness from Mengele's youth. His BDC file clearly indicates that in "1926/27" he had suffered from a string of infections: sepsis, nephritis, and osteomyelitis,[29] conditions that were likely linked, with blood-borne bacteria infecting kidney and bone and causing a systemic inflammatory response. In the days before antibiotics, such infections could have been quite serious, and osteomyelitis (infection of the bone marrow) might have had a significant and lasting impact, leaving evidence in the afflicted bone. The fact that the experts could find no trace of osteomyelitis was troubling indeed.

The issue of osteomyelitis was highlighted for the forensic team by a memorandum I had drafted and sent to them shortly after they arrived in São Paulo. The memo incorporated details of Mengele's osteomyelitis, which I had learned from my friend, the British film-maker Bill Bemister; he had called me to report on an interview he had recently conducted with Kurt Lambertz, a school friend of Mengele's, who provided details about the severity and location of Mengele's bone infection. Lambertz described it as having been in Mengele's leg and having caused a sequestrum (where a piece of necrotic bone breaks away from the site of the infection), which was removed in a surgical procedure called a sequestration.[30] Although these specifics of Mengele's osteomyelitis turned out to be inaccurate, the focus on the disease that originated with his call became an enduring theme for those who would come to doubt the conclusion of the experts in São Paulo.

The German team, significantly outnumbered by the Americans and certainly more insular and circumspect, now introduced their own dramatic and innovative technique to the identification effort. Helmer had arrived in São Paulo with a crate of equipment including video cameras, lighting, and an image processor; nearly a decade earlier, he and a colleague had published the first paper describing a technique made possible by emerging video technology.[31] It required high-quality antemortem photographs of the individual in question. In Mengele's case, there were the photographs in his BDC file from 1938 and a series of portraits taken of Mengele by Bossert in the 1970s, one of which was used on the altered identity card originally belonging to Wolfgang Gerhard. These photographs could be compared to the skull found in Embu, after, of course, it had been repaired by Helmer.

The technique compared the shape, topography, and landmarks (tip of the chin, orbits of the eyes, prominent points on the brow ridge) of the discovered skull with photographs of the individual in question, but it also extrapolated the actual contours of the individual's face. To determine these facial contours, Helmer placed a dab of modeling clay at a number of key landmarks on the skull and inserted a pin. He then put a white plastic disk on the pin, which could be adjusted to be closer to or farther from the skull by sliding it up or down the pin. Based on anthropometric tables, Helmer was then able to adjust the distance between the disk and the skull based on the average soft tissue depth at that selected landmark for a central European male of Mengele's age at the time the comparative photograph was taken. By positioning the disks at a number of different spots on the skull, Helmer was able to approximate the contours of the face that would have formed over the bones of the skull.

The next step was to focus one high-resolution video camera on a photograph of Mengele and another on the skull, making sure that the skull was captured with the precise orientation as that of Mengele's head in the photograph. The two images were adjusted to ensure that the video of the skull matched the scale of the video of the photograph. At this point, the two video images were superimposed, using an image processor and a TV monitor, allowing the observer to note any discrepancies or consistencies between the skull and the photograph. Helmer conducted his analysis using two photographs from the BDC file—Mengele at twenty-seven, profile and full face—and the portraits taken of Mengele when he was in his sixties, adjusting the soft tissue markers to correspond to the older Mengele. There were absolutely no discrepancies. The bony landmarks corresponded perfectly with the facial features, and the extrapolated facial contour created by the movable disks followed the facial lines of the photographs. Using the image processor, Helmer was able to manipulate the images so that, for instance, the top half of the composite could display the image of the skull while the bottom half displayed the photograph, enabling him to analyze particular areas of the skull more carefully.

Eric Stover described Helmer inviting his colleagues from Brazil and the United States to observe the results of his analysis:

> The German flicked on the cameras. The pin-cushion skull came into focus on the television monitor with the photo superimposed onto it. The sight was unnerving. It took a moment for the eye and brain to process the peculiar image. They were seeing a human as no one in life could, as if the skin were a ghostly film. The contours of the face in the photo—the angles of the jaw, the slope

of the forehead, the placement of the nose over the aperture—perfectly matched the shape of the skull. They scanned the face pinpoint to pinpoint. At each spot, the white marker lay at the skin line.[32]

Kerley later told the *New York Times* that the demonstration was "most convincing." "As we watched the monitor we could see the upper half of the picture being replaced by the skull and we could see the contours of the skull in complete agreement with the face. Everything fit."[33]

I saw Helmer's presentation a few days later, after I arrived in São Paulo, and was quite moved by the power of the visual presentation. One need not understand anatomy or be an expert in the degenerative impact of age on bones to make a judgment about the identity of the Embu skull; you simply had to stare at a TV screen. Even so, I wasn't sure how to understand this powerful visual demonstration. It seemed on the face of it incontrovertible, but after discussions with the American experts, I understood that Helmer's method, its stunning visual power notwithstanding, would have to be subjected to rigorous tests before it could be relied upon as a confident indicator of identity.

In addition to the work done by the German team in São Paulo, experts at the German Federal Police in Wiesbaden conducted a sophisticated comparison of the photographs from 1938 in Mengele's BDC file with the one in his 1956 passport application in Argentina and with those taken by Bossert in the 1970s. In developing their method, they studied nineteenth-century techniques, like those of Alphonse Bertillon, the famous French criminologist, based on anthropometrics—examinations of angles, ratios, and dimensions of facial characteristics, focusing on the eyes, ears, and mouth—and perfected and updated them. They claimed that their method was effective even in cases where disguises had been used to obscure identity. In comparing the Mengele photos, they were able to make a positive identification.[34]

Beyond examining the bones of the Embu skeleton, and gathering all available documentary and photographic evidence about Mengele's medical history and antemortem appearance, the forensic experts requested of Tuma that they be allowed to interview key witnesses concerning Mengele's habits, medical issues, and appearance. On the afternoon of June 19 at four p.m., Gitta Stammer was ushered into a meeting room at the IML. She supplied a number of anecdotal details about Mengele, including that he had had some kind of injury during the war, suffered from migraines and swollen finger joints, and complained of a toothache but did not go to the dentist. Of particular interest was her description of periodic swelling of the left side of Mengele's face, which he treated with hot compresses, a detail that provided a possible explanation for the defect in the zygomatic bone. Stammer also described a condition that Lukash interpreted as being consistent with thrombosed hemorrhoids, which led Mengele to visit a hospital. Stammer stated that Mengele had had a wide gap between his two upper front teeth and a ten-centimeter curved, depressed scar above his right wrist. She noted that his lower left leg was swollen and that he complained of pain there, explaining that he had had an infection in Paraguay. She also said that he had had a slight limp but had not worn special shoes.[35]

At five p.m. it was the Bosserts' turn. Like Gitta Stammer, they were already practiced in telling their stories thanks to the near-insatiable appetite of the press, but the experts at the IML had a particular focus. The Bosserts confirmed Gitta Stammer's observation that Mengele had had periodic swelling on the left side of his face. They could not, however, confirm that he had had a diastema, since he had been fitted with a denture in that area of his mouth. They claimed that he had suffered a wartime injury from a grenade but knew no other details. Mengele's fingers were swollen at the joints, an indication to the experts that he had had osteoarthritis. The Bosserts also added a new detail to Mengele's medical history: he had had a stroke within one and a half years of his death and had been treated at the Santa Maria Hospital in São Paulo. The experts' questions also zeroed in on the circumstances surrounding Mengele's death, much as a coroner's inquiry would have done, pressing the Bosserts for exact details of the drowning and burial.

"Reasonable Certainty"

By Thursday, June 20, the forensic experts had completed their analysis. They had proceeded as they would have in any case but for the added complications introduced by their own sheer numbers and by the delicate diplomatic context. In the end, the challenge had been basic and familiar: read the biography encoded in the bones, and compare that story with what was known about Mengele. After a week of focused work, all the morphological and anthropometric observations and values had been collected and noted, and all the antemortem evidence—photographic, documentary, and testimonial—that could be found to form the basis of a comparison had been presented and digested. And as an added bonus, thanks to the Helmer method, a comparison of bones and antemortem evidence had been distilled into a stunning visual display.

What remained was for the American teams to draft a report to present to Tuma. They all clearly believed to some extent that the remains were Mengele's, but they needed to reach an agreement about the degree of probability they would assign to their judgment. Dachi had cabled Washington the day before, claiming that the "USG-sponsored forensic scientists are now convinced that the remains exhumed on June 6 are those of Josef Mengele" and were confident that their findings were "sufficient to prove identity in a U.S. Court." Nonetheless there might be "varying opinions" on the "degree of probability" of the identification, as well as continued concern on the part of some scientists about the "age and sparsity" of data from "currently available medical records."[36]

The six American experts gathered at the U.S. consulate that evening to hammer out their report. Stover, who accompanied them, described a certain tension between members of the Wiesenthal and Justice Department forensic teams, noting that the scientists might "decide that there simply isn't enough physical evidence to say one way or another." "Remember," Lukash said, "this isn't an ordinary case and the public, and especially the skeptics, aren't going to accept just ordinary evidence." They had a responsibility to base their analysis on physical evidence, and he maintained that there simply wasn't enough to be *certain*. There was a "tremendous amount of circumstantial evidence," and the anthropological evidence, the Germans' video demonstration, and "to a limited degree" the dental evidence allowed a conclusion that the skeleton was Mengele's to a reasonable degree—but "the absolute is missing."[37]

What at first appeared to some in the room to be simple contrariness on Lukash's part took on a new light when he read aloud a telex that he had received from Rabbi Marvin Hier of the Simon Wiesenthal Center:

> Communique [*sic*] to Tuma and forensic experts my suggestions that before release of their findings they call a press conference to demand that JM's family make public intimate medical details they promised the German prosecutor last week but never gave. Such medical disclosures prior to forensic teams report could help render conclusion. Otherwise the family will merely echo what they read in public forensic reports. Wiesenthal Center already concerned that basic information has already reached the JM family.
>
> This is not a typical case. More than satisfying the people of Brazil, JM's victims must be satisfied to the greatest degree of certainty.[38]

Among the scientists, temperatures were rising. Levine dismissed the Wiesenthal Center's request, which Lukash believed to be reasonable, as "pure politics." Snow stepped in to try to ease the tension and suggested that they systematically assess their findings and the evidence.[39]

The group ultimately agreed that all the anthropological findings— race, sex, age, stature, and handedness—were consistent with the skeleton of Josef Mengele. The dental findings of the skeleton were consistent with the BDC records, and the dental appliances found in the grave and matching the skeleton were consistent with the testimony of the Bosserts, who had described Mengele's dentures. In addition, the condition of the skeleton's upper jaw and its wide incisive canal matched the diastema evident in the photographs of Mengele. Although they believed that the evidence of a fracture in the skeleton's right hip might be connected to a reported motorcycle accident that Mengele had had in 1943, they acknowledged that there was no real proof. Similarly, they raised the possibility that the defect in the cheek bone of the skeleton might have been connected to the swelling on the left side of Mengele's face reported by both the Bosserts and Stammer.[40] They agreed that the handwriting experts' findings had placed a living Mengele in Brazil, and they were extremely impressed by the German skull-photo superimposition. The only major inconsistency was the absence of any clear evidence of osteomyelitis in the skeleton. Although Mengele's SS records were unambiguous about its presence, the scientists sought to explain away the discrepancy by suggesting that it had been a misdiagnosis or that the infected bone had "remodeled itself over the years."

The six paragraphs of their modest report, finally delivered to Tuma on the morning of June 21, concluded: "Based on the above, it is the opinion of the undersigned that the exhumed remains are definitely not those of Wolfgang Gerhard. It is further our opinion that the skeleton is that of Josef Mengele within a reasonable scientific certainty. A more detailed report will be issued at a later date." Although, according to Stover, Lukash quibbled over language, arguing for "reasonable probability" rather than "reasonable scientific certainty," all six of the U.S. scientists signed the report.

I had arrived in São Paulo on the morning of June 20, just in time for this final act in the two-week drama.[41] The denouement played out in a third-floor conference room at the federal police headquarters in São Paulo, where the huge contingent of print and broadcast media that had descended on the city gathered to receive the verdict of the international group of scientists. While the TV crews set up their cameras and microphones and everyone jockeyed for position, Tuma met with the scientists at ten a.m. on another floor. Only Fitzpatrick was there representing the Wiesenthal team, Snow and Lukash having opted to sleep in after the long night spent debating and drafting. The Germans were present, as were the Brazilian forensic experts. I sat next to Menachem Russek, who seemed out of place with his modesty and quiet reserve.

Tuma used this meeting of the scientists to ensure that everyone was on the same page. He announced the unanimous conclusion of Brazilian team[42] and called upon Levine and Helmer, representing the U.S. and German teams, who reaffirmed without reservation the Brazilian conclusions as well as the excellent cooperation.[43] The Brazilians intended to continue the investigation in several areas, including an attempt to determine blood type from an analysis of the hair that was found in the coffin, a closer examination of the defect in the cheekbone, and an inquiry into Rolf Mengele's visit to Brazil under a false name. Tuma concluded the meeting, "Gentlemen, this is like what you say at a wedding, speak now or forever hold your peace."[44] No one spoke.

Following this preliminary meeting, which lasted two hours, we all moved to the press conference, which was, in the words of Levine, "a zoo." Emotions were high and tempers short among the two hundred or so journalists who had been waiting for hours in an overcrowded space. A fistfight erupted, there were cases of hysteria, and a flimsy partition wall was damaged.[45] Tuma announced the conclusions of the international team and asked Levine to read aloud the last paragraph of the U.S. report. Tuma then read a Portuguese translation of the American report, identifying it as the Brazilian conclusion. Following questions and multiple photo ops, the American team left for its own briefing.[46]

The Maksoud Plaza, the hotel where we all stayed and the informal headquarters for the major American news outlets, served as the venue for the U.S. briefing, during which the press was able to interview individual scientists. From the start, relations between the experts and the press had been good, generally comprising off-the-record comments made with clear ground rules. Such restrictions were now lifted. American news broadcasts that evening led with the story from São Paulo featuring Tuma's press conference, with cutaways to images of the X-rays and the bones. Of particular interest was the eerie half-face, half-skull composite that was the hallmark of the Germans' innovative method. NBC presented a one-on-one interview with Levine, during which he intoned, "Those are the bones of Josef Mengele. I think they can let the ghost go to rest and go after the rest of them." When asked how he would respond to someone who claimed to have seen Mengele recently in Paraguay, Levine responded, "You *think* you saw Josef Mengele in Paraguay, I identified him in São Paulo, Brazil."[47]

Despite the compelling evidence and the unwavering confidence of the experts who had completed their examination, the coverage of the scientists' findings did include some dissenting views. Roger Mudd, then at NBC, reported, "The Israeli Justice Ministry is not yet convinced beyond a reasonable doubt and will keep Mengele's file open until it has studied the full report of the forensic experts in Brazil. . . . Many people who survived Josef Mengele and his cruelties say they will take their time before accepting the forensic report from Brazil. This has less to do with scientific fact than with the enormity of Mengele's atrocities. The survivors want to be 100 percent certain that the Angel of Death is dead."

Menachem Russek was much sought after as the sole representative of the State of Israel. To me, privately, he offered no opposition to the findings of the experts, but he was clearly conflicted. He was too modest, and perhaps a bit intimidated, to openly defy the avalanche of expert opinion, so he offered ambiguous comments. The Germans claimed that Russek had reported at the meeting that, for him personally, ample evidence had been collected.[48] After the press conference, a reporter for the *South Florida Sun Sentinel* got to Russek and described him as finding "no fault with the conclusion" and quoted him as saying that there was a "high probability" that it was Mengele: "That's what the experts say, and I accept their opinion." But he refused to say unequivocally that he believed the bones were Mengele's, or that "the search for him should be canceled."[49]

I learned later that Russek and his colleague, "N," remained in São Paulo after the other international consultants had left the country. They conducted an interview with the Bosserts on June 24 and continued to investigate the case that had for all intents and purposes been closed by Romeu Tuma and the team of international experts.[50]

CHAPTER 12

DOUBTS

(July 1985–March 1986)

I was personally concerned that the forensic experts had been rushed—or had rushed themselves—to reach a conclusion that communicated more certainty than the evidence warranted. In my view, they should have left the case open pending a continued search for new evidence and an opportunity to carefully analyze the evidence that had already been found. By expressing such certainty and effectively closing the case, they removed any incentive for investigators to look further. The conclusion of "reasonable scientific certainty" might have been sufficient in an ordinary case, I argued, but as Rabbi Hier and Lukash had warned, this was no ordinary case. There were serious people who accepted the possibility of a hoax, however far-fetched—that Mengele, in league with the Bosserts, had arranged for a body resembling his in all the measurable ways to be buried. Such a ruse might have succeeded and met what seemed a relatively low standard. An ordinary case might well be decided on powerful circumstantial evidence and layers of consistency, but in the case of a person who might have attempted to mislead investigators, a higher standard should apply. Mengele certainly had the motive, and as a physician and anthropologist, he arguably had the means as well, to engineer a sophisticated fraud.

Perhaps more important, public interest in the identification had been vastly underestimated, amid ignorance of the spectacle that often surrounds the deaths of the famous and infamous. One need only recall the debate and speculation over the deaths of Adolf Hitler, John F. Kennedy, Marilyn Monroe, and Elvis Presley to understand that the Mengele case needed to be handled with a high degree of sensitivity. Holocaust survivors deserved a sober, thorough, and patient investigation, and I feared that the one just concluded in São Paulo had not met those conditions. My colleague Phil Sunshine and I made essentially these arguments to Sher at the end of June 1985 in Washington, and he permitted us to continue to look for more conclusive evidence. Since we had yet to finish the historical part of the investigation into Mengele's whereabouts after the war, Sher could justify travel and other expenses. Still, he was going out on a limb: the attorney general had already accepted the identification of the Embu skeleton.

The German magazine *Bunte* had purchased from Rolf, for a reported one million Deutschmarks, the right to publish the correspondence and notebooks he had retrieved from Brazil in 1979, and it assigned journalist Inge Byhan to write a series of articles about Mengele and his secret postwar history.[1] The June 20 issue of *Bunte* hit the streets before the forensic experts issued their findings in São Paulo. Four more articles appeared in successive weeks, revealing that Mengele had been taken prisoner of war by the Americans and had escaped from Europe to South America in 1949. Reading this article made clear to me that the material Rolf Mengele had sold to *Bunte* would be crucial for the historical investigation. I was able to reach Norbert Sakowski, the deputy editor-in-chief of *Bunte,* by phone, and he invited me to come to the Munich headquarters of Burda Verlag, the publisher of *Bunte,* promising me unfettered access to the Mengele material.[2]

Sakowski and his colleagues could not have been more welcoming or helpful. I was given a comfortable conference room in their modern headquarters building in Arabella Park, on the other side of the Isar River from downtown Munich. It was an area I knew well since I had spent a year in Munich in the late 1970s working on my dissertation, and Egon Hanfstaengl, whose father, Ernst "Putzi" Hanfstaengl, was the subject of my dissertation, lived nearby. The *Bunte* collection consisted of Mengele's correspondence, mostly typewritten, dating from his time in Brazil, along with a series of diaries—more like datebooks— from the 1960s and '70s. In addition, a collection of notebooks of various sizes, written in Mengele's distinctive and relatively legible hand, contained Mengele's autobiographical novel begun in the 1960s, which chronicled his student days, his life on the farm near Rosenheim immediately after the war, and his escape to Argentina.

Reading carefully through this voluminous collection, I found new evidence that might lead to a more conclusive identification of the skeleton. I recorded every mention of any medical or dental treatment that Mengele had noted. Of particular importance were seemingly mundane details like the precise dates and cost of dental treatments, along with clues to the identity of those who had treated him. I discovered that Mengele had been treated by one dentist between 1976 and 1978, while another dentist had performed root canal treatment in December 1978. There was also information about X-rays and a surgery for an intestinal blockage in 1972. I returned to Washington at the end of July with a briefcase full of notes and concrete leads that would, in many ways, define our activity, and that of our colleagues in Germany and Israel, for the next phase of the case. I also read and digested Mengele's autobiographical novel, which would lead to a significant breakthrough a few months later in our investigation of Mengele's postwar movements.

After I returned from Germany, we learned that the American forensic experts had decided to meet as a group to review their findings thoroughly and in a less charged atmosphere than had been possible in São Paulo. Dr. Ali Hameli, chief medical examiner for the State of Delaware, hosted the meeting at the medical examiner's office, a multistory office building in the middle of downtown Wilmington. Present were all the experts who had been in Brazil, as well as Michael

Baden, former chief medical examiner of New York City. Hameli also invited Phil Sunshine and me, and we drove up together from Washington. The first order of business was a session with a photographer from *Life* magazine, whose photo of the experts appeared in the 1985 "Year in Review" issue.

When I shared the results of my recent review of the files from *Bunte,* those assembled agreed there might be additional important evidence yet to be discovered and encouraged me to forward my findings to Tuma. Over the next week, I distilled my notes into a memorandum that offered concrete investigative leads in Brazil, including the names of doctors and dentists whom Mengele had visited "within a year of his death," and cabled it to Dachi in São Paulo. Sher spoke with Dachi, who told him that he had passed on the "new information" to Tuma, who expressed "great interest" and promised to do everything he could to follow up on the information provided.[3]

I SAW SOME of the experts again at the beginning of August when the Juvenile Justice Subcommittee of the Senate Judiciary Committee held its third and final hearing on the Mengele case, this one intended to examine the evidence that Mengele was dead. Most of the forensic experts testified, as did Sher and Howard Safir. Sher announced the Justice Department's position: "The Department of Justice accepts the conclusion by . . . [the] scientific experts that, based on the information available in the forensic examination, the body recently exhumed in Brazil was that of Josef Mengele within a reasonable scientific certainty." Safir summarized the U.S. marshals' involvement and reported that his office, having accepted the forensic experts' findings, had closed the "fugitive investigation," concluding its efforts to locate Mengele.

When the panel of experts testified, however, they offered surprisingly lukewarm support for their own conclusion, relying chiefly on the dental evidence and the anthropological findings of consistency. Under questioning by Senator Specter, a seasoned former prosecutor, and Senator D'Amato, an admitted skeptic on the findings, the scientists emphasized that they had not relied on the testimony of witnesses, who might have been motivated to mislead them. Their conclusions were based solely on their examination of the skeletal remains. Hameli went so far as to suggest the case be kept open and called for further supporting evidence. Although the hearing provided the expected senatorial grandstanding on the importance of searching for Nazi war criminals and corresponding dismay about the lost opportunity to bring Mengele to justice, it did little to address the concerns of those with even the slightest discomfort about the identification of the skeleton in Brazil.

The CANDLES "Inquest"

Doubts were certainly beginning to solidify within the survivor community. In August 1985, CANDLES, the organization of Mengele's twin victims that had helped to organize the mock trial of Mengele in Jerusalem in February, began to plan an "inquest" into Mengele's purported death, to be held in Terre Haute, Indiana, at the end of October. CANDLES executive director Eva Kor wrote to Hans-Eberhard Klein to invite him to participate. The inquest, she said, was intended to find the "truth, and nothing but the truth":

> We have lived for forty years without knowing what Josef Mengele has done to us. Since the facts surrounding his life and death directly influence our lives, we feel that we deserve an opportunity to view and question the evidence, talk to, and cross examine the witnesses in person.[4]

In addition, Kor asked Klein to pass on an invitation to Rolf and Dieter Mengele, Jens Hackenjos (Rolf's stepbrother), and Hans Sedlmeier, saying that Mengele had "taken away everything" and that his family owed them "an opportunity to talk to them."[5]

Although Klein clearly had sympathy for Eva Kor and her colleagues, he feared that the inquest would develop a certain unpredictable "momentum" that would leave him either "falling between two stools" or sitting in the wrong one.[6] He was therefore not inclined to accept the invitation or to pass it on as Kor had requested.

The Germans' decision to decline the CANDLES invitation appears to me now to have been correct, and I regret that my own Justice Department did not act in a similar fashion. Instead of politely declining, Sher decided to send me to "testify" on behalf of OSI and the department. In the past when I had represented the office before community groups, I had been greeted with respect and appreciation, but when I arrived at the CANDLES "Inquest in Terre Haute," I experienced open hostility and suspicion. On entering the hotel where the inquest was taking place, Gerald Posner, who had been asked by Kor to chair the panel, approached me and said, somewhat ominously, that I should have come earlier so that he could have briefed me on what was happening.

The entire event had an antic quality, with outsize personalities and preposterous stories. A mysterious "Mr. G" claimed to have seen Mengele after his purported death, and a former model told of taking off her blouse to entice a suspected Mengele to show himself at the window of a beach house off the coast of West Africa the year before. And always there was the steely resolve of Eva Kor. She had emerged from her tragic experience at Auschwitz as a vital and engaged activist who pursued her various causes with abundant energy and single-minded commitment. Following the Mengele investigation, the findings of which she never accepted, she attracted worldwide attention with her well-publicized decision to "forgive" Josef Mengele; I am not certain she ever forgave me for my role in proving that Mengele had died in Brazil.

In my "testimony" before the tribunal, I summarized the investigation, stressing that the forensic experts had revealed only their preliminary findings and that a comprehensive final report was forthcoming. I emphasized that the timing of the "inquest" was unfortu-

nately premature, since I was not in a position to present or defend
any findings. The response to my testimony was impassioned. The
first question posed by someone on the panel was whether the Justice
Department had approved my remarks before I left Washington and
included the admonition that I "tell the truth." It went downhill from
there. Kor asked for whose benefit the investigation was being conducted: "for the US government or for the victims?" She revealed her
decided antagonism for the Simon Wiesenthal Center and for what
appeared to her to be the privileged role they had been allowed to play
in the inquiry. She alleged that those involved in the investigation,
never having dealt with Nazis, had been hoodwinked by the testimony
of those who had helped Mengele in Brazil:

> We were their victims; we know that they are notorious liars and
> you cannot believe one single word. Yet . . . the report is rein-
> forced by their testimony, and this is what really tied the whole
> thing in. If we would have been there, or anybody representing
> us, that would have not been possible because we would have
> been able to show that these people are liars, and that is a very
> important point.[7]

She revealed perhaps her most serious problem with our investigation:
we had stopped her momentum.

> If I would have held a conference before June 6, I can tell you that
> that place would have been packed with reporters and with peo-
> ple. You, the Justice Department's report and the Simon Wiesen-
> thal seal of approval, killed every single thing that we the victims
> were trying to find out.

She continued to lash out at having been pushed back into a powerless-
ness that had marked the lives of survivors, and from which they had
worked so hard to emerge:

[The preliminary] report was presented to the press for the purpose of killing the investigation and killing the efforts of these
miserable little guinea pigs who for forty years were suffering
and finally were trying to make some sense of their life. Until
the big, the big bullies come around with all their power and
say you're getting another one, here, goodbye. And that's what
we got.[8]

My appearance at the inquest perhaps called for more tact and sensitivity than I was able to muster at the time. I do regret my lack of
patience with some of the people who attended.

Thanks perhaps to Posner's temperate hand, the panel's conclusions and recommendations, in contrast to much of its proceedings,
were reasonable. They called for, among other things, a determination
of the blood type of the skeleton and whether it was compatible with
Rolf's, and a serious evaluation of the "numerous sightings of Mengele"
reported since 1979. Despite the poor timing and unfortunate tone of
the inquest, as well as some of its dubious characters, I agreed with
many of the points raised by the skeptics and worked hard to locate
additional clarifying evidence.

Breakthrough in the Historical Investigation

As the doubts around the forensic investigation crystallized, I made
substantial progress in elucidating important aspects of the historical
inquiry by successfully identifying the pivotal character in Mengele's
autobiography. Mengele had chosen to use the name "Hans Ulmeier"
as a pseudonym for the Wehrmacht doctor who had provided him
with a duplicate copy of his discharge certificate, which he had then
altered to create his new identity for use in the early postwar years. In
attempting to identify the real-life Ulmeier, I approached the name-
change puzzle as a math student would solve an algebraic equation
for an unknown value. I knew three elements of the equation: two

from the realm of Mengele's fiction, "Hans Ulmeier," which Mengele changed to "Hans Holmeder," and a third from the confirmed fact that Mengele had used the name "Fritz Holmann" while working on the farm.[9] "Fritz Holmann" had been formed by Mengele's altering the unknown fourth—the real name of the Wehrmacht doctor. It did not take me long to develop a list of possible alternatives.

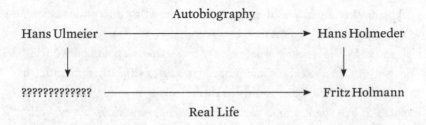

Autobiography

Hans Ulmeier ────────────────────► Hans Holmeder

????????????? ────────────────────► Fritz Holmann

Real Life

I hypothesized that the individual's real first name was "Fritz," since "Hans" remained unchanged in the autobiographical account. Likewise, it seemed logical that his real last name would begin with a *U*, probably followed by an *l* and an *m*. It was, however, extremely challenging to determine whether one of the various reasonable alternatives was right. We have become accustomed to locating people with relative ease through various Internet and social media applications. But what now can be accomplished with a few keystrokes took a great deal of time and shoe leather in the past.

There was another epic source of accumulated knowledge and information—the Library of Congress. Fortunately, one of the perks I enjoyed while working for OSI was a stack pass to the wondrous warrens that shelved the library's enormous collection. The cast iron switchback stairs connecting the cramped decks of the shelving system seemed like those of some vast ocean liner that could transport you anywhere you wanted to venture. In 1985 they led me to a 1950 telephone directory for Munich—Mengele, in his autobiography, indicated that "Ulmeier" came from that area—that had a list of physicians in a kind of professional directory. It was against the names in this directory that I first compared my list of hypothesized names for the real man behind the pseudonym "Hans Ulmeier."

I found a Dr. Fritz Ulmann, a neurologist, among the fifteen or so names on the list. This discovery gave me encouragement and a sense that somehow, I was on the right track. My next step was to determine whether a Dr. Fritz Ulmann had ever been in the Wehrmacht. At that time, on the fourth floor of the National Archives on Pennsylvania Avenue in Washington, was the sprawling microfilm reading room, populated on most days by a seeming army of genealogists who, inspired by the recently broadcast TV series *Roots*, spent hours poring over U.S. Census records and passenger lists of ships that might have brought their ancestors to this country. During my first several years at OSI, I had spent a good part of every week, sometimes every workday, in this room searching Nazi Party as well as German military and ministerial records that had been captured or seized by Allied forces during and after World War II and microfilmed.[10] Among them, I knew, was a card file of German military medical officers, from which I confirmed that a Fritz Ulmann (born January 23, 1910) had been a physician in the German military. But final confirmation that Ulmann was my man did not occur until near the end of September 1985, when I interviewed Dr. Otto-Hans Kahler at his home in the Schwarzwald. I had learned about Kahler from my friend Bill Bemister, who in turn had learned of him from the prominent German geneticist Benno Müller-Hill.[11] I asked Kahler if he had known a Dr. Fritz Ulmann. He responded dramatically, *"Ja! Er war da!,"* Yes! He was there! He claimed to have completely forgotten the name, but my question stirred his memory, and he proceeded to explain Ulmann's important role in relation to Mengele's story.

Now, with a date of birth from the National Archives, I could make further inquiries. The Wehrmacht Auskunftstelle (WASt) in West Berlin was a biographic research center housing German military personnel records of all sorts and was used to verify military service, calculate pensions, and confirm disabilities and other matters relating to a German citizen's military service. I requested, through the State Department, a records check at WASt for any material on Fritz Ulmann, and when I reviewed the record they had found on him, I discovered that he had been on the staff of Field Hospital (Kriegslazarettabteilung) 2/591, the same unit as Kahler. I had, in other words, established that Fritz Ulmann was Hans Ulmeier.

All this work, as exciting and satisfying as it was, might have been of little value if Ulmann had been dead or if I had been unable to find him. To begin, I turned to Gerry Charig, an attorney with the Justice Department who was assigned to our consulate in Munich.[12] A wonderful man, Charig had a ribald sense of humor, and my colleagues and I always looked forward to seeing him when our travels took us to Munich. When I called him and asked for his help in determining whether Fritz Ulmann was still alive and where he lived, he asked for Ulmann's name, date of birth, and last known address (which I had found in the WASt record).

Within the hour, Charig called to tell me that one Dr. Fritz Ulmann, retired, lived in a small village, Eglfing, south of Munich, and gave me his address and telephone number. I appreciated but was not really surprised by how quickly Gerry had uncovered this information: I knew it was much easier to locate someone in Germany than in the United States, especially given the contacts that Charig possessed. Everyone living in Germany—citizen and noncitizen—is obliged to register with an office of the police known as the resident registration office (Einwohnermeldeamt) and provide not only their address and profession but also their religion, used for assessing taxes to be distributed to the various religious communities. These records had allowed for the efficient identification of Jews during the Nazi period.

The next step was to try to talk to Ulmann, or rather, to get Ulmann to talk to me. I made the call on September 27, 1985, from Stuttgart, where I was with Sher. When a man answered, I asked in German whether I was speaking with Dr. Ulmann. "*Ja*," he replied, and I identified myself as a historian with the Department of Justice in the

United States who wanted to meet with him to ask a few questions. When he inquired about the subject of my questions, I responded that they dealt with Josef Mengele. There was a profound silence on the other end of the phone. He finally responded that it had been "forty years" since he had thought about that "matter," and that it was "over" for him. I stressed that only he had the information I was seeking, and that he had a responsibility to talk with me. It may have been my appeal to his sense of duty that led him to agree, telling me he would meet with me in Munich on Tuesday, October 1.

I drove to Munich—only to learn that Ulmann had changed his mind. When I called and heard the strident tone of his wife in the background, I understood that she had persuaded him to change his mind. There was, however, a hint in his voice that suggested his resolve was not so solid. I again emphasized his unique position and his responsibility, and he finally relented. This time the meeting was to be in Murnau, a town south of Munich near his home in Eglfing. He told me to meet him in the lobby of the Hotel Seidlpark at noon the next day.

I arrived early and waited for nearly an hour and a half, during which time I called him twice with no answer. Ready to give up, I finally reached him by phone. He had gone to the hotel, he said, but claimed I was not there. The issue was now closed for him. In fairness to Ulmann, I realized that daylight saving time, which Germans call summer time, had ended two days earlier on Sunday, September 29, and he may have confused the time and arrived and left the hotel before I got there. Nonetheless, I was angry and felt he was simply avoiding me. Having him on the phone, I began to question him. He seemed to warm to the questions, answering them clearly and without hesitation. At this point, I asked him to meet with me, knowing the importance of a face-to-face encounter. When he firmly rejected the entreaty, I increased the pressure. I explained that he had a choice: either he could meet with me and continue the interview in person, or I would release his name to the news media, and they would undoubtedly converge on him in great numbers. The prospect of a gaggle of reporters on his front lawn had the desired effect, and he directed me to drive to the small village of Spatzenhausen, where I would find a small café near the road. I was to sit at an outside table where I would be visible.

I did as instructed, and a few minutes after I arrived in Spatzenhausen, I noticed an elderly man with a cane slowly descending a small hill on the other side of the road. When it became clear that he was heading in my direction, I was both relieved and excited. My frustrating search for him had ended, and I was finally going to have a chance to clarify two key issues—one for the historical investigation, and one for the forensic.

I knew from reading Mengele's autobiography that Ulmann had suffered from osteomyelitis, and through the disease, which they had discussed during their time together in the POW camp, they shared a common bond. I interviewed Ulmann carefully about his association with Mengele and his experience as a POW. He had a good memory and responded intently to my questions, offering a cogent narrative of his movements and, by extension, Mengele's. He was able to provide telling details about Mengele's early medical condition by supplying specific answers concerning the nature, extent, and location of Mengele's osteomyelitis. "Yes, Mengele did suffer from the disease as a child," he confirmed. "No, it was not a serious case," he said, and "No, there had been no sequestrum." When I asked him where the osteomyelitis had been located, he slapped his right hand against his right hip and declared, "Right here." I quickly produced a crude sketch of the hip, placing an arrow at the location he had demonstrated with his own slapping gesture, and he confirmed the location on the drawing. My last question to him proved to be the most important: Did he have his own discharge certificate, the one that he had kept and used in the postwar period? He immediately answered that he did and agreed to my request that he send it.

I should have anticipated—his apparent willingness notwithstanding—his reluctance to follow through. Once I returned to Washington, I waited in vain for the copy of the discharge certificate. It took several more phone calls and attendant pressure, but finally I received a one-page certificate (Control Form D-2) that supplied the full name and unit of the American officer who had signed it, providing me with a whole new avenue of research. I would be able to identify and locate the very individuals who had guarded and released Ulmann and—more important—Mengele. I could also date their release. I immediately contacted Maj. Nick Ruiz at the Pentagon and submitted my requests for the file of Capt. Claudius J. Walker, the army officer who had signed the form. I also requested records for his unit, the 400th Armored Field Artillery Battalion, from the Military Personnel Records Center in St. Louis, which would provide a listing of personnel. I was able to extend my research to other U.S. Army personnel assigned to the POW camp that had held Mengele.

Perhaps most satisfying, however, was looking at Ulmann's signature on the discharge certificate. I could easily track how Mengele had altered its twin, which had been affixed to the duplicate certificate Ulmann had given him: one could see how, as Mengele described in his autobiography, the U in "Ulmann" could have been transformed into an H (for "Holmann") through the addition of a horizontal stroke, and how the space between the U and the l (in "Ulmann") permitted the easy insertion of an o (to form "Holmann"). The deciphering was complete. Thanks to Mengele's autobiographical project, and with the help of Kahler and Ulmann, I was able to reconstruct Mengele's early movements after the war and provide confident answers to the question that gave rise to our investigation in the first place.

More Doubts

In August 1985 Hans Klein believed that he would soon be petitioning the Frankfurt court to close the case on Mengele by concluding that he was dead,[13] but by early October, he was convinced that he could not take that step "before the New Year."[14] The delay was not an indi-cation that Klein had developed doubts or had lost confidence in the "high degree of probability" that he believed the identification war-ranted. Rather, he was concerned that he might be vulnerable to the accusation of having ignored proffered evidence or having acted in an overly hasty manner. He still had a list of open items on the German side that needed to be resolved.[15]

Most important for Klein, however, were the "doubts" raised by "influ-ential parties" abroad. Such doubts had to be taken seriously to counter any possible charge of carelessness; for example, statements provided by CANDLES from witnesses who claimed to have seen Mengele alive after February 7, 1979, should be investigated. Klein was also concerned about a book, *The Angel of Death* by a Brazilian writer of Jewish origin named Ben Abraham, that raised questions about Mengele's death, and that was being translated by his office into German so it could be ana-lyzed. Finally, Klein was aware that the Brazilian authorities were tak-ing additional investigative steps, referring to our request to Tuma in August. Since June, when the identification had been announced with such certainty, much had taken place to give Klein pause about closing the case; the doubts emerging from certain quarters could powerfully undermine even the most assured and confident German prosecutor.

The Israelis continued their own investigation. Russek had returned to Brazil in September as a member of "a team of Israeli experts." The Israeli Justice Ministry spokesman refused to elaborate on the focus of their inquiry but stressed that "as far as Israel is concerned the Mengele file is not closed," and added that the file could be closed only "when the State of Israel declares that Mengele is dead."[16] Russek had arrived in Brazil with Victor Cohen, an experienced interroga-tor who was traveling under an assumed name. Their visit was sup-posed to be secret but was soon leaked, presumably by the attorneys of the Bossert and Stammer families, whom the Brazilian police had summoned for questioning on behalf of the Israelis. The Israelis were keenly interested in the testimony of both families, especially of Lisel-

otte Bossert; Russek, an experienced police officer, had found a number of discrepancies in her previous accounts of Mengele's death and
burial. Victor Cohen was a polygraph expert and brought the necessary equipment to administer the "lie detector" test to the Brazilian
witnesses. Although the accuracy and validity of the polygraph examination had been long debated, the Israelis relied upon it under certain
circumstances and believed that it was essential in establishing the
credibility of the witnesses in the Mengele case.

Victor Cohen found Mrs. Bossert's story consistent with her testimony from June, with the addition of only minor details, but she
refused to submit to a polygraph, invoking her right under Brazilian
law. The Stammers, on the other hand, agreed to the test. Geza Stammer, who had been absent from São Paulo in June, was reportedly
"calm and relaxed" during his questioning, while his wife's "excitement and nervousness" made the results of her test more difficult to
analyze. Nevertheless, it was determined that both were being truthful when they responded to the direct and straightforward questions
posed to them:

Question: Are you convinced that Mengele died on February 7,
          1979?
Answer: Yes.
Question: Have you had any contact with Mengele since February
          7, 1979?
Answer: No.
Question: Did Mrs. Bossert tell you that Mengele died and was
          buried in Embu?
Answer: Yes.
Question: Have you conspired to hide the fact that Mengele is
          alive?
Answer: No.[17]

The answers offered by the Stammers, however truthful, were not necessarily dispositive of the question of Mengele's death, since the Stammers were not eyewitnesses but rather had learned all they knew of the alleged event from the Bosserts.

Cohen and Russek questioned a number of other witnesses—including the gravedigger and the director of the cemetery where "Wolfgang Gerhard" had been buried—who could neither verify nor disclaim the identity of the skeleton. The director of the cemetery also submitted to a polygraph examination. For the Israelis, however, the question of whether it was Mengele's body in the Embu grave could not be answered conclusively unless and until Mrs. Bossert was examined by polygraph. Her refusal offered a powerful reason, in and of itself, for some to doubt her veracity.

According to the Mossad report, although Cohen concluded that Mengele was dead, Russek disagreed with his colleague. He believed the events described after the drowning of the person said to be Mengele were part of an "imaginary story invented by Mrs. Bossert," and that the burial in Embu was a "fake." There was, reportedly, significant tension between him and Cohen. Igo Sommer, a Mossad officer, shared Russek's skepticism.[18]

Other expressions of doubt emerged. In September, at the annual meeting of the German Society for Forensic Medicine in Hamburg, an American doctor, W. P. Mulloy, presented a paper entitled "The Mengele Case: A Dissenting Opinion," in which he argued that there was insufficient identifying information to warrant the conclusion that the skeleton was that of Josef Mengele, and that one could reasonably conclude only that the skeleton was of a white male of a certain age and height. The Germans were concerned enough about the presentation that Klein, Helmer, and Endris attended. Helmer later addressed Mulloy's argument in a journal article about the case, claiming that Mulloy had missed the point: "The question is not whether identified features can apply to some other person, but rather to a specific individual."[19]

On September 26, 1985, Phil Sunshine, Neal Sher, and I interviewed Mengele's medical school friend, Dr. Kurt Lambertz, in his home in Bad Münstereifel. Bill Bemister had located Lambertz the previous May, and Lambertz had described Mengele's osteomyelitis to Bemister as a serious case with a sequestrum and a subsequent operation to remove the necrotic bone. But when we spoke to Lambertz, he related a different story. He claimed that Mengele had never told him directly about the severity of the osteomyelitis or about the formation of a sequestrum. He maintained, rather, that he had assumed these details, since that was the likely course of the disease prior to the advent of antibiotics.[20] A month or so later, I received a copy of Bemister's taped interview with Dr. Lambertz, which had him clearly describing a serious case of osteomyelitis with sequestrum and a deformation of Mengele's leg. When I phoned Lambertz on November 20 and played him the tape, he labeled it a "forgery" and maintained that he had never spoken the words, seriously compromising his credibility.

On October 8 I received a call from Gerald Posner, who passed on information that had come from Irene Mengele. Posner, with whom I regularly exchanged information, was close to Rolf Mengele and through him had gained access to his mother. I had asked Posner to find out all he could about Mengele's medical history, especially about any scars he might have had, or any recollections Irene might have had about Mengele's childhood illnesses. Irene had told Rolf that his father had suffered from a serious "blood infection" as a child, which resulted in a "big scar" on his upper leg, "probably his left leg." She also indicated that she had no recollection of Mengele ever having had a pelvic fracture. Both his legs were the same length, as far as she could remember, and he did not wear "special shoes."[21] The German prosecutor had no authority to compel Rolf or his mother to aid in the investigation; our indirect approach was the only way to acquire this useful information from a reliable source.

Jerusalem Meeting

In early December 1985, Sher and I traveled to Israel to attend a two-day meeting at the Israeli Ministry of Justice. It was the first time that the principals of the tripartite investigation had been in the same room since the Frankfurt meeting the previous May,[22] and it provided an opportunity to take stock and to determine a future course, especially in light of the doubts that had emerged since the identification of the body in June.

We explained that the American forensic experts had not yet completed their final report and that OSI had met with each of the experts separately in the course of the last few months. None of the U.S. experts expected to change their conclusions, and they were planning to complete their final report and present their findings to the annual meeting of the American Academy of Forensic Sciences in March 1986 in New Orleans.[23] We expressed to our colleagues some ambivalence about how the identification of Mengele had been handled. Although we might accept the overall conclusion of the experts, we had concerns that the U.S. authorities had "hurried to accept" the results and make them public "without waiting for the completion of the investigation and the exhaustive analysis of the findings."[24]

Klein reported that German experts had concluded the body was Mengele's but had not yet made their findings public. "In view of the historical significance of the subject of Mengele and its ramifications," the Germans would wait until all the documents and data had been analyzed and all possible witnesses had been interrogated.[25] At the same time, he rejected out of hand an Israeli proposal to form an international commission to analyze and review all the forensic evidence.[26]

Shifting from medical to other forms of evidence, Russek reported on his impressions of the individuals who had protected Mengele and described Liselotte Bossert as the "key to the solution," indicating that her description of the alleged death of Mengele was not without its contradictions. In this connection, the Israelis raised the question of employing the polygraph in their questioning of witnesses in Brazil, a prospect that Klein flatly rejected. He went so far as to stress that the Germans would neither acknowledge nor place value on any interrogation conducted with the polygraph; nor would they draw any negative inferences about the reliability of any witness who refused the use of one.

The Israelis raised two pieces of purely circumstantial evidence that loomed large in their thinking in a way that was confounding to my colleagues and me. The first dealt with a 1982 meeting, arranged by Hans Sedlmeier, between Karl-Heinz Mengele and Dr. Hans Münch, an SS physician who had served with Mengele at Auschwitz.[27] Sedlmeier had told the Germans that the purpose of the meeting was to hear from an eyewitness what Mengele had done at Auschwitz.[28] When German authorities questioned Münch in February 1985, he remembered Karl-Heinz asking about Mengele's "chances" if he were to be tried in West Germany, and claimed to have responded that Mengele's chances would have been "slim." Münch recalled concluding from the question itself that Mengele was alive and that his visitors knew his current whereabouts. It was not an unreasonable inference, especially since, at the time of the meeting, there was a common belief that Mengele was still living. Indeed, Klein himself, in discussions with us at the beginning of the investigation, had used Münch's comment as supporting evidence for his own conviction that Mengele was alive. But it was not difficult to understand the evidence in a different way, and to conclude that the true meaning of the question had been misunderstood.[29] If the purpose of the visit to Münch had been, as reported, to learn from an unbiased source the real nature of Mengele's Auschwitz service, a hypothetical question about Mengele's chances before a court of law might conceivably have been posed.

The second piece of circumstantial evidence, although a bit more difficult to make sense of, still did not deserve, in my opinion, the weight the Israelis had placed on it. Rolf's wife, Almuth, had written a letter to Mengele, dated March 8, 1979, wishing him a happy birthday. Mengele, Rolf, and Almuth shared March 16 as their birthdays, and the day therefore held a special meaning for the three of them. Almuth's letter, which referred to "our day" when "all three of us will be especially thinking of each other," brought her father-in-law up to date on family news, including Rolf's job and the "funny sounds" that their seven-month-old daughter had started to make. Almuth had written the letter before the news of Mengele's death had reached them.

Rolf, instead of discarding the letter after receiving the news of his father's death, sent it on to the Bosserts along with a handwritten postscript in place of what was to have been his own contribution to his father's birthday greeting. He explained how the letter had lain around for some time while he "absorbed the sad news," and he expressed his profound gratitude, "free from sentimentality and bombast," for the help the Bosserts had rendered to his father, not only for himself but also "in the name of him," clearly referring to his father, who had accepted the Bosserts' help "as a matter of course." Rolf seemed to be apologizing for his father's apparent lack of gratitude for all the Bosserts had done for him, explaining that his father "sometimes found it difficult to be simply human."

Rolf also informed Bossert that he would like any writings that his father might have left behind and announced that he would like to visit Brazil later in the year. The Israelis believed this letter was important evidence that Mengele might still be alive, pointing out that it was strange indeed to send a letter intended for a man who you knew to be dead.[30] Rolf's explanation was that Almuth's note contained a great deal of family news which had also been intended for the Bosserts. It was certainly odd, and perhaps a bit macabre, but in the context of a correspondence that had always passed through the hands of intermediaries, the "birthday letter" failed to raise serious concerns for my colleagues or me.

During the course of the meeting, I received the specific assignment to prepare detailed memoranda, based on my review of Mengele's diaries and correspondence, on the possible existence of X-rays, and on investigative strategies relating to Mengele's osteomyelitis. I provided a thorough account of Mengele's 1972 rectal surgery and the X-rays taken pursuant to it, as well as his 1978 root canal treatment. In noting the importance of finding an X-ray, I stated that if we were successful, we could conclusively close the case. Including photocopies of all relevant letters and diary excerpts as attachments, I intended the memo as a useful guide for further investigation. Suggesting that the evidence of the root canal treatment offered the best possibility of success, I wrote, "Since we know the exact dates of Mengele's visits, it would be possible to check [the dentist's] files for each patient who received treatment on those days. . . . It is possible that this avenue of investigation might prove the most fruitful in locating medical records that could yield a conclusive identification in the Mengele matter."[31]

Following the meeting in Jerusalem, Dennis Gouldman, who claimed that Israel had relied exclusively on foreign experts up to that point, recommended that they reach out to Dr. Maurice Rogev, the director of the Pathology Institute in Abu Kabir and the chief pathologist of the Israel Defense Forces, to request that he "set up a team of medical experts" to review the material and provide an independent Israeli opinion.[32] Gouldman briefed Rogev on the Israelis' "grave doubts," based on their beliefs that the American conclusions rested on "rather general findings," and that the Germans had relied, perhaps unreasonably, on the skull-photo superimposition method.[33]

Ortner Consultation

In mid-January 1986 a brilliant consultation by Dr. Donald Ortner gave us a different understanding of the osteomyelitis issue. A curator of anthropology at the Smithsonian Institution's National Museum of Natural History, Ortner would later head the department of anthropology there and also serve for two years as acting director of the museum. His specialty was paleopathology, "the study and application of methods and techniques for investigating diseases and related conditions from skeletal and soft tissue remains." Ortner explained that he could, by examining bones, discover evidence of disease that might otherwise escape detection. A certain degree of change in the density of a bone is necessary before it becomes visible on an X-ray. Forensic pathologists simply did not have the expertise that Ortner possessed, and we were very fortunate he was willing to cooperate with us.

Working at a furious pace, Ortner spent a day and a half in São Paulo studying the purported remains of Josef Mengele "for evidence of skeletal pathology that might be helpful in resolving some of the remaining questions related to a positive identification of the remains."[34] His most important findings, which would have a lasting impact on the way I saw the case, were his "observations on the pelvic girdle and lower extremity." The bones likely revealed a traumatic event in the skeleton's youth—a crushing injury to the hip that might have led to infection. Moreover, Ortner highlighted the "boney spur" that the experts in Brazil had also noted, and he identified it as likely to have been ossified muscle. He described a condition known as myositis ossificans, occurring typically during youth, when, as a result of an injury that disrupts blood flow, muscle tissue can ossify or turn to bone. The location and shape of the bony projection led Ortner to identify it as part of the rectus femoris muscle, the longest muscle in the body, connecting the hip with the knee. The angle of the muscle-turned-bone indicated that the injury would likely have been followed by a period of prolonged inactivity, during which the individual would have been forced to keep his leg in a flexed position.[35] When asked about the kind of injury that would have caused the particular trauma he identified, Ortner suggested something like a fall from a tree. In a twist on Snow's osteobiography metaphor, Ortner accounted for how an entire chapter might be written when flesh turns to bone.

Ortner provided what might have been a solution to the osteomyelitis question as well. He was able to confirm that the "lytic focus" in the hip area noted by forensic experts in June might very well have been an indication of osteomyelitis—an observation that held particular interest for me, since it was precisely that location that Ulmann had pointed to when we met in October.

A meeting in January at our offices in Washington, to which all the American experts as well as Helmer and Dachi had been invited, provided an opportunity for an open discussion of all the available evidence but did not advance the case. Helmer mounted a broad-based and confident defense of his skull-photograph superimposition method, suggesting that if carried out properly under the right conditions, it could deliver a result with reliability on par with fingerprints. Dachi, who had been a professor of dentistry before joining the State Department, gave a presentation on his theory that the hole in the zygomatic bone was in all likelihood the result of a chronic sinus infection that led to the formation of a fistulous tract. He explained how an untreated infection of an upper tooth might invade the sinus and become notoriously difficult to control. The body, in response to such an untreated infection, could create a pathway through bone and soft tissue allowing the infection to drain. He pointed to a blemish on Mengele's cheek, clearly evident in photographs, located directly over the cheekbone, suggesting that it was the terminus of a fistulous tract, which made its way from the sinus, through the zygomatic bone, to the cheek. Others still believed the hole was a postmortem artifact. Despite his passionate advocacy, Dachi was not able to persuade them of his view.[36]

Around the time of the meeting in Washington, word got out that Eli Rosenbaum, my former colleague and future boss at OSI, had undertaken his own investigation into Mengele's death in his capacity as general counsel of the World Jewish Congress (WJC). Rosenbaum had left OSI in 1984 to take a job at a large law firm in New York City. Unhappy at the firm, he went to the WJC, where he broke the case against Kurt Waldheim. According to a column by Jack Anderson appearing in the *Washington Post* on January 29, Rosenbaum was "dissatisfied with the findings of the international team of forensic medical experts" and began to look into the Mengele case. The reporter who actually wrote the article was Lucette Lagnado, who claimed to have read "internal WJC correspondence about the WJC's Mengele investigation and interviewed some of the people involved in it, as well as other experts in the field."[37] Rosenbaum apparently believed that it was "highly probable" that Mengele was dead, but that the examination by the medical team in Brazil was inadequate and that the experts would be "lucky" if their work had led to the correct conclusion." He based his criticism of the experts on their reliance on "mostly circumstantial evidence," without having anything "concrete," such as X-rays or fingerprints, and also noted the "crucial discrepancy" of the lack of evidence of osteomyelitis.[38]

The U.S. experts, preparing to present their findings to their colleagues at their upcoming professional meeting in New Orleans, were arming themselves against this very charge. John Fitzpatrick, believing there might be "static concerning the question of osteomyelitis,"[39] prepared a report addressing the question by dismissing the reference to osteomyelitis in Mengele's BDC file: "It is my opinion (our opinion) that Josef Mengele had some sort of illness at the age of 15. The skeleton revealed no evidence of osteomyelitis. The changes in the hip are those of a fracture. The diagnosis of osteomyelitis is a misdiagnosis."[40] Ellis Kerley concluded:

> The absence of identifiable evidence of osteomyelitis in the skeleton identified as Josef Mengele should not be given undue importance or significance. There is no real description or any radiographs of the condition for comparison with the remains. More specific evidence of osteomyelitis in the living Mengele is necessary before there can be any discussion of the significance of there not being discernible evidence in the skeleton over 50 years

after Dr. Mengele recalled having had "osteomyelitis," while he had been an adolescent, much of whose bone would have been replaced by normal growth and remodeling by age 69.[41]

The experts had, at least, come around to taking the issue seriously enough to offer an explanation.

The combined U.S. forensic team convened in New Orleans in March 1986 to present their findings. Within a month of their presentation, new evidence would be discovered that would provide, at last, a welcome measure of certainty in the case. It is ironic that the very confidence displayed by the forensic experts in Brazil had removed any incentive for the authorities to look for more conclusive evidence. Had a more sober and judicious judgment been delivered, it would probably not have taken so long to complete the necessary investigative work.

CHAPTER 13

PROGRESS AND STALEMATE

(March 1986–Spring 1988)

"Dr. Gama from Sama"

Before he returned to São Paulo following our late January meeting, Steve Dachi received a copy of my December 24 memo on X-ray evidence with my analysis of certain entries in Mengele's diaries. Although Mengele described extensive dental work over the years in his diary, only his entries about his December 1978 root canal treatment provided clues to the identity of the endodontist who performed the treatment:

> [December 5, 1978] Went to dentist who discovered a big, stinking hole in my tooth, which he could not fill without a root canal treatment. Therefore, he sent me to another (Dr. Gama), who wants me back tomorrow at 3:00 pm. Bald and round-faced. . . .
> [December 6] After eating, travel to Sama to the dentist. . . . The "canal specialist" wants 3000 Crz for the one tooth, of which I paid him 2000 Crz. He wants me back on Monday. Naturally there were problems again with the old Swiss.[1]

In these entries, Mengele provided not only a name, "Dr. Gama," and location, "Sama," but also a description, "bald and round-faced." His comment about the "old Swiss" undoubtedly refers to his use of his own former pseudonym, "Pedro Hochbichler," which he had abandoned sometime before when he took on the name "Wolfgang Gerhard." Since Mengele had commenced his treatment with the referring dentist before he had established his "Wolfgang Gerhard" alias, he would have needed to revert to the name "Hochbichler" when he sought treatment from Dr. Gama.

When Dachi got back to Brazil, he set out to locate Dr. Gama. With the help of the most senior foreign service national at the consulate, Eva Reichmann, a German-Jewish émigré, he pored over the diary excerpts.[2] They were stumped; there was no place in the São Paulo area with the name Sama. After considering the problem, Dachi had an epiphany:

> It finally came to me in a flash that Sama could very possibly stand for Santo Amaro, the name of a suburb of São Paulo where I was living, and where he [Mengele] was known to have lived with the Bosserts and the Stammers. And so I got very excited at this thought, so Fred Kaplan and I . . . picked up a phone book . . . [and] we looked under dentists in Santo Amaro and there was the name of a Dr. Gama.[3]

Reichmann contacted the dentist's office, purportedly to make an appointment, and learned two crucial facts: Dr. Gama specialized in root canals, and according to his assistant, he was bald.[4]

After calling Tuma and getting a federal police officer to accompany them, Dachi and Fred Kaplan, an American diplomat at the consulate, set off to meet the dentist. An anxious Dr. Gama received the trio, and although he remembered the Mengele case from the previous summer's press coverage, he had no recollection of having treated the man seven years before. Gama's obvious nervousness, which led Kaplan to suspect that he was lying, might have instead been because of the presence of the Brazilian police officer. Just a few months following the end of military rule, the federal police still inspired fear.

Dachi asked Gama whether he had patient records going back to 1978 and was relieved to hear that the dentist had retained complete treatment and financial records from that period. They divided the charts into three piles, and Dachi, Kaplan, and the police officer each examined their assigned pile in search of a male patient who had received treatment on December 6, 11, 13, and 18 in 1978. The search was made easier because Gama had written the first date of treatment on the upper-left corner of each chart; one could go through a stack very quickly. The police officer hit the jackpot, discovering a patient chart for a Pedro Hochbichler, who had undergone treatment on precisely the dates recorded in Mengele's diary.[5]

When Dachi asked the surprised Gama, who had to admit that he had treated the patient, whether he would have any X-rays for Hochbichler, the dentist replied that although he certainly would have taken X-rays in the course of the treatment, it was his practice to send them to the referring dentist to include in the patient's file. According to the chart, the referring dentist was his colleague, Dr. Kasumasa Tutiya.[6] Dachi, Kaplan, and the police officer set out to find Tutiya, whose office turned out to be a block and a half away. Dachi later described the scene with great drama:

> The three of us walked out of there and crossed the street and . . . the adrenaline was just pumping like crazy and there was a record store there that was playing . . . loud music on the loudspeaker for the street and that sort of enhanced the sort of trance-like or movie-like atmosphere as we were . . . brimming with excitement walking the block and a half . . . to get to the office of Dr. Tutiya.

Once there, the police officer showed Tutiya one of the photographs of Mengele taken by Bossert, and Tutiya immediately recognized him as "the man with the hat." Tutiya retrieved a chart indicating that he

had performed a lot of dental work for the man, then went to a fil-
ing cabinet and removed an envelope containing eight X-rays taken
in conjunction with the patient's extensive treatment, which included
extracting teeth and producing dental protheses.

Dachi was extremely pleased with this discovery and immediately
called us in Washington. We were on the cusp of discovering definitive
proof of Mengele's death—we just needed to have the X-rays examined
and compared to the remaining teeth of the Embu skeleton.

Within five days, Lowell Levine was in São Paulo to evaluate the
new findings. His one-page report, countersigned by the Brazilian
forensic odontologist, Dr. Carlos Valerio, indicated that the "Hochbichler X-rays" were of excellent quality and exhibited "multiple,
unique, and individual characteristics" that were also present in the
X-rays taken of the teeth belonging to the Embu skeleton. There were
"no inconsistent characteristics." In a longer "analysis of the dental
evidence," Levine indicated that "radiographically, the skeleton is
absolutely the dental patient who identified himself as Pedro Hochbichler."[7] Levine concluded that the "skeleton identified by an international panel of forensic scientists as Josef Mengele with reasonable
scientific certainty may now be identified as Josef Mengele with an
absolute certainty."

April Mission

Even before the discovery of the X-rays in March, the Germans had
been contemplating a follow-up trip to São Paulo. Although their
forensic experts were supremely confident about the identification
of the Embu skeleton, Hans Klein understood that it was necessary
to chase down all the outstanding leads and respond to the concerns
raised by various interested parties, and he believed that the discovery
of the new dental evidence only increased the relevance of the proposed investigative trip to São Paulo. At the end of March, he issued
a formal tasking memorandum to the German Federal Police and the

Hessian Criminal Police, outlining the objectives of a renewed investigation in São Paulo. It should focus on five areas, he wrote, including evidence associated with Mengele's various medical treatments and information relating to Mengele's use of the alias "Peter Hochbichler," which had emerged as much more significant since the discovery of the Tutiya records and X-rays. The Germans had to retrace Dachi's steps and examine the circumstances surrounding the X-rays for themselves, and interview Drs. Tutiya and Gama. They also wished to interview Geza Stammer, who had been absent from São Paulo the previous summer, as well as the Bossert children. Finally, they wanted to visit the beach in Bertioga where Mengele was said to have drowned, in order to reconstruct the events of that day in 1979.[8] Klein stressed the importance of the mission and wanted it to take place "as soon as possible."[9]

Our efforts to analyze Mengele's correspondence and diaries, and Dachi's personal interest and engagement, had significantly advanced the case. The Germans could not be seen as passive while others not only raised doubts but also located meaningful new evidence. The Israelis, who had contributed little new to the case besides their negative view of the assembled evidence, also felt they needed to be part of the undertaking. The U.S. Department of Justice was initially lukewarm; it was hard to commit additional resources to the investigation, especially following the discovery of the dental records and with the expense of sending Levine to São Paulo for a second time. The Israelis, however, were adamant that OSI should participate and, impressed by the work I had done in deciphering Mengele's writings, pushed hard for my inclusion.

I arrived in São Paulo on April 16[10] and joined my Israeli and German colleagues, Horst Gemmer of the Hessian State Police, Dieter Sack of the BKA, Dennis Gouldman from the Israeli Ministry of Justice, and Igo Sommer, who introduced himself as Yitzchak Ben Meir, from the office of the Israeli prime minister, his cover identity. They had already met with the Brazilian police and agreed upon a schedule for our work, which was to proceed as a cooperative effort with each of the delegations represented at each of the interviews. The Germans provided an excellent interpreter, who translated from the Portuguese into German and English, and our consulate provided a car and driver. The Brazilian police assigned two officers to accompany us and to make all the necessary arrangements.[11]

There was tension between the Germans and the Israelis. In part, it could be attributed to the differences in age and personality of the two countries' representatives. The Germans were young, experienced, and no-nonsense police professionals, while the Israelis were older men, one of whom, Gouldman, was a high-ranking Justice Ministry official, and the other, Sommer, an intelligence officer more comfortable operating in the shadows. Add to this that the Germans had essentially closed the case in their minds and were looking to address the doubts of others, while the Israelis were, at best, highly skeptical about the evidence that had been adduced in support of Mengele's death. Finally, it is difficult to ignore the history that loomed over the relationship between Germans and the Jews, especially in the context of the Mengele case. I entered this potentially fraught situation as a bridge between the two sides. I told friends afterward that I would drink coffee with the Israelis and beer with the Germans. My good relationship with both allowed me to play a unifying role in the unusual band of investigators who slipped mostly unnoticed into São Paulo in the spring of 1986.

Our first interview, on April 16, was with Tutiya, a pleasant man of Japanese descent, whose office was on a busy commercial street in the Santa Amaro section of São Paulo. Precise and orderly, Tutiya kept his examination room tidy and clean and took pride in his fastidiousness, a characteristic that led him to maintain his well-organized files. He recalled that Hochbichler, whom he described as "taciturn" and "grumpy," arrived with teeth that were in very poor condition, with only three molars in good enough condition to remain and the others either missing or in need of extraction. The patient, who spoke very little, did so in a mixture of Portuguese, Spanish, English, and German. Although he had come expecting to need a full prosthesis, thanks to the remaining molars, Tutiya recommended two partial protheses. The patient card was filled out, and Hochbichler had not needed to present his identity card since he was paying in cash.[12]

Tutiya made a very favorable impression, and his testimony was useful. The Israelis determined, after examining the records, that Mengele had visited Tutiya twenty-three times in the course of his treatment and that there were identical references in Mengele's diaries. The Germans concluded their report on the interview as follows:

> Through detailed questioning and examination there was no doubt as to the truthfulness of the information and the authenticity of the evidence. Dr. T. has kept an above-average record of accounts and kept nearly every record since the beginning of his practice.
>
> The Israeli and American officials, according to their own statements, arrived at the same evaluation.[13]

Although the Israelis were clearly impressed with Tutiya's apparent honesty and forthrightness, this did not stop them from requesting that he undergo a polygraph. He refused the request, referring to his "professional honor," and said he would get in contact with the physicians' professional organization. Gama made a similarly good impression as a witness, although his relatively limited contact with the patient, consisting of one treatment over four visits, had not made a significant impression on him.

The Hairball

On Friday, April 18, we pursued evidence of a surgical procedure that Mengele had undergone to clear an intestinal blockage. I had first learned of Mengele's odd condition the previous summer in a letter that I had found amid the correspondence I reviewed in Munich. Mengele had written Rolf in August 1972, describing his complaint and its resolution:

> About five weeks ago I once again experienced a violent liver-gallbladder attack, and, at its conclusion, a blockage of the rectum by a fecal stone [fecaloma]. After long-term self-treatment, I was forced to visit a doctor in a neighboring city, who wanted to operate to remove the "hardened section of bowel." After complicated X-rays in a hospital, which were then presented to a professor in the capital (as an interesting case), the treating physician then removed a polyp from the colon via the rectum. For this I had to be taken again to another hospital for two days. Two days after that, I gave birth to the *corpus delicti,* which had been pushed up during the polyp operation. The solitary polyp had prevented the natural elimination of the stone. The pathological examination of the polyp indicated a benign representative of intestinal neoplasm, and the stone consisted of 80% hair (probably my beard).[14]

Although the Brazilians had located and deposed the surgeon and radiologist who had worked on Mengele's case at our request in the fall of the previous year,[15] we believed that there might still be undiscovered X-rays or medical records relating to the case and wanted our own chance to speak with his doctors.

The patient was a "very different kind of person," the radiologist, Dr. Antonioi Furtado de Albuquerque Cavalcanti, recalled: "very well dressed" in a velvet suit with a "Tyrolean hat." The first set of X-rays, which were taken using barium for contrast, were negative. When these normal results were reported to the patient, he tried to explain that he had a "real problem." In a mixture of Portuguese, Spanish, German, and English, he told the radiologist that he had difficulty moving his bowels and that the problem was intermittent: sometimes everything was normal, and other times he felt an impediment. He described it as a "ball that prevented the feces from getting out." When this occurred, he forced himself to insert his finger into his rectum and push the blockage up. Cavalcanti told us that in considering the patient's description, he decided to repeat the X-rays, only this time without the use of contrast medium. The second set revealed a mass that had been obscured the first time by the barium.

Cavalcanti explained to us that the mass had actually been a trichobezoar, or hairball, and represented a highly unusual case. It was not unusual for a hairball to form—more commonly in mental hospitals, where patients would tear out and eat their own hair—but it would normally remain in the stomach and would rarely pass through the digestive system and find its way to the rectum. Cavalcanti, who taught at a medical school, asked the patient whether he might be permitted to use the X-rays in presenting this rare case to his students and colleagues. The patient had been reluctant to lend the X-rays, which technically belonged to him, but he relented under the condition that his name not be mentioned in connection with the X-rays or the case. Cavalcanti told us that the patient had carefully counted the X-rays as he lent them out and again when they were returned to ensure that none were missing.

We then traveled to the city of Jundiaí, about thirty miles northwest of São Paulo, to interview Dr. Eduardo Fredini Jr., the surgeon who had performed the operation on Mengele. In contrast to his more conservative colleague, Fredini wore blue jeans, cowboy boots, and an open-necked shirt, which made him look like an aging hipster. Fredini remembered the case and described his patient and the procedure he had performed in essentially the same way as had his colleague, also confirming Cavalcanti's description of the case as very rare. He claimed not to possess any records relating to it, although when we asked him if we could look through his patient files, he agreed, perhaps because of the presence of the Brazilian police officers.

We were shown into a small file room lined with metal cabinets containing what seemed like tens of thousands of records. Before we had searched for very long, one of the police officers, Dieter Sack, the BKA colonel, reached into a file drawer and retrieved a record for one Pedro Hochbichler. Not until we got back to the car and were able to go through the record with our interpreter did I realize we had a significant find. The patient file described the condition and treatment along with a brief medical history. Under the heading "previous surgeries" appeared "Hernia operation 48 years ago." In the back seat of the Suburban, I checked the BDC file, a copy of which I had carried with me, and confirmed that in Mengele's SS medical record he had had a hernia operation in 1924—forty-eight years before the date of the Hochbichler's 1972 patient record. For me, this small detail offered powerful confirmation of the identity of the Embu skeleton, beyond the calculation of even the most resourceful and clever hoaxer.

Stalemate

On July 22, 1986, the Germans received word that the Brazilian Federal Police had closed their case on Mengele. In September, Klein told both Sher and Gouldman that the Germans had reached a similar point; having concluded all "investigative activities," they were now planning to declare Mengele dead. Klein informed his colleagues before making a public announcement and, in an abundance of caution, asked for any evidence that might contradict the Germans' conclusion, especially the identity of any individuals who claimed to have seen Mengele since February 1979.[16]

Gouldman responded in early November that it was "premature for the German authorities to close their file on Mengele." While he acknowledged that the discoveries made earlier in the year in Brazil, by which he meant the dental X-rays and other medical evidence, "took [them] closer to the conclusion that the body buried in Embu [was] indeed that of Josef Mengele," there still remained "a number of questions" to which they did not have the answers.[17] Gouldman stressed that until "these difficulties" had been "satisfactorily resolved," the case could not be "regarded as closed." He added that Dr. Maurice Rogev, after carefully reviewing all the medical evidence, including the reports by the U.S. and German experts, shared this conclusion.[18]

Gouldman wrote again ten days later and included specific questions posed by Rogev that related to Helmer's photo-skull comparison and details about the hip fracture.[19] It took the Germans until early February 1987 to respond, and when they did, they could barely disguise their frustration.[20] The Israelis had not understood Helmer's method, and the hip fracture was "close to meaningless" in significance for the identification. Dr. Rolf Endris, who drafted the German response, felt it necessary to suggest that his Israeli colleagues needed to be instructed in the principles of the identification of a body.[21]

After receiving the German responses, the Israelis decided to send Rogev to Brazil to examine the bones himself and to confer with the Brazilian experts.[22] He spent a week in São Paulo at the end of July 1987, marking the first time that an Israeli expert had laid eyes on the actual skeleton. On his way back to Israel, Rogev met with us at OSI and with Don Ortner from the Smithsonian. Rogev had no dispute with the anthropological findings related to age, sex, height, and race,[23] but he disagreed on the issues relating to the right hip, offering a dramatically different and far more detailed explanation for the condition of the relevant bones than that reached by the other experts in June 1985; he agreed, in essence, with Ortner, judging the hip fracture to have likely occurred between the ages of twelve and sixteen. The kind of damage he saw in the hip area was characteristic of a fall from a height of three to six meters, "where a person falls on the legs and the force of the impact is transferred to the pelvis." Such an injury, he estimated, would have required at least a month or two of bed rest and might have resulted in osteomyelitis.[24] Rogev also interpreted the fractures of the clavicle and scapula as having occurred in adolescence, and as being consistent with the kind of fall that caused the hip injury.[25]

Rogev called for a search for additional evidence—specifically, for
any indication that Mengele had suffered a "fall in adolescence, that
could have caused the fractures that were found." He emphasized that
his findings did not "reveal any facts that contradict the possibility"
that the skeleton belonged to Mengele. Rather, he believed that "if we
can solve the problems of the osteomyelitis and the fall, there is no jus-
tification for not accepting the identification of Mengele."[26]

Gouldman took up Rogev's suggestions with Klein in November,
recommending that the Germans try to determine whether there
was any evidence of an accident in Mengele's adolescence. Gouldman noted that such an accident had not been recorded in Mengele's SS medical file; nor was the hip fracture that was supposed to
have resulted from it. Rogev's estimate that the mishap would have
occurred between the ages of twelve and sixteen and would have
resulted in a prolonged period of bedrest led Gouldman to suggest
a search for attendance records from Mengele's primary school and
Gymnasium, as well as records from local hospitals and clinics. If the
son of one of the most prominent men in a town like Günzburg were
involved in such an accident, Gouldman believed that someone would
surely be able to confirm its occurrence, and it might even have been
mentioned in the local newspaper. He also suggested that Klein pursue records from the family physician and question former Mengele
family household staff. Finally, he recommended that Mengele's first
wife, Irene, be interviewed.[27]

CHAPTER 14

CASE CLOSED

(Spring 1988–April 1992)

"We would have preferred to present you with a living Mengele. . . ."

In the summer of 1988, the Mengele investigation was at a standstill. OSI had completed its report and put to rest the doubts that had clung to the case following the spectacle in São Paulo three years before. With a careful and diligent effort to review all the available material and with success in locating significant new evidence, we raised the degree of certainty beyond what "reasonableness" demanded. The Germans, among themselves, had been prepared for several years to close the case, keeping it open only with a sharp eye on public opinion and concern for the positions taken by their partners. It was the Israelis who refused to accept the evidence as conclusive, and their doubts kept the case open. Given the effort and expense that had already been devoted to discovering unassailable evidence and given the broad expectation from the public for a conclusion to the case, Hans Klein was understandably impatient. His colleagues in the prosecutor's office and the police were clear about the facts; they thought the case should be closed.

The Israelis' doubts still centered on the lack of evidence from Mengele's youth of the hip fracture. No medical records or witness testimony had confirmed it, and the recently discovered school records, which corroborated the fact that Mengele had been out of school for an extended period when he was sixteen, only added to Israeli doubts, since they referenced an illness and not an accident.[1] When Klein spoke with Sher in an apparent effort to gauge the latter's reaction to a German closing of the case, Sher told him, off the record, that it would not be seriously contested by the Americans. Klein, however, decided to pursue one last possibility, raised by Gouldman, who wrote that the Israelis believed a "properly executed DNA fingerprinting test could give a conclusive answer to the question of identity."[2] Knowing that the Israelis would make public their doubts, Klein understood how a reluctance on his part to follow every possible lead would be received. Around this time, Klein privately confided to me that no one would believe a German prosecutor who declared Mengele to be dead if the Israelis presented a contrary position. His superiors agreed with his reasoning, and the final phase of the forensic investigation got under way.

We agreed with the initiative and decided to evaluate whether the new technique of DNA typing could be employed in the Mengele case. The FBI was at the time conducting tests and establishing guidelines and protocols for using DNA as a forensic tool. I visited Dr. Bruce Budowle, the FBI biochemist responsible for this project, in his laboratory in Quantico, Virginia, and received a quick course in DNA "fingerprint" technology, which was then in its infancy.[3]

DNA "fingerprinting" relies on the inherent differences in the DNA of individuals. The greatest variability between humans can be found in that part of the genome that is noncoding and therefore does not determine specific physical characteristics. Although the function of noncoding DNA is not well understood, we know that it is not subject to evolutionary pressures and is therefore highly variable among humans. At specific locations within the noncoding DNA, there are repeated sequences of the components that make up the genetic code, and the number of repetitions of the sequences differs significantly between people. Alec Jeffreys, the British geneticist, was able to develop a method whereby an enzyme introduced to the DNA would cut the DNA molecule at the end of the repetitive sequence, resulting in DNA fragments of different lengths depending on the number of repetitions. The fragments of DNA would then be subjected to a process known as electrophoresis, which separates them according to length, as a function of how far they travel through a gel when an electrical current is introduced, with the shortest fragments traveling the farthest in a given time period. The fragments are treated so that they create an image when exposed to X-ray film. The result is a graphic presentation of the DNA in the form of a series of separated bands resembling a bar code, corresponding to the lengths of the targeted sequences.

By the summer of 1988, the technique had been more or less standardized, and a great deal of testing had been done to ensure that reliable and repeatable results could be obtained and defended in a court of law. One of the limitations, Budowle explained to me, was that high-molecular-weight DNA was necessary in order to perform a meaningful analysis. This requirement had to do with the length of the DNA sequences that were analyzed as well as the sensitivity of the electrophoresis/gel technique. Whereas obtaining high-molecular-weight DNA was no problem if one was conducting a paternity test and had blood samples from the parents and the child in question, in criminal cases the DNA evidence was often severely degraded. Moreover, there was no precedent for what we wanted to accomplish. I was told that while it was theoretically possible to extract DNA from bones and hair, any sample would likely have been degraded by the conditions in the wet grave and the length of time that had passed. But hair samples could contain usable DNA, since at the base of each strand of hair, there is a plug of tissue, and the hair shaft itself had DNA. We believed that as unlikely as successful DNA testing appeared to be, it was worth a shot. We cabled our consulate in São Paulo to request that samples of Mengele's hair be delivered to Washington.

When the samples arrived—some scalp and moustache hair—I took them to FBI headquarters, where a new area of their lab was being renovated to house a newly established DNA section. The analyst carefully prepared them for examination under his microscope, taking time to arrange the slide and attain the proper focus. He peered through the eyepiece, then slowly lifted his head, turned to me, and said softly, "This does not appear to be human hair." A number of thoughts rushed to mind, including how apt the judgment might be considered in characterizing Josef Mengele. He added quickly that the sample was so degraded that it was not possible to identify it properly, and there was no chance of extracting any useful DNA. With that conclusion, the search for a conclusive scientific imprimatur for our findings seemed to have run its course—straight into a dead end.

While we explored DNA profiling in the United States, Klein was investigating resources available in Germany. He turned first to Helmer, who, in turn, suggested Dr. Christian Rittner, the head of the Institute for Forensic Medicine at the University of Mainz, the recognized German expert in the field.[4] Horst Gemmer met with Rittner in early December 1988, along with Dr. Andreas Sonnberg, who was the head of the biology/seriology section of the Hessian Criminal Police.

Rittner's assessment of the prospects for DNA analysis in the Mengele case was not encouraging. He considered it "an extremely time-consuming, extensive examination, whose prospects for success are judged to be remote."[5] The hurdles were significant. Even if suitable material could be obtained from the skeleton—Rittner believed pulp from a tooth was the most likely source—current science would permit an exclusionary probability of only 60 percent—a level of certainty that would do nothing to persuade the skeptics.

Referring to Rittner's pessimistic evaluation, Sonnberg suggested, "Given the extraordinary nature of this matter, we should seek the opinion of another expert in the area of genetic testing" and recommended contacting Alec Jeffreys at Leicester University.[6] Klein, apparently influenced by Rittner's pessimism concerning DNA's prospects, would not reach out to Jeffreys for more than nine months.

Bossert Polygraph

In the meantime, the Israelis had again taken up their long-sought effort to subject Liselotte Bossert to a polygraph test, something she had refused in September 1985. Later, in February 1987, they had conceived of a ruse in which a Mossad agent, posing as a German journalist, would approach the Bosserts through their attorney, Flavio Marx. This journalist, seeking the "whole truth about Mengele," would be willing to make a substantial payment to the Bosserts for their cooperation, which would have to include a polygraph test.[7] The Bosserts' attorney was willing to consider the proposal in principle, but it would have to wait until after the trial of Liselotte Bossert. The Brazilians had charged her with "false ideology" for "providing information that resulted in the preparation of a fraudulent death certificate," a charge that could result in a sentence of one to five years in prison.[8] The trial began on April 9, 1987, but would not be finished quickly; the judge informed her on the first day of trial that she would not be called again until May 1988.[9] The Israelis put their plan on hold.

In March 1989 the Israelis revisited the Bossert polygraph issue and decided to forget the earlier "journalist" ruse and to use a more direct approach. They enlisted the help of Pinchas Bar, who had once served in the Israeli consulate in São Paulo and had good relations with Tuma and other police officials. Bar contacted Tuma and communicated the Israelis' persistent doubts and the fact that "for moral reasons" they could not close the Mengele case. Bar proposed to go to Brazil and talk with Liselotte Bossert and verify her testimony with a polygraph. Tuma had Marco Veronesi, his successor as chief of the Brazilian Federal Police in São Paulo, contact Bossert, who referred him to her lawyer. He responded that the entire Bossert family was willing to be questioned and that Liselotte Bossert would agree to a polygraph examination. What remained was to negotiate an acceptable price.

Bar headed to São Paulo to meet with police officials. Much to his consternation, his presence in São Paulo and the purpose of his mission had been leaked to the press, likely by Bossert's lawyer. The bright light of publicity almost scuttled the Israelis' plan by provoking the judge in the Bossert case to raise serious reservations about the appropriateness of the Israelis operating on Brazilian soil and the ethics of paying a witness. The judge, however, relented and agreed the plan could proceed if he received a formal request from the police and a formal statement from Bossert confirming her voluntary participation. Negotiations with Bossert and her lawyer yielded agreement on a price of $45,000, which was nearly double that which had been approved by the Mossad, albeit less than half of what Bossert had originally requested.

Given the four years of lead-up and the seemingly high price that was paid, the actual questioning was surprisingly straightforward when it was finally conducted on March 27, 1989. Although Liselotte Bossert was very tense at the start of the examination, she provided clear answers to the three key questions posed to her: Was it Josef Mengele who drowned at Bertioga? Was the man you brought to the Pathology Institute in Santos Josef Mengele? And is Josef Mengele alive? Her answers—yes to the first two questions, and no to the last—were judged by the polygraph expert to be unequivocally truthful.

Bossert's polygraph removed the last remaining investigative step that the Israelis had identified. With the prospect of using DNA still remote, Gouldman drafted a long memorandum outlining in some detail every step taken in the investigation and evaluating the state of the case.[10] He determined that he and his colleagues should "conclude" their "professional and operational" work. He did not, however, recommend that the case be closed. "From the public aspect, we think that the government should assume responsibility for [that] decision, and it also has to decide what it chooses to release to the public."[11] In his judgment and recommendation, Gouldman had captured the complexity of the Mengele case for the Israeli government. He was admitting that the decision about how to handle the case going forward was a political one.

Just a few days before Bossert underwent the polygraph examination, a number of survivor groups, including CANDLES, published a full-page advertisement in the March 24 issue of the *New York Jewish Week*, with the bold headline, "Is Mengele Dead?"[12] Addressed to OSI, the ad quoted extensively from Simon Wiesenthal's annual report, dated January 31, 1989, in which the famous Nazi hunter indicated that although he had once accepted the findings of the "highly trained medical examiners" who had identified the "mortal remains that were dug up in the Embu cemetery" as Mengele's, he was no longer so certain. Relying heavily on the work of Russek and Ben Abraham from Brazil, Wiesenthal repeated the inventory of inconsistencies and doubts that had kept the Israelis from closing the case. The appearance of the advertisement was proof of the enduring nature of the doubts about Mengele's death. At the same time, it seemed to be evidence of an insurmountable challenge to any notion that the case could ever be closed, even with the proof, now in hand, that Bossert had not lied.

Jeffreys

Klein met with Sher and me in Frankfurt over the summer of 1989. I was then director of the Berlin Document Center and had been kept informed of the progress, or lack thereof, in the Mengele case. I had received successive drafts of the report and maintained regular contact with Sher. We sat down with Klein in his office on August 29, and he informed us of his intention to pursue DNA testing at the urging of Israel.[13] Klein intended to contact Alec Jeffreys in England to seek his opinion on the possibility of successful DNA testing and to ask Tuma in Brazil to obtain appropriate samples from Mengele's skeleton. He secured from Sher a commitment to hold off on publishing our report until Jeffreys had rendered his opinion.[14]

Tuma agreed to bring the requested material to Germany himself during a stopover on a planned visit to Italy in mid-September.[15] Once they were certain they could obtain the bone samples, the Germans had Sonnberg reach out to Alec Jeffreys at Leicester University.[16] Jeffreys was willing to consider working on the case but sought to manage Sonnberg's expectations:

> While we would obviously have to discuss in detail the feasibility of carrying out DNA fingerprint analysis on the exhumed remains, I should perhaps mention at this stage that such an analysis would be far from guaranteed to be successful. I would imagine that the state of deterioration of the remains is such that any DNA remaining would be severely degraded and not readily amenable to typing analysis. It may well be necessary to use DNA amplification by the polymerase chain reaction to carry out typing on this material.[17]

Sonnberg traveled to Leicester in November 1989 to discuss in detail the unprecedented undertaking they were considering and returned in March 1990 carrying parts of three of Mengele's bones and two of his teeth. Samples of the bones were cut and retained by Jeffreys and his colleague, Erika Hagelberg, for use in the analysis.[18]

Near the end of July, Jeffreys wrote to Sonnberg to report very slow progress, owing in part to competing claims on his time, but also to "formidable technical problems." He and his colleagues had restricted the work to the humerus and femur, since the scapula was far too degraded to offer any chance of successful extraction. "Reasonable quantities" of DNA had been extracted from both bones, but the proportion of human DNA was "exceedingly small," one part in one thousand from the femur and little, if any, from the humerus sample, which was "severely degraded."[19] The resulting "tiny amounts and degraded state of the human DNA" would force the team to use PCR amplification techniques that would pose a number of "significant challenges."[20] All in all, however, Jeffreys expressed excitement at the progress they had made. They had shown "in principle [that] it may be possible to obtain typing information on this DNA sample," but he cautioned that the work ahead would likely take "several months."[21]

Within a month, however, Jeffreys reported that the "first stage" of the DNA analysis had been completed. "To our astonishment," he wrote with obvious satisfaction, "it has proven possible to obtain unambiguous typing information." Because the length of the extracted strands would not allow them to use minisatellite locations for analysis, they would be forced to deploy a newer technique, using microsatellites that compared shorter repetition sequences.[22] By the end of August, he submitted a comprehensive report on the extraction of the DNA and its analysis. It described the painstaking care the British scientist and his colleagues employed at every step of the process as they made their way into uncharted territory.

Although the use of microsatellites was less "informative" than minisatellite DNA typing systems, they could unquestionably be probative in parentage testing. This was good news, since a type of parental testing was precisely what Jeffreys had in mind. Jeffreys provided a "rough" estimate of the statistical power of using microsatellites in the Mengele case, claiming, in somewhat tortured language, that the probability that a "non-father of Rolf Mengele would not be identified as such (i.e., possibility of chance non-exclusion of a non-father)" was 0.0006. In other words, they could identify the questioned remains as being those of Josef Mengele to a 99.94 percent degree of certainty. The next and necessary step would be to obtain blood samples from both Rolf and Irene.

What seemed like a minor requirement turned out to be far more complicated; the case—poised as it was at a breakthrough—would remain open for nearly another two years. Klein's entreaties to Rolf and Irene were rebuffed. Although we do not know Rolf's precise motive for refusing to give his blood, I do recall Klein telling me that Rolf had "had enough" of the whole affair and did not wish to cooperate any further. Rolf's early engagement and willingness to put himself in the public eye had vanished. In the weeks and months after the body was discovered, and after the series in *Bunte,* he had become a public figure of sorts. He had agreed to meet with Sher and me in Freiburg in March 1986 and had then appeared to be interested in helping; he had even traveled to the United States to appear on *The Phil Donohue Show* to help Gerald Posner promote his new book about Mengele.[23] But by the early 1990s, things had changed, the most obvious sign of which was Rolf's decision to drop the name Mengele and take his wife's maiden name, Jenckel. I was told that he had invested in a children's clothing business in Freiburg and had tried to settle into a quiet life with his wife and three children.

Under German law, Rolf and his mother enjoyed specific protection against compulsion to provide testimony or evidence in connection with the criminal proceedings against Josef Mengele. In a conversation with Klein in mid-December, Rolf informed him that he was invoking his rights under this provision of the German criminal code to refuse to cooperate with the investigation, and specifically he would not provide a blood sample.[24] He let a German magazine know of his position in response to an interview request in March:

> I am not available for interviews, questions, information, telephone calls, etc. The Staatsanwaltschaft in Frankfurt is aware that I am making use of my legal rights to refuse to provide evidence or testimony in the investigative proceedings against Josef Mengele. One does not require a reason to exercise his rights under Section 52 of the Criminal Code.[25]

In April, Klein wrote to Fritz Steinacker, an attorney who had represented Josef Mengele and the Mengele family in the past, bemoaning Rolf's refusal to cooperate and suggesting that it would not be in the best interest of the Mengele family for him to do so: "You can well imagine what sort of interpretations and speculations this refusal will invite." He asked Steinacker to intercede with the Günzburg Mengeles to influence Rolf to change his mind.[26]

Klein, however, decided not to rely on the Mengele family to persuade Rolf. He knew there was tension between the branches of the family and that Rolf might not be moved by a request from his cousins, who were motivated to put the case to rest once and for all. He went public with his frustration in an interview with the *Mail on Sunday* in mid-October, complaining that he had written to Rolf many times:

> Jenckel simply refuses to give a blood sample, asserting his right to decline to give evidence. I have no legal means to force him to help us in the investigation. It is disappointing and inexplicable. Jenckel holds the key to the case in his hands. He is Mengele's only child and the only living person who can enable the use of definitive scientific proof that the remains are actually those of his father.[27]

Alfred Streim, a prominent West German investigator and prosecutor of Nazi war crimes, was also quoted:

> I find it amazing, that he refuses to cooperate. It is obvious that it is in the interest of the Mengele company that Josef should be declared dead. I personally do not believe that Mengele is dead. That is the obvious conclusion that one must draw from Jenckel's passivity.[28]

Rolf and his wife, Almuth, were interviewed for the same article. After emphasizing that he had no doubts that the skeleton exhumed in June 1985 in Brazil was that of his father, Rolf made clear that he did not want to be drawn into the case anymore, "now and for the rest of my life." "That is my right under German Law. For me the matter is closed." His wife told the interviewer, "We are aware of the new scientific development, but you must understand that we wish to be left in peace."[29]

When pressure from the family and pressure from the weight of public opinion did not have the desired effect on Rolf, Klein hatched another plan. He concocted a clever ruse, which two members of the police unit assigned to Klein's office described to me in confidence a year or two after the events.[30] They told me, with undisguised admiration, of Klein's careful instructions: they were to travel to Günzburg, locate the town gravedigger, and ask him to point out the grave of Karl Mengele, Josef's father. They were then to leave, after explicitly warning the gravedigger not to mention their visit to anyone. Dutifully, the police carried out their orders.

After a few days, when it became clear that the desired result of Klein's scheme had failed to materialize, Klein refined his plan; he called in the police officers once more and instructed them to return to Günzburg, this time to seek out the retired gravedigger and ask him the same question and impart the same warning. This time, within a few days, Rolf Mengele contacted Klein, saying he would provide the desired blood sample. Klein had had the exquisite psychological sensitivity to understand the dynamics of an insular company town, where a secret can become gossip; in spite of his desire to be left alone, Rolf would not want his grandfather's grave disturbed.

On January 9, 1992, Rolf and his mother each had 0.5 milliliters of blood drawn from their arms in a doctor's office in Freiburg. Klein and Sonnberg were in attendance as witnesses. Then they met in Rolf's nearby office to execute the necessary paperwork to document the provenance for the blood and to ensure that both Rolf and Irene had acted willingly and with the understanding that they had the legal right to refuse. Klein now had the last piece of evidence that would allow him to close the case once and for all.[31]

Jeffreys and his colleagues in Leicester wasted no time in processing the blood from Rolf and his mother, and by March they had concluded their examination. They had improved the level of confidence in their findings by doubling the number of comparison sites, or loci, on the genotype from five to ten. Their findings:

> For every locus typed, the genotype of the bone DNA was fully consistent with that expected for the father of Rolf Jenkel [sic]. No genotype combinations were found which excluded paternity. Statistical evaluation of the evidence using published Caucasian allele frequency tables suggested that only one person in 36,000 individuals unrelated to Rolf Jenkel [sic] would by chance show alleles over all 10 loci compatible with paternity. Even after compensating for the limited sizes of the current allele databases, this frequency remained low (1 in 1,800 individuals). We therefore conclude that, beyond reasonable doubt, the skeletal remains are those of the father of Rolf Jenkel [sic], namely Josef Mengele.[32]

Klein had his answer. It remained only for him to officially close the case.

In a press conference held at the Frankfurt Prosecutor's Office on April 9, 1992, seven years after our first tripartite meeting in Frankfurt, Klein announced the results to the international press corps. I had taken the U.S. Army's duty train from Berlin early that morning to be present at the formal closing of the case that had occupied me in one way or another for more than seven years. The occasion also permitted me to spend some time with my German colleagues, whom I had not seen for a number of years. In his formal remarks, Klein stated:

> We, the prosecutors in Frankfurt am Main, who have for decades been trying to elucidate the crimes committed in Auschwitz and assure a just atonement, assure the surviving victims of the Holocaust as well as the survivors of Mengele's inhuman experiments: We would have preferred to present you with a living Mengele in order to establish Mengele's guilt in a trial and to satisfy the needs of the victims for closure.[33]

Still, one of the Israeli reporters posed a final question about how the level of certainty would be affected if the analyzed DNA had come not from the bones of Josef Mengele but rather from those of his brother.

Despite that sliver of implied suspicion that even the DNA test could not deliver a clear and definitive answer, the conclusion that the Embu skeleton was indeed Josef Mengele's was widely accepted by the public and has survived without serious assault for more than a quarter of a century. No credible new evidence, no deathbed revelation from a family member, and no hoax-enacting conspirator has emerged to challenge it. That is not to say, however, that everyone believed it. Indeed, in August 1992, a few months after Klein's press conference, the Knesset, the Israeli parliament, held a session during which members grilled the minister of justice, David Labai, about the government's decision to close the Mengele case. Dov Shilansky, deputy and former speaker of the Knesset and a member of the Likud Party, responded that he was "utterly convinced that the body exhumed from the grave is not Mengele's body."[34]

Russek, who had effectively been marginalized due to his outspoken opposition to the consensus view of the Israeli interagency committee on Mengele, had written a comprehensive report in December 1986 that one journalist described as "a sweeping attack on the Embu skeleton story," one that "chronicled inconsistency, inaccuracy and demonstrable falsehood in the testimony of witnesses."[35] In May 1991 someone handed the once-secret report to Eva Kor, and she provided it to the press.[36] It seems that Russek also gave a copy of his report to Ben Abraham in São Paulo, who published a second book about the Mengele case, *Mengele: The Truth Exposed,* in 1994, which is dedicated to Russek and quotes liberally from his work. Abraham opens the book with the "revelation" that Mengele actually died in "early 1992 in the United States."[37]

In March 1996 the German news magazine *Focus* published an article entitled "Haunted by Evil Doubts" (*Gejagt von bösen Zweifeln*), which featured Russek and his continued suspicions:

Five years after his retirement, [Russek] is speaking out for the first time publicly about his doubts concerning the death of the most searched-for Nazi criminal. Many victims, and the offspring of those murdered, listen to him—and believe his arguments. They are now demanding that the worldwide search for Josef Mengele, who would have been 85 years old last Saturday, be taken up again.[38]

The article's author, Wilhelm Dietl, wrote to Klein in late February to give him a chance to respond to the issues raised in the article: "The Israelis believe they can recognize a political conspiracy. They speak of American interest in Mengele's research papers and the US government's influence on the Israeli government." He informed Klein that Russek believed Klein had closed the case "against his better judgment" because of an "order from above."[39] The article concludes with Klein describing the doubts as "nonsense." The only way the conclusive DNA tests could be overturned, he said, would be if "Mengele comes in the door and says, 'You were wrong. Here I am.'"

On October 1, 1992, Sher forwarded OSI's Mengele report, entitled simply *In the Matter of Josef Mengele*, to Robert S. Mueller III, the assistant attorney general for the criminal division and future FBI director and special counsel for the investigation of Russian interference with the 2016 presidential election. A week later Mueller forwarded the report to his boss, Attorney General William Barr, formally ending, for the United States, the eight-year investigation.

ROBERT JAY LIFTON, whose book *The Nazi Doctors* was published in 1986, tried to account for the difficulty many survivors had in accepting that Mengele was dead. The discovery of a body and not a living person "was psychologically unsatisfactory, especially for Auschwitz survivors," he wrote. "The need was to capture him and put him on trial, to hear his confession, to put *him* at *their* mercy. Failing that, many survivors refused to believe that the remains in the Brazilian grave were Mengele's."[40] Soon after the initial identification of the skeleton in São Paulo in June 1985, Lifton spoke with a surviving twin, who had been one of Mengele's subjects. She told Lifton that she simply could not accept that "the arrogant, overbearing figure she had known in Auschwitz could have undergone a 'change in personality' and become the frightened hermit in Brazil." Lifton suggested that her difficulty stemmed from her not having "been provided with a psychological experience of that 'metamorphosis' from evil deity to evil human being."[41]

Examining the responses of each of the three nations involved in the search for Mengele in 1985 reveals much about their own individual connections to the case and their respective histories. The United States, the least likely of the tripartite group to have become involved in the case in the first place, given that it had no clear jurisdiction, was the most active in moving the case beyond the initial hasty conclusion offered in São Paulo in the summer of 1985. Responding to the purely political hijinks of politicians performing for the ballot box, on the one hand, and attempting to set the record straight on the other, we were sensitive to the survivor community and to what we considered our responsibility to history. It is true that the U.S. Marshals Service dropped the case as soon as it appeared to be robbed of its promised glory, but OSI persisted until every lead had been pursued and every opportunity examined, often spurring our colleagues in Germany and Israel to action.

The Germans, on the other hand, were convinced very quickly by the evidence. Their experts had little patience with the endless objections, and they generally seemed relieved that Mengele had finally been removed as the most visible and provocative reminder of a difficult and tragic history. Only the refined judgment of Hans-Eberhard Klein kept them from closing the case too early and made them wait until the science was able to catch up to their conclusions. The Germans had reason to be self-conscious about their lack of effective advocacy, given that Mengele had lived more or less openly in Argentina and Paraguay and could have been caught. Although they responded to leads that came their way and undertook relatively modest actions to surveille the family on several occasions, their overall effort was lackluster until the final phase, when they collaborated with Israel and the United States in 1985.

The Israelis were the most reluctant to close the case. Part of their skepticism, I am convinced, related to their own long and, until recently, unpublicized history in trying to find Mengele. We now know the Mossad came agonizingly close to finding him in the 1960s but elected at the time to abort its operation. It considered and rejected any number of proposed operations that might have led to his capture, though it engaged in creative schemes and devoted significant resources to his pursuit. The Mossad professionals' reluctance to accept what seemed like too neat a conclusion to the prolonged and vexing case was the result of their long experience with an adversary who had eluded them time and again. As a form of compensatory exaggeration, they could not afford to be wrong. On the other hand, on a political and psychological level, the Israelis seemed unable to accept the evidence for many of the reasons that Lifton attributed to individual survivors.

And all along, Mengele—and all he represented—loomed over the investigation, exerting a commanding influence on those who conducted it and those who followed it. A totem of regrettable inaction, unanswered-for crimes, and unfinished business, he robbed both his victims and his pursuers of their day in court.

EPILOGUE

FATHER AND SON

Shortly before his death, Mengele did have the sort of confrontation that so many had hoped for: with his son, Rolf, who pressed his father for answers about what he had done. There was much at stake for young Rolf, who could not escape the biological connection to this man who was both father and fugitive. Rolf was hostage to his heritage, and it exercised an elemental and unwanted emotional sway over him, though he had grown up largely free of his father's influence in terms of how he thought and how he saw the world.

As an adult, Rolf Mengele came face to face with his father only when he was thirty-three years old, the same age his father had been in the summer of 1944. The 1977 visit had been long planned, and it came after Mengele had suffered a stroke. It would be their first and likely last chance to meet as father and son and man to man.

Although Rolf had met Josef Mengele before, when he was twelve, Mengele had been known to him then as his entertaining and dashing "Uncle Fritz" visiting from South America and not as his father, who—he thought—had been killed during the war. Not until the time of the Eichmann trial, when the name Mengele began to appear in the press, did his stepfather reveal to him the real identity of Uncle Fritz.

It was a double shock for Rolf. He learned that his father was not only alive but was charged with horrific crimes.

When Mengele learned that Rolf had been informed of his true identity, he wrote in his diary:

> It is painful that I do not even have the faintest idea of R.'s reaction to the "Enlightenment." . . . If I imagine the middle-class and pseudo-cosmopolitan world in which my growing son now has to live, then I am dizzy at the thought of "Enlightenment" at this time.[1]

Rolf's family told him that the accusation that his father was a murderer was not true. As he later explained to Gerald Posner, "It was not murder in the sense that he is murdering by his own hand personally. . . . They just said to me that he was a cog in the system, in the machinery, and this time—I was 15, 16—I accepted it."[2] But of course the revelation took its toll on the young Rolf, who began an awkward correspondence with the man he now knew was his father, receiving and sending letters from and to Mengele through the elaborate cutout system that Sedlmeier had devised with Mengele's protectors in Brazil.

> I got letters from him, and my mother forced me to answer his letters. I didn't like it. So I wrote to him in a sense you write to someone who is a prisoner. I just wrote him . . . as my mother told me, to help him. You must have these human feelings somehow . . . it was an obligation for me.

Rolf had a close relationship with Irene's second husband, and there was little warmth in his "unwilling" exchanges with Mengele over the two decades or so that they corresponded.

Rolf's ambivalence toward his father was informed by his emotional connection at an elemental level, and his revulsion was fueled by an intellectual understanding of the crimes that had been attributed to his father. Born in 1944, Rolf grew up in a Germany that was consumed with coming to terms with its Nazi past. This struggle with understanding the past and its impact on the generation that came of age after the war spawned its own literary genre—*Vaterliteratur*. Rolf and his story played an unanticipated role in one exemplar of this highly personal category. Peter Schneider, the German writer, after reading the five-part series that appeared in *Bunte* magazine in the summer of 1985 featuring Rolf and his relationship with his father, wrote a novel that so mirrored the circumstances and language of the *Bunte* story that Schneider was taken to court for plagiarism. Indeed, "Vati" (Daddy) tells the story of a young man who learns as a teenager that his father is accused of monstrous crimes. The father in the story fled to South America and found refuge in Brazil, where the son decides to visit him. Although no names are revealed, it is absolutely clear that the novel deals with Josef Mengele and Rolf. Schneider even used the same literary approach that Mengele used in his own autobiographical novel as a vehicle to examine larger, more universal themes. Schneider's novel, in turn, became the basis for a 2003 feature film starring Charlton Heston, in his final role, as Mengele, and Thomas Kretschmer playing Rolf. The film, *My Father, Rua Alguem 5555*, also includes a character, played by F. Murray Abraham, who appears to be a composite of Gerald Posner and Marvin Hier.

Although there had been little focus on Nazi crimes in the Germany of his youth, by the time Rolf was a teenager, his father and his crimes began to be widely known and, over time, became a symbol of the Holocaust and a touchstone for evil. Whereas his father's political pedigree included membership in right-wing and Nazi organizations, Rolf came of age in the 1960s with that era's progressive and radical politics that shunned convention and consciously (and unconsciously) strove to represent a counterweight to the generations that gave birth to the Nazi State. Father-son relationships, even in intact families, were strained under these powerful forces, so it is no wonder that Mengele and Rolf faced gale-force headwinds as they attempted to forge their long-distance relationship.

Through their strained correspondence, Mengele kept up with Rolf's activities, though he often received more detailed news of his son through reports from Sedlmeier and Karl-Heinz, who were more faithful correspondents than Rolf. The surviving and available letters, most of which were recovered in Brazil after the discovery of Mengele's body, date almost entirely from the last six years of Mengele's life and include only Mengele's side of the exchange, in the form of copies of the letters he sent. According to Rolf, the earlier correspondence, beginning in 1956, was burned by mutual agreement. The aging Mengele was clearly a man with time on his hands and a profound need to connect with Rolf, an effort that was often marked by a clumsy earnestness. A quote from a letter to Rolf concerning Rolf's first marriage provides some insight into their relationship. Sounding both aggrieved and out of touch, Mengele wrote:

Unfortunately, I hardly know [Rolf's new wife] or rather I only know as much as the few photographs revealed. But do I know the son any better? . . . [I] know so little about you, my fantasies and wishful thinking revolve around your happiness and future and knows no limits. . . .

One more little contribution I do nevertheless want to make to your new start: I will forget the pain and bitterness, which was caused by the inexplicable fact that I was ignored and not informed of anything for years.

The first I heard about this [the marriage] was from Ha [Sedlmeier] and then came a report of the ceremony from KH [Karl-Heinz]. . . . Now I have been waiting for several months [7] for a letter from you.[3]

In addition to expressing hurt and regret for the lack of closeness between them, Mengele offered fatherly advice:

> Your professional development stays a worry of mine since I can't recognize any progress and I don't see any systematic planning in your development. I doubt that a legal practice in Freiburg, which doesn't have an amount of industry worth mentioning (thank God!) will be to your financial advantage! Maybe you should establish a practice in a little town in Baden.[4]

In this way, Mengele claimed a role in his son's life, offering comments on life events, correcting grammar, opining on family relationships, and providing updates on his health and the complicated relationships he maintained with his Brazilian friends and protectors.

With only one side of the correspondence, it is difficult to assess the full complexity of the relationship between Mengele and his son. A leitmotif in Mengele's letters was certainly his frustration at Rolf's inattention, and one can see, increasingly, that Rolf seemed to be most interested in engaging his father about the past. In the latter half of 1975, perhaps to broach the subject of the Nazi period, Rolf mentioned in a letter to his father the newly published book by Albert Speer, *Spandau Diaries*. Mengele responded that he had read Speer's first book, *Inside the Third Reich*, the year before, and launched with some bitterness into a critical review:

> Concerning his memoirs, I'd like to say that it's a pity that so little of the greatness of the time has stayed in the memory of a man who was allowed to play in the game in such a preferred position. . . .
>
> He made his contribution as an opportunistic technocrat, which is how he describes himself, but he gives a totally insufficient, at times, half-true and mostly deliberately falsified

description of an epoch, which can be compared with that of
Alexander the Great, Charles XII of Sweden, Frederick the Great,
or Napoleon. . . .

He takes on guilt which at times he isn't even accused of, and
then he believes, or so he hopes, that this can be amended by sitting in prison for a few years, now that the head has been pulled
out of the noose. But such "admissions of guilt" should lead normally to different consequences. To be a "Schinkel"* of one's
time, one also simply needs the qualities of a great artist and not
just technical knowhow.[5]

Mengele's letters included long discursions into politics, history, eco-
nomics, science, and occasionally—and carefully—his own experience,
with no expression of remorse.

Rolf discussed the correspondence with Gerald Posner in 1986:

You see in the end, there had been some normal discussions in
these letters between son and father or between generations. . . .
And I learned in a political sense or a historical view, we had
really diametrical positions. We had these passions. . . . We had
debates through these letters. In the end I saw it was useless,
and he always turned it around and it did come to an end. To a
solution somehow. We had been really opposite. Diametrical.[6]

At some point, perhaps in late 1976, the plan emerged for the two
to meet. Rolf explained that the motivation was "curiosity" and also a
certain frustration with the ponderous correspondence: "I felt it was
useless to write. I want to speak to him face to face and I expected
then to get more out of him, more explanation. That was the reason I
decided to make this visit."[7]

---

* Karl Friedrich Schinkel was a famous Prussian architect and city planner.

Mengele responded to the idea warmly:

> I'm sure I don't have to stress how much a meeting between us would mean to me. For want of a better way, I have always tried to be in close contact with you by writing to you. If this [visit] would be possible, nobody would be happier than me.

And he seemed to understand both the objective and challenge of such a meeting:

> It is quite natural and understandable, that you want to get to know me through personal contact, and that you want to find out, independently from all that you have heard and read, for yourself what I am like. I after all feel the same about you. Such a dialogue . . . does, of course, presuppose a certain *niveau,* free of stenciled prejudices, biased wishful thinking, uncritical simplification, cheap resentment, and patronizing arrogance.[8]

What remained was to prepare for the risky and consequential journey. This "adventure," Mengele wrote, would have to be "planned very well in advance. A faultless passport in a different name would be an essential prerequisite. If one has that, then one doesn't need to make any great contortions." He cautioned, without any hint of irony, that "you have to plan this undertaking right down to the last detail without self-deception." "We must not make the smallest mistake," he wrote to Rolf in April 1977, and admitted that it was difficult for him to express how much he was looking forward to the visit, confessing that it was "the next goal" of his life.[9]

Sedlmeier wrote to Mengele on May 27, 1977, and relayed the plan for Rolf's trip, which was to take place at the end of September.[10] To prepare Rolf for the encounter, Sedlmeier arranged for him to meet with Karl-Heinz in August. Rolf's cousin had maintained a more faithful correspondence with Mengele and, having lived with him for several years in Argentina as a youth, had a useful perspective not only on the details of the planned trip but also on Mengele himself. Sedlmeier sought to control all aspects of the visit as well to prepare Mengele for the encounter with his son by advising him to accept that the world had changed:

> You have no right to criticize . . . from afar, without having gone through the decades of internal development with us, and without having seen the causes through the eyes with which we view this. The visit from Rolf will offer you the best opportunity to get to know a representative of today's youth and to study their attitudes. I will leave it to him to carry on with these views in all openness, to get more understanding from you for the blame and the failure of the old ones and for the attitude of the youth. . . .
>
> I know one thing for sure, namely the preconditions that you take as a basis for all actions and thoughts simply no longer exist. The world, especially here with us, has changed tremendously, and these changes have passed you by. You are stuck in the concepts of the old days, which unfortunately, yes, I use the word, unfortunately, are no longer valid. I only have to think of the endless disputes I have with my boys, who definitely are not outsiders, and the accusations that are made about our generation, which to a very large extent are justified. In this context I am reminded of a comment made by your father, who always said to me: "It doesn't matter what one wanted to do, what matters is what one has achieved."[11]

After at least one postponement, Rolf boarded a Varig Airlines jet in Frankfurt departing for Rio de Janiero on October 10, 1977.

To make the trip to Brazil, he used the passport of a friend, Wilfried Busse, who bore a close resemblance to him. He had swiped the passport earlier in the year, never revealing to Busse that he had done so or the reason why. Rolf traveled with another friend, who carried Rolf's real passport should a need for it arise and, leaving him in Rio "to find girls on Copacabana Beach," flew on to São Paulo. Upon arrival, taking three taxis to throw off any surveillance, he made his way to the Bosserts' home. Mr. Bossert then drove him to his father's place, located not too far away.

The encounter was bound to be highly charged. For Rolf, it promised a direct confrontation, unmediated by the delays and labored quality of written exchanges. He would be able to use all his senses—not just his mind—in evaluating his father's responses to the catalog of questions he planned to ask about his past. Rolf was intent on not allowing Mengele to talk around an issue and wanted to pursue him doggedly.

For Mengele, the encounter promised to be no less emotionally fraught, coming as it did after a longer period of anticipation and in the context of a profound deprivation, resulting from having been cut off from everything that really mattered to him—his home, his culture, his family, his profession, and his very past. Although he had been consumed by the question of heredity, he had never experienced firsthand the surprise, delight, or even disappointment that every parent feels when observing the animated impact they may have had on the appearance, personality, and behavior of their children. He had closely examined the lower jaws of long-dead people searching for clues to heredity, and he had compiled and analyzed family trees for evidence of physical traits that were handed down from one generation to another. He had searched the faces of many, including Heinz Alexander, in a high-stakes exercise to link father and son in opinions before the court. He had reviewed thousands of cases of ethnic Germans from the Baltics to determine the racial traits passed from one generation to another. And he had worked at Auschwitz to test the impact of nature as opposed to nurture in the characteristics of his twin subjects. Now he stared into the face of his own son.

Rolf described their discussions "concerning ideological and political subjects," the examination of which he had hoped would reveal "the key" to his father's "essence, to his nature." He was most interested "in hearing about the time in Auschwitz," wanting to know what his father had done there and how he responded to the charges leveled against him. Having had a great deal of time to plan his strategy, and after long experience engaging in long-distance debates by letter, Rolf approached this subject very cautiously. He knew that his father's tendency to launch into long explanations of things, such as "human development with all its cultural and political aspects" from ancient times, but failing, in the end, to address the original question. He realized that he had to be persistent and tactical, rather than confrontational, in pursuing his line of inquiry.

He began by approaching directly the main undercurrent of the Nazi worldview: the assignment of value to certain races and racial characteristics. He asked his father how, if it was the ability of humans to think that set them apart from other forms of life, a proposition that he held to be unassailable, could it be that many who were deemed racially flawed or even subhuman were often more brilliant than those considered to be racial paragons? He added, "Isn't it true that sometimes only disease, physical deficiency, and crippled conditions make the man realize and see the essential independently?" According to Rolf, his father could not provide a "proper answer" and was "contradictory and not convincing."[12]

When he asked his father for evidence that certain races—Jews, for instance—were different or abnormal, Mengele "alleged" that he had such evidence but did not, according to Rolf, furnish any convincing proof. Rolf then raised the issue of Auschwitz and told his father that he believed it to have been immoral and deeply inhuman. What mattered was not only what one did or did not do there; one's mere presence there made one an "accessory within the meaning of the deepest humanity."

Mengele tried to explain Auschwitz politically and sociologically, claiming that when he came there, he "had to do his duty, to carry out orders. Everybody had to do so to survive. . . . He was not a shirker."

From his point of view, he is not personally responsible for the incidents there. He didn't "invent" Auschwitz. It already existed. He couldn't help anyone. On the platform, for instance. What was he to do, when the half-dead and infected people arrived? It was beyond imagination to describe the circumstances there. His job was to clarify only: "able to work" and "unable to work." He has tried to grade the people "able to work," as often as possible. He thinks he saved the lives of thousands of people in that way. He hasn't ordered extermination and he is not responsible. Also the twins owe their lives to him. He has never harmed anybody personally.

Rolf described his father as getting very excited, angry, and even crying, asking whether "I—his son believe in lies told in the newspapers?" At this point, the conversation ended. There was nothing to be gained for either father or son in continuing. Rolf would not get the answers he needed from his father. There would be no admission of guilt or responsibility. Mengele must have realized that his son could not be convinced that his actions had been justified or even understandable. A tense standoff replaced the raised voices and raw emotion.[13]

For the rest of Rolf's visit, Mengele took him on a tour of the various places where he had lived and introduced him, with much fatherly pride, to the few friends and acquaintances he had made. After two weeks, Rolf returned to Rio, rejoined his friend, and after some sightseeing, returned to Germany. Rolf summed up what he believed his father felt about the visit:

He was proud of his son, like a soldier after a successful reconnaissance patrol. After all he was his son; even if different, pigheaded and spoiled by the post-war propaganda and by the stepfatherly home and education. All that will settle down. At

last the son had found the right wife. Soon he'll become a grandfather. That visit gave a fresh impetus and hope to him.[14]

When they parted, Mengele told his son that they would meet "very
soon again."

Their correspondence continued for a short period, up until
Mengele's death fifteen months after Rolf's return. Reclaiming the
calm and dispassionate mien of the letter writer, Mengele wrote to
Rolf after the visit:

In the weeks following your departure, I kept asking myself
whether I am happier or, to put it another way, whether I can
die more easily. . . . On the basis of my worldview and my specific
profession, I attach, more than most, of course, special meaning to the terms offspring, inheritance, son. On the other hand,
I understand, as well, the power of environment. If the laws of
heredity can produce a significant difference in psycho-physical
characteristics between father and son, this dissimilarity can be
intensified by a completely different milieu, especially during the
period of development. A man with my fate, especially, tends to
hope too much for the fulfillment in his son of all that he had
failed to do. That may range from the simplest details of life to
great professional and public success. Against this—and in our
case drastically so—is the disruption (encouraged by the *Zeitgeist*)
of the father's experience of the son. Apart from the material
security provided by my paternal inheritance, there is nothing
significant in my life that could have had a favorable influence
on your relationship with me. Not because such . . . achievements
were lacking, but because they were pushed into obscurity by a
larger event, and you could not recognize them. Inherited qualities, as well as education and environmental influences, force
you to view the content of my life incorrectly, if not intentionally
negatively. In and of itself, this does not bother me all that much

since, given the circumstances, I can understand it, but where it should have objectively or subjectively impeded your material or spiritual progress, it causes me a tormenting pain.

If, on one hand, I cannot hope for understanding and empathy from you, on the other hand, I am not moved in the slightest to "justify" or even excuse any decisions, actions, or behavior in my life beyond the objective explanation. I have already expressed this to you and others in other unmistakable words. If you have recognized—even to your amusement—our only "inherited" similarity in "unconditionally defending our respective positions and ideas," that's not much. But perhaps it is the reality. My tolerance really has a limit, and that is where unquestionably traditional values are concerned and where I fear threats to those close to me or to my *völkische* community.[15]

Among the last written words of his life, Mengele was unrepentant to the end and expressed no remorse. His *Weltanschauung,* or worldview, was little changed from that summer day in 1944 when he had stalked the ramp at Auschwitz-Birkenau.

POSTSCRIPT

If Mengele had not advanced in his thinking, the science that was so important to him progressed well beyond his understanding of it and its implications for his worldview. In 1953, as Mengele was establishing his life in Argentina, James Watson, Francis Crick, and Rosalind Franklin were deciphering the structure of DNA. In 1972, as Mengele was holed up in Brazil, writing a fictionalized account of his life, Richard Lewontin was publishing his landmark paper, *The Apportionment of Human Diversity,* in which he suggested that attaching a "great significance to variations between groups" was a "bias" that "necessarily flows from the process of classification itself since it is an expression of the perception of group differences." The differences we perceive in others—the color of their hair, skin, and eyes; the shape of their nose and lips; the quality and amount of their hair—are those differences "to which human perceptions are most finely tuned," and to which we consequently give "tremendous emphasis."[1]

The mapping of the human genome, completed in 2003, decades after Mengele's death, has permitted an understanding of the human family that would have shaken Mengele to his very core. As Siddhartha Mukherjee wrote in his magisterial book *The Gene: An Intimate History,* the "racial categorization of humans is an inherently limited proposition. . . . Given our rather brief tenure on earth as a spe-

cies, we are much more alike than unlike each other." This is not to
say that Mengele would have found nothing of use in the new science.
The analysis of a single drop of blood can reveal "rather deep insights
into a person's ancestry, or place of origin," a prospect that Mengele
and his colleagues had only dreamed about. "The problem," Mukherjee writes, "is not the inference of a person's race from their genetic
characteristics. It is quite the opposite: it is the inference of a person's
characteristics from their race." When we get beyond skin and hair
color, and those characteristics that Mengele was so concerned about,
and we consider "more complex features such as intelligence, habits, personality, and aptitude," there is very little that can be inferred.
"The most recent estimates suggest that the vast proportion of genetic
diversity (85–90 percent) occurs *within* so-called races . . . and only a
minor proportion (7 percent) between racial groups."[2] The genome is,
as Mukherjee puts it, "strictly a one-way street"; it can tell us where a
person comes from, but knowing where a person comes from can tell
us precious little about him beyond superficial characteristics.

Expressing a satisfying symmetry, Mukherjee writes: "Genetics
unleashed the specter of scientific racism in the nineteenth century.
Genomics, thankfully, has stuffed it back into its bottle."[3] The science
that had occupied such a crucial place at the center of Josef Mengele's
life had developed to the point where it made bankrupt the tenets by
which he had lived.

ACKNOWLEDGMENTS

A great many people and institutions provided crucial assistance in helping me to research and write this book. I am grateful to the Joseph and Rebecca Meyerhoff Center for Jewish studies at the University of Maryland in College Park for appointing me a visiting associate research scholar. Many thanks to professors Charles H. Manekin and Marsha Rozenblit, and to the very kind Jaclyn K. Hopkins. I want to thank the staff of the university's McKeldin Library, who helped me gain access to its rich resources. The heroic members of the interlibrary loan department were as patient as they were skilled in tracking down my often-obscure requests; I am extremely grateful to them all.

I consulted a number of archives and research collections in search of the primary sources for this book. I spent several weeks in 2016 at the Hessian State Archives in Wiesbaden and wish to thank Dr. Carina Schmidt for her assistance then and for her help in the several follow-up requests. Her colleague Dr. Johann Zilien also deserves mention. Alex Rankin from the Gotlieb Archival Research Center at Boston University was helpful and accommodating in my search through the rich Posner Papers. Cara Dellatte, of the New York Public Library's Manuscripts, Archives, and Rare Books Division, provided access to the Robert Jay Lifton Papers. Caitlin Haynes and her colleagues at the National Anthropological Archives of the Smithsonian Institution were a great help. I thank Dr. Haim Gersten and his colleagues at Yad Vashem Archives and the staffs of the Israeli State Archives and the National Library. In addition, I wish to thank Susanne Uebele of the Archiv der Max-Planck-Gesellschaft in Berlin; Janine Aures (University Archives, Goethe University, Frankfurt); Dr. Claudius Stein (Munich University Archives); Linda Mosig (Bonn University Archives); Thomas Maisel (Vienna University Archives); Walter Grabert (Günzburg City Archives); Imke Brünjes (Bremen State Archives); the staff of the L. C. Dunn Papers, American Philosophical Society; and Elisa Ho at the Jacob Rader Marcus Center of the American Jewish Archives.

My former colleagues at the Department of Justice's Office of Special Investigations deserve special thanks for the role they played in this story and for their interest and support in helping me to share it. Thanks to Michael Wolf and Philip Sunshine. Neal M. Sher, OSI's director at the time, shared his recollections about the case with me, and Eli M. Rosenbaum, OSI's last director, was extremely helpful and accommodating.

The following people shared important details of their involvement in the Mengele story: Ralph Blumenthal; Stephen Dachi, who passed away not long after our interview; Dennis Gouldman, who sat with me for several hours in Jerusalem; Elizabeth Holtzman; Fred Kaplan; Lucette Lagnado, who died shortly before this book went to print; Barry and Leilane Mehler; and Menachem Rosensaft.

Other assistance was provided by the following generous individuals: Hermann Abmayr (Germany), Dr. Kai-Uwe Eckardt (Germany), Ted Greene, Dr. Sven Keller (Germany), Dr. Rick Lukash, Thiago Medaglia (Brazil), Ruth Rix (UK), Eric Scheinkopf, Gerald Steinacher, Michael Stöppler (Germany), Eric Stover, Tilman Taube (Germany), Bill Wanlund, John Ware (UK), Dr. Bertram Wiedenmann (Germany), Markus Wolter (Germany), and Adriana Valobra (Argentina).

My colleague Ruth Winter deserves a paragraph to herself. A skilled researcher with impressive linguistic and investigative skills,

Ruth, who lives in Tel Aviv, conducted research on my behalf in Israel. Persistent and resourceful, thoughtful and meticulous, Ruth provided crucial assistance, and I owe her more than I can adequately describe.

Charlie Rattan from the UK, who once embarked on his own Mengele book project, was generous with his knowledge and shared some important research material that he collected more than three decades ago. Betina Anton, who lives in São Paulo, is writing a book about Mengele and generously shared her thoughts and research. My friend Gerald Posner, whom I met during the Mengele investigation and whose own book on Mengele continues to impress me, was uncommonly generous with his insights and advice.

My editor, John Glusman, and his team at Norton, especially Helen Thomaides, were invariably patient and skilled guides who led me through the process of producing this book. My agent, Tracy Brown, did far more than place this book; his calm, good counsel was essential at every stage.

After a long career of stimulating and challenging positions with hectic schedules of travel and social engagements, I found myself at the beginning of 2016 pursuing a quiet life of writing with few distractions or excursions, apart from occasional trips to the archives or the library. This solitary life was, however, crowded with the encouragement and support of family, friends, and colleagues too numerous to mention, but a few need to be singled out. My friend, the poet Jason Sommer, whose brilliant poem about Mengele continues to move me, read several drafts and provided thoughtful comments. My teacher and friend Carole Fink was characteristically encouraging and insightful in her close reading of an early draft. Kate Deery, Caroline Earp, Yitzchak Mais, David Goldman, and Judah Gribetz were attentive and loyal cheerleaders. I salute my brother, Josh Marwell, whose expertise and experience were so important to me, and our siblings and their families, whose frequent check-ins and warm support were a welcome tonic. My children and grandchildren, Nathan and

Haley, and their daughter, Grace; and Gabe and Shea, and their son, Benjamin, continue to be a constant source of, yes, pride and joy.

Finally, I thank my wife, Judith Marwell, sounding board, editor, and critic. She got me down off the ledge—and out of the clouds—when it was necessary, lifted me up as she always has, and overfunctioned in countless ways that allowed me the time and space to contemplate the difficult topic I had chosen. She is, I know, as relieved as I am to get Josef Mengele out of our home.

NOTES

BDC	Berlin Document Center
BKA	Bundeskriminalamt (Federal Criminal Police)
BMJ	Bundesministerium der Justiz (Federal Ministry of Justice)
DGM	David G. Marwell
DOJ	Department of Justice
FOIA	Freedom of Information Act
GARC	Gotlieb Archival Research Center at Boston University
HLKA	Hessisches Landeskriminalamt (Hessian Office of Criminal Investigations)
HMdI	Hessisches Ministerium des Innerns (Hessian Ministry of Interior)
HMdJ	Hessisches Ministerium der Justiz (Hessian Ministry of Justice)
ISA	Israel State Archives
JAG	Judge Advocate General
JTA	Jewish Telegraphic Agency
LG	Landesgericht (State Court)
NAA	National Anthropological Archive
NARA	National Archives and Records Administration
NYPL	New York Public Library
OSI	Office of Special Investigations
UAF	Universitätsarchiv Frankfurt (Frankfurt University Archives)
UAM	Universitätsarchiv München (Munich University Archives)
UPI	United Press International
USHMM	U.S. Holocaust Memorial Museum
YVA	Yad Vashem

CHAPTER 1: "BRILLIANT LUMINOSITY"

1. There is an entire literature focused on Nazi perpetrators with manifold explanations for what produced them. One scholar, Gunnar Heinsohn, "has tallied forty-one different theories." See Lewy, *Perpetrators*, p. 118.

2. Loewenberg, "Psychohistorical Origins."

3. Zofka, "Der KZ-Arzt Mengele," p. 248.

4. Mengele Autobiography, Notebook 3, pp. 19–20, HHStAW 544/2572/Ordner 70.

5. Keller, *Günzburg und der Fall Mengele*, p. 76n21.

6. Völklein, *Der Arzt von Auschwitz*, p. 50.

7. Zofka, "Der KZ-Arzt Mengele," p. 249.

8. Denazification Court Ruling on Karl Mengele, July 29, 1947, HHStAW 461/37976/069.

9. Mengele Diary, entry for June 23, 1977, quoted in Völklein, *Der Arzt von Auschwitz*, p. 48.

10. Völklein, *Der Arzt von Auschwitz*, p. 47.

11. Keller, *Günzburg und der Fall Mengele*, p. 76.

12. Keller, *Günzburg und der Fall Mengele*, p. 79.

13. Keller, *Günzburg und der Fall Mengele*, p. 79.

14. Völklein, *Der Arzt von Auschwitz*, p. 54.

15. Weiss, *Nazi Symbiosis*, pp. 12–13.

16. "Betrachtungen zu unserer geistigen Situation," quoted in "Comments on Chapter 1," Posner Papers, Box 18, Folder 3, GARC.

17. "Betrachtungen zu unserer geistigen Situation," quoted in "Comments on Chapter 1," Posner Papers, Box 18, Folder 3, GARC.

18. Mengele Autobiography, Notebook 21: "Studium 1," n.d., p. 42, HHStAW 461/37976/139.

19. Mengele Autobiography, Notebook 21: "Studium 1," n.d., p. 41, HHStAW 461/37976/139.

20. Mengele Autobiography, Notebook 21: "Studium 1," n.d., p. 42, HHStAW 461/37976/139.

21. Proctor, *Racial Hygiene*, p. 64.

22. Proctor, *Racial Hygiene*, p. 73.

23. Quoted in Bruns, "Turning Away," p. 216.

24. Reiter, *Das Reichsgesundheitsamt*, p. 6.

25. Reiter, *Das Reichsgesundheitsamt*, p. 286.

26. "Ternon," Lifton Papers, Box 134, NYPL. Quoted from Drs. Yves Ternon and Socrate Helman, *Les médecins allemands et le national socialisme*.

27. Proctor, *Racial Hygiene*, p. 64.

28. Proctor, *Racial Hygiene*, p. 38.

29. Proctor, *Racial Hygiene*, p. 39.

30. He shared the prize with Nikolas Tinbergen and Konrad Lorenz.

31. Munz, *Dancing Bees*, p. 77.

32. Mengele Autobiography, Notebook 21, "Studium 1," n.d., p. 70, HHStAW 461/37976/139.

33. Mengele Autobiography, Notebook 22, n.d., p. 32, HHStAW 461/37976/139. Three years after Mengele encountered Frisch in the lecture hall, the Nazis passed legislation that required that all civil servants be able to prove that their racial background was free of Jewish influence. Although Frisch submitted paperwork showing he had no Jewish blood, and was initially allowed to remain in his position, he was later denounced by student activists and could not provide adequate proof of the racial background of his maternal grandmother, who, it happened, had been born Jewish and was converted to Catholicism as a child. Given his status as a so-called *Mischling*, or mixed breed, Frisch faced expulsion from his position but was saved by the interventions of important people in the scientific establishment; his expulsion was ultimately postponed for the duration of the war thanks to his active research on combating Nosema, a parasitic infection that was threatening the German bee population. Munz, *Dancing Bees*, chaps. 3 and 4.

34. Mengele Autobiography, Notebook 21, "Studium I," n.d, p. 70, HHStAW 461/37976/139.

35. During the First World War, Wieland headed the department of chemical weapons at the Kaiser Wilhelm Institute for Chemistry in Berlin, where he worked on mustard gas and so-called mask-breaker agents that caused such irritation that affected soldiers would tear off their gas masks and then fall victim to other chemical agents.

36. Gerlach was famous for his work with physicist Otto Stern and for their experiment, conducted in 1922, that discovered spin quantization in a magnetic field. It became known as the "Stern-Gerlach Effect." Stern, a Jew who emigrated to the United States after the Nazis took power, was awarded the Nobel Prize in 1943, while the important discovery he made with Gerlach, who remained active in Germany, was not mentioned in the Nobel citation. Gerlach's contribution to experimental physics is recognized today by the Stern-Gerlach Medal, which is awarded by the German Physical Society and is the most prestigious German award for experimental physicists.

37. Mengele Autobiography, Notebook 21, "Studium 1," pp. 72–76, HHStAW 461/37976/139.

38. Mengele Autobiography, Notebook 22, p. 30, HHSTaW 461/37976/139.

39. Mengele Autobiography, Notebook 22, p. 38, HHSTaW 461/37976/139.

40. Forsbach, *Die Medizinische Fakultät*, p. 71. In the summer semester 1931, 1,401 as compared to 2,177.

41. Mengele Autobiography, Notebook 22, p. 19, HHSTaW 461/37976/139.

42. Keller *Günzburg und der Fall Mengele*, p. 82; Völklein, *Der Arzt von Auschwitz*, p. 67. A friend of Mengele's described how he had met Mengele: "I was a medical student in Bonn in 1931. I worked for the student council. One day a medical student came to see me, introduced himself as a member of the *Stahlhelm*, and asked me to post an announcement for a public meeting of the *Stahlhelm* in the student council display case. There was to be a speech by von Seeckt. I had to refuse because it did not conform to the rules and asked the student to go to the director of anatomy and ask for permission. We both knew that it would not be allowed. The student, it was Mengele, nonetheless invited me to come to the meeting myself. I went there. The meeting was a disaster. V. Seeckt laboriously read from the paper. I had the impression, and M[engele] later confirmed, that v. Seeckt was drunk. A disaster." Kurt Lambertz, "Mein Freund Mengele," n.d., HHStAW 461/37976/179.

43. Opitz, *Leitfaden der Prüfungsordnungen*, p. 23.

44. Opitz, *Leitfaden der Prüfungsordnungen*, p. 76.

45. Archiv der Rheinischen Friedrich-Wilhelms-Universität to Kirn C. Rattan and Simon Jones, August 7, 1984, provided by K. C. Rattan.

46. Mengele Autobiography, Notebook 21, "Studium 1," p. 59, HHStAW 461/37976/139.

47. "In memoriam Prof. Dr. Dr. h. c. Wolfgang Denk," in *Acta chirurgica Austriaca: Organ der Österreichischen Gesellschaft für Chirurgie und der angeschlossenen Fachgesellschaften*, February 1970; Mengele Autobiography, Notebook 2, pp. 55ff.

48. H. Czech, "Beyond Spiegelgrund und Berkatit," p. 152. Some years later Mengele was called upon to issue an opinion in a case involving Feix's paternity.

49. H. Czech, "Beyond Spiegelgrund und Berkatit," p. 140.

50. Quoted in H. Czech, "Beyond Spiegelgrund und Berkatit," p. 140.

51. H. Czech, "Beyond Spiegelgrund und Berkatit," p. 140.

52. "Wien 1945, Kriegsende," in Aichinger, *Film und Verhängnis*, p. 56.

53. Ruth Rix to DGM, February 13, 2018.

54. Berta Aichinger, who was Jewish, lost her ability to practice medicine after Austria was incorporated into Germany in 1938. At the start of the war, Berta and Ilse became forced laborers in a leather factory. Helga was taken to England on a Kindertransport. Berta's own mother and siblings were

deported to Minsk, where they were murdered. Ilse survived the war and afterward became an acclaimed author in Vienna, joining the writers' group Gruppe 47, and Helga became an actress in England.

55. Mengele offered clinical details of his "nephrosis" in his autobiography: "loss of 0.5 to 1 percent protein, isolated epitheliums, completely isolated erythrocytes, no edema, no elevated blood pressure." He posited that it "might have been an isolated abscess in a kidney, resulting from the sepsis, which emptied into the urinary tract after it was perforated through the extreme sporting effort and vibration." A German nephrologist, whom I contacted to review Mengele's symptoms, advised that Mengele's diagnosis was unlikely since such a condition would likely have been fatal. He suggested, rather, that Mengele might have suffered from "post-infectious glomerulonephritis."

56. Teicher, "Racial Zigzags," pp. 31–32.

57. Kamp, "In Memoriam Mollison."

58. Massin, "From Virchow to Fischer," pp. 106–7.

59. Teicher, "Racial Zigzags," p. 32.

60. Teicher, "Racial Zigzags," p. 32.

61. Mollison, *Rassenkunde und Rassenhygieniker,* quoted in Weingart, Bayertz, and Kroll, *Rasse, Blut und Gene,* p. 390.

62. Quoted in Massin, *Anthropologie und Humangenetik,* p. 18.

63. Massin, *Anthropologie und Humangenetik,* p. 18.

64. Massin, *Anthropologie und Humangenetik,* p. 18.

65. Courses with Mollison represented 192 hours out of a total 289 hours of instruction. Mengele's Student File, UAM.

66. Evans, *Anthropology at War,* p. 223.

67. Quoted in Evans, *Anthropology at War,* p. 223.

68. Evans, *Anthropology at War,* p. 224.

69. Evans, *Anthropology at War,* p. 224. See Mollison, "Eine Schausammlung für Anthropologie," for a description of the exhibition.

70. Mengele, *Rassenmorphologische Untersuchungen,* p. 60.

71. Mengele, *Rassenmorphologische Untersuchungen,* pp. 60–61. He mentions Jankowsky and Rasche.

72. Teicher, "Racial Zigzags," p. 32.

73. Mengele, *Rassenmorphologische Untersuchungen,* p. 84.

74. Mengele, *Rassenmorphologische Untersuchungen,* p. 111.

75. Benzenhöfer, Ackermann, and Weiske, "Wissenschaft oder Wahn," pp. 40–41.

76. Kater, "Der Krise der Ärzte," pp. 362–63.

77. "Votum Informativum," October 31, 1935, Mengele Promotion, UAM.

78. Mengele had successfully petitioned in November 1934 to be allowed to have

anatomy as his second minor field. He argued that after he had chosen it as his minor, the faculty had voted that it should no longer be an option. Mengele claimed that he was too far along in his studies, and that it would be a financial hardship for him to have to prepare a new minor field, especially when anatomy had been suggested to him when he began his studies and was accepted at that time as an appropriate field. Despite his successful petition, which was agreed to by the faculty and endorsed by Mollison, Mengele developed a new second minor in physiology. Mengele Promotion, UAM.

79. Broemser, an expert in the circulatory system, developed new methods for measuring blood pressure. In 1938 he became the rector, or chief academic officer, at the University of Munich, a position he retained until his death in 1940.

80. In Leipzig, Mengele likely encountered Werner Catel, who would later play an important role in the euthanasia program. Massin, "Mengele, die Zwillingsforschung," p. 218.

81. Ehrenreich, "Otmar von Verschuer," p. 57.

82. Ehrenreich, "Otmar von Verschuer," p. 57.

83. Verschuer, "Vier Jahre Frankfurter Universitäts-Institut," p. 57.

84. Verschuer, "Vier Jahre Frankfurter Universitäts-Institut," p. 58.

85. Verschuer, "Aufgaben und Ziele," pp. 99–100.

86. Verschuer, "Aufgaben und Ziele," pp. 99–100.

87. Founded by the widow of William G. Kerckhoff, an American businessman of German origin, the foundation was located in Bad Nauheim, a spa town in Hesse, where Kerckhoff had been treated for a heart ailment. Its current website indicates that "for more than 80 years, the William G. Kerckhoff Foundation has supported young scientists with their research . . . making it possible for particularly young scientific talent to experiment and to make advances in the dimensions of fundamental research" (http://www.kerckhoff-stiftung.de, accessed on December 8, 2016).

88. Twin research had been used with unsatisfactory results. First, it was difficult to find a sufficient sample of suitable twins—between 1922 and 1939, for example, only 36 pairs could be identified. Although a significantly larger number of identical twins shared the condition than that of fraternal twins, which would normally be an indication of a genetic determination, in two-thirds of the cases, the identical twin partner failed to display any sign of the condition that his sibling possessed. It was an indication that the anomaly did not present itself in a regular way. Massin, "Mengele, die Zwillingsforschung," p. 208.

89. Massin, "Mengele, die Zwillingsforschung," p. 209.

90. A critique of Mengele's dissertation, written in 2012, points out that his inclusion of microforms in his examination of family members was flawed since

it confused these microforms with morphological findings which "cannot be considered solely to be related" to cleft formation. Moreover, Mengele's data collection was based on "speculative assumptions" about the significance of certain characteristics, such as a high-vaulted palate, which Mengele cites thirty-eight times in the genealogical tables that accompany his dissertation. Mengele's use of other morphological abnormalities, such as those relating to the shape and size of the uvula, "underline the tendentious aim" of the undertaking. Thieme, "Gedemütigt, entwürdigt," p. 63.

91. Schmuhl, *Kaiser Wilhelm Institute*, p. 362; Mengele, "Sippenuntersuchungen," p. 42.

92. Kater, "Der Krise der Ärzte," p. 363.

93. Verschuer, *Gutachten über die Abstammung und Rassenzughörigkeit des Beschuldigten*, June 20, 1938, quoted in Benzenhöfer, *Mengele, Hirt, Holfelder*, p. 10.

94. For a discussion of other dissertations on oral clefts during the Nazi period, see Paprotka, "Zwangssterilisation."

95. Vol. 23, no. 1, pp. 2–42.

96. Roth, "Die wissenschaftliche Normalität," p. vi; Lehmann, "Erbpathologie," p. 568.

97. Steiniger, "Die Entstehung," p. 116.

98. Akasaka, "Statistical and Cytogenic."

99. Dixon and Newton, "Minimal Forms."

100. Roth, "Die wissenschaftliche Normalität," p. vi.

101. Quoted in Benzenhöfer, *Mengele, Hirt, Holfelder*, p. 17.

102. Wyszynski, "Fifty Years After," pp. 523–24.

103. Mengele, "Tagung der Deutschen Gesellschaft."

104. See the middle photograph on the second page of the photograph gallery.

CHAPTER 2: SCIENTIST AND SOLDIER

1. Otmar von Verschuer to Kuratorium der Universität Frankfurt am Main, May 10, 1938, UAF 4/1502/15R-V.

2. Mengele, "Zur Vererbung der Ohrfisteln."

3. Otmar von Verschuer to Kuratorium der Universität Frankfurt, April 13, 1939, UAF 50:2130:27R. During the war, Grosse-Brockhoff was involved as a physician for the German Air Force (Luftwaffe) in a series of experiments on dogs relating to the effects of extreme cold. He participated in the infamous "Cold Conference" held in Nuremberg in October 1942, during which Dr. Sigmund Rascher described the experiments he conducted on prisoners at Dachau concerning methods of rewarming humans after prolonged exposure to extreme

cold. The research was designed to help the Luftwaffe determine best practices in rewarming downed flyers who ended up in frigid water.

4. Otmar von Verschuer to Kuratorium der Universität Frankfurt, March 12, 1940, UAF 4/1502/29R.

5. Ehrenreich, *Nazi Ancestral Proof,* p. 58.

6. Verschuer, "Die Vaterschaftsgutachten," p. 26. See Weiss, "Loyal Genetic Doctor," p. 645.

7. After its establishment, the Frankfurt Institute had been able to secure for itself the responsibility of providing such expert opinions with jurisdiction for a part of the city of Frankfurt.

8. Weiss, "Loyal Genetic Doctor," pp. 651–52.

9. Weiss, "Loyal Genetic Doctor," pp. 659–62.

10. "Urteil, Strafsache gegen Heinz Alexander wegen Rassenschande (6b Kls 11/37)," September 14, 1937, HHStAW, Abt. 484, Nr. 738.

11. *Gutachten über die Abstammung und Rassenzughörigkeit des Beschuldigten,* July 9, 1937, HHStAW, Abt. 484, Nr. 738.

12. Weiss, "Loyal Genetic Doctor," p. 661.

13. Weiss, "Loyal Genetic Doctor," p. 662.

14. The Berlin Document Center (BDC), where I became director in 1989, was an important repository in West Berlin for captured Nazi personnel-related records. Among its holdings was a huge collection of marriage files created by the Race and Settlement Main Office of the SS (RuSHA) pursuant to the SS Engagement and Marriage Order. Representing one of the columns on the SS organization chart, RuSHA was charged with establishing and enforcing racial standards for the SS. An application for membership in the SS required a racial examination, as did a proposed marriage. Housing one of the most interesting collections at the BDC, the RuSHA file room was a mandatory stop when I gave tours of the center.

15. Georg Schlick response to SS-Pflegestelle, RuSHA, November 27, 1938, Mengele File, BDC.

16. Dr. Rudolf Schwarz response to SS-Pflegestelle, RuSHA, November 23, 1938, Mengele File, BDC.

17. Physical Examination Form for Irene Schoenbein, December 26, 1938, Mengele File, BDC.

18. Excerpt from Darmstadt Court record, December 2, 1886, Mengele File, BDC.

19. Friedrich Wilhelm Osiander (b. 1903) was chief of the Department of Family Research in the *Sippenamt* of RuSHA. In 1942 he became head of the Family Tree Office (*Ahnentafelamt*) in RuSHA. See Heinemann, "Rasse, Siedlung, deutsches Blut," p. 628.

20. Note in Irene Schoenbein's Marriage Application, February 28, 1939, Mengele File, BDC.

21. This is the date that Mengele entered in official forms for his engagement.

22. Kurt Lambertz, "Mein Freund Mengele," n.d., HHStAW 461/37976/179.

23. Irene Hackenjos to Kirn C. Rattan and S. W. Jones, April 14, 1984, Posner Papers, Box 19, Folder 1, GARC.

24. "Verfügung des Kuratoriums vom 5.9.1939," September 5, 1939, UAF 50/2126/26r.

25. "Lebenslauf," July 18, 1940, Mengele's SS Officer File, NARA, BDC Records, SSO Reel 308A, frames 395ff.

26. Kurt Lambertz, "Mein Freund Mengele," n.d., HHStAW 461/37976/179.

27. "Erlaß des Führers und Reichskanzlers zur Festigung deutschen Volkstums vom 7. Oktober 1939," in *Themenportal Europäische Geschichte*, January 1, 2007, www.europa.clio-online.de/quelle/id/artikel-3303.

28. "Darlegungen Himmlers in Posen vor den SS-Führern über die Siedlung am 24.10.39," in Müller, *Hitlers Ostkrieg*, pp. 119–21.

29. The situation in Lithuania was different, and the resettlement of its ethnic Germans took place later.

30. Fiebrandt, *Auslese*, p. 182.

31. Fiebrandt, *Auslese*, p. 182.

32. Dr. Heidenreich, "Taetigkeits- und Erfahrungsbericht," October 7, 1940, NARA, T-81/310/2413758-762.

33. Heinemann, "Another Type of Perpetrator," p. 400.

34. When ethnic Germans applied for German citizenship and filled out the necessary paperwork, they had to account for their previous political and professional activities. The Germans were concerned about the political reliability of prospective settlers and wanted to know of any associations with Communist organizations. In some cases, applicants had worked for the Germans in their home areas before resettling, serving perhaps as policemen or translators. This activity would have been duly noted in the EWZ file. When I was at OSI, they served as probative evidence of involvement in persecution.

    After I arrived at the BDC in 1988, the EWZ files began to take on an unexpected, ironic new importance. With the fall of the Berlin wall and the dismantling of the Soviet empire, a huge wave of individuals claiming German background made their way to Germany in pursuit of German citizenship and the generous benefits that came with it. Under German law at the time, anyone who could prove German heritage had a claim to German citizenship. The EWZ records at the BDC provided excellent proof for the thousands of people who could now make their way to Germany. These people were, in many cases, the sons and daughters, and grandsons and granddaughters, of the very individuals who had been resettled by the Germans during the war.

My work with the EWZ files, first at OSI and later at the BDC, equipped me to serve as an expert witness for Canadian and Australian prosecutors in several war crimes trials.

35. Historian Sven Keller, in *Günzburg und der Fall Mengele*, provides a much-needed correction to all previous works that deal with Mengele's military career. Most biographers have understated the length of Mengele's service with the Viking Division, mistakenly giving weight to evidence in his SS file that notes a transfer out of the unit in July 1942. No other evidence exists that such a transfer took place, and much contradicts it, leaving some to suggest that the transfer was planned and ordered but did not occur because of changed circumstances within the Viking Division during the hectic summer of 1942. One piece of evidence to support this possibility is the SS file of Dr. Hubert Schopper, who was named on the same transfer order as Mengele. That order, dated July 17, 1942, indicates that Schopper was to be transferred from the *Reichsarzt SS* to the SS Viking Division and that Mengele was to be transferred from the Viking Division to the *Reichsarzt SS*, suggesting that one would replace the other. In Schopper's file, however, it is clear that he was assigned not to Mengele's unit, the Fifth SS Engineers Battalion, but to the Fifth SS Artillery Regiment in the division. BDC File for Dr. Hubert Schopper, born October 3, 1912, in Vienna. Even if Mengele had been transferred in July 1942, it would have been a brief assignment, since Mengele's superior on the battalion staff, Hugo Eichhorn, made clear, in a postwar work, that Mengele was in place with the battalion as of July 27, 1942. See *Pioniereinheiten der 5. SS-Panzerdivision "Wiking,"* p. 154.

36. Charles Trang, in his three-volume work on the Viking Division, indicates, without specific reference, that Mengele was an assistant doctor [*Hilfsarzt*] on the staff of the Fifth SS Engineers Battalion as of December 31, 1940. Trang, *Wiking,* 1:34. Irene Mengele implies in a letter she wrote in the summer of 1941 that Mengele had been assigned to the Viking Division sometime after Christmas 1940.

37. Dr. Wilhelm Müller, Dentist for the Battalion, Diary, October 16, 1941, quoted in *Pioniereinheiten der 5. SS-Panzerdivision "Wiking,"* p. 329.

38. Mengele to Irene, January 17, 1942, in Wolter, "Der SS-Arzt Mengele," p. 181.

39. Peter Strassner, *Europäische Freiwillige–Die 5. SS-PzDiv "Wiking,"* p. 30, quoted in *Pioniereinheiten der 5. SS-Panzerdivision "Wiking,"* p. 18.

40. Struve, *Deutsche Herrschaft,* p. 562.

41. Struve, *Deutsche Herrschaft,* pp. 562–63.

42. Quoted in Struve, *Deutsche Herrschaft*, p. 565.

43. Struve, *Deutsche Herrschaft*, p. 565.

44. Struve, *Deutsche Herrschaft*, p. 565.

45. Quoted in Struve, *Deutsche Herrschaft*, p. 573.

46. Struve, *Deutsche Herrschaft*, pp. 586–87.

47. August von Kageneck, *Examen de Conscience*, quoted in Trang, *Wiking*, p. 1:128.

48. "Verleihungsliste E.K.II, Verliehen am 14.7.1941," reproduced in *Pioniereinheiten der 5. SS-Panzerdivision "Wiking,"* p. 343.

49. Irene to Herr Wahl, August 15, 1941, copy provided by Charles Rattan.

50. Quoted in *Pioniereinheiten der 5. SS-Panzerdivision "Wiking,"* p. 325.

51. Quoted in *Pioniereinheiten der 5. SS-Panzerdivision "Wiking,"* p. Wi 28.

52. Liedtke, *Enduring the Whirlwind*, table 3.9.

53. *Pioniereinheiten der 5. SS-Panzerdivision "Wiking,"* p. Wi 331.

54. Mengele to Irene, January 4, 1942, in Wolter, "Der SS-Arzt Mengele."

55. Mengele to Irene, January 17, 1942, in Wolter, "Der SS-Arzt Mengele."

56. Mengele to Irene, February 18, 1942, in Wolter, "Der SS-Arzt Mengele."

57. Quoted in Liedtke, *Enduring the Whirlwind*, Kindle locs. 4438–40.

58. At some point in August 1942, Mengele went on home leave. The evidence can be found in one of the best-known photographs of Mengele in his SS uniform, which shows him standing next to a house. Markus Wolter, a historian from Freiburg, has analyzed this photograph and makes a strong argument for it having been taken in August 1942 in Freiburg, during a home leave. In 2013 Wolter was able to examine the apartment where Irene and her parents were living during the war and claims that the window frame and roof details match those in the photograph. In addition, their apartment had a balcony that matched the depth and orientation of the one in the photo; the hill in the background was also a match. These observations make it all but certain that the photo was taken in Freiburg. There is evidence that supports the August date for Mengele's home leave. In his autobiography, Mengele describes a meeting he had with Eugen Fischer "during a visit," shortly after Fischer had learned about the death of his son in the war. Fischer's son died in mid-July 1942, and Fischer moved back to Freiburg in August. Lösch, *Rasse als Konstrukt*, p. 392. It seems likely that Mengele visited him there during his leave.

59. Mengele to Irene, September 2, 1942, in Wolter, "Der SS-Arzt Mengele."

60. "Beförderung in der Waffen-SS," October 13, 1942. Mengele File, BDC.

61. *Pioniereinheiten der 5. SS-Panzerdivision "Wiking,"* p. Wi 95

62. *Pioniereinheiten der 5. SS-Panzerdivision "Wiking,"* p. 102.

63. The date for the award of the medal is listed as January 1, 1943, in "EK I—*Ver-*

leihungsliste, (verliehen am 1.1.43)," *Pioniereinheiten der 5. SS-Panzerdivision "Wiking,"* p. 354. Mengele was on the train moving toward Salsk, so we must conclude that the act for which he was being recognized occurred during the period his unit was withdrawing from Alagir. Posner and Ware have dated the award as being in the summer of 1942, during fighting for the recapture of Rostov; they quote Irene as saying that he received it for having rescued "two wounded soldiers from a burning tank under enemy fire." Posner and Ware, *Mengele: Complete Story,* p. 17. Irene's explanation may indeed have been her recollection of what her husband had told her, but the heroic act likely occurred later, much closer to the end of Mengele's service on the front.

64. Lifton, *Nazi Doctors,* p. 376.
65. Verschuer to Fischer, January 25, 1943, Archiv der Max-Planck-Gesellschaft. III/86A/291-5.
66. Schmuhl, *Kaiser Wilhelm Institute,* p. 365.
67. Fischer to Verschuer, February 2, 1943, quoted in Schmuhl, *Kaiser Wilhelm Institute,* p. 365n501.
68. Weingart, "German Eugenics," p. 277.
69. Schmuhl, *Kaiser Wilhelm Institute,* p. 250.
70. Schmuhl, *Kaiser Wilhelm Institute,* p. 283.
71. Schmuhl, *Kaiser Wilhelm Institute,* p. 286.
72. Weiss, *Nazi Symbiosis,* p. 117.

CHAPTER 3: THE CAPITAL OF THE HOLOCAUST

1. Hayes, "Auschwitz."
2. Rolf Mengele, interview by John Ware, September 2, 1985, notes, Posner Papers, Box 16, Folder 2, GARC.
3. Sedlmeier Interrogation, December 6, 1984, HHStAW 461/37976.
4. Massin, "Mengele, die Zwillingsforschung," p. 225.
5. Lifton, *Nazi Doctors,* p. 346.
6. Lifton, *Nazi Doctors,* p. 378.
7. Wirths served in Auschwitz from September 1942 until the camp was evacuated in January 1945, then was transferred to several other camps. He committed suicide in September 1945, while in British custody.
8. Lingens-Reiner, *Prisoners of Fear,* pp. 64–65.
9. Kubica, "Crimes of Mengele," p. 328.
10. Lasik, *Organizational Structure of Auschwitz,* pp. 243–58.

11. Strzelecka, *Medical Crimes*, p. 10.

12. Strzelecka, *Medical Crimes*, p. 13.

13. Strzelecka, *Medical Crimes*, p. 14.

14. Strzelecka, *Medical Crimes*, p. 15.

15. Strzelecka, *Medical Crimes*, pp. 15–16.

16. Weindling, "Genetik und Menschenversuche," p. 265.

17. Strzelecka, *Medical Crimes*, p. 16.

18. Dirks, *"Die Verbrechen der Anderen,"* p. 135.

19. Rzesnitzek and Lang, "Material History."

20. Massin, "Mengele, die Zwillingsforschung," p. 220; Lifton, *Nazi Doctors*, p. 358.

21. Pukrop, *SS-Mediziner*, p. 152.

22. Lifton, *Nazi Doctors*, p. 311.

23. Langbein, *People in Auschwitz*, p. 374.

24. Lifton, *Nazi Doctors*, p. 150.

25. Demant, *Auschwitz*, p. 47.

26. Landgericht Frankurt am Main 1964, transcript, p. 26.

27. His testimony was later challenged, and he was accused by some of concocting the story of his having observed the gassing and substituted what he had heard from others as his own memory.

28. Dr. Mauritius Berner, testimony, August 17, 1964, quoted in Wojak, *Auschwitz-Prozeß 4Ks*.

29. Dr. Mauritius Berner, testimony, August 17, 1964, quoted in Wojak, *Auschwitz-Prozeß 4Ks*.

30. When Capesius was convicted at the Frankurt Auschwitz trial in 1965 for accessory to murder, this encounter on the ramp was cited by the judges as one of the grounds. Steinbacher et al., *Der Frankfurter Auschwitz-Prozess*, p. 1251.

31. Zofka, "Der KZ-Arzt Mengele," p. 246n5.

32. Langbein, *People in Auschwitz*, pp. 295–96.

33. Bergen, "No End in Sight?," p. 299.

34. Quoted in Kushner, "Saul Friedlander," p. 78n19.

35. Zofka, "Der KZ-Arzt Mengele," p. 247.

36. Browning, *Remembering Survival*, p. 236.

37. Lower, "Distant Encounter," p. 108.

38. Sofsky, *Order of Terror*, pp. 243–44.

39. Quoted in Langbein, *People in Auschwitz*, p. 364.

40. Lifton, *Nazi Doctors*, p. 345.

41. Lifton, *Nazi Doctors*, p. 346.
42. Langbein, *People in Auschwitz*, p. 360.
43. Dirks, *"Die Verbrechen der Anderen,"* pp. 158–59.
44. Dirks, *"Die Verbrechen der Anderen,"* pp. 158–59.

CHAPTER 4: "SERENDIPITOUS TRANSFER"

1. Massin, "Mengele, die Zwillingsforschung," pp. 237–38.
2. Kubica, "Crimes of Mengele," p. 320.
3. Ostałowska, *Watercolours*, pp. 50–51.
4. Massin, "Mengele, die Zwillingsforschung," p. 234.
5. Enwonwu, "Ulcer," pp. 221–22.
6. Enwonwu, "Ulcer," p. 223.
7. Dr. Jan Cespiva, recollections recorded by Vlasta Klavdiva, September 11, 1963, quoted in Kubica, "Crimes of Mengele," pp. 333–34n10.
8. Adelsberger, "Medical Observations," p. 318.
9. Seidler, *Jüdische Kinderärzte*, pp. 411–12.
10. Kubica, "Crimes of Mengele," p. 338.
11. Weindling, *Victims and Survivors*, p. 130.
12. Adelsberger, "Medical Observations," p. 318.
13. Brasse, *Wilhelm Brasse*, p. 86.
14. Kubica, "Crimes of Mengele," p. 323.
15. Langbein, *People in Auschwitz*, p. 338.
16. Kubica, "Crimes of Mengele," p. 320.
17. Kurt Lambertz, "My Friend Mengele," HHStAW 461/37976/022.
18. Turda, "Ambiguous Victim," pp. 49–50.
19. Nyiszli, *I Was Mengele's Assistant*, p. 44.
20. Segal, "Twin Research," p. 287.
21. Verschuer, "Twin Research," pp. 62–81.
22. Francis Galton, "The History of Twins as a Criterion of the Relative Powers of Nature and Nurture," *Fraser's Magazine* 12 (1875): 566–76.
23. Schmuhl, *Kaiser Wilhelm Institute*, p. 61.
24. Massin, "Mengele, die Zwillingsforschung," p. 202.
25. For an interesting discussion of contemporary zygosity diagnosis, see Segal, "Zygosity Diagnosis."
26. Kranz, "Zwillingsforschung," pp. 149–50.
27. Massin, "Mengele, die Zwillingsforschung," p. 203.
28. Proctor, *Racial Hygiene*, p. 42.

29. Massin, "Mengele, die Zwillingsforschung," p. 206.

30. Proctor, *Racial Hygiene,* p. 42.

31. Proctor, *Racial Hygiene,* p. 349n115; Rende, Plomin, and Vandenberg, "Who Discovered?"

32. Proctor, *Racial Hygiene,* fig. 8, pp. 38–39.

33. Massin, "Mengele, die Zwillingsforschung," p. 210.

34. Massin, "Mengele, die Zwillingsforschung," pp. 210–14.

35. Quoted in Schmuhl, *Kaiser Wilhelm Institute,* p. 306.

36. Quoted in Lifton, *Nazi Doctors,* p. 367.

37. Quoted in Dirks, *"Die Verbrechen der Anderen,"* pp. 153–54.

38. Krzysko, "Jan Czekanowski," p. 166.

39. Martyna Puzyna, interview, October 31, 1972, Protokoll, HHStAW 461/37976/052.

40. Lifton, *Nazi Doctors,* p. 357.

41. Frau Gardonyi Ferenc (née Erzsebet Fleischmann), "Zeugenvernehmungsprotokoll," October 12, 1972, HHStAW 461/37976/26.

42. Lifton, *Nazi Doctors,* p. 357.

43. Martyna Puzyna, interview, October 31, 1972, Protokoll, HHStAW 461/37976/052.

44. Lagnado and Dekel, *Children of the Flames,* pp. 59–60.

45. Heller, *History of Zvi Spiegel,* p. 82.

46. Quoted in Heller, *History of Zvi Spiegel,* p. 83.

47. Quoted in Heller, *History of Zvi Spiegel,* p. 83.

48. Kubica, "Crimes of Mengele," p. 323.

49. Thomas Simon, Interview 3085, June 7, 1995, Shoah Foundation. A former inmate named Maria Hanel-Halska described how Mengele had assigned her to examine the teeth of the twins and claimed that, right before the liquidation of the camp, she gave Mengele a "descriptive study of the subject, accompanied by tooth models." Kubica, "Crimes of Mengele," p. 335n27.

50. Ostałowska, *Watercolours,* p. 50.

51. Kubica, "Crimes of Mengele," p. 324; Frau Gardonyi Ferenc (née Erzsebet Fleischmann), "Zeugenvernehmungsprotokoll," October 12, 1972, p. 2, HHStAW 461/37976/26.

52. Massin, "Mengele, die Zwillingsforschung," pp. 214–15.

53. Massin, "Mengele, die Zwillingsforschung," pp. 214–15.

54. Massin, "Mengele, die Zwillingsforschung," p. 216.

55. Schwerin, *Experimentalisierung,* p. 244.

56. For instance, Lucette Lagnado, in *Children of the Flames,* wrote of the "eye

studies," describing them as "especially gruesome," and explaining that the Nazis "in their desire to create a race of perfect Aryans . . . wanted to produce children with lustrous blond hair and blue eyes." Lagnado and Dekel, *Children of the Flames*, p. 65.

57. Schmuhl, *Kaiser Wilhelm Institute*, p. 372.

58. Quoted in Schmuhl, *Kaiser Wilhelm Institute*, pp. 372–73.

59. Schmuhl, *Kaiser Wilhelm Institute*, p. 375.

60. Schmuhl, *Kaiser Wilhelm Institute*, p. 374.

61. Schmuhl, *Kaiser Wilhelm Institute*, p. 375.

62. Quoted in Schmuhl, *Kaiser Wilhelm Institute*, p. 375.

63. Schmuhl, *Kaiser Wilhelm Institute*, p. 376.

64. Schmuhl, *Kaiser Wilhelm Institute*, p. 377.

65. Schmuhl, *Kaiser Wilhelm Institute*, pp. 377–78.

66. Müller-Hill, *Murderous Science*, p. 71.

67. Hesse, *Augen aus Auschwitz*, p. 92.

68. Karin Magnussen Interrogation, May 25, 1949, Staatsarchiv-Bremen, 4,66-I-6922.

69. Quoted in Klee, *Deutsche Medizin im Dritten Reich*, p. 364.

70. The chart is reproduced in Klee, *Deutsche Medizin im Dritten Reich*, p. 364.

71. Karin Magnussen Interrogation, May 25, 1949, Staatsarchiv-Bremen, 4,66-I-6922.

72. Quoted in Klee, *Deutsche Medizin im Dritten Reich*, p. 364.

73. Karin Magnussen Interrogation, May 25, 1949, Staatsarchiv-Bremen, 4,66-I-6922.

74. Nyiszli, *I Was Mengele's Assistant*, p. 47.

75. Massin, "Mengele, die Zwillingsforschung," p. 240.

76. "Protokoll," June 21, 1972, HHStAW 461/37976/052.

77. Nachtsheim to L. C. Dunn, February 14, 1961, L.C. Dunn Papers, American Philosophical Society.

78. Massin, "Mengele, die Zwillingsforschung," pp. 247–49.

79. Karin Magnussen Interrogation, May 25, 1949, Staatsarchiv-Bremen, 4, 66-I-6922.

80. Massin, "Mengele, die Zwillingsforschung," p. 250.

81. Hesse, *Augen aus Auschwitz*, p. 78.

82. Hesse, *Augen aus Auschwitz*, p. 96.

83. Grant W. Morton, *Toxicology of the Eye* (1986), p. 398, quoted in Hesse, *Augen aus Auschwitz*, p. 78.

84. Massin, "Mengele, die Zwillingsforschung," p. 251.

85. Massin, "Mengele, die Zwillingsforschung," p. 252.

86. Trunk, *Two Hundred Blood Samples*, p. 130.

87. Massin, "Mengele, die Zwillingsforschung," p. 229.

88. Massin, "Mengele, die Zwillingsforschung," p. 229.

89. Gausemeier, "Rassenhygienische Radikalisierung," p. 187.

90. Massin, "Mengele, die Zwillingsforschung," p. 230.

91. That he so abruptly changed his mind, organized the project, and got it funded suggests to Benoît Massin that Verschuer knew in advance that his star student was going to be assigned to Auschwitz and may have had a hand in the transfer. Massin, "Connection," 230–31.

92. Müller-Hill, *Murderous Science*, p. 155.

93. Gausemeier, "Rassenhygienische Radikalisierung," pp. 188–89.

94. Quoted in Trunk, *Two Hundred Blood Samples*, p. 122.

95. Quoted in Trunk, *Two Hundred Blood Samples*, p. 123.

96. Trunk, *Two Hundred Blood Samples*, pp. 137–38.

97. Trunk, *Two Hundred Blood Samples*, p. 138.

98. Müller-Hill, *Murderous Science*, pp. 155–56. Trunk's reconstruction of the project is convincing and accounts for all the relevant evidence that has survived. It is not the only interpretation, however. Benno Müller-Hill suggests that Mengele's contribution to the project was, on the face of it, far more sinister than Trunk's version. But Müller-Hill appears to have conflated two projects funded by the DFG and connected to the KWI-A. Around the time that the Specific Protein Project, led by Verschuer, had been funded, a project on tuberculosis, under the leadership of Verschuer's colleague Karl Diehl, was also supported. Müller-Hill believes that the blood samples from Auschwitz collected by Mengele were for the tuberculosis project, and that the individuals from whom the blood was taken were intentionally infected with the disease beforehand so that their relative susceptibility could be studied. Trunk marshals a number of technical details to maintain convincingly that Müller-Hill is simply incorrect in his interpretation, not the least of which is that the infected person's urine and not their blood would have been necessary for the experiment Müller-Hill describes.

99. Anja Kühne, "Einfach eigeäschert," *Der Tagesspiegel*, January 26, 2015, https://www.tagesspiegel.de/wissen/umgang-mit-den-skelettfunden-in-dahlem-einfach-eingeaeschert/11278454.html, accessed March 22, 2018.

100. Nyiszli, *I Was Mengele's Assistant*, p. 47.

101. Nyiszli, "SS Obersturmführer Mengele (Conclusion)," pp. 64–66. This article is an English translation of fragments, published in Jean-Paul Sartre's *Le temps moderne* in 1951, of the 1946 Hungarian edition of Nyiszli's memoirs.

102. Perl, *I Was a Doctor*.

103. Massin, "Mengele, die Zwillingsforschung," p. 239.
104. Massin, "Mengele, die Zwillingsforschung," p. 220.
105. Kubica, "Crimes of Mengele," p. 324.
106. Kor, "Mengele Twins," p. 57.

CHAPTER 5: "I'LL NEED TO BUY A CRIB FOR ROLF . . ."

1. Setkiewicz, *Private Lives*, pp. 79ff. Marco Pukrup indicates that they regularly included Drs. Rohde, Kitt, Willy Frank, and Fritz Klein as well. Pukrop, *SS-Mediziner*, p. 189.
2. Radvanský, *Trotzdem*, pp. 56–58.
3. One historian dates the visit earlier, to late June, suggesting that Rolf was conceived then, accounting for his birth the following March. Wolter, "Der SS-Arzt Mengele." Such a visit would have come within a few short weeks of Mengele's arrival and seems unlikely for a number of reasons. Three weeks after he arrived at Auschwitz, Mengele, riding his motorcycle, was struck by an oncoming tractor, throwing him onto the railroad tracks that ran alongside the road. The report of the accident stated that Mengele's uniform was torn, that his Iron Cross was ripped from his tunic, and that he had suffered injuries; it included no details concerning their extent or gravity. SS- und Polizeigericht XV Breslau, "Einstellungsverfugung," August 1943, Mengele File, BDC. During the investigation into the identity of the skeleton found in Brazil, this accident was cited as a possible cause for the hip fracture that was identified in the remains, but there is no evidence that Mengele suffered such an injury. The SS and Police Court investigated Mengele for his role in the accident and concluded the proceedings without charges since they could determine no culpability. A visit by Irene at this time would have to have occurred after the June 21 accident and during Mengele's convalescence, and she would likely have recalled the accident. Moreover, dating the visit in connection with her pregnancy seems problematic. Far more likely Irene became pregnant on the eve of her husband's departure for Auschwitz in late May 1943, with Rolf's birth coming some forty-two weeks later, at the very end of the period for a normal pregnancy, especially for a first child.

   The timing of Rolf's conception remains uncertain; a German prosecutor even speculated that Rolf might not be Mengele's son given the absence of clear evidence that husband and wife were together at the relevant time. Galm to HLKA, Ordner 1. But the date is, in the end, unimportant, except perhaps for Rolf Mengele, who, according to one version, is spared the added burden of having been given life in the place on earth most associated with death.

4. Laboratory register indicating Mengele had a value of 1:400 on the Weil-Felix test, December 24, 1943, copy provided by Charles Rattan.

5. Beischl, *Dr. med. Eduard Wirths*, p. 194.

6. Mengele to Irene, April 26, 1944, in Wolter, "Der SS-Arzt Mengele."

7. Mengele to Irene, April 26, 1944, in Wolter, "Der SS-Arzt Mengele."

8. Ostałowska, *Watercolours*, p. 69.

9. D. Czech, *Auschwitz Chronicle*, p. 677.

10. Mengele File, BDC.

11. "Gespräch mit Frau Irene Maria Hackenjos, geschiedene 1. Ehefrau von Josef Mengele," Freiburg, September 20, 1985, Posner Papers, Box 18, Folder 3, GARC.

12. "Gespräch mit Frau Irene Maria Hackenjos, geschiedene 1. Ehefrau von Josef Mengele," Freiburg, September 20, 1985, Posner Papers, Box 18, Folder 3, GARC.

13. Dirks, *"Die Verbrechen der Anderen,"* p. 147. Czech indicates the date was December 26, 1944. D. Czech, *Auschwitz Chronicle*, p. 768.

14. "Gespräch mit Frau Irene Maria Hackenjos, geschiedene 1. Ehefrau von Josef Mengele," Freiburg, September 20, 1985, Posner Papers, Box 18, Folder 3, GARC.

15. D. Czech, *Auschwitz Chronicle*, pp. 725–26.

16. Heller, *History of Zvi Spiegel*, p. 107.

17. Heller, *History of Zvi Spiegel*, pp. 107–8.

18. Koren and Negev, *In Our Hearts*, p. 144; Heller, *History of Zvi Spiegel*, p. 109.

19. "Gespräch mit Frau Irene Maria Hackenjos, geschiedene 1. Ehefrau von Josef Mengele," Freiburg, September 20, 1985, Posner Papers, Box 18, Folder 3, GARC. Camp records indicate that on October 17, "SS Camp Doctor Mengele" employed female Jehovah's Witness inmates as domestic workers. D. Czech, *Auschwitz Chronicle*, p. 733.

20. "Gespräch mit Frau Irene Maria Hackenjos, geschiedene 1. Ehefrau von Josef Mengele," Freiburg, September 20, 1985, Posner Papers, Box 18, Folder 3, GARC.

21. D. Czech, *Auschwitz Chronicle*, p. 736.

22. Mengele Autobiography, Notebook 3, pp. 19–20, HHStAW 544/2572/Ordner70.

23. Josef Mengele to Irene, November 6, 1944, revision of the version in Wolter, "Der SS-Arzt Mengele," provided to the author by Markus Wolter.

24. Mengele, n.d., quoted in Zofka, "Der KZ-Arzt Mengele," p. 266.

25. Mengele to Irene, December 1, 1944, in Wolter, "Der SS-Arzt Mengele," p. 186.
26. Mengele to Irene, December 3, 1944, in Wolter, "Der SS-Arzt Mengele," p. 187.
27. Mengele to Irene, December 6, 1944, in Wolter, "Der SS-Arzt Mengele," p. 188.
28. Mengele to Irene, December 14, 1944, in Wolter, "Der SS-Arzt Mengele," pp. 188–89.
29. Martina Puzyna, Witness Protocol, October 31, 1972, German Embassy London, HHStAW 461/37976/052.
30. Dr. Horst Fischer, interrogation, January 24, 1966, in Dirks, *"Die Verbrechen der Anderen,"* p. 181n475.
31. Quoted in Dirks, *"Die Verbrechen der Anderen,"* p. 181.
32. Dr. Horst Fischer, interrogation, June 14, 1966, in Dirks, *"Die Verbrechen der Anderen,"* p. 181.
33. Dirks, *"Die Verbrechen der Anderen,"* p. 182.
34. Keller, *Günzburg und der Fall Mengele,* pp. 43–44.
35. Gutterman, *Narrow Bridge,* p. 163; D. Czech, *Auschwitz Chronicle,* p. 736.
36. Gutterman, *Narrow Bridge,* p. 265n24.
37. Gutterman, *Narrow Bridge,* p. 265n24.
38. Ulrich Völklein believes, based on witness testimony, that Mengele went to Ravensbrück after Gross-Rosen.

CHAPTER 6: CUSTODY AND CONCEALMENT

1. Otto-Hans Kahler, interview by DGM, September 22, 1985.
2. Mengele may have already shed his SS uniform before meeting Kahler.
3. Mengele Autobiography, HHStAW 544/2572/Notebook 70, *"Bauernzeit."*
4. Mengele Autobiography, HHStAW 544/2572/Notebook 70, *"Bauernzeit."*
5. Kahler, interview by DGM, September 22, 1985. This fact, mentioned in Mengele's autobiography, offers a tantalizing clue to his actions following his eventual release from captivity and also to the fate of his Auschwitz research records.
6. OSI, *In the Matter of Mengele,* p. 33.
7. Headquarters, 302nd Field Artillery Battalion, History: July 1, 1945 to July 31, 1945; Ziemke, *U.S. Army in the Occupation*; NARA, RG94, World War II Operations Reports 1940 to 1948, 76th Infantry Division, Box 11518.
8. In Mengele's autobiography, he described the process through which he altered the fictional name, *Ulmeier*: "The name on the certificate of the person released from the POW camp was originally Ulmeier and had been cleverly changed into Holmeder. The original signature had been hastily written,

leaving an open space between the *U*, which received a cross stroke and the *L*, so that one could easily insert an *O* in between, and it was simple to make the *I* into a *D*." With this explanation, one can see how Mengele altered the real name "Ulmann" into the alias "Holmann."

9. It is possible, as Mengele claims in his autobiography, that the Helmbrechts camp was in the process of being disbanded and that their release was part of the liquidation of the camp.

10. By the time I left OSI in December 1988, Phil Sunshine and I had completed a draft of the Justice Department's report on the Mengele case. After my departure, it benefited from review and emendation by OSI staff, and I continued to receive subsequent drafts while I was serving at the Berlin Document Center. The final version's conclusions were essentially unchanged from what we had written at OSI, but a few points were altered or emphasis shaded. One change was the question of whether Mengele had been released from Helmbrechts under his own name. The final report takes no firm position but suggests that it was unlikely that Mengele was released under his own name. Both Ulmann and Kahler had claimed to me in interviews, independently and without consultation, that although Mengele had used a pseudonym in the early days of his confinement, he was released under his own name. Therefore I think the report's ultimate suggestion is incorrect. There is no plausible explanation for why they would have misled me on this point, and logic seems to support their version. If Mengele had been released under a pseudonym, with a valid discharge certificate, why would he have needed to take the duplicate of Ulmann's and gone through the cumbersome and risky process of altering it?

11. The following paragraphs are a summary of, and quote from, the Department of Justice report that I drafted. OSI, *In the Matter of Mengele*, pp. 38–43.

12. The vast majority of these prisoners were classified as "disarmed enemy forces," taken prisoner after the war was over—not technically POWs and hence not subject to the provisions of the Geneva Conventions.

13. As luck would have it, many of the low-pointers ended up at home first, having been redirected while on the high seas after the Japanese surrender in August 1945.

14. Cable, Hq., 12th Army Group, to SHAEF Forward, May 16, 1945, in SHAEF SGS 370.01, quoted in Ziemke, *U.S. Army in the Occupation*, p. 293.

15. Some discharge directives had already been issued, including "Disbandment Directive No. 1," issued May 15, 1945, which authorized the release of "Agricultural workers, coal miners, transport workers and such other key person-

nel as are urgently needed," and Directive No. 2, also issued May 15, 1945, which authorized the discharge of women who were not members of the SS, concentration camp guards, or German. Ziemke, *U.S. Army in the Occupation*, p. 293.

16. Quoted in Ziemke, *U.S. Army in the Occupation*. This attitude was reflected in the 12th Army Group's release rate, which averaged thirty thousand prisoners a day. The 21st Army Group hoped to increase its discharge rate from 13,000 to 20,000 POWs a day. SHAEF G-1 Division, Subject: Disbandment Directive No. 5, NARA, 387.4/12, June 14, 1945. The Third Army alone had released over a half-million disarmed enemy troops by June 8. Ziemke, *U.S. Army in the Occupation*, p. 293.

17. Ziemke, *U.S. Army in the Occupation*, p. 294.

18. Melvin G. Kidder to Col. P. S. Lauben, memorandum, Subject: CROWCASS, October 12, 1945. NARA, RG332, ETO, Records of the Secretary, General Staff Classified General Correspondence 1944 to 1945 000.1-000.5, Box 1.

19. The earliest mention of Mengele in the files of the JAG, the military justice unit in the U.S. Zone of Occupation, was a "Report on War Crimes," dated April 30, 1945, written by a French officer, which listed individuals responsible for crimes at Auschwitz. The second name on the list was "Mengele, called Mephisto," who had a "hobby about twins." According to the report, Mengele "made surgical experiences [*sic*] on them, but taking good care of them," and that "any sick person of an anti-pathetic looking [*sic*] would have [been] noted on the sick call card, by Mengele, 'uncurable,' that ment [*sic*] death!" JAG Auschwitz File 000-50-3, quoted in OSI, *In the Matter of Mengele*, p. 98. Mengele's name was marked with the letter *A*, which meant that he was to be considered an "accused" in the Auschwitz investigation. Another reference to Mengele, this one from the Czech physician Dr. Kurt Grunwald, made on May 13, 1945, included this description: "Chief physician in Auschwitz II, Birkenau—responsible for the organization of man murder [*sic*]. He did for years the deary [*sic*] job of selections. He also was responsible for the 'scientific' experiments made on healthy people. Millions have been murdered during his office." JAG Auschwitz File 000-50-3, quoted in OSI, *In the Matter of Mengele*, p. 98.

I found what appeared to be a radio script prepared by the psychological warfare detachment of the U.S. Ninth Army, dated April 1945, in which a "Dr. Mengels" and his activity at Auschwitz are described in some detail: "[He] was one of the chief selectors in the camp. In the hospital he used to joke with the patients whom he would condemn to the gas chambers a minute later.

While he put the sign of death on a patient's chart he amused himself by whistling and singing popular tunes. His hobby was to select particularly all twin and liliputians for the gas chamber. He also used these types for his famous experiments and was assisted by a couple of women physicians who had specialized in dentistry, ophthalmology, and anthropology." JAG Auschwitz File 000-50-3, quoted in OSI, *In the Matter of Mengele*, p. 99.

None of the witness accounts, however, included sufficient personal details to be the basis for a meaningful search. Often Mengele's name was misspelled, no first name was supplied, and no further identifying details like date or place of birth were available. The fact that the name *Mengele* was not uncommon—there were at least seventeen men named *Josef Mengele* in the German armed forces during World War II—helps to illustrate how difficult it would have been to identify and locate him without additional information.

20. In the U.S. Army, the blood type is included on a soldier's dog tag for the same reason.

21. I discovered an analysis of blood type tattoo procedures conducted by the U.S. Army that concluded many SS men did not receive the mark. In fact, of 102 POWs included in the study who were known to be members of the SS, twenty did not have one. "Report on Interrogation of 102 SS and other POWs at Devizes, 12 Oct to Nov 44," NARA, RG332, ETO MIS-4; Misc. Interrogation Records, 1944–46, Box 128.

22. DGM, "Conversation with Otillie Miller," January 31, 1986, DOJ FOIA, OSI, *In the Matter of Mengele*, pp. 62ff.

23. DGM, "Conversation with Otillie Miller," January 31, 1986, DOJ FOIA, OSI, *In the Matter of Mengele*, p. 63.

24. Gerald Posner and John Ware write, based on information they received from Rolf Mengele, that Mengele arrived in Munich at the end of September and went directly to the apartment of someone he had known in the Viking Division—a pharmacist, who was "an ethnic German from Romania." According to Posner and Ware, the pharmacist and his wife took in Mengele, who was exhausted and run down from his stay in the Soviet zone. Mengele, reportedly, defended himself against the charges that he had done terrible things during the war and indicated his desire to turn himself in and be "cleared in a trial." The couple counseled against this course of action and warned Mengele that he would never get a fair trial and would be executed. Instead they introduced him to Dr. Hans Weigel, the brother-in-law of Fritz Ulmann, the man with whom Mengele had been interned as a POW. It is Weigel who then helped Mengele find refuge as a worker on a farm not far from his own

home near Rosenheim. Posner and Ware, *Mengele: Complete Story,* pp. 66–67. Apart from Rolf's account of this couple and their assistance to Mengele, there is no independent corroboration, and Mengele makes no mention of the couple in his autobiography.

25. "Der Bauernhof," Posner Papers, Box 34, Folder 13, GARC.

26. The handwritten notebooks were transcribed in typescript in the course of the investigation for the German police.

27. "Alois Fischer," Posner Papers, Box 34, Folder 13, GARC.

28. Maria Fischer, interview by K.H.K. Schöller and K.H.M. Schönig, May 14, 1986, HHStAW 461/37976/091.

29. When I spoke to Rolf Mengele in March 1986, he told me that his mother regularly visited his father: "He indicated to us that she visited her husband approximately once a month and that the visits were very dangerous. She said she would go at night and meet him in a forest. In order to establish that she was not being followed, they would pass each other as strangers first and then double back and meet." "Interview with Rolf Mengele," March 25, 1986, DOJ FOIA.

30. One reference to Mengele in the Auschwitz investigative file provided accurate and actionable identifying information. The memorandum recommending Mengele for the War Service Cross, which he received at the end of April 1944, described his activities in Auschwitz, including his handling of "urgent scientific problems in research concerning the racial identification of Gypsies," and his carrying out of "special tasks." The document included Mengele's birthplace and bore a handwritten note indicating that it had been "carded," meaning that the information contained in it had been added to an investigative card file, on May 31, 1945. This document proved that by the beginning of June, the U.S. authorities had sufficient information to lead them to Günzburg in search of an SS officer who had served as a physician at Auschwitz.

31. "Gespräch mit Frau Irene Maria Hackenjos, geschiedene 1. Ehefrau von Josef Mengele," Freiburg, September 20, 1985, Posner Papers, Box 18, Folder 3, GARC.

32. The Poles held two trials of Auschwitz personnel, the first involving Rudolf Höss, the former commandant of Auschwitz, who had been extradited to Poland in May 1946. The proceedings, which took place between March 11 and 29, 1947, in Warsaw, drew international attention with simultaneous translation into English, Russian, French, and German. Gen. Telford Taylor led the American delegation. The verdict, which was handed down on April 2, 1947, found Höss guilty, and he was executed on the grounds of the Auschwitz camp, not far from his former office, two weeks later. The second, larger

trial, this one with forty defendants, including Dr. Hans Münch, took place between November 25 and December 16, 1947, in Cracow, and resulted in twenty-three death sentences, six life sentences, a number of lesser sentences, and Münch's acquittal; he was saved by his purported refusal to participate in selections. Had Josef Mengele been located and arrested, he almost certainly would have been found guilty and executed.

33. Mengele describes, in his autobiographical novel, completing his *Fragebogen* and that of others at the farm, but I was unable to locate the questionnaires in German archives.

34. OSI, *In the Matter of Mengele*, p. 110.

35. Taylor to Young, December 8, 1947, quoted in OSI, *In the Matter of Mengele*, p. 85.

36. Karl Mengele Denazification Files, September 10, 1946, July 29, 1947, HHStAW 461/37976/69.

37. Martina Bleicher to Kurt Lambertz, April 12, 1946, HHStAW 461/37976/179.

38. Völklein, *Der Arzt von Auschwitz*, p. 225.

39. The Mengele family invested a reported seven thousand newly minted Deutschmarks to purchase a fake passport for Josef, which turned out to be of such poor quality that it could not be used. Keller, *Günzburg und der Fall Mengele*, p. 49.

40. Posner, *Hitler's Children*, p. 86.

41. Völklein, *Der Arzt von Auschwitz*, p. 226.

42. Steinacher, "'Cape of Last Hope,'" p. 208.

43. Aldo G. Ricci, ed., *Verbali del Consiglio dei Ministri. Luglio 1943–Maggio 1948* (Rome: Presidenza del Consiglio del ministri, Dipartimento per L'informazione e l'editoria, 1995), p. 4:21, quoted in Steinacher, "'Cape of Last Hope,'" p. 208.

44. Steinacher, "'Cape of Last Hope,'" p. 209.

45. Steinacher, *Nazis on the Run*, p. 52.

46. Steinacher, *Nazis on the Run*, p. 52.

47. Posner and Ware accept Rolf Mengele's assertion, related in the *Bunte* magazine article appearing in the summer of 1985, that Erwin was a cover name for Hans Sedlmeier, the trusted family friend and business associate. Posner and Ware, *Mengele: Complete Story*, p. 88. Ulrich Völklein, on the other hand, in his 1999 biography of Mengele, disputes this claim. He bases his conclusion on the lack of any indication either in the investigative files or in Mengele's notes themselves. He suggests that Erwin was much more likely a former SS member from Steinach, who worked for the Nazi refugee organization and organized and supervised border crossings to Italy. Völklein reports that a resident of Steinach had told him this, although he was not provided with the identity of

Erwin. Völklein, *Der Arzt von Auschwitz*, p. 322. We receive no unambiguous help from the internal clues within the autobiography. On one hand, Erwin is described as a local, which was not the case with Sedlmeier. On the other hand, he is described as having a close connection with the Mengele family and firm, which would support the Sedlmeier proposition. Mengele may have sought to obscure the true identity of Erwin in order to protect Sedlmeier, but writing in the early 1970s—a quarter-century after the events—it is hard to imagine that Sedlmeier would have been exposed to any real threat if his participation in Mengele's escape had been revealed. On balance, I would suggest that Erwin was not Sedlmeier but perhaps one of the Steiner brothers, who would later become business associates of the Mengele firm when they founded the South Tyrolean branch.

48. Mengele Autobiography, Notebook 5, p. 53, HHStAW 544/2572/Ordner 70.
49. Steinacher, "'Cape of Last Hope,'" p. 211.
50. Steinacher, "'Cape of Last Hope,'" p. 212.
51. Steinacher, "'Cape of Last Hope,'" p. 212.
52. *Glastäbchen*.
53. DGM, Notes taken during *Bunte* visit, 1962 Tagebuch.
54. Mengele Autobiography, Notebook 5, p. 76, HHStAW 544/2572/Ordner 70.

CHAPTER 7: CALM AND STORM

1. Völklein, *Der Arzt von Auschwitz*, p. 236; Posner and Ware, *Mengele: Complete Story*, p. 94.
2. Quoted in Völklein, *Der Arzt von Auschwitz*, p. 236.
3. Völklein, *Der Arzt von Auschwitz*, p. 238.
4. At this point, Mengele's diary ends abruptly and does not resume until a decade later. Although there is evidence that he wrote about his Argentine experience, no diaries or notebooks that deal with this period have been discovered, leading some to suspect that he destroyed them when he left Argentina to protect those who had helped him, or else they were lost in some other way. It is possible, however, to track Mengele's movements in Argentina without them, and to reconstruct in general terms the life he led there.
5. The tapes and their transcripts became very useful evidence against Eichmann when he stood trial in Jerusalem.
6. Stangneth, *Eichmann*, p. 110.
7. Posner and Ware, *Mengele: Complete Story*, pp. 101ff.
8. Keller, *Günzburg und der Fall Mengele*, p. 51. Rolf Mengele spoke to *Bunte* magazine about the visit but supplied no date. Sven Keller discovered a letter in

the Günzburg city archives, dated July 5, 1952, from Mengele's father, then on the city council, informing the mayor that he would be unable to attend meetings since he would be traveling for three weeks.

9. Hans Sedlmeier, interview, March 10, 1964, HHStAW 461/37976; Keller, *Günzburg und der Fall Mengele*, p. 51.

10. Posner and Ware maintain that it was Frederico Haase who introduced Mengele to Jung. Posner and Ware, *Mengele: Complete Story*, p. 105.

11. Keller, *Günzburg und der Fall Mengele*, p. 51.

12. Quoted in Posner and Ware, *Mengele: Complete Story*, p. 105.

13. Posner and Ware, *Mengele: Complete Story*, p. 102.

14. See Meding, *Der Weg.*

15. Helmuth, "Die Vererbung," pp. 815–20.

16. Record of Court Proceeding 3R 40/54, March 25, 1954, HHStAW 461/37976/067.

17. Posner and Ware, *Mengele: Complete Story*, p. 110; Keller, *Günzburg und der Fall Mengele*, p. 52.

18. Marc Turkow to Nehemiah Robinson of the World Jewish Congress, August 12, 1960, Posner Papers, Box 18, Folder 10, GARC.

19. Rolf says Geneva, while Sedlmeier in a different context says Zurich.

20. Rolf Mengele, interview, February 15, 1986, Posner Papers, Box 16, Folder 2, GARC.

21. Sedlmeier Interrogation, December 6, 1984, HHStAW 461/37976.

22. Otto Hans Kahler told me that he had learned from Verschuer's secretary, Dora Gross, that Mengele had visited with Verschuer after the war in Solz, where the family estate was located. That visit must have occurred during this incognito trip to Europe. Kahler, interview by DGM, September 22, 1985.

23. John Ware, memo of Rolf Mengele Interview, September 2, 1985, Posner Papers, Box 16, Folder 2, GARC. In their book, Posner and Ware report that it was Mengele's father who paid off not the driver but the police.

24. Völklein, *Der Arzt von Auschwitz*, p. 250.

25. Quoted in Keller, *Günzburg und der Fall Mengele*, p. 53n201.

26. Quoted in Posner and Ware, *Mengele: Complete Story*, p. 115.

27. Truppel, interview transcript, Posner Papers, Box 18, Folder 1, GARC.

28. Elsa Haverich, interview transcript, Posner Papers, Box 18, Folder 1, GARC.

29. For this reason, many Argentinians traveled to Uruguay or Mexico to get married, ensuring that the union was legal and that they would not be open to the charge of bigamy. I am grateful to Adriana Valobra for her help in explaining the technicalities of marriage and divorce in Argentina. See Valobra and Giordano, "Absolute Divorce."

30. Carlos Peláez y Gabriel Monteagudo, "El trabajo y los apoyos del nazi en Nueva Helvecia," *LaRed21*, October 3, 2000, http://www.lr21.com.uy/politica/23843 -el-trabajo-y-los-apoyos-del-nazi-en-nueva-helvecia; "Oficina del Registro del Estado Civil de la 109 Seccion en Nova Helvecia, Expediente No. 63, Matrimonio de José Mengele y de Marta Maria Will, 1958," downloaded August 15, 2017, from https://elecoweb.files.wordpress.com/2008/07/acta_casamiento_ mengele1.pdf.

31. Pablo Cribari, "De Eso No Habla: Mengele en Nueva Helvecia," *Nueva Helvecia*, January 4, 2018, p. 21, https://www.slideshare.net/Nuevahelveciamagazine/de -eso-no-se-habla-joseph-mengele-en-nueva-helvecia, accessed May 22, 2018.

32. Quoted in Prins, "Foreword."

33. Anonymous to Ernst Schnabel, July 8, 1958, HHStAW 461/37976/0010.

34. Wojak, *Fritz Bauer,* pp. 310ff; Völklein, *Der Arzt von Auschwitz,* pp. 252ff; Keller, *Günzburg und der Fall Mengele,* pp. 53, 120ff.

35. Schnabel to Oberstaatsanwaltschaft Ulm, August 3, 1958, HHStAW, 461/ 37976/001.

36. Schnabel to Oberstaatsanwaltschaft Ulm, August 3, 1958, HHStAW, 461/ 37976/001.

37. Pendas, *Frankfurt Auschwitz Trial,* pp. 53ff.

38. Herf, *Divided Germany,* p. 296. A powerful irony in the story of Erwin Schüle was revealed in February 1965, while he was in Warsaw in connection with an investigation. There he was confronted with an allegation that he had been a member of the Nazi Party. He denied the allegation, although it was in fact true. A year later he had to step down from his position as director of the Central Office (Zentrale Stelle) because of allegations that he had himself committed war crimes while serving with the Wehrmacht in the Soviet Union. Although the charges did not lead to indictment or trial, due to lack of evidence, they affected Schüle's reputation and served to undermine the results of his important work.

39. Bayerische Landpolizei, Kriminalaußenstelle Günzburg, to Staatsanwaltschaft Memmingen, August 25, 1958, HHStAW, 461/37976/001.

40. Posner and Ware, *Mengele: Complete Story,* p. 118.

41. Memorandum, January 1978, Posner Papers, Box 18, Folder 3, GARC.

42. Henry Ormond to Hermann Langbein, November 12, 1958, in Ortmeyer, *Jenseits.*

43. A check for files on Mengele at the BDC was made by a German intelligence agency on November 11, 1958, indicating investigative interest, HHStAW 461/37976/001.

44. Stahl, *Nazi-Jagd,* p. 116.

45. Schowingen to Auswärtiges Amt, March 3, 1959, quoted in Stahl, *Nazi-Jagd*, p. 116.

46. N. Robinson to N. Goldman, March 15, 1960, American Jewish Archives, MS-361, Box C191, Folder 12.

47. U.S. Embassy Buenos Aires to Secretary of State, June 24, 1960, Posner Papers, Box 18, Folder 3, GARC.

48. Extradition Request, Note No. 179/59, German Embassy Buenos Aires to Argentine Foreign Ministry, September 30, 1959; Archivo General de la Nación: Caja José Mengele, Ramón Lascano to Foreign Minister, November 17, 1959, http://www.argentina-rree.com/portal/archivos/justicia03.htm, accessed May 2, 2018.

49. Stahl, *Nazi-Jagd*, p. 117.

50. Ramón Lascano to Foreign Minister, June 24, 1960, http://www.argentina-rree.com/portal/archivos/justicia03.htm, accessed May 2, 2018.

51. "Chronology," Posner Papers, Box 33, Folder 18, GARC.

52. "Generalvollmacht des Herrn José Mengele an seine Ehefrau Mara Will-Mengele," September 29, 1958, in Keller, *Günzburg und der Fall Mengele*, p. 53n202.

53. Elsa Haverich, interview transcript, Posner Papers, Box 18, Folder 1, GARC.

54. A few years later, while visiting Germany, Dr. Ernesto Timmerman revealed that Fadrofarm had lost all its contracts with the Argentine state following the revelation that Mengele had had a business interest in it. StA Frankfurt to Hessische Ministerium der Justiz, February 10, 1992, telefax, HHStA 461/37976/64.

55. "Chronology," Posner Papers, Box 33, Folder 18, GARC.

56. José Mengele—Carta de Naturalización, November 27. 1959, copy (with translation) in Posner Papers, Box 18, Folder 6, GARC.

57. Völklein, *Der Arzt von Auschwitz*, p. 258.

58. Hans Sedlmeier, interrogation, December 6, 1984, HHStAW 461/37976/110.

59. "Protokoll über die Beweisaufnahme im Ermittlungsverfahren," July 12, 1985, HHStAW 461/37976/095.

60. Völklein, *Der Arzt von Auschwitz*, p. 263.

61. Keller, *Günzburg und der Fall Mengele*, p. 55n215.

62. Chen, *Looking for a Needle*, pp. 52–53.

63. Chen, *Looking for a Needle*, pp. 79–80

64. Chen, *Looking for a Needle*, pp. 82–83

65. Chen, *Looking for a Needle*, pp. 83–84

66. Chen, *Looking for a Needle*, p. 100.

67. Ronen Bergman, "The Hunt for Dr. Death," *Yedioth Ahronoth*, September 6, 2017, https://www.yediot.co.il/articles/0,7340,L-5012708,00.html, accessed September 8, 2017.

68. Chen, *Looking for a Needle*, p. 103.

69. I knew Peter "Zvi" Malkin in New York City in the early 2000s. He was a close friend of the late Robert Morgenthau, the storied Manhattan district attorney and chairman of the Museum of Jewish Heritage, where I was director at the time. Malkin, a talented painter, had retired from the Mossad and had an apartment in New York where he pursued his art. I recall bumping into Peter one evening in Battery Park City, in Lower Manhattan, where he had been visiting his son, who was living in the neighborhood. Animated, Peter described to me an idea he had just developed for a device that would foil suicide bombers. The encounter took place in mid-August 2001, just three weeks before 9/11 and a block or so from the World Trade Center. I never discussed Mengele with Peter, who died in 2005.

70. Chen, *Looking for a Needle*, p. 104.

71. Aharoni and Dietl, *Operation Eichmann*, p. 151. The Schumacher case took on political significance, and David Ben-Gurion asked the Mossad to help find the boy and return him to his parents. Yossele was eventually located in Brooklyn and was sent back to Israel.

72. "Yossele Schumacher, Reunited with Parents, Called as Court Witness," *Daily News Bulletin*, JTA, July 6, 1962, p. 2.

73. Chen, *Looking for a Needle*, p. 105.

74. Chen, *Looking for a Needle*, p. 137.

75. Harrecker, *Degradierte Doktoren*, pp. 233–34.

CHAPTER 8: PRELUDE

1. Ralph Blumenthal, "3 Nations Joining to Hunt Mengele," *New York Times*, May 11, 1985.

2. An allegation made by Simon Wiesenthal in July 1960, for instance, that after the Eichmann capture Mengele had been taken to Egypt by the "Nazi underground" occupied the Mossad for a number of weeks that summer. Wiesenthal claimed that the Egyptians demanded that Mengele leave the country until the Eichmann storm died down, and Mengele was then taken by ship to Piraeus and from there to the island of Kythnos, where he was hiding in an orthodox monastery. On July 30 Mossad officer Shlomo Cohen-Abarbanel went to Kythnos accompanied by a local El Al worker and toured the island for two days but found no evidence that Mengele was there. Two weeks later

a second Mossad team visited the island to conduct a more thorough investigation, came up empty, and suspended the search. Wiesenthal recounted this incident in his memoir, *The Murderers Among Us*, which I read in the summer of 1971 and credit with giving birth to my interest in the entire subject of Nazi war criminals. Wiesenthal, *Murderers Among Us*, pp. 160ff. Wiesenthal, however, puts the date as 1961, while Alan Levy says it was 1962. Levy, *Wiesenthal File*, p. 230.

3. Chen, *Looking for a Needle*, p. 62.

4. Bergman, *Rise and Kill*, p. 666n.

5. Bergman, *Rise and Kill*, p. 209.

6. Bergman, *Rise and Kill*, p. 666n.

7. Chen, *Looking for a Needle*, p. 160.

8. Ronen Bergman, "Auschwitz-Arzt: Mengeles Glück," *Die Zeit*, September 6, 2017. Heidemann was to be in the headlines for another Nazi-related story a few years later, when he was convicted for his role in the Hitler Diary forgeries.

9. Chen, *Looking for a Needle*, p. 205.

10. Chen, *Looking for a Needle*, p. 240.

11. Chen, *Looking for a Needle*, p. 243.

12. Chen, *Looking for a Needle*, p. 244.

13. Many twins suffered persistent medical problems, which they believed were the results of experiments Mengele performed on them at Auschwitz. There was precious little evidence of the nature of the experiments beyond their own childhood recollections, but they were sufficiently convinced of the link that they interested a New York attorney, Gerald Posner, in taking on a pro bono lawsuit against the Mengele firm in Günzburg for damages the twins had suffered. Posner never filed the suit, but he became an expert on Mengele and a friend of mine. Posner's resourcefulness and ability to operate outside the strictures that confined me as a government employee allowed him to collect significant and valuable evidence.

14. Quoted in *New York Times*, January 28, 1985.

15. Quoted in *New York Times*, January 28, 1985.

16. By the end of the 1980s, *Parade* was included as a supplement in some 330 newspapers nationwide and had a circulation of more than 35 million, http://www.pophistorydig.com/topics/tag/parade-magazine-history/, accessed June 11, 2017.

17. Two months after its publication, Lagnado was invited to accompany Brooklyn district attorney Elizabeth Holtzman on a trip to Paraguay to pressure the government of Alfredo Stroessner to cooperate in the apprehension and extradition of Mengele, who was widely believed to have found refuge there.

Holtzman's delegation included Beate Klarsfeld; Bishop Rene Valero of the Brooklyn Archdiocese, who Holtzman thought might prove effective in visiting the overwhelmingly Catholic Paraguay; and Menachem Rosensaft, a child of Holocaust survivors and chairman of the International Network of Children of Jewish Holocaust Survivors, who helped raise the money for the trip. Rosensaft's mother, Hadassah, had encountered Mengele many times at Birkenau where, as an inmate, she served in a medical capacity and helped shield a number under her care from Mengele's deadly selections in the camp's infirmaries. See Rosensaft, *Yesterday*.

18. Quoted in *New York Times*, February 10, 1985.

19. Quoted in *New York Times*, February 7, 1985.

20. StA Ffm (Galm) to Russek, November 23, 1984, HStA Wiesbaden 37976/102.

21. German Embassy in Tel Aviv to BPA, BMJ, HMdJ, LG Ffm, March 6, 1985, HStA Wiesbaden, 37976/102.

22. This arrest warrant was replaced by the same court with a revised one on June 5, 1959.

23. "Begründung der Zuständigkeit für die Auschwtiz-Untersuchung beim Landesgericht/Staatsanwaltschaft Frankfurt am Main," HHStAW 461/37976/212.

24. "Tabellarische Zusammenstellung der Fahndungsmaßnahmen nach Josef Mengele von 1959 bis 1984 durch die Gerichte und Behörden der Bundesrepublik Deutschland," n.d., HHStAW 461/37976/068.

25. When Bill, who became a dear friend of mine, told me this story shortly after we met in 1985, I frankly thought he was exaggerating, but among the records of the Mengele investigation in the State Archives in Wiesbaden, I found a surveillance photo of Bill taken by the German police while he was secretly filming them. Bill died suddenly and unexpectedly several years ago, and seeing him "in action" in this photo reminded me of his brilliance, creativity, and determination. Bayerisches Landeskriminalamt, memorandum describing stakeout, June 28, 1984, HHStAW, 461/37976/086.

26. Löw to HMdI, January 28, 1985, HHStAW 461/37976/62.

27. Von Hoerschelmann to HMdJ, January 30, 1985, HHStAW 461/37976/62.

28. Mitscher to HMdJ, January 30, 1985, HHStAW 461/37976/62.

29. Haueisen to HMdJ, January 31, 1985, HHStAW 461/37976/61.

30. Kulenkampff to Haueisen, January 31, 1985, HHStAW 461/37976/62.

31. HMdJ, press release, January 31, 1985, HHStAW 461/37976/62. For its part, the Mossad had begun discussing the possibility of offering a reward for information that would lead to the capture of Mengele in early September 1984 and

decided in December to set the figure at $1 million. It planned for Serge and Beate Klarsfeld, the "Nazi-hunting" couple who lived in Paris, to announce the reward offering at a press conference in Günzburg and claim that it was funded through a bequest of an anonymous Holocaust survivor. The Mossad made it clear to the Klarsfelds that any information would have to be handed over directly to itself, and that only information that led directly to Mengele's capture would qualify for the reward. The Klarsfelds required that the money be deposited in advance in a Swiss bank as a condition of their participation. The Mossad then turned to the Anti-Defamation League as a possible front for the reward. This avenue failed as well. Only in early May 1985 did Israel finally make public its reward, this time offered by the State of Israel and the World Zionist Organization.

32. Hier, *Meant to Be*, p. 82; Zuroff, *Occupation*, p. 95; Gorby Memorandum, in OSI, *In the Matter of Mengele*, p. 85.

33. Rabbi Marvin Hier, statement, U.S. Senate, *Searching for Dr. Josef Mengele*, p. 64.

34. Rabbi Marvin Hier, statement, U.S. Senate, *Searching for Dr. Josef Mengele*, pp. 64–65. See also Jay Matthews, "Former Officer Backs Report on Mengele: War Criminal Believed Detained by U.S.," *Washington Post*, January 26, 1985, p. A14.

35. Ralph Blumenthal, "U.S. May Investigate Mengele Case," *New York Times*, January 24, 1985.

36. Rabbi Marvin Hier, statement, U.S. Senate, *Searching for Dr. Josef Mengele*.

37. Ralph Blumenthal, "U.S. May Investigate Mengele Case," *New York Times*, January 24, 1985.

38. Jay Matthews, "Ex-GI Tells of Seeing Josef Mengele in a U.S. Prisoner-of-War Camp," *Washington Post*, February 15, 1985. p. A4.

39. Robert A. Martin, "Former Soldier Says He Saw Mengele," UPI, February 15, 1985.

40. Jay Matthews, "Ex-GI Tells of Seeing Josef Mengele in a U.S. Prisoner-of-War Camp," *Washington Post*, February 15, 1985, p. A4; Robert A. Martin, "Former Soldier Says He Saw Mengele," UPI, February 15, 1985.

41. "Formal Senate Hearings on the Mengele Case to Be Convened in Washington February 19," JTA, February 13, 1985.

42. David Shribman, "Sen. Arlen Specter Succeeds in Getting Headlines in an Effort to Boost His Prospects for Reelection," *Wall Street Journal*, October 25, 1985, p. 64.

43. See Stone, *Jews of Capitol Hill*, p. 405.

44. D'Amato to Casey, January 24, 1985, Mengele File, CIA.
45. Assistant General Counsel, "DDO Files Pertaining to Dr. Josef Mengele," February 1, 1984, CIA memorandum, Mengele File, CIA.
46. Ambassador Davis, "Memorandum to the File," December 14, 1984, Mengele File, CIA.
47. "Query About Possible Location in Portugal of Dr. Mengele," February 1, 1985, CIA cable, Washington 240794, Mengele File, CIA.
48. "Allegation that Mengele was in Portugal," [Redacted (Lisbon?)] 58930, February 25, 1985, CIA cable.
49. "Dear Fellow New Yorker," c. February 1985, HHStAW 461/37976/184.
50. "D'Amato Calls for Increased Efforts to Apprehend Mengele," JTA, February 18, 1985.

CHAPTER 9: THE INVESTIGATION

1. Leslie Maitland Werner, "U.S. Launches Investigation of Mengele Case," *New York Times*, February 7, 1985.
2. U.S. Senate, *Searching for Dr. Josef Mengele*, p. 39.
3. OSI, *In the Matter of Mengele*, p. 4.
4. Philip Shenon, "U.S. Is 'Optimistic' on Nazi's Capture," *New York Times*, April 23, 1985.
5. P. Weiss, "True Story," pp. 33ff; Joyce and Stover, *Witnesses*, pp. 155ff.
6. Joyce and Stover, *Witnesses*, p. 156.
7. Joyce and Stover, *Witnesses*, p. 156.
8. P. Weiss, "True Story," p. 38.
9. The Mossad had also learned of the allegation and sent its own team to Uruguay, which concluded that the story was bogus.
10. The Roger Channel was reserved for classified messages dealing with intelligence matters. It owed its name to Roger Hilsman, a former State Department official under John F. Kennedy who directed the Bureau of Intelligence and Research.
11. State Department Cable, STATE 092234, March 27, 1985.
12. CIA Cable, DIRECTOR 324470, April 5, 1985.
13. Varon, *Diplomat and Dr. Mengele*.
14. Varon, *Professions of a Lucky Jew*, p. 380.
15. CIA Cable, Asunción 24380, May 22, 1985.
16. State Department "Roger Channel" Cable, Asunción 3160, May 24, 1985.
17. CIA Cable, Asunción 24380, May 22, 1985.
18. State Department "Roger Channel" Cable, Asunción 3160, May 24, 1985.

19. CIA Cable, Asunción 24380, May 22, 1985.

20. CIA Cable, Asunción 24380, May 22, 1985.

21. CIA Cable, Asunción 24380, May 22, 1985. The consequences of such a discovery were troubling: "The Paraguayans would certainly consider such activities to be a violation of their sovereignty. Beyond that, however, they might put an even darker interpretation on them. The Paraguayan government, from the president on down, has repeatedly insisted that it has searched for Mengele and that he is not here. Government officials might conclude that the USG effort represented an attempt to discredit or even destabilize the Stroessner regime, by revealing embarrassing facts about Mengele's connections in Paraguay." State Department "Roger Channel" Cable, Asunción 3160, May 24, 1985.

22. CIA cable, "Meeting with U.S. Marshals re: Mengele," May 24, 1985.

23. CIA Cable, DIRECTOR 395921, SUBJ: "Meeting with U.S. Marshals re Josef Mengele," May 31, 1985.

24. State Department "Roger Channel" Cable, Secret State 171152, June 5, 1985.

25. Safir went on to become fire commissioner, then police commissioner of New York City under Mayor Rudy Giuliani.

26. "Besprechung am 09.05.1985 bei der Staatsanwaltschaft Frankfurt/Main in Sache MENGELE," May 10, 1985, HHStAW 461/37976/074.

27. March 10, 1964, December 9, 1971, December 6, 1984, February 5, 1985, March 12, 1985.

28. Segev, *Simon Wiesenthal*, pp. 169–70.

29. File Memorandum, March 29, 1985, HHStAW 544/2572/Ordner 64.

30. File Memorandum, March 29, 1985, HHStAW 544/2572/Ordner 64.

31. Gemmer, "Search in Günzburg on 31.05.85," May 29, 1985, cable, HHStAW 544/2572/Ordner 64.

32. *Ablaufkalendar*, June 1, 1985, HHStAW, 544/2572/Ordner 64.

33. MUS to Messerle, n.d., HHStAW, 544–2572/Ordner 64; English translation from Mengele File, CIA.

34. MUS to Messerle, n.d., HHStAW, 544–2572/Ordner 64.

35. *Ablaufkalendar*, June 1, 1985, HHStAW, 544/2572/Ordner 64.

36. "Go-Between Tells of Trips to Brazil," *New York Times*, June 13, 1985.

37. Dieter Sack, "Report: Evaluation of Correspondence Secured During the Search of the Sedlmeier House on 31.05.85 in Günzburg," June 3, 1985, HHStAW 461/37976/214.

38. I later learned that the nickname *Messerle*, which means "little knife," was supplied to Sedlmeier by Mengele, after Sedlmeier gave a "Karl Mengele & Sons" penknife to one of the Stammer children as a gift during one of his visits—a surprising lapse in operational security.

39. MUS to Messerle, n.d., quoted in Dieter Sack, "Report: Evaluation of the Correspondence Secured During the Search of the Sedlmeier House on 31.05.85 in Günzburg," June 3, 1985, HHStAW 461/37976/214.

40. Dieter Sack, "Report: Evaluation of the Correspondence Secured During the Search of the Sedlmeier House on 31.05.85 in Günzburg," March 3, 1985, HHStAW 461/37976/214.

41. Vermerk, June 4, 1985, HHStAW 461/37976/280.

CHAPTER 10: SÃO PAULO

1. CIA Cable 90684, June 6, 1985, Box 89, Folder 1.

2. CIA Cable DIRECTOR 405001, June 6, 1985, Box 89, Folder 1.

3. German Police in São Paulo to BKA Wiesbaden and StA Frankfurt, telex, June 7, 1985, HHStAW 461/37976/119.

4. German Police in São Paulo to BKA Wiesbaden and StA Frankfurt, telex, June 7, 1985, HHStAW 461/37976/119.

5. State Department Cable, São Paulo 1432, June 7, 1985.

6. State Department Cable, São Paulo 1432, June 7, 1985.

7. Alan Riding, "The Man in the News; Key Man in Mengele Case: Romeu Tuma," *New York Times*, June 16, 1985.

8. The Brazilian Supreme Court refused to grant extradition requests for Wagner from Israel, Poland, Austria, and West Germany because the statute of limitations had expired. Although he reportedly expressed no remorse for his crimes, Wagner is said to have committed suicide in Brazil in October 1980.

9. Alan Riding, "Exhumed Body in Brazil Said to Be Mengele's," *New York Times*, June 7, 1985.

10. Neal Sher, interview by DGM, February 2017.

11. Alan Riding, "Exhumed Body in Brazil Said to Be Mengele's," *New York Times*, June 7, 1985

12. *Fernschreiben*, June 12, 1985, HHStAW, 461/37976/119.

13. *Fernschreiben*, June 12, 1985, HHStAW, 461/37976/119.

14. Cable, São Paulo 1462, June 10, 1985, Box 89, Folder 1.

15. Confidential Cable, Brasilia 06019, June 8, 1985.

16. Gouldman notes on telephone conversation with Neal Sher, June 9, 1985, YVA Tr.11/32.4. Dennis called me as well, and I filled him in on all the details that I had concerning the Sedlmeier search, the Germans' conduct, and the exhumation.

17. Although Tuma's changed attitude eased tensions, the strains among the Americans—between OSI and the U.S. Marshals Service—intensified. From

the moment the attorney general assigned them to the case, the marshals seemed more motivated by competition than cooperation. The extent of this rivalry was not clear to me until I gained access to the CIA file more than twenty years later. The division of responsibility in the case had been clear before the body was discovered: the USMS was to locate the international fugitive and was organizing its ambitious effort in South America just as the body was discovered. OSI was to account for Mengele's postwar activities and, through this effort, had gathered important knowledge and developed key relationships that would prove essential in helping to identify the body. Rather than cooperating, the USMS sought to monopolize. The tension reached a crescendo in São Paulo, and the declassified file provides clear indication that the marshals were often working against us. Evidence of their efforts can be seen in their consistent attempts to exert their authority and claim sole responsibility for the investigation in Brazil.

18. Posner and Ware, *Mengele: Complete Story*, p. 321.

19. Posner and Ware, *Mengele: Complete Story*, p. 321.

20. Posner and Ware, *Mengele: Complete Story*, p. 322.

21. Rolf Mengele, statement, June 11, 1985, HHStAW, 461/37976.

22. Alan Riding, "Brazil Is Seeking Proof on Mengele," *New York Times*, June 12, 1985.

23. "Body Is Mengele's, His Son Declares," *New York Times*, June 12, 1985.

24. I recall accompanying Cantu on a trip to the National Archives, where he harvested small samples, the size of the dot of an *i*, from original documents to use in one of our cases.

25. We had obtained the original of this document from Geneva in April and had asked Epstein to compare the signature with that of Mengele's from his BDC file.

26. Cable, São Paulo 1476, June 11, 1985.

27. It turned out that the handwriting analysis used forged "known" samples of Hitler's writing for comparison, and that some of the historians, whose imprimatur was so important, had changed their opinions.

28. Cantu Report, July 31, 1985, in OSI, *In the Matter of Mengele*, pp. 298ff.

29. Earlier in the investigation, we had requested that the original of the BDC file on Mengele be sent to Washington so that we could have it examined for fingerprints. We needed special permission to have the original removed from the BDC. The only other instance in which this had been allowed, I was told, was for the Eichmann case, when the original was loaned to Israel but had not been returned. Although BDC director Daniel Simon, whom I succeeded in the position, was most reluctant to release the file, we persisted, and the

original arrived in Washington. A key document in Mengele's file was a hand-written *Lebenslauf*, or autobiographical statement. We reasoned that when Mengele was writing on the form, he might have placed his hand on another part of it, which consisted of several oversize pages that had been folded and opened like a brochure. Unfortunately, no useful prints could be detected, but having the original file turned out to be extremely important for the document analysis in São Paulo.

30. Epstein, "Examination of Handwriting," pp. 108–9.

31. Crown, "Identification of Handwriting," pp. 110–17.

32. Ralph Blumenthal, "Handwriting Experts Say Letters Found in Brazil Were Mengele's," *New York Times,* June 15, 1985. The Germans brought over a fingerprint specialist, who joined the three Americans and attempted to lift latent prints from the documents using the chemical ninhydrin; he was unable to lift any prints matching those of Mengele, perhaps because the document he was analyzing had become wet at one point. Telefonnotiz, "Betr.: Fahndung nach Josef Mengele; hier: weitere Erkenntnisse aus São Paulo," June 11, 1985, HHStAW, 544/2572/Ordner 52.

CHAPTER 11: "A BIOGRAPHY OF BONES"

1. Joyce and Stover, *Witnesses,* p. 159.

2. Joyce and Stover, *Witnesses,* p. 160.

3. Joyce and Stover, *Witnesses,* p.161.

4. Quoted in Joyce and Stover, *Witnesses,* p. 161.

5. Joyce and Stover, *Witnesses,* p. 163.

6. Joyce and Stover, *Witnesses,* p. 163.

7. Keenan, Weizman and Portikus (Gallery), *Mengele's Skull,* pp. 18–19.

8. Joyce and Stover, *Witnesses,* p. 144.

9. Keenan, Weizman, and Portikus (Gallery), *Mengele's Skull,* p. 19.

10. Keenan, Weizman, and Portikus (Gallery), *Mengele's Skull,* p. 19.

11. Joyce and Stover, *Witnesses,* p. 171.

12. William R. Long, "Skull Bones in Brazil Found Damaged: Experts Sift Dirt from Grave in Search for Mengele Clues," *Los Angeles Times,* June 18, 1985.

13. "Final Report of Forensic Consultants," November 6, 1986, in OSI, *In the Matter of Mengele,* p. 350.

14. "Final Report of Forensic Consultants," November 6, 1986, in OSI, *In the Matter of Mengele,* p. 350.

15. Cable, São Paulo 1511, June 14, 1985.

16. Jonathan Broder, "Israelis Refuse to Fall for Nazi 'Trick,'" *Chicago Tribune*, June 16, 1985.

17. Chen, *Looking for a Needle*, p. 289.

18. Joyce and Stover, *Witnesses*, p. 175.

19. Joyce and Stover, *Witnesses*, p. 175.

20. Richard Helmer to StA Galm, 121987, ISA 7373/16: "Nach fugenlosen und spannungsfreiem Zusammenfügen mußte der Schädel dadurch wieder seine ursprüngliche Gestalt zurückerhalten."

21. "Final Report of Forensic Consultants," November 6, 1986, in OSI, *In the Matter of Mengele*, pp. 353–54.

22. Ford Burkhart, "Ellis Kerley Is Dead at 74; A Forensic Sherlock Holmes," *New York Times*, September 12, 1998.

23. Joyce and Stover, *Witnesses*, p. 184.

24. "Final Report of Forensic Consultants," November 6, 1986, in OSI, *In the Matter of Mengele*, p. 352.

25. See Ubelaker and Zarenko, "Can Handedness."

26. He also suggested that since Mengele himself may have supplied the measurement, he might have inflated it so that he would be issued a slightly larger and more comfortable steel helmet.

27. Clyde Snow, "Estimation of Head Circumference of the Embu Skull," in OSI, *In the Matter of Mengele*, pp. 363ff.

28. Shortly after the grave was discovered, a potentially important detail concerning Mengele's medical history was released to the press by Simon Wiesenthal, who reported that soon after Mengele's arrival at Auschwitz in June 1943, he had had a motorcycle accident. Although this report attracted much attention and inspired the speculation that Mengele had fractured his hip or pelvis in the accident, the document in his file offers no such information about the severity or location of his injury. SS- und Polizeigericht XV, Breslau, Einstellungsbericht, August 1943, BDC.

29. While I was in the final stages of writing this book, I received a photocopy of a medical form prepared when Mengele had first applied to enter the SS in July 1938. The form contains a brief medical history that differs slightly from the one in Mengele's SS file from the BDC: it mentions measles, scarlet fever, and diphtheria, which are missing from the other form, and the following description of an ailment: "Sepsis with bone suppuration [*Knocheneiterung*] (healed)." This new information, had we had it at the time, would not likely have altered the opinion of the forensic experts. But it is evidence that Mengele, using different terms to describe the malady, had some understanding of it and was not

blindly repeating what had been told to him. "Untersuchungsbogen für Neue-instellung in die SS," July 1, 1938, copy provided by Charles Rattan.

30. DGM Memo, quoted in Joyce and Stover, *Witnesses*, pp. 172–73.

31. Helmer and Grüner, "Vereinfachte Schädelidentifizierung," p. 202.

32. Joyce and Stover, *Witnesses*, p. 196.

33. "Scientists Decide Brazil Skeleton Is Josef Mengele," *New York Times*, June 22, 1985.

34. Cable, São Paulo 1534, June 17, 1985.

35. Lukash, Notes of Stammer Interview, June 19, 1985, Lukash Papers.

36. Cable, São Paulo 1556, June 19, 1985.

37. Joyce and Stover, *Witnesses*, pp. 196–97.

38. Hier's cable and its cautionary content had been reported to the USMS in Washington earlier in the day by U.S. Marshal John Pascucci, who indicated that Rabbi Abraham Cooper from the Wiesenthal Center, who had arrived in Brazil the week before, had requested that the Wiesenthal scientists not render an opinion or "adopt any other team's opinions." Pascucci had warned headquarters that "part or all" of the Wiesenthal team might withdraw from a joint U.S. conclusion. CIA Cable 30014, June 20, 1985.

39. Joyce and Stover, *Witnesses*, pp. 197–98.

40. Some believed that Mengele had suffered from a chronic sinus infection that resulted in a fistulous tract that made its way through the bone, providing a way for the infection to drain. Others believed the cheekbone defect was a postmortem artifact.

41. A few days before, Joe Lynch, a senior trial attorney at OSI, had arrived to replace Mike Wolf, who left on June 19, as the senior OSI representative. Upon my arrival, it became obvious to me that the marshals were seeking to dominate the investigation. During one encounter with Pascucci, he shoved a tape recorder in my face and told me I should be careful what I said and threatened that I should keep my mouth shut. Indeed, in reviewing the declassified CIA Mengele file, I discovered a cable written by Pascucci in which he indicated that Mike Wolf had been advised that he would be "excluded from all meetings" that involved security, requests from the medical team, or "investigative matters," and that any information "relevant to Mr. Wolf" would be made available him. Pascucci had clearly been given marching orders to control the situation in São Paulo, keep the doctors in line, and ensure that a final report was delivered to Tuma. CIA Cable 30010, June 20, 1985.

42. German Cable 101, São Paulo to Bonn, June 21, 1985, HHStAW 461/37976/119.

43. Fitzpatrick spoke for the Wiesenthal team and emphasized its independence from the other teams but made no substantive comments on the case.

44. Joyce and Stover, *Witnesses,* p. 202.
45. German Cable 101, São Paulo to Bonn, June 21, 1985, HHStAW 461/37976/119.
46. Cable, São Paulo 1592, June 21, 1985.
47. *NBC Evening News,* June 21, 1985.
48. German Cable 101, São Paulo to Bonn, June 21, 1985, HHStAW 461/37976/119.
49. Mark Prendergast, "Experts: Body Mengele's," *Sun-Sentinel,* June 22, 1985.
50. Chen, *Looking for a Needle,* p. 290.

CHAPTER 12: DOUBTS

1. Freisinger, *Hubert Burda,* pp. 203–4.
2. Note Verbal No. 311, July 19, 1985, HHStAW, 461/37976/281.
3. Neal Sher to Ali Hameli, August 20, 1985, Ellis Kerley Papers, NAA.
4. Eva Kor to Hans-Eberhard Klein, August 1, 1985, HHStAW 461/37976/064.
5. Eva Kor to Hans-Eberhard Klein, August 1, 1985, HHStAW 461/37976/064.
6. Klein to Hessischer Minister der Justiz, August 13, 1985, memo, HHStAW, 461/37976/064.
7. CANDLES Inquest transcript.
8. CANDLES Inquest transcript.
9. The Germans had discovered the "Holmann" pseudonym under which Mengele had lived after the war while on a farm near Rosenheim and told me about it during our meetings in May.
10. These records, microfilmed in the 1950s during a huge project managed by the American Historical Association, provided researchers with unprecedented access to the records of a regime within a decade and a half of its end.
11. Müller-Hill had been researching the Kaiser Wilhelm Institute for a book he was writing, and he had tracked down Kahler, a colleague of Mengele's in Verschuer's Frankfurt institute. Müller-Hill learned, to his surprise, that Kahler had met with Mengele in the Sudetenland during the last days of the war, when Mengele had joined Kahler's Wehrmacht hospital unit.
12. Charig, a German-Jewish émigré who had settled in the States, was then representing U.S. interests in the activities of the Mixed Claims Commission, an agency that dealt with property matters arising out of World War II. Charig's role was that of legal coordinator for U.S. cases pending in European courts. He retained and directed local counsel, maintained U.S. policies, reviewed legal positions and defenses, and located and deposed witnesses. His office sought money due to the United States and its citizens and, when necessary, defended and sought to reduce the claims against it.
13. See his correspondence with the Hessian minister of justice about how to

respond to Eva Kor's invitation to the CANDLES "Inquest," August 13, 1985, HHStAW 461/37976/64.

14. Klein to HMdJ, October 9, 1985, HHStAW 461/37976/191.

15. This list of open items included the translation from Portuguese of voluminous interrogations, reports, and expert opinions from Brazil, the final report from Dr. Endris, and the findings on blood type, from analysis of the hair and the age of the dental filling from one of the teeth found in the grave.

16. AP Report quoted in telex to Klein, October 7, 1985, HHStAW 461/37976/185.

17. Chen, *Looking for a Needle*, p. 293.

18. Chen, *Looking for a Needle*, p. 294.

19. "Die Frage ist aber nicht, ob die festgestellten Identitätsmerkmale auf irgendeinen Menschen zutreffen, sondern konkret auf ein ganz bestimmtes Individuum." Helmer, *Identifizierung der Leichenüberreste des Mengele*, p. 141.

20. Schriftsatz, "Mengele's Osteomyelitis: New Evidence," October 16, 1985, DGM Memo (translated by the Germans), HHStAW 544/2572/Ordner 05.

21. "New Information from Irene Mengele," October 9, 1985, DGM Memo (translated by the Germans), HHStAW 544/2572/Ordner 05.

22. Howard Safir had ceased to be involved at this point.

23. Dennis Gouldman to Minister of Justice, "Joseph Mengele—Report on a meeting of the staffs from the USA, Germany, and Israel," December 22, 1985, ISA 130.3/3/1110.

24. Classified cable, December 17, 1985, ISA Folder 130.3/3/790.

25. Classified cable, December 17, 1985, ISA Folder 130.3/3/790. Hans Klein's experts had drawn clear conclusions concerning the identification of the Embu skeleton, yet he had decided not to close his investigation and had undertaken to respond to additional research requests. Nonetheless both Neal Sher and Dennis Gouldman thought it appropriate to provide support in the form of a message to Klein's superior, the Generalstaatsanwalt Dr. Hans Gauf. On December 18, the Israeli ambassador wrote to Gauf stating that the "representatives of both Israel and the United States recognize" the "significant activity" of Klein during the recent consultations in Jerusalem, and that his contribution was especially valued. Ambassador Jitzhak Ben-Ari to Generalstaatsanwalt Dr. Horst Gauf, December 18, 1985, HHStAW 461/37976/64.

26. "Memorandum about the Discussions at the Israeli Ministry of Justice on the Mengele Investigation," December 17, 1985, HHStAW 461/37976/76.

27. Sedlmeier had arranged the meeting and accompanied Karl-Heinz, much as he had done for Alois Mengele, Josef's brother, for a similar meeting a decade or so earlier.

28. Hans Sedlmeier, interrogation, December 6, 1984, HHStAW 461/37976/.

29. Dennis Gouldman to Minister of Justice, "Joseph Mengele—Report on a meeting of the staffs from the USA, Germany, and Israel," December 22, 1985, ISA 130.3/3/1110.

30. When I interviewed Rolf in March 1986 and asked why he didn't simply write a new letter to Bossert, he replied, "Perhaps I am a lazy man."

31. "Mengele X-Rays: Investigation in Brazil," December 24, 1985, DGM memorandum, HHStAW 461/37976/76; "Mengele's Osteomyelitis: Research in Germany," December 24, 1985, DGM memorandum, HHStAW 461/37976/76.

32. Dennis Gouldman to Minister of Justice, "Joseph Mengele—Report on a meeting of the staffs from the USA, Germany, and Israel," December 22, 1985, ISA 130.3/3/1110.

33. Gouldman to Rogev, December 31, 1985, memorandum, ISA 7373/18 (883–886).

34. "Observations on the Purported Remains of Josef Mengele, 14 January 1986–15 January 1986," revised August 19, 1986, in OSI, *In the Matter of Mengele*, pp. 305ff. The skull and mandible had been taken to the University of Campinas, where a "clay restoration of the soft tissue was being attempted," so he was not able to examine the hole in the zygomatic bone itself.

35. Cognizant of the theory that the hip injury was associated with the motorcycle accident that Mengele had suffered early in his tenure at Auschwitz, Ortner wrote, "If Mengele were mobile and active four weeks following his motorcycle accident," as had been established, "the probability is that the injury to the hip region is associated with another traumatic event early in life."

36. Since Don Ortner had been unable to examine the zygomatic bone when he was in Brazil, he had been forced, instead, to review X-rays and photographs, which led to his inability to deliver a definitive opinion. His observations provided support for both sides of the question about whether the hole in the bone was the result of a fistulous tract draining a sinus infection, as Dachi and some of the Americans believed, or was a postmortem artifact, as the Germans maintained. He failed to find evidence in the X-rays of "the typical response of bone to chronic inflammatory drainage, including a relatively thick zone of compact bone and thickened spongy bone." He noted further that the "morphology seen on x-ray film and photographs, including the very irregular shape of the border of the defect, is more compatible with a diagnosis of postmortem bone destruction." On the other hand, he observed that the "suggestion of a circular pattern of what appears to be the exposed trabeculae surrounding the defect" argued for "the possibility of a fistula communicating between the maxillary sinus and an external surface." He concluded that the presence of some postmortem damage and the "destructive . . . procedures

used as part of the forensic analysis" might have eliminated the possibility of an absolute resolution of this issue. Ortner Report.

37. "Jewish Group Questions Mengele Probe," *Washington Post*, January 29, 1985.

38. "Jewish Group Questions Mengele Probe," *Washington Post*, January 29, 1985.

39. Fitzpatrick to Kerley, January 26, 1986, Ellis Kerley Papers, NAA.

40. Dr. John Fitzpatrick, "Osteomyelitis," January 24, 1986, ISA 7373/3.

41. Ellis Kerley, Ph.D., "Osteomyelitis," in OSI, *In the Matter of Mengele*, pp. 413–14.

CHAPTER 13: PROGRESS AND STALEMATE

1. Mengele Diary Entries; "Mengele X-Rays: Investigation in Brazil," December 24, 1985, DGM memo, appendix, HHStAW 461/37976/076.

2. Fred Kaplan to DGM, March 3, 2017.

3. Dachi Oral History, USHMM.

4. Fred Kaplan to DGM, March 3, 2017; Dachi Oral History, USHMM.

5. Fred Kaplan to DGM, March 3, 2017.

6. Brazil is home to the largest Japanese community outside Japan, with more than a million people.

7. "Analysis of the Dental Evidence Re: Josef Mengele," n.d., ISA 7373/3. Levine did, however, point to one possible inconsistency. In Tutiya's chart, the left upper first bicuspid was marked for extraction, a tooth that was listed as missing in the SS dental chart from the BDC. Levine dismissed this apparent problem by referring to the X-rays, which show a "hard tissue fragment" in the "soft tissue of the first bicuspid area." It might have been the root tip of the first bicuspid that broke off during extraction earlier in life, or it could be explained by any of a number of other conditions.

8. "Sachstandsbericht zum Ermittlungsverfahren der Staatsanwaltschaft Frankfurt/M.—50/4 Js 340/68—gegen Josef Mengele wegen Mordes (NSG)," March 12, 1986, HHStAW 461/37976/124.

9. "StA F/M Fernschreiben an BKA, HLKA, betr. Fahndung nach Josef Mengele," March 27, 1986, HHStA/461/37976/282.

10. The night before I left, President Reagan had ordered the bombing of Libya, during which Qaddafi's infant daughter was killed. The attack was in response to a number of recent terrorist incidents that had claimed American lives, the latest being the bombing of a Berlin discotheque on April 5. The air raid may have provided the motivation for the downing of Pam Am 103 over Lockerbie, Scotland, in December 1988, in which my friend and OSI colleague Michael Bernstein was killed.

11. "Ermittlungsverfahren Mengele; Tagesablauf vom 14.04.1986," April 14, 1986, HHStAW 461/37976/124; "Trip to Brazil, April 16–23, 1986," May 6, 1986, DGM Memorandum, USDOJ.

12. DGM Notebook; "Befragung des Dentisten Dr. Kasumasa Tutitya," April 16, 1986, HHStAW 461/37976/124.

13. "Befragung des Dentisten Dr. Kasumasa Tutitya," April 17, 1986, HHStAW 461/37976/124.

14. Mengele to Sedlmeier (most likely), 1972, attached as appendix to "Mengele X-Rays: Investigation in Brazil," December 24, 1985, DGM Memorandum, HHStAW, 461/37976/076.

15. I had included a description of the surgery in my cable to Brazil the previous August, and Tuma and his men were able to locate the surgeon, Dr. Fredini, as well as the radiologist, Dr. Cavalcanti. They interviewed both physicians, and both men recalled the unusual case and the patient.

16. Klein to Neal Sher, Dennis Gouldman, September 10, 1986, HHStAW 461/37976/194.

17. He specified, as well, the lack of a satisfying explanation for the "severe hip fracture" evident in the Embu skeleton and the difference in length of the skeleton's legs. He also explained that the Israelis had wanted to polygraph Liselotte Bossert when they were in São Paulo in April, and she had refused even to meet with them, as had Rolf Mengele, about whom they had wished to form their own impression. Their unwillingness, itself, raised questions for the Israelis.

18. Gouldman to Klein, November 6, 1986, HHStAW 461/37976/194.

19. Gouldman to Klein and Sher, November 16, 1986, HHStAW 461/37976/194.

20. Endris and Ritter to Galm, February 5, 1987, HHStAW 461/37976/194.

21. Endris and Ritter to Galm, February 5, 1987, HHStAW 461/37976/194.

22. Gouldman to Klein, July 9, 1987, HHStAW 461/37976/214.

23. Dr. M. Rogev, "Preliminary Medical Opinion," enclosed with Dennis Gouldman to Hans Klein, October 6, 1987, HHStAW 461/37976/179.

24. Rogev claimed to have found another possible focus of osteomyelitis in the left cheekbone—the site of the fistula that Dachi had theorized.

25. Concerning the difference in the length of the skeleton's legs, an issue that was noted by the experts in June 1985, Rogev made a significant contribution. He noted that the difference in the length of the femurs was mitigated by differences in the relative length and angle of the necks of the femurs. Rogev saw these differences as the result of changes that could only have occurred during adolescence and that compensated for the damage to the hip socket and the infraction of the pelvic bone. The damage to the hip, caused by a fall,

would have induced compensatory changes to the neck of the femur and its angle relative to the femur shaft, allowing the individual to walk without a limp.

26. Dr. M. Rogev, "Preliminary Medical Opinion," enclosed with Dennis Gould-man to Hans Klein, October 6, 1987, HHStAW 461/37976/179. I should note here that Dr. Rogev was far less cautious in his remarks to me about the case when he visited our office on his return from São Paulo to Israel. Although our conversation was informal and off the record, it was clear to me that he was convinced that the Embu skeleton was Mengele.

27. Gouldman to Klein, November 23, 1987, HHStAW 461/37976/193.

CHAPTER 14: CASE CLOSED

1. Gouldman to Klein, May 16, 1988, HHStAW 461/37976/22.
2. Gouldman to Klein, May 16, 1988, HHStAW 461/37976/22.
3. Alec Jeffreys of Leicester University had made "the accidental discovery of unique genetic patterns which led to the development of the technique in 1984." "DNA Testing Will Speed Up in Future," *British Medical Journal* 307, no. 6907 (Sept. 25, 1993), p. 758.
4. Klein to Gemmer, draft, November 14, 1988, HHStAW 461/37976/196.
5. Rittner to Gemmer, December 28, 1988, HHStAW 461/37976/196.
6. Dr. Sonnberg to K. D. Gemmer, January 5, 1989, HHStAW 461/37976/196.
7. Chen, *Looking for a Needle*, p. 308.
8. The court ruled that the charge of "harboring an illegal alien" could not be brought because the statute of limitations had expired. Cable, AMCONSUL São Paulo to SECSTATE, SÃO PAULO 00953, April 17, 1987.
9. Bossert was convicted in 1994 of perjury and sentenced to two years in prison, plus a fine. Her appeal of the conviction was not ruled on until 1997, and although the conviction was confirmed, she spent no time in prison. I am grateful to Betina Anton in São Paulo for tracking down the court files in this case.
10. Gouldman to Aharon Scharf, "Re: Josef Mengele–Summary of the Investiga-tion," May 1, 1989, reproduced (with the exception of page 9) in Chen, *Looking for a Needle*, p. 355fd.
11. Chen, *Looking for a Needle*, p. 10.
12. *New York Jewish Week*, March 24, 1989, HHStAW 461/37976/214.
13. Neal provided Klein with a copy of a letter he had received from Roger Castonguay, the FBI's assistant director in charge of the laboratory division.

The letter reported on attempts by the FBI to evaluate new DNA techniques and their suitability for the Mengele case. Castonguay reviewed the effort by my colleague, Phil Sunshine, beginning in "late 1988," after my departure from OSI, to pursue DNA testing after the dead end I encountered the previous summer. Phil had met with FBI specialists and discussed the use of the polymerase chain reaction (PCR) dot-blot technique, which could amplify minute quantities of DNA to the point where they could be analyzed—an important step forward in forensic DNA analysis, given the often-degraded samples that were available for testing. Castonguay indicated that the FBI had conducted research in early 1989 with the help of bone samples from the Smithsonian Institution and concluded that it was not then possible to extract testable human DNA from aged bones. They then attempted the PCR dot-blot procedure on "500 pooled hair roots" from Mengele that OSI had supplied, and likewise were unable to extract any detectable human DNA. Castonguay concluded that it was not "appropriate to apply the PCR dot-blot DNA typing procedure to the Mengele bones." He emphasized, however, that DNA testing was continually developing and that the future might hold the possibility of some success. Castonguay to Sher, June 22, 1989, HHStAW 461/37976/196.

14. Note to the File, September 1, 1989, HHStAW 461/37976/193.

15. Tuma–Gemmer correspondence, August 25, August 30, and September 1, 1989, HHStAW 461/37976/196.

16. Sonnberg to Jeffreys, September 12, 1989, HHStAW 461/37976/196.

17. Jeffreys to Sonnberg, September 27, 1989, HHStAW 461/37976/196.

18. Alec J. Jeffreys and Erika Hagelberg, "Report on the Investigation of the Mengele Case by DNA Analysis," August 21, 1990, HHStAW 461/37976/195.

19. "A mean single strand size of approximately 150 nucleotides and with more than 90% of DNA being less than 500 nucleotides in length."

20. The small size of the extracted sample would essentially eliminate all the markers that they would normally have used, and the presence within the sample of a "potent inhibitor" of PCR, which would have to be eliminated if the extremely small sample were to be amplified for analysis.

21. Jeffreys to Sonnberg, July 6, 1990, HHStAW 461/37976/196.

22. Jeffreys to Sonnberg, August 3, 1990, HHStAW 461/37976/196.

23. See the video of Rolf's appearance at https://www.youtube.com/watch?v=JFQaDSvlIKg.

24. Klein to Fritz Steinacker, April 4, 1991, HHStAW 461/37976/195.

25. Rolf Jenckel to Kneissler, Heinrich Bauer Spezialzeitschriften Verlag, KG, March 24, 1991, in Abraham, *Mengele: The Truth Exposed*, p. 32.

26. Klein to Fritz Steinacker, April 4, 1991, HHStAW, 461/37976/195.

27. "Eine Frostige Erbschaft des Dr. Tod," German translation of article in *Mail on Sunday*, October 13, 1991, HHStAW 461/37976/183.

28. "Eine Frostige Erbschaft des Dr. Tod," German translation of article in *Mail on Sunday*, October 13, 1991, HHStAW 461/37976/183.

29. "Eine Frostige Erbschaft des Dr. Tod," German translation of article in *Mail on Sunday*, October 13, 1991, HHStAW 461/37976/183.

30. I no longer feel compelled to keep this confidence since the story of the threatened exhumation has already been divulged to the press. See Constance Holden, "Mengele's DNA," *Science*, new series, vol. 255, no. 5046 (February 14, 1992), p. 801.

31. Vernehmungsniederschrift, January 9, 1992, HHStAW 461/37976/195.

32. "Second Report on the Investigation of the Mengele Case by DNA Analysis," March 13, 1992, HHStAW 461/37976/195.

33. Quoted in U. Renz, "Die Spurensuche nach Mengele."

34. "The Nazi Criminal Josef Mengele," 11th session of the 13th Knesset, August 5, 1992.

35. Michael Sheridan, "The Monster Who Will Not Die," *Independent*, July 21, 1991, p. 10.

36. "Indiana Woman Claims Weighty Allies in Hunt for Facts on Mengele," *Indiana Jewish Post & Opinion*, June 26, 1991, p. 2.

37. Abraham, *Mengele: Truth Exposed*, p. 9.

38. Dietl, "Gejagt von bösen Zweifeln," *Focus Magazin*, no. 12, March 18, 1996.

39. Wilhelm Dietl to Hans Klein, February 23, 1996, HHStAW 461/37976/216.

40. Lifton, *Nazi Doctors*, p. 382.

41. Lifton, *Nazi Doctors*, p. 382.

EPILOGUE: FATHER AND SON

1. Quoted in *Bunte*, no. 30, July 18, 1985.

2. Rolf Mengele, interview by Posner (in English), February 15, 1986, Posner Papers, Box 16, Folder 2.

3. Mengele to Rolf, n.d., HHStAW 461/37976/135.

4. Mengele to Rolf, n.d., Posner Papers, Box 17, Folder 1, GARC.

5. Mengele to Rolf, n.d., c. 1975, HHStAW 461/37976/35.

6. Rolf Mengele, interview by Posner (in English), February 15, 1986, Posner Papers, Box 16, Folder 2.

7. Rolf Mengele, interview by Posner (in English), February 15, 1986, Posner Papers, Box 16, Folder 2.

8. Mengele to Rolf, n.d., HHStAW 461/37976/135.

9. Mengele to Rolf, April 1977, Posner Papers, Box 17, Folder 1, GARC.

10. Sedlmeier to Mengele, May 27, 1977, HHStAW 461/37976/135.

11. Sedlmeier to Mengele, August 10, 1977, HHStAW 461/37976/135.

12. "The Meeting," September 30, 1985, Posner Papers, Box 34, Folder 13, GARC.

13. "The Meeting," September 30, 1985, Posner Papers, Box 34, Folder 13, GARC.

14. "The Meeting," September 30, 1985, Posner Papers, Box 34, Folder 13, GARC.

15. Mengele to Rolf, n.d., HHStAW 461/37976/135.

POSTSCRIPT

1. Lewontin, "Apportionment," p. 382.

2. Mukherjee, *Gene*, pp. 341–42.

3. Mukherjee, *Gene*, p. 343.

SS OFFICER RANKS

SS-Untersturmführer	2nd Lieutenant
SS-Obersturmführer	1st Lieutenant
SS-Hauptsturmführer	Captain
SS-Sturmbannführer	Major
SS-Obersturmbannführer	Lt. Colonel
SS-Standartenführer	Colonel
SS-Oberführer	Senior Colonel
SS-Brigadeführer	Brigadier General
SS-Gruppenführer	Major General
SS-Obergruppenführer	Lt. General
SS-Oberstgruppenführer	General

SELECTED BIBLIOGRAPHY

Abmayr, Hermann G. "Der Auschwitz-Arzt, das dämonische Wesen." *Kontext: Wochenzeitung*, December 18, 2003.

Abraham, Ben. *The Angel of Death: The Mengele Dossier*. São Paulo: Sherit Hapleita, Brazilian Associaton of Survivors of Nazism, 1986.

———. *Mengele: The Truth Exposed*. São Paulo: Sherit Hapleita, 1994.

Adelsberger, Lucie. *Auschwitz: A Doctor's Story*. Boston: Northeastern University Press, 1995.

———. "Medical Observations in Auschwitz Concentration Camp." *Lancet* 247 (1946): 6392.

———. "Typhus Fever in Auschwitz Concentration Camp." *Journal of the American Medical Womans Association* 7, no. 3 (1952): 102–3.

Afiero, Massimiliano. *The SS-Division Wiking in the Caucasus 1942–1943*. MMP Books, 2017.

Aharoni, Zvi, and Wilhelm Dietl. *Operation Eichmann: The Truth about the Pursuit, Capture, and Trial*. New York: John Wiley & Sons, 1997.

Aichinger, Ilse. *Film und Verhängnis: Blitzlichter auf ein Leben*. Frankfurt am Main: S. Fischer Verlag, 2001.

Akasaka, Yoko. "Statistical and Cytogenic Study on the Cleft Lip, Aveolus and/or Palate." *Japanese Journal of Human Genetics* 15 (1970): 35–96.

Aly, Götz, and Susanne Heim. *Architects of Annihilation: Auschwitz and the Logic of Destruction*. Princeton: Princeton University Press, 2002.

Baron, Jeremy Hugh. *The Anglo-American Biomedical Antecedents of Nazi Crimes: An Historical Analysis of Racism, Nationalism, Eugenics and Genocide*. Lewiston, N.Y.: Edwin Mellen Press, 2007.

Beischl, Konrad. *Dr. med. Eduard Wirths und seine Tätigkeit als SS-Standortarzt im KL Auschwitz.* Würzburg: Verlag Königshausen & Neumann, 2005.

Benzenhöfer, Udo. "Bemerkungen zum Lebenslauf von Josef Mengele unter besonderer Bücksichtigung seiner Frankfurter Zeit." *Hessisches Ärzteblatt* 4 (2011): 228–30, 239–40.

———. *Mengele, Hirt, Holfelder, Berner, von Verschuer, Kranz: Frankfurter Universitätsmediziner der NS-Zeit.* Münster: Klemm & Oelschläger, 2010.

Benzenhöfer, Udo, Hanns Ackermann, und Katja Weiske. "Wissenschaft oder Wahn? Bemerkungen zur Münchener Dissertation von Josef Mengele aus dem Jahr 1935." In *Studien zur Geschichte und Ethik der Medizin mit Schwerpunkt Frankfurt am Main,* edited by Udo Benzenhöfer, 31–41. Wetzlar: GWAB-Verlag, 2008.

Bergen, Doris. "No End in Sight? The Ongoing Challenge of Producing an Integrated History of the Holocaust." In *Years of Extermination: Saul Friedlander and the Future of Holocaust Studies,* edited by Christian Wiese und Paul Betts, 289–309. New York: Bloomsbury, 2010.

Bergman, Ronen. *Rise and Kill: The Secret History of Israel's Targeted Assassinations.* New York: Random House, 2018.

Böck, Richard. Testimony to Frankfurt Auschwitz trial, March 8, 1964. "Tonbandmitschnitt des 1. Frankfurter Auschwitz-Prozesses, Audiofiles und Transkriptionen." Fritz Bauer Institute, accessed August 22, 2017. http://www.auschwitz -prozess.de/index.php?show=Boeck-Richard.

Braese, Stephan, and Dominik Groß, eds. *NS-Medizin und Öffentlichkeit: Formen der Aufarbeiten nach 1945.* Frankfurt: Campus Verlag, 2015.

Brasse, Wilhelm. *Wilhelm Brasse, number 3444: Photographer, Auschwitz, 1940–1945.* Portland, Ore.: Sussex Academic Press, 2012.

Browning, Christopher R. *Remembering Survival: Inside a Nazi Slave-Labor Camp.* New York: Norton, 2010.

Bruns, Florian. "Turning Away from the Individual: Medicine and Morality Under the Nazis." In *Nazi Ideology and Ethics,* edited by Wolfgang Bialas und Lothar Fritze, 211–36. Newcastle upon Tyne: Cambridge Scholars, 2014.

Cesarani, David. *Becoming Eichmann: Rethinking the Life, Crimes, and Trial of a "Desk Murderer."* Cambridge, Mass.: Da Capo Press, 2006.

Chen, Yosef (Yossi). *Looking for a Needle in the Haystack.* Jerusalem: Mossad History Department, 2017.

Cottebrune, Anne. "Erbforscher im Kriegsdienst? Die Deutsche Forschungsgemeinschaft, der Reichsforschungsrat und die Umstellung der Erbforschungsförderung." *Medizinhistorisches Journal* 40, no. 2 (2005): 141–68.

Crown, David A. "The Identification of the Handwriting of Josef Mengele." *Journal of Forensic Sciences* 32, no. 1 (1987): 110–17.

Czech, Danuta. *Auschwitz Chronicle, 1939–1945.* New York: Henry Holt, 1990.

Czech, Herwig. "Beyond Spiegelgrund und Berkatit: Human Experimentation and Coerced Research at the Vienna School of Medicine, 1939 to 1945." In *From Clinic to Concentration Camp: Reassessing Nazi Medical and Racial Research, 1933–1945,* edited by Paul Weindling, 138–62. New York: Routledge, 2017.

Deichmann, Ute. *Biologists under Hitler.* Translated by Thomas Dunlap. Cambridge, Mass.: Harvard University Press, 1996.

Demant, Ebbo. *Auschwitz—"Direkt von der Rampe weg...": Kaduk, Erber, Klehr, Drei Täter geben zu Protokoll.* Hamburg: Rowohlt, 1979.

Dirks, Christian. *"Die Verbrechen der Anderen": Auschwitz und der Auschwitz-Prozeß der DDR: Das Verfahren gegen der KZ-Arzt Dr. Horst Fischer.* Paderborn: Ferdinand Schöningh, 2006.

Dixon, D. A., and I. Newton. "Minimal Forms of the Cleft Syndrome Demonstrated by Stereophotogrammetric Surveys of the Face." *British Dental Journal* 132, no. 5 (1972): 183–89.

Drob, Sanford L. "The Lessons from History: Physicians' Dual Loyalty in the Nazi Death Camps." In *Review of Clinical Psychiatry and the Law,* Volume 3, edited by Robert I. Simon, 167–71. Washington, D.C.: American Psychiatric Press, 1992.

Ehrenreich, Eric. "Otmar von Verschuer and the 'Scientific' Legitimization of Nazi Anti-Jewish Policy." *Holocaust and Genocide Studies* 21, no. 1 (2007): 55–72.

———. *The Nazi Ancestral Proof: Genealogy, Racial Science, and the Final Solution.* Bloomington: Indiana University Press, 2007.

Enwonwu, Cyril O. "The Ulcer of Extreme Poverty." *New England Journal of Medicine* 354, no. 3 (2006): 223.

Epstein, Gideon. "Examination of the Josef Mengele Handwriting." *Journal of Forensic Sciences* 32, no. 1 (1987): 100–9.

Evans, Andrew D. *Anthropology at War: World War I and the Science of Race in Germany.* Chicago: University of Chicago Press, 2010.

Feigin, Judy. *The Office of Special Investigations: Striving for Accountability in the Aftermath of the Holocaust.* Washington, D.C.: U.S. Department of Justice, 2006.

Fiebrandt, Maria. *Auslese für die Siedlergesellschaft: Die Einbeziehung Volksdeutscher in die NS-Erbgesundheitspolitik im Kontext der Umsiedlungen 1939–1945.* Göttingen: Vandenhoeck & Ruprecht, 2014.

Fischer, Eugen. "Versuch einer Phänogenetik der normalen körperlichen Eigenschaften des Menschen." *Versammlung der Deutschen Gesellschaft für Vererbungswissenschaft in Würzburg, 24. September 1938.* Berlin-Dahlem: Kaiser-Wilhelm-Institut für Anthropologie, menschliche Erblehre und Eugenik, 1939.

Forsbach, Ralf. *Die Medizinische Fakultät der Universität Bonn im "Dritten Reich."* Munich: R. Oldenbourg Verlag, 2006.

Frankfurter, Bernhard. *The Meeting: An Auschwitz Survivor Confronts an SS Physician.* Syracuse, N.Y.: Syracuse University Press, 2000.

Freisinger, Gisela. *Hubert Burda: Der Medienfürst.* Frankfurt am Main: Campus, 2005.

Galle, Helmut. "Os escritos autobiogáficos de Josef Mengele." *Estudos Avançados* 25, no. 71 (2011): 269–86.

Garré, Carl, A. Borchard, R. Stich, and K. H. Bauer. *Lehrbuch der Chirurgie.* 13th ed. Berlin: Springer-Verlag, 1944.

Gausemeier, Bernd. "Rassenhygienische Radikalisierung und Kollegialer Konsens." In *Die Verbindung nach Auschwitz: Biowissenschaften und Menschenversuche an Kaiser-Wilhelm-Instituten,* edited by Carola Sachse, 178–200. Göttingen: Wallstein Verlag, 2003.

Goñi, Uki. *The Real Odessa: How Perón Brought the Nazi War Criminals to Argentina,* rev. ed. New York: Granta Books, 2002.

Gutterman, Bella. *A Narrow Bridge to Life: Jewish Forced Labor and Survival in the Gross-Rosen Camp System, 1940–1945.* New York: Berghahn Books, 2008.

Halpin, Ross. *The Essence of Survival: Jewish Doctors in Auschwitz.* Sydney: Sydney Jewish Museum, 2014.

Harrecker, Stefanie. *Degradierte Doktoren: Die Aberkennung der Doktorwürde an der Ludwig-Maximilians-Universität München während der Zeit des Nationalsozialismus.* Munich: Herbert Utz Verlag, 2007.

Haumann, Heiko. *Die Akte Zilli Reichmann: Zur Geschichte der Sinti im 20. Jahrhundert.* Frankfurt am Main: S. Fischer Verlag, 2016.

Hautval, Adélaïde. *Medizin gegen die Menschlichkeit: Die Weigerung einer nach Auschwitz deportierten Ärztin, an medizinischen Experimenten teilzunehmen.* Berlin: Karl Dietz Verlag, 2008.

Hayes, Peter. "Auschwitz, Capital of the Holocaust." *Holocaust and Genocide Studies* 17, no. 2 (2003): 330–50.

Heim, Susanne, Carola Sachse, and Mark Walker. *The Kaiser Wilhelm Society Under National Socialism.* New York: Cambridge Univerity Press, 2009.

Heinemann, Isabel. "'Another Type of Perpetrator': The SS Racial Experts and Forced Population Movements in the Occupied Regions." *Holocaust and Genocide Studies* 15, no. 3 (2001): 387–411.

———. *"Rasse, Siedlung, deutsches Blut": Das Rasse- und Siedlungshauptamt der SS und die rassenpolitische Neuordnung Europas.* Göttingen: Wallstein Verlag, 2003.

Heitz, Caroline, and Eveline Schüep. *Annäherung an die soziale Wirklichkeit der SS-Ärzte; Sprachanalysen und sozialpsychologische Untersuchungen anhand von Hans Münchs Erinnerungserzählungen.* Frankfurt am Main: Peter Lang, 2011.

Heller, Yoav. *The History of Zvi Spiegel: The Experience of Mengele Twins and Their Protector During the Holocaust.* Dissertation. Department of History, Royal Holloway, University of London, 2013.

Hellman, Peter, Lili Meier, and Serge Klarsfeld. *The Auschwitz Album.* New York: Random House, 1981.

Helmer, Richard. "Identifizierung der Leichenüberreste des Josef Mengele." *Archiv für Kriminologie* 177, nos. 5–6 (1986): 129–44.

Helmer, R., und O. Grüner. "Vereinfachte Schädelidentifizierung nach dem Superprojektionsverfahren mit Hilfe einer Video-Anlage." *Forensic Science* 7, no. 3 (1976).

Helmreich, E. C. "The Return of the Baltic Germans." *American Political Science Review* 36, no. 4 (1942): 711–16.

Helmuth, G. "Die Vererbung als biologischer Vorgang." *Der Weg* (1953): 815–20.

Herf, Jeffrey. *Divided Germany: The Nazi Past in the Two Germanies.* Cambridge, Mass: Harvard University Press, 1997.

Hesse, Hans. *Augen aus Auschwitz: Ein Lehrstück über nationalsozialistischen Rassenwahn und medizinische Forschungen: Der Fall Dr. Karin Magnussen.* Essen: Klartext Verlag, 2001.

Hier, Marvin. *Meant to Be: A Memoir.* New Milford, Conn.: Toby Press, 2015.

Hördler, Stefan. *Ornung und Inferno: Daz KZ-System im lezten Kriegsjahr.* Göttingen: Wallstein Verlag, 2015.

International Auschwitz Committee. *Nazi Medicine: Doctors, Victims and Medicine in Auschwitz.* New York: Howard Fertig, 1986.

Ivanovic, Christine. "Inkubation—Vom langen Weg der Erfahrung in die Texte oder Die Wiederkehr der Zwillingsforschung bei Ilse Aichinger und Hans-Ultich Treichel." In *NS-Medizin und Öffentlichkeit: Formen der Aufarbeitung nach 1945,* edited by Stephan Braese und Dominik Groß, 301–22. Frankfurt am Main: Campus Verlag, 2015.

Jäger, Herbert. *Verbrechen unter totalitärer Herrschaft:.* Frankfurt am Main: Suhrkamp Verlag, 1982.

Joyce, Christopher, and Eric Stover. *Witnesses from the Grave: The Stories Bones Tell.* Boston: Little, Brown, 1991.

Jukes, Geoffrey. *Hitler's Stalingrad Decisions.* Berkeley: University of California Press, 1985.

Kalisky, Aurélia. "Ein Teufel in christlichen Kegelspiel: Der Doktor in Hochhuths Stellvertreter." In *NS-Medizin und Öffentlichkeit: Formen der Aufarbeitung nach 1945,* edited by Stephan Braese and Domnik Groß. Frankfurt am Main: Campus Verlag, 2015.

Kamp, P. "In Memoriam Theodor Mollison (1874–1952)." *Zeitschrift für Morphologie und Anthropologie* 45, no. 3 (1953): 416–32.

Kater, Michael H. "Das Böse in der Medizin." *Jahrbuch zur Geschichte und Wirkung des Holocaust,* Fritz Bauer Institut (1998–99): 219–39.

———. "Der Krise der Ärzte und der Medizin im Dritten Reich." In *Der Wert des Menschen: Medizin in Deutschland 1918–1945,* edited by Christian Pross and Götz Aly, 357–71. Berlin: Edition Hentrich, 1989.

Kaul, F. K. *Ärzte in Auschwitz.* Berlin: VEB Verlag Volk und Gesundheit, 1968.

Keenan, Thomas, Eyal Weizman, und Portikus (Gallery). *Mengele's Skull: The Advent of a Forensic Aesthetics.* Berlin: Sternberg Press, 2012.

Keller, Sven. *Günzburg und der Fall Josef Mengele: Die Heimatstadt und die Jagd nach dem NS-Vebrecher.* Munich: Oldenbourg Wissenschaftsverlag, 2003.

Klarsfeld, Beate, and Serge Klarsfeld. *Hunting the Truth: Memoirs of Beate and Serge Klarsfeld.* New York: Farrar, Straus & Giroux, 2018.

Klee, Ernst. *Auschwitz, die NS-Medizin und ihre Opfer.* Frankfurt am Main: S. Fischer Verlag, 1997.

———. *Deutsche Medizin im Dritten Reich: Karrieren vor und nach 1945.* Frankfurt am Main: S. Fischer Verlag, 2001.

Klietmann, K.-G. *Die Waffen-SS: Eine Dokumentation.* Osnabrück: Verlag "der Freiwillige," 1965.

Koehl, Robert L. *RKFDV: German Resettlement and Population Strategy, 1939–1945.* Cambridge, Mass.: Harvard University Press, 1957.

Kor, Eva. "The Mengele Twins and Human Experimentation: A Personal Account." In *The Nazi Doctors and the Nuremberg Code,* edited by George J. Annas and Michael A. Grodin, 53–59. New York: Oxford University Press, 1992.

Koren, Yehuda, and Eilat Negev. *In Our Hearts We Were Giants: The Remarkable Story of the Lilliput Troupe—A Dwarf Family's Survival of the Holocaust.* New York: Carroll & Graf, 2004.

Kramer, Helgard, ed. *Die Gegenwart der NS-Vergangenheit.* Berlin: Philo, 2000.

Kranz, Heinrich. "Zwillingsforschung." *Klinische Fortbildung* 4 (1937): 134–95.

Kriegel, Vera. " '. . . endlich den höchsten Berg gefunden.' " In *Die Verbindung nach Auschwitz: Biowissenschaften und Menschenversuche an Kaiser-Wilhelm-Instituten,* edited by Carola Sachse. Göttingen: Wallstein Verlag, 2003.

Krogh, Christian von. "Schausammlung für Abstammungs- und Rassenkunde des Menschen in München." *Volk und Rasse* 13 (1938): 193–94.

Krzysko, Miroslaw. "Jan Czekanowski (1882–1965)." *Statistics in Transition,* new series, 13, no. 1 (March 2012): 161–68.

Kubica, Helena. "The Crimes of Josef Mengele." In *Anatomy of the Auschwitz Death Camp,* edited by Yisrael Gutman und Michael Berenbaum, 317–37. Bloomington: Indiana University Press, 1994.

Kushner, Tony. "Saul Friedlander, Holocaust Historiography and the Use of Testimony." In *Years of Extermination: Saul Friedlander and the Future of Holocaust Studies*, edited by Christian Wiese und Paul Betts, 67–80. New York: Bloomsbury, 2010.

Lagnado, Lucette, and Sheila Cohn Dekel. *Children of the Flames: Dr. Josef Mengele and the Untold Story of the Twins of Auschwitz.* New York: William Morrow, 1991.

Langbein, Hermann. *People in Auschwitz.* Chapel Hill: University of North Carolina Press, 2004.

Lasik, Aleksander. "Die Personalbesetzung des Gesundheitsdienstes der SS im Konzentrationslager Auschwitz-Birkenau in den Jahren 1939–1945." *Hefte von Auschwitz* 20 (1997): 290–368.

———. *Organizational Structure of Auschwitz Concentration Camp.* Oświęcim: Auschwitz-Birkenau State Museum, 2000.

Lee, Henry C., and Frank Tirnady. *Blood Evidence: How DNA Is Revolutionizing the Way We Solve Crimes.* Cambridge, Mass.: Perseus, 2003.

Lehmann, W. "Erbpathologie der Lippen-Kiefer-Gaumenspalten." In *Erbbiologie des Menschen*, vol. 4, *Erbbiologie Erbpathologie Körperlicher Zustände und Funktionen II*, edited by K. H. Bauer, E. Hanhart, and G. Just, 568–70. Berlin: Verlag Juilus Springer, 1940.

Leniger, Markus. *Nationalsozialistische "Volksarbeit" und Umsiedlungspolitik 1933–1945: Von der Minderheitsbetreuung sur Siedlerauslese.* Berlin: Frank & Timme, 2006.

Levy, Alan. *The Wiesenthal File.* Grand Rapids, Mich.: William B. Eerdmans, 1994.

Lewontin, R. C. "The Apportionment of Human Diversity." *Journal of Evolutionary Biology* 6 (1972): 381–98.

Lewy, Guenter. *The Nazi Persecution of the Gypsies.* New York: Oxford University Press, 2000.

———. *Perpetrators: The World of the Holocaust Killers.* New York: Oxford University Press, 2017.

Liedtke, Gregory. *Enduring the Whirlwind: The German Army and the Russo-German War, 1941–1943.* Wolverhampton Military Studies. Solihull, U.K.: Helion, 2016.

Lifton, Robert Jay. "Mechanized Killing in Auschwitz." *Psychiatry* 45, no. 4 (1982): 283–97.

———. *The Nazi Doctors: Medical Killing and the Psychology of Genocide.* New York: Basic Books, 1986.

———. "What Made this Man?" *New York Times*, July 21, 1985.

———. *Witness to an Extreme Century: A Memoir.* New York: Free Press, 2011.

Lingens-Reiner, Ella. *Prisoners of Fear.* London: Victor Gollancz, 1948.

Loewenberg, Peter. "The Psychohistorical Origins of the Nazi Youth Cohort." *American Historical Review* 76, no. 5 (1971): 1457–502.

Lösch, Niels C. *Rasse als Konstrukt: Leben und Werk Eugen Fischers.* Frankfurt am Main: Peter Lang, Europäischer Verlag der Wissenschaft, 1997.

Lower, Wendy. "Distant Encounter: An Auschwitz Survivor in the College Classroom." In *Approaching an Auschwitz Survivor: Holocaust Testimony and Its Transformations,* edited by Jürgen Matthäus, 95–118. New York: Oxford University Press, 2009.

Lumans, Valdis O. *Himmler's Auxiliaries: The Volksdeutsche Mittelstelle and the German National Minorities of Europe, 1933–1945.* Chapel Hill: University of North Carolina Press, 1993.

Massin, Benoît. "Anthropologie und Humangenetik im Nationalsozialismus oder: Wie schreiben deutsche Wissenschaftler ihre eigene Wissenschaftsgeschicte?" In *Wissenschaftlicer Rassismus: Analysen einer Kontinuität in den Human- und Naturwissenschaften,* edited by Heidrun Kaupen-Haas and Christian Saller, 12–64. Frankfurt: Campus Verlag, 1999.

———. "From Virchow to Fischer: Physical Anthropology and 'Modern Race Theories' in Wilhelmine Germany." In *Volksgeist as Method and Ethic: Essays on Boasian Ethnography and the German Anthropological Tradition,* edited by George W. Stocking, 79–154. Madison: University of Wisconsin Press, 1998.

———. "Mengele, die Zwillingsforschung und die Auschwitz-Dahlem Connection." In *Die Verbindung nach Auschwitz: Biowissenschaften und Menschenversuche an Kaiser-Wilhelm-Instituten,* edited by Carola Sachse, 201–54. Göttingen: Wallstein Verlag, 2003.

Meding, Holger M. *Der Weg: Eine deutsche Emigrantenzeitschrift in Buenos Aires, 1947–1957.* Berlin: Wissenschaftlicher Verlag, 1997.

Mengele, Josef. "Rassenmorphologische Untersuchungen des vorderen Unterkieferabschnittes bei vier rassischen Gruppen." In *Gegenbaurs Morphologisches Jahrbuch. Eine Zeitschrift für Anatomie und Entwicklungsgeschichte* 79 (1937): 60–116.

———. "Sippenuntersuchungen bei Lippen-Kiefer-Gaumenspalte." *Zeitschrift für menschliche Vererbungs- und Konstitutionslehre* 23, no. 1 (1939): 17–42.

———. "Tagung der Deutschen Gesellschaft für Physische Anthropolgie." *Der Erbarzt* 4 (1937): 140–41.

———. "Zur Vererbung der Ohrfisteln." *Der Erbarzt* 8 (1940): 59f.

Mildenberger, Florian. "Race and Breathing Therapy: The Career of Lothar Gotlieb Tirala (1886–1974)." *Sign System Studies* 21, nos. 1–2 (2004): 253–75.

Miquel, Marc von. *Ahnden oder Amnestieren? Westdeutsche Justiz und Vergangenheitspolitik in den Sechzigerjahren.* Göttingen: Wallerstein Verlag, 2004.

Mollison, Theodor. "Eine Schausammlung für Anthropologie in München." *Anthropologischer Anzeiger* 15, no. 1 (1938): 78–82.

———. "Rassenkunde und Rassenhygieniker." In *Erblehre und Rassenhygiene im völkischen Staat,* edited by Ernst Rüdin. Munich: J. F. Lehmann, 1934.

Muensterer, Olivier J., Walter E. Berdon, Ralph S. Lachman, und Stephen L. Done. "Pseudoachondroplasia and the Seven Ovitz Siblings Who Survived Auschwitz." *Pediatric Radiology* 42 (2012): 475–80.

Mukherjee, Siddhartha. *The Gene: An Intimate History.* New York: Scribner, 2016.

Müller, Rolf-Dieter. *Hitlers Ostkrieg und die deutsche Siedlungspolitik: Die Zusammenarbeit von Wehrmacht, Wirtschaft und SS.* Frankfurt am Main: Fischer Taschenbuch Verlag, 1991.

Müller-Hill, Benno. *Murderous Science: Elimination by Scientific Selection of Jews, Gypsies, and Others, Germany 1933–1945.* New York: Oxford University Press, 1988.

Munz, Tania. *The Dancing Bees: Karl von Frisch and the Discovery of the Honeybee Language.* Chicago: University of Chicago Press, 2016.

Naumann, Bernd. *Auschwitz.* New York: Frederick A. Praeger, 1966.

Nyiszli, Miklós. *I Was Doctor Mengele's Assistant: The Memoirs of an Auschwitz Physician,* edited by Franciszek Piper. Oświęcim: Frap-Books, 2010.

———. "SS Obersturmführer Doktor Mengele (Conclusion)." *Merlin* 2, no. 1 (Spring–Summer 1953): 48–72.

Office of Special Investigations (OSI). *In the Matter of Josef Mengele: A Report to the Attorney General of the United States.* Washington, D.C.: U.S. Department of Justice, 1992.

Opitz, K. *Leitfaden der Prüfungsordnungen für Ärzte und Zahnärzte.* Berlin: Springer Verlag, 1921.

Ortmeyer, Benjamin. *Jenseits des Hippokratischen Eids: Josef Mengele und die Goethe-Universität.* Frankfurt am Main: Forschungsstelle NS-Pädagogik an der Goethe-Universität, 2014.

Ostałowska, Lidia. *Watercolours: A Story from Auschwitz.* New Delhi: Zubaan, 2016.

Paprotka, Stefan. "Zwangssterilisation bei Lippen-Kiefer-Gaumenspalten. Zahnärztliches und kieferchirurgisches Handeln im Nationalsozialismus." Berlin: Medizinische Fakultät Charité—Universitätsmedizin Berlin, 2017.

Pascucci, John, und Cameron Stauth. *The Manhunter: The Astounding True Story of the U.S. Marshal Who Tracked Down the World's Most Evil Criminals.* New York: Pocket Books, 1996.

Pendas, Devin O. *The Frankfurt Auschwitz Trial, 1963–1965: Genocide, History, and the Limits of the Law.* Cambridge, U.K.: Cambridge University Press, 2010.

Perl, Gisella. *I Was a Doctor in Auschwitz.* 1948; rpt. Salem, N.H.: Ayer, 1984.

Pioniereinheiten der 5. SS-Panzerdivision "Wiking," n.d.

Posner, Gerald L. *Hitler's Children: Sons and Daughters of Leaders of the Third Reich Talk About Themselves and Their Fathers*. New York: Random House, 1991.

Posner, Gerald L., and John Ware. *Mengele: The Complete Story*. New York: McGraw-Hill, 1986.

Prins, Erika. "Foreword." In *The Footsteps of Anne Frank*, edited by Ernst Schnabel. London: Southbank, 2015.

Proctor, Robert. "From Anthropologie to Rassenkunde in the German Anthropological Tradition." In *Bones, Bodies, Behavior: Essays on Biological Anthropology*, edited by George W. Stocking Jr., 138–79. Madison: University of Wisconsin Press, 1988.

———. *Racial Hygiene: Medicine Under the Nazis*. Cambridge, Mass.: Harvard University Press, 1988.

Pross, Christian, and Götz Aly. *Der Wert des Menschen: Medizin in Deutschland 1918–1945*. Berlin: Edition Hentrich, 1989.

Przyrembel, Alexandra. *Rassenschande: Reinheitsmythos und Vernichtungslegitimation im Nationalsozialismus*. Göttingen: Vandenhoeck & Rupprecht, 2003.

Pukrop, Marco. *SS-Mediziner zwischen Lagerdienst und Fronteinsatz. Die personelle Besetzung der Medizinischen Abteilung im Konzentrationslager Sachsenhausen 1936–1945*. Dissertation. Hanover: Gottfried Wilhelm Leibnitz Universität, 2015.

Radvanský, Artur. *Trotzdem habe ich überlebt: Lebensbericht eines Menschenfreundes*. Dresden: DDP Goldenbogen, 2006.

Reichert, Ottwil. "Zur Erbbedingtheit der Thrombangitis obliterans." *Zeitschrift für menschliche Vererbungs- und Konstitutionslehre* 23 (1939): 53–66.

Reiter, Hans. *Das Reichsgesundheitsamt, 1933–1939: Sechs Jahre Nationalsozialistische Führung*. Berlin: Springer Verlag, 1939.

Rende, Richard D., Robert Plomin, and Steven G. Vandenberg. "Who Discovered the Twin Method?" *Behavioral Genetics* 20, no. 2 (1990): 277–85.

Renz, Ulrich. "Die Spurensuche nach Josef Mengele: Die Ermittlungsakten können nunmehr endgültig geschlossen werden." *Tribüne* 31 (1992): 132–37.

Renz, Werner. "Der 1. Frankfurter Auschwitz-Prozess." *Hr Online*, n.d., accessed June 5, 2017. http://www.hr-online.de/website/static/spezial/auschwitz-prozess/downloads/vorgeschichte.pdf.

Rosensaft, Hadassah. *Yesterday: My Story*. Washington, D.C.: U.S. Holocaust Memorial Museum, 2004.

Roth, K. H. "Die wissenschaftliche Normalität des Schlächters." *Mitteilungen der Dokumentationsstelle zur NS-Sozialpolitik* 2 (1985): i–viii.

Rzesnitzek, Lara, und Sascha Lang. "A Material History of Electroshock Therapy: Electroshock Technology in Europe Until 1945." *Zeitschrift für Geschichte der Wissenschaften, Technik und Medizin* 24, no. 3 (2016): 251–77.

Sachse, Carola. 2011. "Was bedeutet 'Entschuldigung'? Die Überlebenden medizinischer NS-Verbrechen und die Max-Planck-Gesellschaft." *Berichte zur Wissenschaftsgeschichte* 34 (2010): 224–41.

Sachse, Carola, and Benoît Massin. *Biowissenschaftliche Forschung an Kaiser-Wilhelm-Instituten und die Verbrechen des NS-regimes: Informationen über den gegenwärtigen Wissenstand*. Berlin: Max-Planck-Gesellschaft zur Förderung der Wissenschaften, 2003.

Sandner, Peter. "Das Frankfurter 'Universitätsinstitut für Erbbiologie und Rassenhygiene' zur Positionierung einer rassenhygienischen Einrichtung innerhalb der 'rassenanthropologischen' Forschung und Praxis wärhrend der NS-Zeit." *Jahrbuch zur Geschichte und Wirkung des Holocaust* (1998): 73–100.

Schafft, Gretchen E. *From Racism to Genocide: Anthropology in the Third Reich*. Urbana: University of Illinois Press, 2004.

Schmuhl, Hans-Walter. *The Kaiser Wilhelm Institute for Anthropology, Human Heredity and Eugenics, 1927–1945*. New York: Springer, 2008.

Schwerin, Alexander von. *Experimentalisierung des Menschen: Der Genetiker Hans Nachtsheim und die Vergleichende Erbpathologie 1920–1945*. Vol. 10 of *Geschichte der Kaiser-Wilhelm-Gesellschaft im Nationalsozialismus*. Göttingen: Wallstein Verlag, 2004.

Segal, Nancy L. "Twin Research at Auschwitz-Birkenau: Implications for the Use of Nazi Data Today." In *When Medicine Went Mad*, edited by Arthur L. Caplan, 281–99. Totowa, N.J.: Humana Press, 1992.

———. "Zygosity Diagnosis: When Physicians and DNA Disagree." *Twin Research and Human Genetics* 18 no. 5 (2015): 614–15.

Segev, Tom. *Simon Wiesenthal: The Life and Legends*. New York: Doubleday, 2010.

Seidler, Eduard. *Jüdische Kinderärzte 1933–1945: Entrechtet/Geflohen/Ermordet*. New York: Karger, 2007.

Setkiewicz, Piotr. *The Private Lives of the Auschwitz SS*. Oświęcim: Auschwitz-Birkenau State Museum, 2015.

Sofsky, Wolfgang. *The Order of Terror: The Concentration Camp*. Princeton: Princeton University Press, 1997.

Sprenger, Isabell. *Gross-Rosen: Ein Konzentrationslager in Schlesien*. Cologne: Böhlau Verlag, 1996.

Stahl, Daniel. *Nazi-Jagd: Südamerikas Diktaturen und die Ahndung von NS-Verbrechen*. Göttingen: Wallstein Verlag, 2013.

Stangneth, Bettina. *Eichmann Before Jerusalem: The Unexamined Life of a Mass Murderer*. New York: Knopf, 2014.

Steinacher, Gerald. "Berufsangabe: Mechaniker—Die Flucht von Gestapo-Angehörigen nach Übersee" (2009). Faculty publication, University of Nebraska at Lincoln, http://digitalcommons.unl.edu/cgi/viewcontent.cgi?article=1133&co ntext=historyfacpub.

———. " 'The Cape of Last Hope': The Postwar Flight of Nazi War Criminals Through South Tyrol/Italy to South America." In *Transatlantic Relations: Austria and Latin America in the 19th and 20th Centuries*, edited by Klaus Eisterer und Günter Bischof, 203–24. Innsbruck: Studienverlag, 2006.

———. *Nazis on the Run: How Hitler's Henchmen Fled Justice.* New York: Oxford University Press, 2011.

Steinbacher, Sybille, Devin O. Pendas, et al. *Der Frankfurter Auschwitz-Prozess (1963–1965): Kommentierte Quellenedition.* Frankfurt am Main: Campus Verlag, 2013.

Steiniger, F. "Die Entstehung und Vererbung der Hasenscharte." *Fortschritte der Erbpathologie, Rassenhygiene, und ihrer Grenzgebiete* 4 (1940): 98–140.

Steinweis, Alan E. *Studying the Jew: Scholarly Antisemitism in Nazi Germany.* Cambridge, Mass.: Harvard University Press, 2006.

Stengel, Katharina. *Hermann Langbein: Ein Auschwitz-Überlebender in den erinnerungspolitischen Konflikten der Nachkriegszeit.* Frankfurt am Main: Campus Verlag, 2012.

Strassner, Peter. *Europäische Freiwillige: Die Geschichte der 5. SS Panzerdivision Wiking.* Osnabrück: Munin Verlag, 1977.

Struve, Kai. *Deutsche Herrschaft, ukrainischer Nationalismus, antijüdische Gewalt: Der Sommer 1941 in der Westukraine.* Oldenbourg: De Gruyter, 2015.

Strzelecka, Irena. *Medical Crimes: Medical Experiments in Auschwitz.* Oświęcim: Auschwitz-Birkenau State Museum, 2008.

Stuchlik, Gerda. *Goethe im Braunhemd: Universität Frankfurt, 1933–1945.* Frankfurt: Röderberg-Verlag, 1984.

Szejnmann, Claus-Christian W. "Perpetrators of the Holocaust: A Historiography." In *Ordinary People as Mass Murderers: Perpetrators in Comparative Perspectives*, edited by Olaf Jensen und Claus-Christian W. Szejnmann, 25–54. Basingstoke, Hampshire, U.K.: Palgrave Macmillan, 2008.

Taube, Tilman. "Der Großvater in Auschwitz: Zur Geschichte einer Fotoserie im Höcker-Album." In *Das Höcker-Album: Auschwitz durch die Linse der SS*, edited by Christophe Busch, Stefan Hödler, and Robert Jan van Pelt, 172–87. Darmstadt: Philipp von Zabern, 2016.

Teicher, Amir. "Racial Zigzags: Visualizing Racial Deviancy in German Physical Anthropology During the 20th Cenutry." *History of Human Sciences* 28, no. 5 (2015): 17–48.

Teo, T., and L. Ball. "Twin Research, Revisionism and Metahistory." *History of the Human Sciences* 22, no. 5 (2009): 1–23.

Thieme, V. "Gedemütigt, entwürdigt, verstümmelt—die 'rassenhygienische Aus-
merze' der Lippen-Kiefer-Gaumen-Spalten im Dritten Reich. Studie zur
Situation der Betroffenen und zur Position der Ärzte im Dritten Reich." *MKG-
Chirurg* 5 (2012): 62–72.

Tobin, Patrick. "No Country for Old Fighters: Postwar Germany and the Origins of
the Ulm Einsatzkommando Trial." Master's thesis, University of North Carolina, 2009.

Trang, Charles. *Wiking,* vol. 1: *Décembre 1940–Avril 1942.* Bayeux: Éditions Heimdal, 2014.

———. *Wiking,* vol. 2: *Mai 1942–Avril 1943.* Bayeux: Éditions Heimdal, 2014.

Trunk, Achim. "Two Hundred Blood Samples from Auschwitz: A Nobel Laureate
and the Link to Auschwitz." In *The Kaiser Wilhelm Society Under National
Socialism,* edited by Susanne Heim, Carola Sachse, und Mark Walker, 120–44.
New York: Cambridge University Press, 2009.

Turda, Marius. "The Ambiguous Victim: Miklós Nyiszli's Narrative of Medical
Experimentation in Auschwitz-Birkenau." *Historien: A Review of the Past and
Other Stories* 14, no. 1 (2014): 43–58.

Ubelaker, Douglas H., and Kristina M. Zarenko. "Can Handedness Be Determined
from Skeletal Remains? A Chronological Review of the Literature." *Journal of
Forensic Sciences* 57, no. 6 (2012): 1421–26.

U.S. Senate. Subcommittee on Juvenile Justice of the Committee on the Judiciary.
*Searching for Dr. Josef Mengele: Hearings to inquire into Dr. Mengele's where-
abouts and on the role of the U.S. Army, if he was in custody of the U.S. Government, February 19; March 19; and August 2, 1985.* 99th Cong., 1st sess., serial
no. J-99-4. Washington, D.C.: Government Printing Office, 1985, http://hdl
.handle.net/2027/purl.32754078038969.

Valobra, Adriana, and Verónica Giordano. "Absolute Divorce in Argentina, 1954–
1956. Debates and Practices Regarding a Short-lived Law." *History of the Family* 18, no. 1 (2013): 3–25.

Varon, Benno Weiser. "The Diplomat and Dr. Mengele." *National Jewish Monthly*
(1979): 6–16.

———. *Professions of a Lucky Jew.* New York: Cornwall Books, 1992.

Varshizky, Amit. "Between Science and Metaphysics: Fritz Lenz and Racial
Anthropology in Interwar Germany." *Intellectual History Review* 27, no. 2
(2017): 247–72.

Verschuer, Otmar von. "Die Ähnlichkeitsdiagnose der Eineiigkeit von Zwillingen."
Anthropologischer Anzeiger 5, no. 3 (1928): 244–48.

———. "Aufgaben und Ziele des Instituts für Erbbiologie und Rassenhygiene zu
Frankfurt a. M." *Der Erbarzt,* nos. 1–2 (1934–35): 97–101.

——. "Twin Research from the Time of Galton to the Present Day." *Proceedings of the Royal Society of London, Series B, Biological Sciences* 128, no. 850 (1939): 62–81.

——. "Die Vaterschaftsgutachten des Frankfurter Universitätsinstituts für Erbbiologie un Rassenhygiene: Ein vorläufiger Überblick." *Der Erbartzt* 2, no. 9 (1941): 25–31.

——. "Vier Jahre Frankfurter Universitäts-Institut für Erbbiologie und Rassenhygiene." *Der Erbarzt* 6, no. 5 (1939): 57–65.

Völklein, Ulrich. *Der "Märchenprinz": Eduard Wirths: Vom Mitläufer zum Widerstand. Als SS-Arzt im Vernichtungslager Auschwitz.* Gießen: Haland & Wirth im Psychosozial-Verlag, 2006.

——. *Josef Mengele: Der Arzt von Auschwitz.* Göttingen: Steidl Verlag, 1999.

Wachsmann, Nikolaus. *KL: A History of the Nazi Concentration Camps.* New York: Farrar, Straus & Giroux, 2015.

Weikart, Richard. "The Role of Darwinism in Nazi Racial Thought." *German Studies Review* 36, no. 3 (2013): 537–56.

Weindling, Paul. *From Clinic to Concentration Camp: Reassessing Nazi Medical and Racial Research, 1933–1945.* New York: Routledge, 2017.

——. "Genetik und Menschenversuche in Deutschland, 1940–1950: Hans Nachtsheim, die Kaninchen von Dahlem und die Kinder vom Bullenhuser Damm." In *Rassenforschung an Kaiser-Wilhelm Instituten vor und nach 1933*, edited by Hans-Walter Schmuhl, 245–74. Göttingen: Wallstein Verlag, 2003.

——. *Victims and Survivors of Nazi Human Experiments: Science and Suffering in the Holocaust.* New York: Bloomsbury Academic, 2015.

——. "Weimar Eugenics: The Kaiser Wilhelm Institute for Anthropology, Human Heredity and Eugenics in Social Context." *Annals of Science* 42, no. 3 (1985): 303–18.

Weingart, Peter. "German Eugenics Between Science and Politics." *Osiris* 5 (1989): 260–82.

Weingart, P., K. Bayertz, and J. Kroll. *Rasse, Blut und Gene: Geschichte der Eugenik und Rassenhygiene in Deutschland.* Frankfurt am Main: Suhrkamp, 1988.

Weiss, Philip. "The True Story of Rupert Murdoch's Search for Josef Mengele." *Spy Magazine* (May 1987): 32–41.

Weiss, Sheila. "After the Fall: Political Whitewashing, Professional Posturing, and Personal Refashioning in the Postwar Career of Otmar Freiherr von Verschuer." *Isis* 101 (2010): 722–58.

——. "Essay Review: Racial Science and Genetics at the Kaiser Wilhelm Society." *Journal of the History of Biology* 38 (2005): 367–79.

——. "The 'Faustian Bargain': The Kaiser Wilhelm Institute for Anthropology,

Human Heredity and Eugenics in the National Socialist Era, 1933–1938/1942." In *The Kaiser Wilhelm Institute for Anthropology, Human Heredity and Eugenics, 1927–1945: Crossing Boundaries*, edited by Hans-Walter Schmuhl, 117–239. New York: Springer, 2008.

———. "Human Genetics and Politics as Mutually Beneficial Resources: The Case of the Kaiser Wilhelm Institute for Anthropology, Human Heredity and Eugentics During the Third Reich." *Journal of the History of Biology* 39, no. 1 (2006): 41–88.

———. "The Loyal Genetic Doctor, Otmar Freiherr von Verschuer, and the Institut für Erbbiologie und Rassenhygiene: Origins, Controversy, and Racial Political Practice." *Central European History* 45 (2012): 631–68.

———. *The Nazi Symbiosis: Human Genetics and Politics in the Third Reich*. Chicago: University of Chicago Press, 2010.

———. "The Race Hygiene Movement in Germany." *Osiris* 3 (1987): 193–236.

Wiesenthal, Simon. *Justice Not Vengeance*. New York: Grove Weidenfeld, 1989.

———. *The Murderers Among Us: The Simon Wiesenthal Memoirs*. New York: McGraw-Hill, 1967.

Wildt, Michael. *An Uncompromising Generation: The Nazi Leadership of the Reich Security Main Office*. Translated by Tom Lampert. Madison: University of Wisconsin Press, 2009.

Wiltshire, Gail. 2015. *A Spatial Reading of Ilse Aichinger's Novel "Die gößere Hoffnung."* Würzburg: Verlag Königshausen & Neumann, 2015.

Wojak, Irmtrud. *Auschwitz-Prozeß 4Ks 2/63 Frankfurt am Main*. Cologne: Snoeck Verlagsgesellschaft, 2005.

———. *Fritz Bauer 1903–1968: Eine Biographie*. Munich: Beck, 2009.

Wolter, Markus. "Der SS-Arzt Josef Mengele zwischen Freiburg und Auschwitz: Ein örtlicher Beitrag zum Banalen und Bösen." *Schau-ins-Land: Zeitschrift des Breisgau-Geschichtsvereins* 133 (2014): 149–89.

Wyszynski, Diego F. 1998. "Fifty Years after the Nuremberg Nazi Doctors' Trial: Reviewing How the Laws of the Third Reich Applied to Individuals with Oral Clefts." *Plastic and Reconstructive Surgery* 101, no. 2 (1998): 519–27.

Ziemke, Earl F. *The U.S. Army in the Occupation of Germany 1944–1946*. Washington, D.C.: Center of Military History, U.S. Army, 1975.

Zimmermann, Michael. *Verfolgt, vertrieben, vernichtet: Die nationalsozialistische Vernichtungspolitik gegen Sinti und Roma*, 2nd ed. Essen: Klartext-Verlag, 1993.

Zofka, Zdenek. "Der KZ-Arzt Josef Mengele. Zur Typologie eines NS-Verbrechers." *Vierteljahrshefte für Zeitgeschichte* 34, no. 2 (1986): 245–67.

Zuroff, Efraim. *Occupation: Nazi Hunter*. Southampton: Ashford Press, 1988.

INDEX

Note: Page numbers after 353 refer to the Notes section.